Gilbert White, Thomas Bell

The Natural History and Antiquities of Selborne, in the County of Southampton

Volume II

Gilbert White, Thomas Bell

The Natural History and Antiquities of Selborne, in the County of Southampton
Volume II

ISBN/EAN: 9783744791014

Printed in Europe, USA, Canada, Australia, Japan

Cover: Foto ©ninafisch / pixelio.de

More available books at **www.hansebooks.com**

THE
NATURAL HISTORY AND ANTIQUITIES
OF
SELBORNE,
IN THE COUNTY OF SOUTHAMPTON.

BY THE LATE
Rev. GILBERT WHITE,
FORMERLY FELLOW OF ORIEL COLLEGE, OXFORD.

EDITED BY
THOMAS BELL, F.R.S., F.L.S., F.G.S., &c.,
PROFESSOR OF ZOOLOGY IN KING'S COLLEGE, LONDON.

VOLUME II.
CORRESPONDENCE, SERMON, ACCOUNT-BOOK,
GARDEN KALENDAR, ANIMALS AND PLANTS, GEOLOGY,
ROMAN-BRITISH ANTIQUITIES, &c.

LONDON:
JOHN VAN VOORST, 1 PATERNOSTER ROW.
MDCCCLXXVII.

LIST OF ILLUSTRATIONS

IN VOL. II.

Sheep-fold . . . . *Half-title*

Front View of the Wakes. The small lower window between the first and second rail-posts belongs to the room in which the 'Natural History' was written . . . . *Frontispiece*

West Portion of the Village, on the road to Newton *Page* 138

Coffin-lid . . . . *Page* 396

Ecclesiastical Tiles found in Selborne Church . . *Page* 398

Facsimile page of 'Expenses,' to show White's distinct and beautiful autograph . . . . . . *Page* 410

CORRESPONDENCE

OF

GILBERT WHITE.

VOL. II.

CORRESPONDENCE OF GILBERT WHITE.

LETTERS TO HIS BROTHER

THE

REV. JOHN WHITE.

LETTER I.*

Selborne, May 26, 1770.

DEAR BROTHER,

I AM to acknowledge first the receipt of your kind letter of February 19, which I should have answered before now, had I not waited for your box of curiosities; concerning which you would naturally expect I should give some account. Farther obligations are now due for a second letter of April 14: but though I have not yet received the box, I must no longer omit to take notice of your agreeable communications. It is probable the box may be in London: but I have lately intimated that I would not wish to have it sent down at present, as I hope to be in town as soon as Whitsuntide is over.

Your *Vespæ* with purple wings are a beautiful and scarce species: they are the *Vespæ crabroni congeneres in Italia captæ* of Mr. Willughby, well described in Ray's *His. Insectorum,*

---

* [The first and second letters were written when his brother was Chaplain at Gibraltar.—T. B.]

p. 250. Pray observe what they feed on; and enquire into their manner of nidification. Your butterfly-like insect with long remiform wings is curious and rare, and proves to be the *Panorpa coa* Lin.: you see it is to be found in few places; and Scopoli knows nothing of it, though Carniola lies in a warm latitude. Send some more specimens. Pray observe how and where they breed. I suspect much that they come from the water, where they perhaps are hatched like the *Ephemeræ* (may flies) and the *Phryganeæ* (cadews).

Here it will be proper to remark that Lin. is too general in some of his assertions: too many exceptions occur under his general rules: as you must have already observed in the course of your reading the *Syst. Nat.*

You will be pleased to observe whether your ant-catching *Sphex* (for a *Sphex* I certainly think it was, though we soon lost our single small specimen) does not carry it's prey to it's nest in order to feed it's maggots: in and with what substance does it make it's nest? I have named it *Sphex formicarum falco*.

The insect with a long slender petiolus between the thorax and abdomen is a fine sort of *Ichneumon*.

Look after the genus of birds called Petrels; they are very peculiar in their way of life, and are in the Atlantic; perhaps may enter the Streights.

I am glad you begin to relish Linn.: there is nothing to be done in the wide boundless field of Nat. Hist. without system. Now you are master of the *ordines*, you must attend to the *genera*, and make yourself well acquainted with the terms. Study well the introductions to the classes, and see how the terms are explained.

Look still for the *Myrmeleon* (lion pismire) *Syst. Nat.* p. 913. It has jaws like a wasp; 4 pretty long *palpi* (feelers), no *stemmata*; pimples like crowns on it's head; **antennæ clavatæ**!! Andalusia, I should think, must produce it.

Your embassy to Morocco, when well drawn up, will make a good chapter in your History. Did you make no remarks on the country? You are to remember that you will want an abundance of matter to fill up 200 or 300 pages: and no publication will make a respectable appearance unless you can swell it to somewhat of such a bulk.

What sorts of Land-tortoises do you find? when do they come forth, and when do they hide*?

Have you no stone-curlews *(Charadrius œdicnemus)*? they certainly leave us for some of the dead months of winter.

You will, I hope, settle that curious article concerning your winter-martin †. In your letter of November last you seemed to be puzzled, and say "that the winter-martins begin to appear in a different dress: they are blacker on the back, and whiter under the belly than last winter:" and "that you suspect they are the real summer martins now undergoing a change of colour, and possibly intending to winter here in a browner habit." And yet in your letter of April 14 you only say in general, "that you saw (March 23) swallows, martins, and your brown winter-martins all flying together." This most curious article of all your intelligence will not, I hope, remain dubious, and unsettled.

Sure you must mistake when you say in your Journal, April 15th, 1769, "that the vines, though their shoots are but 6 or 8 inches long, have a good many grapes set." Do you not mistake the buds of bloom for fruit? Vines are late blowers in most climates: they show the rudiments of bloom with us in April; but do not blow 'til about July 1: 'til the shoots are two or three feet long. When in bloom they smell sweetly. Are not some of your foxes jackalls (*Lupus aureus*)? that animal wants to be better described.

Don't be too hasty in pronouncing any species a nondescript.

Scopoli is very ingenious: he is publishing on birds.

Mr. Pennant has heard of your pursuits, and desires to promote them. As to fishes, he says you must get Brünnich's history of those of Marseilles; and Gouan on fish: the last lives at Montpellier. Can't you contrive to correspond with him? He has written to Mr. Pennant. He expects the

---

* [The only species likely to be found in North Africa are *Testudo mauritanica* and *T. marginata*.—T. B.]

† [*Hirundo rupestris*; see next page.—A. N.]

birds and fishes of Leghorn and Naples soon, and is ready to communicate them.

Mineralogy must not be neglected.

In order to assist your enquiries Mr. Pennant sends you a list of such animals as are known to belong to the southern parts of Europe.

Your wine proves very sound and good.

LETTER II.

Selborne, Jan. 25, 1771.

DEAR BROTHER,

I RECEIVED your kind letter of October 19, and wrote you an answer on November 6. I should have been very glad to have seen Mr. Twisse: he just came to London, called on Bro. Ben, and set out for Gibraltar again. No. five is Ray's *Junco*, and the *Turdus arundinaceus* of Lin.* The *Merula passer solitarius* of Ray is said to be a fine songster, and is supposed to be the bird mentioned Psalm cii. 7 †. Your winter swallow is undoubtedly the *Hirundo rupestris* of Scopoli: you however will have the credit of discovering it's winter quarters.

Brisson mentions a tridactyl quail‡ from Madagascar: he calls it " Perdix infernè cinerea, supernè e cinereo rufo, & nigro variegata, gutture & collo inferiore nigris; coturnici nostrati *paululum crassitie cedens*." His 'Ornithology' is ex-

* [See note to p. 9.—A. N.]
† [The Rock-Thrush, *Monticola cyanus* of modern ornithologists.—A.N.]
‡ [This seems to show that John White had met with the " Gibraltar Quail," which was first described by Latham (Gen. Synops. ii. p. 790) from a specimen in the Leverian Museum. At the same time he also described (*tom. cit.* p. 791) the "Andalusian Quail," though that had previously been mentioned by Shaw (Trav. p. 300), and both are now known to be specifically identical. A few years afterwards Desfontaines described and figured the species (Mém. de l'Acad. des Scien. 1787, p. 500) as *Tetrao sylvaticus*; and it is the *Turnix sylvatica* of modern ornithologists. The type of Latham's " Gibraltar Quail " passed at the sale of the Leverian Museum to that of Vienna, but, says Herr von Pelzeln (Ibis, 1873, p. 36), " is no longer in the collection."—A. N.]

travagantly dear; 7 or 8 guineas. Geoffroy will set you right by means of his cuts in many genera of insects.

The motto from the Odyssey, Book iv. 566, is a description of the Elysian fields, and will suit the climate of Andalusia well.

> Ου νιφετος, ουτ' αρ' χειμων πολυς, ουτε ποτ' ομβρος·
> Αλλ' αιει Ζυφυροιο λιγυπνειοντας αητας
> Ωκεανος ανιησιν, αναψυχειν ανθρωπ*ς*.
>
> Stern winter smiles on that auspicious clime;
> The fields are florid with unfading prime:
> From the bleak pole no winds inclement blow,
> Mould the round hail, or flake the fleecy snow;
> But from the breezy deep the blest inhale
> The fragrant murmurs of the western gale.

The prose motto is perfectly suitable to your present situation, and prophetic of your undertaking.

"Certe si aliquis naturæ consultus in maxime australi Hispaniâ aves observaret, quando accedant aut recedant austrum et septentrionem versus, notatis scilicet diebus mensis et speciebus; res hæc adeo obscura brevi maxime illustraretur."—*Amœnitates Academicæ, Lin.* vol. iv.

Now Mr. Twisse is returned, be sure get his conjectures on the currents of the Streights: you will want dissertations for your work. Your embassy to the Emp. of Morocco with a description of his person, manners, troops, &c. will make a very good chapter. Have you not in Spain some crown-flocks of sheep which migrate with the seasons from N. to S. Get some anecdotes of them. Mr. Pennant makes his artist take all your most curious birds; and promises the drawings shall be forthcoming if wanted to engrave from. Describe the *Vultur percnopt.* most minutely, and learn if you have an opportunity the difference of the sexes. Get the skin of the *Lupus aureus* from Barbary, and describe it well. Scopoli's new *Hirundo alpina* is nothing, I think, but the *Hirundo melba*, which is indeed a noble swift: get all the anecdotes you can about them. Write to Scopoli, he is very clever: but ask him as gravely as you can how he is sure that the woodcock, when pursued, carries off her young in her bill. I have just sent your cargo, which I received in August, to Mr. Pennant: but as to your collection shipped in October, I have never seen it yet; for brother Thomas writes word that it has been performing quarantine in Stangate-creek. Just as I had penned the last sentence a letter arrived from brother Tho. informing me that the box was got safe to his house; which is good news: for I was in pain for the curiosities and Jack's shirts. When the *Mantis* casts his skin he is in his pupa state, and advancing to perfection by casting aside those exuviæ. Scopoli's *icones* will probably disappoint you; Linnæus's engravings of insects are miserable: Geoffroy's are the best I have seen. The bird you call a *Parus* (if it be not the common black-cap) is a nondescript: if it should prove new, call it *Motacilla atricapilloides:* Mr. Pennant thinks it a new bird*. Your purple-winged *Vespa* is no doubt the *Crabroni congener* Raji; and if you can find that it has "thorax ad latera postice utrinque dente notatus," I shall acknowledge it to be the *Sphex bidens* Linn. I am sending all your insects to nephew Ben. White in town, and shall get Mr. Lee the botanist of Hammersmith to inspect and ascertain them, because he is the best entomologist that I know. The reason that Linn. mentions so many insects from Barbary is, because Mr. Brander the Swedish Consul at Algiers sent him vast collections. In the little box which you sent me with the sliding lid are two species of *Myrmeleones*. Geoffroy seems to have a good cut of one. You will now be able to measure the rain of your climate: the mean quantity *per ann.* in Rutland is 20¾ inches. Learn as much as possible the manners of animals; they are worth a ream of descriptions. You must produce some ingenious dissertations to entertain the unsystematic reader. What do the *Panorpæ cow* do with their long remiform wings? Frequent your markets, and see what birds are offered to sale. Get some account of the prickly heat, or fever, and the exact height of your mountain.

* [Mr. Pennant seems to have been quite right. The bird was most likely that which is now known as *Sylvia melanocephala*, and was first described in 1776 by Cetti, who found it in Sardinia (Uccelli di Sard. p. 218), but did not receive a name till Gmelin gave it one. If John White's specimen, as his others appear to have been, was deposited in the Leverian Museum, it must have been overlooked by Latham.—A. N.]

It seems to me no doubt that your *Motacilla* No. 5 is the *Junco* of Ray; but he does not seem to be so exact as usual, and talks of a stiff tail, and omits mentioning the white and black bars at the end of it's tail*. It will be worth our while to find out Mr. Moore the botanist, or his representatives; and to endeavour to procure his flora of your district.

Ray does not take notice that the thighs of the *Merops* are naked.

I had written thus far when your curious box of birds shipped in October, and Jack's shirts and sweetmeats arrived: the insects were left in town for the reason above mentioned. Your kind letter of December 9 came the same day. Geoffroy no doubt is too verbose; so are all his countrymen. Mr. Pennant makes sad complaint of Gouan's book of fishes, and of the obscurity of the *Labrus* and *Sparus* genera. Dr. Shaw's Natural part of his travels is said to be good.

You will do well to have two columns of thermometer observations, especially as 1769 and 1770 were both on the extremes. As matter flows in upon me I begin to think of composing a Natural History of Selborne in the form of a journal for 1769; we shall then be able to compare the climates. You mention the great eagle owl, and send me, I think, a wing and claw of that majestic bird; and yet you call it *Strix otus;* sure you mean *Strix bubo:* the *otus* is our common horned owl. I see none of your plants; perhaps they are lost: the sweet-smelling clammy shrub must be, I suppose, a cistus; has it not a single, rose-like, fugacious flower? You have classed all your last fine cargo of birds so justly that there is no room for objection; where you doubt, I doubt, though I think there is little room to doubt about the *Alauda cristata;* but the pair of birds (if they are a

* [This statement of White's proves that this bird (already mentioned p. 6) was not the *Junco* of Ray, which is the Great Reed-Warbler (*Acrocephalus arundinaceus*); but it is doubtless the Reed-Thrush, var. A, of Latham (Gen. Synops. ii. p. 33), who described a specimen from Gibraltar in the Leverian Museum—most likely the very one sent by John White. The species did not receive a name till 1820, and is the *Aedon galactodes* of modern ornithologists. See Yarrell, 'Brit. Birds,' Ed. 4, i. p. 355.—A. N.]

pair) which, I suppose, you call *Alauda non-cristata*, seem rather some species of the genus *Motacilla**. Get the *Pratincola* when you can. At present I am a stranger to your *Œnanthe*†. The *Oriolus galbula* must be a fine bird when in perfection. Your barometer fluctuates much more than I could have expected in so low a latitude and warm a climate: in the tropics it hardly varies at all. Your last quail seems to be a male, the former a female. You will pardon the didactic air of my letters, which in our present way of correspondence is perhaps unavoidable. The wing of the *Strix bubo* is "*remigibus primoribus serratis:*" had Linn. remarked that, he would not have made that a specific difference to his *Strix aluco*‡. See Fauna Suec. p. 25.

I am, &c. &c.

LETTER III. §

Selborne, June 17 [1773].

DEAR BROTHER,

As you knew that the measles obtained very much in this village, you could not much wonder if you were to hear that

* [It would, of course, be useless to attempt any identification of these birds.—A. N.]

† [Besides our common *Saxicola œnanthe*, three other species of Wheatear, according to Col. Irby ('Ornithology of the Straits of Gibraltar,' p. 79), frequent the Rock. It would, of course, be impossible to say which of them John White's bird was; but Latham gives Gibraltar as a locality for that which he calls the Russet Wheatear, and described a specimen in the Leverian Museum. This is *S. stapazina*.—A. N.]

‡ [Herein White seems to have fallen into the error of supposing that each particular feature included in the diagnosis given of a species by Linnæus needs be peculiar thereto. On the contrary it is the aggregate of these features that forms a specific character; and by naming certain other features Linnæus sufficiently guarded himself from such a mistake as is imputed to him in the text. As to what his *S. aluco* may have been, see 'Ibis,' 1876, pp. 101, 102.—A. N.]

§ [This and the following letters were written after John White's return to England, which took place in May 1773.—T. B.]

your son had got them; but you will be agreeably surprised to be informed that he has had them, and got up this morning for the first time. He drooped a little on Saturday and Sunday, and went to bed on Monday, where he lay 'til this morning without any cough, or fever, or any bad symptom at all. Thomas lay in the little bed by him to help him to balm tea, &c. in the night; but last night he slept without taking any thing at all. Tomorrow he takes physic. Mr. Budd and Mr. Webb (who both came to neighbours) called in and said he was in a fine way. Jack has behaved like a philosopher all through, submitting to his confinement without reluctance or murmuring. In general the neighbourhood has been severely handled by this disorder; and poor Nanny Woods had such a fever afterwards, and was so reduced, that I thought we should have lost her; she is still so weak as not to be able to walk. Give my respects to my sister, whom I congratulate on this event. I will write again in about a week.

I am not sure yet that I shall be able to procure timber for my new building.

Your affectionate brother,
GIL. WHITE.

LETTER IV.

Selborne, June 26 [1773].

Dear Brother,

Your favour of the 17th reached me Wednesday; and about the same time, I presume, you received my account about Jack's measles. My nephew continues perfectly well, and has not, through the distemper nor since, had the least cough. From the time that he came home he had somewhat of an hoarseness in his voice, which I took at first to be a cold; but, upon considering the matter, it is owing no doubt to a cause incident to young men about his time of life.

It pleases me much to find that you have heard the sibilous, or shivering wren, since you know all the species; and that you have heard the sedge-bird, which for variety of notes, and swift transitions from the song of one bird to that of another is, I think, a wonderful fellow; and was it not for the hurrying manner, would be an elegant warbler. It is plain Mr. Lever knows nothing of the grasshopper-lark; if he did he could not confound it with the sedge-bird, to which it bears not the least resemblance, either in person, song, or manner of life. Did the shivering wren make its noise in the tops of tall trees? Mr. Lever is, I perceive, a very adroit *natural* naturalist; it is therefore pity he does not allow himself the advantage of books, and call in the assistance of system.

The sedge-bird sings all night when it is awake; therefore when you throw stones or dirt into the bushes you rouse it from its slumbers, and set it to work again.

You will be very busy, no doubt, in your repairs; and will meet, I hope, with no disappointments. I thought a fortnight ago that I was going to build a chamber full speed. I had bespoke a mason in the room of Long, who was pre-engaged; and Jack was to have been comptroller general of my majesty's works; but just as I was going to lay in all materials my mason sent me word he had got another job, and could not do mine 'til after harvest.

For these three days past we have had the king at Portsmouth; and heard continual firing, which shook my house. My st. foin is down; but the weather is unsettled. Mr. Lever has procured the canne petiere * in Lancashire; Mr. Pennant mentions one shot in Cornwall. Some boys killed lately at Oakhanger-ponds some flappers or young wild-ducks; among the rest they took some young teals † alive; one I saw, and turned into James Knight's ponds. Till now I never knew that teals bred in England. So you see information crowds in every day.

Was not the sibilous bird that you heard the real grasshopper-lark? did it haunt the tops of the tallest trees, or low bush-hedges? did it sing by night or by day? Many children continue to die of the measles, amongst the rest the youngest

---

* [*Otis tetrax*, Linn.—T. B.]
† [*Anas crecca*.—T. B.]

of Mrs. Hale's this morning; and the whooping cough rather gets worse than better. Poor Nanny Wood's cough is very bad; and she is very weak and mends very slowly. Mr. Knight of Street House is dead. With respects to my sister I remain,

Your affectionate and obliged brother,
GIL. WHITE.

LETTER V.

Selborne, Aug. 2, 1773.

DEAR BROTHER,

I FIND you still, as well as when you resided on the other side of the Pyrenean mountains, my most steady and communicative correspondent; and therefore it will be my own fault if our epistolary intercourse should languish.

Jack* behaves very well and is very obliging, and, in his readiness to assist and put an helping hand, often puts me in mind of a gentlewoman that is very nearly related to him †. Mr. and Mrs. Etty take a great deal of notice of him, and have him to dine every Sunday ‡.

No doubt your wren that you saw was the shivering wren. So Mr. Lever does not know the grasshopper lark; that is plain: but as it has done whispering there will be no procuring one till next season. He seems also to be unacquainted with the laughing sort. If you were to recollect, you would call to mind that my letters to Mr. Pennant are full of accounts of the sedge-bird. It was by my means that that bird, when omitted totally in the *Zool.* was inserted in the Appendix. Mr. P. had seen it in Lincolnshire, but did not at all know what to make of it, nor how to ascertain it. He was misled

---

* [Now aged 15.—T. B.]

† [Alluding to Jack's mother, who, after her husband's death, resided with Gilbert White. See Memoir.—T. B.]

‡ [Gilbert White, being at this time curate of Faringdon, of course did not dine at Selborne on Sundays. The Rev. Andrew Etty was vicar of Selborne at that time.—T. B.]

by Ray's classing it among the "*Picis affines*." Your appellative of polyglott pleases me so much that I shall adopt it. It has the notes of many birds; and could it be persuaded not to sing in such a hurry, it would be an elegant songster. They abound with us, especially on the verge of the forest, and are sometimes at James Knight's ponds—in short, wherever there are pools or streams.

Mr. Lever may very probably be right with respect to the short-eared owl. I have always suspected that Mr. S.'s tawny owl and brown owl were only different sexes of the same species. I am sorry that you met with such a rebuff at Midsummer, such a cold and dreary summer solstice; for if these things be done in the green tree, what will be done in the dry? Indeed we had at that season cold, wet, black weather; but from July 7th to this time have enjoyed the most lovely season that ever was seen, both as to sun for our hay, and, since, soft showers for our meadows, gardens and turnips. I have a prospect of a very fine crop of grapes on the walls of my house. Pray revise your journal without loss of time. The wind was very far from being constantly N. with us for a month before you wrote; it was very much so indeed from June 27th to July 3rd inclusive, but the week before was all S.W. to a day; but then again from June 13th to the 19th it was pretty much N.E. and N.W. at different ends of the week.

I shall write to Mr. Twisse soon and repeat my invitation.

From the time that the widow returned from her bathing in the sea, she began to be less cruel; and last week she consented to make Mr. Webb happy. They kept their wedding at Newton. Mr. Y[alden] was so delighted with the event, that he made verses on it, the strangest verses you ever saw. He made also a copy on his new alcove; they are alexandrines and wonderfully unwieldy; and very much like those before 'Pilgrim's Progress.' It is a pity that so worthy a man should be troubled with such an infirmity*!

The story of the aurora is all contradicted. It is a pity that you can't hear from Linnæus. You had better write again.

---

* [I have seen these lines; it is almost a libel on Bunyan to compare them with his, grotesque as they are.—T. B.]

Some boys went to hunt flappers (young wild ducks) last month in the forest: among the ducks they caught some minute wild fowls alive. I examined them, and found them to be young teals, but never had supposed that teals ever bred in our parts till now. I redeemed one and turned it into J. Knight's ponds.

Thomas Corston has brought Berriman a certificate of his marriage with Mary Gregory in the church of St. George's, Hanover Square, February 1771. The extract was taken April 24, 1773. It is on a 5s. stamp and looks as if it were genuine. Corston has called since.

This evening I expect from Fyfield brother Thomas and master Brocket, and brother Henry and Tho. Holt White: the two former are on their way to London. When did you get into your house? Jack joins in respects.

Your affec. brother,
GIL. WHITE.

Brother Harry was told in Oxford that Linnæus was certainly dead*.

Harvest does not begin 'til next week.

LETTER VI.

Selborne, Sept. 11, 1773.

DEAR BROTHER,

YOUR last letter but one, and my last letter, crossed, I believe, on the road. I am now to thank you for your frank of August 25.

As to Jack he is no trouble or inconvenience to me, but of real use; and therefore I desire he may stay as long as ever you can spare him. Moreover I wish you and my sister,

---

* [This was a false report. Linnæus died January 8, 1778, aged 71. Five out of the six letters from John White to Linnæus were written after the return of the former to England. The last is dated October, 1774.—T. B.]

while your house drys, would come and spend one more winter with me. You might put in an elderly, grave person for that period to make fires, and take care of your goods, and defer the hiring of servants 'til spring. I will endeavour to do everything to make the winter as easy to you as possible; you shall have a bed put up in the drawing-room, and a grate where you shall have a constant fire, by which you may instruct your son, and fabricate your *Fauna*. As my sister, I know by agreeable experience, is of an active disposition, she shall, if she please, manage my house, and see to provisions; and we shall, if it please God to bless us with health, pass the dead season of the year in no uncomfortable way; and at the season of spring I will let you depart in peace, and will follow you in the summer into Lancashire. All this proposal is the result of a sincere intention; and therefore I hope you will think of it in earnest, and not let the consideration of a long coach journey (which is not so formidable to you as to some others) prevent the comfort and satisfaction I propose from such an undertaking. When you write again I hope to discover that you have considered this matter, and will be so kind as to think of putting it into execution.

Mr. Derham in his 'Physico-theol.' incidentally mentions Dr. Leigh's 'Natural History of Lancashire,' which perhaps Mr. Lever has got, and you shall see. If I err about the *Mot. ficedula*, I err in good company; for your bird is indisputably the bird that Lin. means by *Mot. f.*; and yet he all the while acknowledges that it has " mandibula superior utrinque emarginata, et latere vibrissata," which are the characteristics of a *Muscicapa*. In Edwards there are cuts of the male and female. As to myself, I can't help thinking that your bird is of a *plumper and shorter habit* than the cock goldfinch with a white forehead; besides you sent many like the cocks that had no white in their foreheads. Mr. Shaw I see is preferred. I am glad he continues to send you new birds. The lark-like bird may probably be as you say.

From August 9 to 14 inclusive was most wonderfully hot. My thermometer on the 13th was up to $78\frac{1}{2}°$: on that day in the evening came a violent thunderstorm, which about London did great damage. Jack and I were all that week at Mr. Mulso's at Meonstoke. In the night between the 18th and 19th of August there was a violent thunderstorm from the north, which damaged all our hops to a great degree, and particularly Sir S. Stuart's, which were very fine. Hops will be dear and bad.

Mrs. W. Isaac is with me at present. She brought her son Bap. that he might stand for a scholarship of Winton College: we went this week and left him with the usher, where he is to continue as a commoner 'til taken into college.

My wall has produced about 10 dozen of most lovely peaches and nectarines; and I have a fine show of grapes.

I have written to Mr. Twisse and invited him to come; but he says he cannot possibly be spared from the fortifications 'til winter.

Swifts left us about the hot week. Young martins continue to come out daily.

Mr. Etty's Portugal brother is here at present. How can Mr. Curtis* leave his shop, and go to Gibraltar in pursuit of natural history?

Jack makes English themes and writes letters. We have gone through Phæd. and now read Virgil's *Georg.* and Sallust.

Mr. Lever, I find, is an excellent ornithologist. If we are to correspond, who is to break the ice? and on what subjects are we to exchange thoughts? He will, I hope, study system.

We have now a very wet and windy season, a sad time for barley-harvest and hop-picking. Most of our wheat was housed in very nice order.

I have some hopes of seeing Skinner soon.

Mrs. Isaac and niece Molly White, who came with her, join in respects.

Your affect. brother,
GIL. WHITE.

* [The well-known nurseryman and botanist, author of the magnificent 'Flora Londinensis' and of 'Lectures on Botany,' in three volumes.—T. B.]

LETTER VII.

Selborne, Nov. 2 [1773].

I CANNOT deny that I did receive your letter while at Oxford; but then my short time was so totally taken up with the accounts, and the common room, and a little visiting, that I never had the resolution to sit down to a regular letter.

Just before I came away, Skinner came up from a twelvemonth's sojourning at Brecknock to a regular residence in college: he made me dine and sup and spend the whole day with him, and is the same chatty, communicative, intelligent, gouty, indolent mortal that he used to be. Moreover he had written me a long letter! just before I saw him; which arrived at Selborne some posts after I got home. He is now first oars with regard to college preferment; and provided Dr. Patten should die (who is in a very dangerous way), he will succeed to a living of more than £400 per annum.

Jack did not go with me to college; for I well knew that if he had I could not have been with him one tenth of the time; however by means of his old friends at the Vicarage and at Newton he was left very little with the servants. We are to set out on Monday next on a visit to Ringmer; and nep. Pen. who is visiting with his father and mother and sisters, is to accompany us. We intend to stay two Sundays. Last week I began taking away the earth of my grass plot and walk at my garden door, so as to destroy the two steps, and to level the ground quite on to the alcove. We were much interrupted at first by rain, but now go on swimmingly. When completed the job will be *tanti*; and the nuisance of two slippery steps removed.

And now as to my visit into Lancashire: I am very desirous, as indeed I ought, to make you a visit. But this cannot be brought about 'til after Christmas; for in the first place our journey to Sussex will take up half the space between this and that, and in the next place I am hampered with a breaking tenant at Greatham whom I want to remove before

I leave these parts. And by Christmas, I fear, the severe weather will much impede our expedition, which will be a sort of migration reversed, to the north instead of the south. However, if it please God to enable me, I hope to get to you some time in January. I rejoice to hear that you have at last got possession of your house; and indeed, was I ready now, some time would be needful for you to settle a little before any visitors came upon you.

It is pleasant to hear that the spirit of natural enquiring subsists still at Gibraltar. There is a muscle, perhaps your dactyl*, that gets into the cliffs on the coasts of Sussex, and terebrates the chalk in a most curious manner. You saw, I think, a piece of chalk so bored at my house. I have received a most violent complimenting letter from Mr. Pennant lately. He is going to publish a second edition of 'Brit. Zool.,' and is to do wonders with the information extracted from my letters. I shall take the opportunity of laying before him the more glaring faults in the first edition. Ice this morning. My grapes are now delicate. Pray write while I am at Ringmer. Jack joins in respects to my sister and yourself. Ring-ouzels in plenty this last September.

Yours affect.
GIL. WHITE.

LETTER VIII.

Ringmer, Dec. 9, 1773.

DEAR BROTHER,

JACK and I arrived here on Thursday, December 2nd, and found that your letter of November 11th had waited for us for more than a fortnight. We were very agreeably surprized to find Mrs. Snooke † so much recovered after so great a plunge. She is cheerful and chatty, free from pain, and able to walk

---

* [*Pholas dactylus.*—T. B.]

† [Mrs. Snooke, Gilbert White's cousin, the owner of Timothy the tortoise.—T. B.]

to all parts of her house without a stick, rides out in her chaise, and is, for her great age, an extraordinary woman.

In my last, as I wrote on a sunny day, I mentioned that my levelling work went on *swimmingly;* but there came immediately upon me a glut of wet for many weeks that spoiled my metaphor, and drowned and floated all my works and sadly embarrassed our operations in the clay, which was all converted to mud and mire. Before we could dig we were obliged to lade. However, by perseverance, in five weeks instead of twelve days I finished my job; which has a very good effect, though neither the turf nor the pavement can be expected to lie quite so smooth and regular as if all had been moved in dry weather. The ground came out to nothing on an hanging level on the grass plot short of the mulberry-tree, and in the broad walk midway between the farther wicket and the alcove on a dead level. I apprehend no harm from the borders; they will be lowered. We went 20 inches deep at the entrance of the long walk. My back front looks higher and better.

I am sorry you have improved your parlor 'till it smokes; it is a common case; but you must exert all your mechanic powers to remove so sad a nuisance.

My horse Miller is very lame, and could not come; as Jack was trotting him in the north field he trod on an old track and strained his knee in a wonderful manner. However, his old friend Mr. Etty has lent Jack his poney, that carries him well. The tortoise went under the ground about November 20, came out again for one day December 3, and now lies in a swamp border in mud and mire!

My letters to Mr. Barrington swell very fast. He has engaged me in the monography of the swallow genus. I have dispatched the *house martin;* and my letter is to be read before the R. S. I wish I knew a little more about the *bank martin.* Does Mr. Lever know anything about the bank martin that can be depended on?

Harry's little folks, all but Har. Woods, are down with the whooping cough. While brother Ben and family were at Newton, Mrs. Pain discovered at London that James White had got a cataract or film in one of his eyes. Brother Harry is going to have a West-Indian boy at £100 per annum. If Mr. H. Woods could be prevailed on to take an apprentice, he would be the best master I know, as he is always at home: but brother B. asked him the question with respect to Edm.; but he has never returned any answer. Jack is taller somewhat than Mr. Yalden, and grows large in his limbs. Poor Mr. John Warnford of C.C.C. is, I see, just dead, and his lecture disposed of. If he had a college living, as I take for granted he had, then there is a parsonage at Skinner's option. I fear Mr. W. has left a widow. Easter I find comes this year very early, and will cruelly intersect the spring, as I must attend an election at Oriel in Easter week. If you don't make haste I shall publish before you. All friends join in proper respects.

Your affect.
GIL. WHITE.

LETTER IX.

Selborne, Jan. 12, 1774.

DEAR BROTHER,

As I make no manner of doubt but that your many kind and repeated invitations were very sincere, you will, I fear, feel a little disappointed when you come to find the purport of this letter. But I desire you would hear what I have to say before you condemn me.

I wrote to Mr. Roman* signifying a desire of being set at liberty from his cure, and fixing a day. He returned me a very handsome friendly answer, in which he wished me still to continue; and as he understood a desire to visit distant friends made me uneasy under restraint, he was ready at once to advance my salary to £50 per annum: hoping that sum would enable me to procure assistance from Oxon or elsewhere whenever I wanted to take a long journey.

* [Whose curate he was at Faringdon.—T. B.]

This proposal concurring, as you know, with my constant wish of reserving an employ to return to, has at present put a stop to my N. expedition, and has put me upon trying every expedient for procuring a substitute by writing to J. Mulso, Bro. H., — Skinner, &c. &c. What I could wish is to be at liberty after Easter to visit you from Oxon. For I must not pretend so totally to disregard College concerns as purposely, and in good health, to decline appearing at an election.

For my own feelings, I often wish myself with you, and make many comparisons between this and the last winter, not much to the advantage of the present. Last winter I look back upon as one of the most pleasant of my life, when I had my friends about me in a family way, and enjoyed the conversation of relations from whom I had been parted so long. When I do come to see you, you may depend on it I should wish to make you a good long visit, besides the stay that I must make in Rutland. As to Jack, I should wish to have him stay as long as ever you and his mother can spare him. He does not altogether lose his time, because he construes and translates, or looks over maps, or writes letters every day. He has read all the three volumes of the 'Spectator' through with that relish that shewed he understood them; and is much pleased with Derham's 'Physico-theology,' and is now embarked in Brydone's and Sir W. Hamilton's Letters, in which I make him refer all the way to maps. J. and I want to go to Fyfield soon; and therefore wish to know from my sister whether he has had the whooping cough, which all Harry's boys labor under at present.

My monography on the house-martin is finished, and in the hands of Mr. Barrington, who is so much prejudiced in its favour, that he proposes soon to have it read before the R. Society. Another on the house-swallow is nearly completed; from which I propose to proceed to the rest of the British *Hirundines*. Can Lever send us any authentic remarks? Pray tell me over again the story of the swallow building on the dead owl's wings, and on the coach, &c.: I think I could make a good use of it. The barometer is very irregular of late; we have now this day hard frost with the mercury at

29·22; and our last frost (which **lasted** from the 30th of December till January 5th inclusive) began with the barometer at 29·4. All last Saturday afternoon and night, and all Sunday there was a most extraordinary rain from the N. which perhaps was snow northward. Mr. and Mrs. Y. **were** here and stayed all Saturday night. On Sunday there was such a flood down at the Pond, that Thomas and I were over the calves of our legs before we got to Peter **Wells's**; where **we** were told that if we proceeded **any** further **our horses** would swim. So we returned back; and the rain followed on so the whole day, that I omitted going to my church at all, the first time for weather since I have undertaken Faringdon cure. People tell me they have known as big **a** flood, but never one that lasted so long. On Sunday evening it snowed, and then froze hard. Pray tell me a little about your **frosts,** and weather; what birds do you see? Wild geese, I suppose: have you any wagtails in winter? and what other small birds? You will enliven, I hope, your fauna with some dissertations **and** an agreeable journal, and some comparisons between the climates, &c. of And[alusia] and Great Britain. **Poor** old Miller is very lame still. Pray write soon. **Jack joins in best** respects.

Yours aff.
GIL. WHITE.

LETTER X.

Selborne, Feb. 4, 1774.

DEAR BROTHER,

BY your writing so very quickly, your last letter arrived much sooner than I could have expected. Since **I wrote to** you I have talked to Mr. Robinson the **curate of Colmer; and** he informs **me** that he **has not the least doubt but at the end of the summer he** shall be able **to take my cure off my hands** for some considerable time by **the following means.** The owner of Colmer **living, a young man in the N. is, it seems,** to take orders this summer, and to supply **his own church.**

This event will remove Robinson to East Tisted, from whence he can with ease undertake the full duty of Faringdon, and will be glad of the emolument, having a large family. You and my sister will therefore excuse me until October, I hope, when I shall, God willing, wait on you with great pleasure. Instead of your making excuses to me, I ought to make many to you for detaining your son so long : but, if you can undergo so much self denial, I should wish you could now spare him until autumn, when we will come down together. He is now of real service to me, a companion in my solitude. We shall ride down to Fyfield soon; and in March I shall carry him to London. It would be cheaper as well as pleasanter for me to travel this summer than to stay at home, because I seem to be in danger of building. But if I do not stay at this place in the summer, when can I think to enjoy it? and was I at liberty now, Easter would cruelly intersect my time, and spoil all. Lever is a generous man, and is of great service to you by lending you all his books: I hope Mr. P. will bethink himself, and wipe off all the imputation of selfishness that he lies under. Mr. Budd has just given his fine harpsichord to Bro. Harry. Your weather and ours accord very much. A neighbour carries this to London. So I am, in some haste,

Your affect. Bro.

GIL. WHITE.

Jack joins &c.

Berriman has paid Th. Gorston the money ordered : I got a bond paper; but not caring to go to an attorney, I drew up as full a receipt on it as I could couch in words. The man seemed staggered at first when he saw he must sign stamppaper: but complying at last he took the money, and getting without the door, cursed us all in a most devout and liberal manner, and so ended the negociation. B. was so provoked at the usage, that he thinks that he should have thrashed him had he been well and able. Let me hear soon.

LETTER XI.

Faringdon, March 6 [not later than 1774].

Dear Brother,

Mr. Webb, as you say, is, I believe, a good natured man, and in good business. I have made some enquiries round about by means of Mr. Yalden; but the answer was, that at present he did not think it convenient to take an apprentice. So it is needless to say anything farther on that subject.

What is become of your friend Gen. Cornwallis? I have never seen any mention of his arrival.

You never let me know whereabout your expences came for the fitting up of your house. I talk of building a parlor: but when it comes to the point I have fears about the trouble; besides green walls will not be habitable till the second year. In what language did you write to Linnæus? and in what did he answer you?

The late decree in the house of Lords concerning literary property will make booksellers shy of publishing new editions, as it renders such property very precarious. There is in London a strange spirit of decrying Linn., which seems to obtain more and more; I think, without any reason. Just as infidels rail at the S. S. tho' at the same time their minds are much enlightened by them. Mr. Twiss had written me word that he would come and see me in the winter. At Xmas I invited him again; but he was gone into Staffordshire on family business, and when he returned had no more time to spare.

By the death of Mr. John Warnford, Skinner is put in the possession of the living of Bassingham in the county of Lincoln, on the Witham, midway between Newark and Lincoln. His living was set in 1663 st 8d per acre; and so it continues; was it let only at 1s. 6d. it would be a noble parsonage, now it rents about 200 guineas. Skinner is to stay in coll. about five weeks longer. If you want to consult him about your fauna why don't you write to him? Direct for Skinner, after five weeks, at Passingham near Newark.

Jack by no means wants a coat and waistcoat yet; he shall have a pair of fustian breeches. Bro. Tho. can hear of no master as yet, but will continue to enquire. Prices are so enormous, that a common seedsman asked him the astonishing deposit of £300! to enable a young man to sell a pennyworth of radish seed!

I could get no *Mus* *, as nobody moved a rick.

Pray write very soon.

Yours affectionately,
GIL. WHITE.

Friends join in respects.

If you have anything for Linn. send it up soon, because the ship is likely to sail shortly. If you have any desiderata with respect to Spain, now is your time, for Mr. Barrington † tells me this morning that he has just compleated a nat. treaty with the King of Spain, who is to send all the curiosities of S. America, and the R. S. are to send him all the nat. productions of N. America.

I remember you wished to know how far the *Hirundo melba* extended up into Spain, and whether the *Hirundo rupestris* was seen in summer in the internal parts.

Mr. B. shewed me and Jack the curiosities of the R. S.; there was a stuffer packing and preparing the productions of N. America for the use of the King of Spain.

Pray write soon.

LETTER XII.

Selborne, March 29, 1774.

DEAR BROTHER,

THE long contested drawings are lodged in Thames Street in order to be sent down to you. I wish they had been better executed, and the owner had behaved more like a gentleman

* [He alludes to the harvest-mouse, *Mus messorius*, of which White was the discoverer in this country: see vol. i. p. 36.—T. B.]

† [Mr. Barrington was at this time commissary of the stores at Gibraltar, residing, however, in England.—T. B.]

on the occasion. He showed me a letter which he intended to send you: and as Benj. and he have literary connections, I hope you will forget and forgive. They always quarrel and squabble by letter, but accord well when they meet.

You do well to send Linn. your most curious specimens, and not only your most curious ones, but also such common ones as by the circumstances of his country he seems to be unacquainted with. He will, I trust, act with candour, and give you the best information he can concerning your nondescripts. No doubt when he sees the *Pratincola* he will remove it from the *Hirundines*.

As to my letters, they lie in my cupboard very snug: if you will correct them, and assist in the arrangement of my journal, I will publish. I have finished the monography of all the *Hirundines* except the swift.

Cromhall is so dismally circumstanced that I think there can be no doubt which way I had best act. The late incumbent insolvent, and too negligent to leave any papers of information behind him; no barn; I believe, no stable; a wretched house; and all the parish offices for years past in the hands of an attorney and a gentleman steward; and to complete all, the manor-farm belonging to Dr. Bosworth's persecuting peer! Mr. Pen told a man a little before he dyed that he had made one year £160 of his living, but that in general it produced only £150. Dr. Bosworth says it may be raised to £200.

Write to Mr. Barrington under cover to the Bishop of Llandaff in London.

I have not been at Hawkley yet: but the falling of the fragment from the cliff is the least part of the story; for a slipping below has disordered and damaged near 100 acres of land, and ruined two houses! The ground is rumpled and forced up as it were into waves[*]. I did not suppose your repairs would inform me about new buildings, I only wished to know what expense would put a good firm shell in comfortable condition. The vexation of workmen, I fear, is great. I bought in town Dr. Campbell's Political Survey of Great

[* [See vol. i. p. 230.]

Britain, a work that has employed his thoughts more than twenty years; 2 vols. 4to, £2 2s. As far as I have seen, I think his style is not so good as in his 'Present State of Europe.' The new work seems to comprise a variety of knowledge.

Some time ago I put Hume's History of England into Jack's hands. The young man is much taken with the work, and reads it with great earnestness and in preference to the 'Spectator' and Fathers, and makes pertinent remarks. ' With respects to my sister we remain

Yours affect.
GIL. WHITE.

LETTER XIII.

Selborne, April 29, 1774.

DEAR BROTHER,

OUT of all my journals I think I might collect matter enough, and such a series of incidents as might pretty well comprehend the natural history of this district, especially as to the ornithological part; and I have moreover half a century of letters on the same subject, most of them very long; all which together (were they thought worthy to be seen) might make up a moderate volume. To these might be added some circumstances of the country, its most curious plants, its few antiquities, all which together might soon be moulded into a work, had I resolution and spirits enough to set about it.

As to your own work, your journal incidents will be the most entertaining part of it. Skinner was much pleased with them. You should moreover, I think, have some letters, or dissertations, for the unsystematic part of your readers, who will not so well relish a fauna alone. The comparative account of the climates (where they will admit) would, I think, be very engaging. You have by you an abundance of your own letters. I should have told you before that I have finished my monography on the British *Hirundines*. If you can procure yourself a frank and will send it to me, Jack shall transcribe you one sheet that you may see how I have acquitted myself, and whether you approve of the manner. My cold and feverish complaint hung so about me at Easter that I did not go at all to the election, expecting every day to be laid up; but I wrote to the Provost, and sent a renunciation of the living of Cromhall; as I have done since of the living of Swainswick near Bath, which Ken also dyed possessed of.

Brother Thomas and Molly will be here, I think, next week in order that Molly may be settled for a while under the care of Mrs. Etty.

As to building, I have not yet absolutely determined about it; the next week will be the last week of asking, because the bark of oaks (as I must cut some timber) will not strip or run after that time. I am quite at a loss about the housemartins, as they do not appear yet: the swallows and bankmartins were early; a pair of swifts came to the church yesterday.

Mr. Lever, I find, continues wonderfully generous, and helpful by means of his books; if it was not for the General, you should, I think, dedicate your work to him. In my monography I have made honourable mention of his museum. Pray where did he get his little mouse? I mean by that to enquire whether it is common in Lancashire. For I concluded, as it had escaped Ray, that it did not extend far northward.

When Brother Thomas comes I will enquire what farther information he has procured with regard to a master for Jack. It is a very difficult matter, it seems, to find a place where all things concur to our wishes. Jack grows stout and tall, but not upright. He says he is five feet six inches and a half without his shoes.

We began to read Horace's Odes together; but found many of them so indecent for a young man, that we have taken to the Epistles, which are a fine body of ethics, and very entertaining, and sensible. Jack construes well; but makes slips with regard to quantity. He is become a very good transcriber. I believe such employ now and then is not bad for a young man, since it teaches him the use and power of stopping; a thing much neglected. Jack has read all the Georgics through. I wish I could read Reaumur and De Geer.

The spring is forward, and we have had some lovely weather; but winter is returned to day. I want to know what Linn. will say to the supposed *Junco* and the *Turdus*.

My wall trees promise much fruit. We join in respects to my sister. Pray write soon.

Your affect. brother,
GIL. WHITE.

LETTER XIV.

Selborne, June 18, 1774.

DEAR BROTHER,

IT pleases me to find that my little monography entertained you; it makes its own excuse for being short. The next will not offend in that way. Pray make *all* the *objections* freely that occur.

Linnæus's letter is polite and entertaining and instructive. But pray what does he mean by saying that your *Hirundo hyemalis* (for so I shall still call it) is - - - *varietas apus?* for the *apus* and *melba* only perhaps have omnibus *quatuor* digitis anticis, while your swallow has a back toe like other birds; besides the bill of your *apus* and *melba* are much *bent;* but that of the *hirundo hyemalis* is *straight*.

I have just received a letter from Mr. Pennant, wherein he says that he has lately sent twenty-nine more drawings to Mr. Ben., being the whole that were copied from your 'Gib.' They are to be kept as long as wanted.

Humbledon is a place that I have a strong dislike to, on account of its morals and dissipation, besides Mr. Hale has a young partner, should he want to leave business by and by*.

* [This remark has reference to the intended apprenticeship of 'Jack,' which at this time was a subject of much anxiety both to his father and uncle.—T. B.]

My anecdote from Valentia is taken from Willughby's 'Ornithology.' In one of your letters you regret the trouble of transcribing your Fauna. A writing master would take this trouble off your hands for a small sum, but with this disadvantage, that no man can transcribe his own without seeing places that he can alter for the better; a benefit which is entirely lost where a stranger is amanuensis. I wish Jack would earn your book; I mentioned the conditions, at which he smiled.

Pray return the printed monography without fail. If Mr. Lever desires to see my papers, let him have them; he is a man of honour, and will not suffer them to be transcribed. I beg his objections and additions. After I have heard from you again I will send your fourth monography with Mr. Willis's receipt &c.

Lin. still allows your *piscis thoracicus* to be a new genus; he should give it a name and you an engraving. When he talks of making honourable mention of you in his future edition you may reply " orna me."

No doubt the 'Voyage to the Hebrides' is an entertaining work; I have seen the cuts, but not the book*. You should observe when your summer birds come and depart, that we may compare notes. It is a sickly time among young folks, especially in Sussex. Thomas has had a pleurisy, and is not yet recovered so as to do any work. Molly White likes Selborne and looks well. Nanny Woods is very stout and very brown; she is all day in the sun.

Wall fruit abounds; and vines promise to blow well.

Harry has just lost his best cart horse; he is most unfortunate in horse flesh.

As my little mouse is so common in your parts and probably in all the intermediate, I am amazed that it should be so long a nondescript.

Printers, I know, some of them get a deal of money; but their state of apprenticeship must be, I should suppose, very

---

* [Johnson's 'Tour to the Western Islands of Scotland,' which took place in the previous autumn, was published only a short time before the date of this letter.—T. B.]

low and servile, and unwholesome; but of all this I am not sure. Chemistry, Bro. Thomas says, is very unwholesome. A packer's was, I have heard, a fine business; but at present they say merchants are their own packers. I have heard no more of the ribbon man. Jack will by no means obstruct my motions this summer, but is of use and service. We never fall out much; and then it is chiefly about *quantity* in verse, and there is no moral turpitude in long and short feet. As to law, I have nothing to say about it; lawyers get all the money. Our father, you know, did not approve of it. Sure London is so large a field, and you have so many friends there, that you cannot be long without hearing somewhat for your son. That you may get a proper place to your mind I heartily wish.

Your affectionate brother,
GIL. WHITE.

We join in respects to my sister. Pray write soon. I do not know that our Coll. is Dutch.

LETTER XV.

Selborne, July 15, 1774.

DEAR BROTHER,

JACK and I went down to Fyfield on June 22d, and stayed there 'til July 6th, and found and left Brother Henry very brisk and very busy; for, what between seven boarders, six children, some farming, three churches, and some building, he has enough to do. He has a one hundred pound boy in the room of Mr. Brocket, who by this time, I fear, is dead; and Jack and Jem from Fleet Street. The house, especially the kitchen, is so small for twenty-two in family, that H. is embarked in building a wing of 36 feet from the kitchen towards the brewhouse: this wing is to consist of a staircase, a large kitchen, a parlor over, and a large garret. The kitchen is to communicate with the new staircase of the brewhouse by a narrow entry running against the chalk wall; and thus the whole house may be made use of without a person's going abroad. The chambers over the brewhouse are finished, and very neat. All these buildings will cost a great sum and prevent the laying up of money; but as more room was absolutely necessary, and things are all done in the way of trade, I hope they will answer in the end.

I am glad to hear H. talk didactically about grammar rules, and moods and tenses; for unless a school master is somewhat of a pedant, and a little self-sufficient in his way, he must expect to be soon jaded with his drudgery.

Swifts, as I suspected, invariably lay but two eggs*; and as they breed but once, their increase is very small. I got Harry's bricklayer one evening to open the tiles of his brewhouse, under which were several nests containing only two squab young apiece; and moreover his workmen all told me that, when boys, they had invariably found only two eggs or two birds. If I lived at Fyfield, I should be more learned in swifts; for as you sit in the parlour you see their proceedings at the brewhouse.

I thank you for your strictures on my printed monog. and wish you would *extend* yours to the rest. I *had* used the pronoun personal to my swallows; but somebody objected; so I put *it* in its place. But I think you are right, and shall replace *she* and *her*; though there is this objection, that in a *pair* a male is implied as well as a female, and yet *he* would sound awkward for a bird.

Linn. is wrong past all doubt with respect to your *Hirundo hyemalis*. The *Melba* is undoubtedly *affinis* to the swift, but not your new swallow; it can by no means be a variety of *apus*. The rest of Mr. Pennant's drawings are here: you shall be sure to have them as soon as I can find a safe method of conveyance. I am glad your Fauna swells so fast. You must publish a quarto work: every man now publishes in quarto. It is not to be wondered at that you do not readily find a master for Jack; for our Bro. B. you see, is under the same

* [This is not invariably the case, as has been shown by the late Mr. Salmon (Yarr. Brit. Birds, ii. p. 235).—T. B.]

difficulty with respect to Edmund. Jack's epistle is of his own composing: I have altered here and there a word, but inserted no sentence.

"Orna me," is a sentence very familiar to me; it is, I think, in Tully's letters. Mrs. Barker writes me word this week, that now she and Mr. B. are come to a determination not to stir from home this summer. They plead the ill health of old Mrs. Barker, and a great deal of repairs to be done to a farmhouse.

We have had continual showers for three weeks past; much hay, especially clover, is totally spoiled; and much meadow-grass, and among the rest my own, is still standing, but growing too old. Harry still preserves your Barbary breed of fowls distinct: but they labour under a disadvantage not very convenient for this climate; for their down comes off before their feathers appear, and so they are stark naked for a fortnight—a condition not very suitable to a cold wet summer. They are taller and more erect than our breed.

As to franks, pray think no more about them; for, unless any thing particular wants to be enclosed, I never wish to receive one again: there is no money that I pay with more satisfaction than postage of letters from friends.

If you will object to the rest of my monog. where you see occasion, I shall be glad.

My neighbour Mr. Robertson is disposed, and thinks he shall be able, to take my curacy in the autumn, when I much wish to see Lancashire. But then it must not be until the beginning of November; for I must be at Oxford in October, and I am embarrassed with a broken tenant at Greatham, by whom I shall lose a year's rent, if I do not look about me, at Michaelmas.

Swifts breed but once in a summer, and but *two* at a time; swallows and martins breed twice in a season, and from *four* to *six* at a time; so the latter increase at an average five times as fast as the former. With respects to my sister, I remain

Your affectionate brother,
GIL. WHITE.

LETTER XVI.

Selborne, Aug. 11, 1774.

Dear Brother,

My best thanks are due for your strictures on my monographies, of which I shall avail myself in many particulars, and hope you will extend them to the swift. But I am greatly disappointed with respect to Mr. L.*, from whom, as a good practical ornithologist, I expected several new remarks and observations, but I don't find that he sent you *one*. Surely that gent.'s scheme with regard to his museum is a strange one; for as I cannot suppose that a man of his spirit will take money, so, if he entertains that great beast of a town for nothing (gratis), it will cost him thousands and be quite a ruinous expence! Swifts may breed twice at Gibraltar, as far as I know, because they arrive there much earlier than with us. But it is past all doubt that with us the case is quite different; for they do not arrive 'til the first week in May, do not hatch 'til the middle of June, and this year and the last departed by the seventh of August. Down at Fyfield I opened the eaves of some roofs on June 30, and found squab helpless young, and invariably but two in a nest; so that their congeners, who lay all round from four to six eggs, and produce invariably two broods in a year, increase five times as fast as they do. Linnæus is wrong even in doubting whether the *Hirundo hyemalis* be a variety of the *apus*; for the feet, the bill, the whole habit bespeak it an absolute swallow, not a swift †. The *melba* is an absolute *apus*. Pray send me a copy of that gent.'s last letter; I love to see the letters of great and able men in any way. Don't regard the want of franks. I pay $2\frac{1}{2}d.$ for a nonsensical newspaper, and shall I hesitate to pay $7d.$ for the sight of an epistle from the greatest naturalist in Europe? He will insert you in the

* [Lever.]
† [See Linnæus's letter of Jan. 2nd, 1774, afterwards printed.—T. B.]

next edition of his 'Syst. Nat.:' say to him in your next, "orna me."

I cannot procure a grass-hopper lark. They are such shy, skulking varlets; such troglodytes, such hedge-creepers, there is no knowing where to have them. When a good opportunity offers, I will send the drawings to town. Poor Nanny White of Fleet Street is in a very declining way. Happening to meet Mr. Edm. Woods lately at Newton, I pressed him very earnestly to lend his assistance in looking out a master for Jack. He promises to do his best, and is a likely man to forward such a business. * * * You must read Lord Chesterfield's letters; they are very entertaining, though in parts very exceptionable.

Bear is a sort of barley: Mr. P.† should have told his readers as much in a note. Mr. and Mrs. Lort are now on a tour round N. Wales. Mr. Leech has lost his cause with respect to the lead-mines, and stands obliged to refund all his gains. Molly White must lose her share, of course. Niece Molly joins in respects

Your loving brother,
GIL. WHITE.

I am mending my tiling and pointing against winter. A stitch in my side makes writing irksome.

LETTER XVII.

Selborne, Sept. 26, 1774.

DEAR BROTHER,

SOME years ago, when I met Sam Barker at Ringmer, I found he had some propensity to poetry, tho' it had not then been called forth. I therefore gave him a few instructions, and this summer sent him some old verses, on Selborne, new furbished up ‡. These small encouragements have occasioned the lines above, which Jack transcribes for your amusement. By all means recollect the specific difference, or else get new spe-

† [Pennant?]
‡ [The 'Invitation to Selborne.' See the Poems at the end of Vol. I.
—T. B.]

cimens of the *Sphex formicarum falco*; for it is a great pity that so diverting an account as that which you give of that insect should be lost to your Fauna.

You must be sure to caution Linn. that the *Œstrus curvicauda* is by no means the parent of the star-tailed water-maggot, though Derham says it is; Swam., Geoffroy, and others have since discovered that wonderful maggot to be the offspring of a *Musca hydroleon*: see Geof.; he calls it *Stratiomys*. You will be the means, I perceive, of correcting many mistakes, and new arranging many misplaced articles in 'Syst. Nat.,' which I wish to see as perfect as possible. I wish you may catch a *curvicauda* before the autumn is over: you will at once be convinced that it is an *Œstrus*. *Os nullum, punctis tribus*, &c.: it sometimes haunts upland fields, and teazes the horses at plow; but is more frequently found in swampy wet places, and is probably aquatic in its larva state. The nits laid on my horses at Meon-Stoke Aug 19th stick on their legs and flanks still. * * * Skinner can if he pleases, send several questions and pertinent enquiries relative to 'Syst. Nat.,' which he well understands, with its comparative merits and defects, as far as the author has borrowed from or imitated Mr. Ray.

Next summer I will, if possible, get a grass-hopper lark: but they are not easily procured; they skulk in the hedges like mice.

When you write to Linnæus next, pray talk to him about tortoises†. There are tortoises whose shells are always open *behind* and *before*—" apertura testæ anterior," as he says himself, " pro capite et brachiis, posterior pro caudâ et femoribus." These apertures are supported as it were by pillars on each side, and can never be closed. Of such construction is the shell of Mrs. Snooke's present living tortoise, Timothy. But then there are tortoises whose under shell has a *cardo* or hinge about the middle of their bellies commanding one lid or flap for-

† [The letter from John White to Linnæus, which was the result of this suggestion of Gilbert's, certainly gave the great Swede the first idea of the two distinct families of *Testudinata* in question; but he failed to name his brother as the real author of the observation. (See note to p. 240, Vol. I.)--T. B.]

ward, and one lid backward (like the double-lidded snuff-boxes), which when shut conceal the head and legs and tail of the reptile entirely and keep out all annoyances. Two such (very small they were) Mrs. Snooke had formerly; the shells lie still in her room over the hall. Now concerning shells of this construction Linn. makes no mention at all; and this construction is certainly the most curious, and perhaps the most uncommon. But what I would infer from all this is that in his genus *Testudo* express mention should be made of this diversity; and the genus should be divided into *testis clausis cardinatis*, and *testis apertis*, or by some such expression. He loves, you know, to subdivide his long genera; and such subdivisions are very consistent with system. I hope I have expressed myself so as to be understood in this matter; and I wish you would mention it to him, and ask if such a subdivision would not be proper. Thus he divides his genus of *Œnas* into " rostro basi gibbo," and " rostro basi æquali," &c. &c. Can't you hear yet where and how the *Panorpa coa* feeds? It is pity that part of its hist. should escape you. I shall transcribe my swift anew before it be read [redde]* to the R. S. I have alterations of some consequence to make, such as the number of its eggs, &c. It is remarkable that none of the martins round my buildings have this year any second broods. Is this owing to the cold, wet, uncomfortable equinox? We had sweet weather this August till towards the end, but since, sad doings —much corn damaged and our fruit spoiled. We have vast quantities of hops; but they are mostly distempered. My thanks are due for your kind letter of Sept. 11th; some of the contents are very strange! Over Leicester-house gate should be written in letters of gold, *Museum Leveriense*.

Our respects to my sister.   Yours affect.
                               GIL. WHITE.

Just as I had finished thus far, your entertaining letter of Sept. 18 came to hand. I am convinced by Reaumur with respect to the *Œstrus bovis* &c., and much pleased that you have

* [" Redde" is the word repeatedly used at that period in the 'Philosophical Transactions.'—T. B.]

discovered and seen with your own eyes, and caught with your own hands a *curvicauda*: but it seems strange that you did not see eggs on the horse's hair. Perhaps the color of the horse might prevent your seeing them. Horses of dark color are quite discolor'd by them. I wish to know the *nidus* of the great *Tabanus* also: it haunts, I know, watery, moor places. The *Sturnus coll.** can't be a *Fringilla*, since it has no conic bill. All grass horses now in *watery* places have nits: I am pleased to find that insect extends to your district. You may see with your own eyes the parent deposit each single egg. Your remark concerning the bivalve straps of the egg is a good one.

Cholderton lies again at my option †.

LETTER XVIII.

Selborne, Feb. 1, 1775.

Dear Brother,

I HAVE been unusually dilatory in my answer to your last letter; and the reason was, tho' I was much vexed and disappointed at your rebuff, which came so unexpectedly, yet I did not know how to come to your assistance. Mr. Pinnock at the same time mentioned a gent. of the law; but that is a profession you do not seem to affect.

Brother Ben says you must have as many plates as possible in your Fauna; for it is the fashion now " to look in picturebooks." Insects being the most laborious, and probably to most readers the most uninteresting part of your work, I am glad you have run thro' them. The birds and quadrupeds will pass off smoothly. I am sorry you will not work up your tour to Mogador into a pretty chapter; it is the fashion now to publish tours: besides, some account of the person, manners, and mode of life of that monarch who at present sets all naval powers at defiance, would take with many readers. The

---

* [This is the *Accentor alpinus*, or more properly *A. collaris*, of modern ornithologists.—T. B.]

† [The living of Cholderton was twice declined by him. See memoir. —T. B.]

practice of gratifying such barbarians with elegant presents, and the Moors turning Dollond's perspectives into walking-sticks, would furnish matters for agreeable reflection. Dr. Johnson has just published his journey through the Western Isles. I have read it; and you should read it. It is quite a sentimental journey, divested of all natural history and antiquities, but full of good sense, and new and peculiar reflections. It does not at all interfere with Mr. Pennant's book.

John Neal and Dame Knight are dead. Berriman lies in the same sad deplorable way. Mrs. Snooke writes me word that she has been better than usual this mild winter.

For some days past we have had great rains and blustering weather. This morning it is very wet and stormy; the thermometer at 50, the barom. 28·7. Every sunny day, insects abound, and in warm lanes and under hedges the air swarms with them. Within doors wood-lice, spiders, and *Lepismæ* are in motion, and many *Muscæ* in the stable; earthworms come forth every mild evening; so that in mild winters insects are not so much laid up as is imagined. Some *Phalænæ* fly also all the winter. * * * On Jan. 20th many rooks were caught, it is said, by a man near Hackwood Park; their wings, as he affirms, were frozen together by a wet sleet then falling. Pray write soon.

Respects as due.   Your affect.
                          GIL. WHITE.

LETTER XIX.

Fyfield, March 9, 1775.

DEAR BROTHER,

As you have long experienced that I am not usually a tardy and negligent correspondent, you will, I suppose, conclude that something has happened to prevent my writing sooner, as really has been the case. I have had an heat and stiffness in my eyes from over much reading, that made writing very irksome for some time; they are now pretty well recovered again.

After your disappointment in town I was glad to hear by your last that you had a prospect of disposing of your son at Manchester; but now I understand that farther difficulties arise. The Scopoli from Mr. Pennant that you mention, is at Selborne; and I will send it, if you desire it; but it affords no information.

As you rather complain of some reserve on Benj.'s side respecting your work, suppose you write to him, and ask him how much he will give you *downright* clear of the plates and printing for your copy; and then you will know your certain gain, and will run no risk. Anything in the nat. way now sells well. Or if he chuses to go shares in profit or loss, enquire of him what proportion he should think would pay him for conducting the sale and publication. Booksellers have certainly a power of pushing books into the world; and it must be a work of great merit to obtain and make its way *invitis bibliopolis*. You mention also a want of books: might you not also apply to Benj. to know on what terms he would furnish you with the *use* of books proper for your purpose 'til you had compleated your Fauna? It is highly proper, it seems, to have a good many cuts. Mr. Curtis will superintend your engravings.

Mrs. Chapone * sold her two first vols. for £50. Now she has made up a third from essays, poems, adventures, &c. and sold that to another for £250; so that it is expected the man will lose considerably by the purchase.

Many thanks for the copies of your 'Gib. Letters,' which are very entertaining. You have the advantage of me now, since you have taken away my amanuensis. I am disturbed that Mr. Shaw takes no manner of notice of the *Hirundines*; nor how far the *melba* and *hybernæ* extend, as might have been expected from his opportunities at Cadiz and elsewhere. Pray let Cap. Shaw know, that if he comes to Alton I should be glad to see him. The spirit for nat. hist. that you left behind you is by no means evaporated; neither is your mantle worn out.

* [This lady was the early object of Gilbert White's regard and addresses when Hester Mulso. (See memoir.)—T. B.]

Lever has opened his museum at half a guinea per head. Harry has got a fine roomy kitchen indeed, and will have a fine parlor over. This addition shuts all his buildings finely together; and nothing is to be regretted but the expense. Sister Harry has got another fine boy, whose name is Edward. Nanny White is in a poor languishing way, still at lodgings near Vauxhall. Edward White is gone on trial to Mr. John Hounsom, linendraper in Fleet Street. The father is to advance with him a fee of £250; and the master makes a merit of taking so little, and says that from a stranger he should have demanded £300.

When opportunity serves, pray read Dr. Johnson's 'Journey thro' Scotland,' and Dr. Burney's 'Tour thro' Europe to make enquiries into the present state of musick.' Thanks for your information about cotton-cups.

Should you not produce in your work a short comparative table of weather at Gib., Selborne, and N. America? Kalm will furnish you with the barom., thermom., &c. of America. I herewith send you my best account of the cobweb shower of 1741. What is said of spiders shooting webs, and flying &c. in Ray's Letters is so much, that it cannot be transcribed. You should consult Ray's Letters *.

When first I came I fully intended to have sent you my account of the cobweb shower: but this house is so full that I have no opportunity of being long enough alone to think accurately on any subject; so I must defer that part till I write again. We have continual wet weather; and farmers are sadly hindered in their spring crop: stormy and wet this day, March 11.

When Hesiod says that the chirping note of the *Cicada* comes from *under its wings*, he expresses himself thus—

$$\text{ἠχέτα τέττιξ}$$
$$\text{Δενδρεω ἐφεζομενος λιγυρην καταχευετ' ἀοιδην}$$
$$\text{Πυκνον ὑπο πτερυγων.} \qquad \text{v. 584.}$$

Is there not a Frenchman who claims this discovery?

Sure insects have been more abroad this winter than usual: and lately, in our little interval of fine weather, many species

* [See p. 182, Vol. I.—T. B.]

of *Musca* came forth. *Chrysomela Gottingensis* begins to come forth.

Bro. Tho., Molly White, and myself came down to this place on Tuesday last; on Wednesday next Harry's boy is to be bapt.; and on Friday we are to return to Selborne.

I have just dug away 40 loads of earth from the end of my kitchen, and have now set my house above ground in all parts.

Mr. Halliday behaves very well, and improves so much, that his friends are well pleased with the pains that have been taken with him. His parts, tho' somewhat backward, and slow, promise to be solid.

Building is very infectious and catching: I am so pleased with H.'s new parlour, that I want to go home and build one.

A certain plea of license against the incumbent's taking all the duty in person can avail him nothing. Every man may, if he chooses, do his own business himself, certainly.

A flock of Spoon-bills was seen last winter near Yarmouth in Norfolk: one was shot and sent to Curtis, who showed it to Bro. Tho. This is a rare bird indeed in England, tho' common in Holland, and must have migrated across the German Ocean, no narrow frith, in spite of all that Mr. Barrington can say to the contrary[*]. That gent. is got into some fracas with the R. S.; so that, I suspect, no more of my *Hirundines* will be redde.

I will send you in my next what Chaucer says about gossamer: it is wonderful that so remarkable and prognostic a phenomenon should escape Thomson, the naturalist poet.

As America is at present the subject of conversation, it may be matter of some amusement to you to send you a quotation from the *Medea* of Seneca, prophetic of the discovery of that vast continent.

veneant annis
Secula seris, quibus *oceanus*
Pateat, *tellus*, Tiphysque novos
Detegat orbes; nec sit terra ultima Thule.

[*] [It is now well known that the Spoonbill used to breed in Norfolk. See Stevenson's 'Birds of Norfolk,' ii. p. 526. Sir Thomas Brown also says that they used to build in the Heronry at Claxton and Rudham, in in that county.—T. B.]

N.B. Tiphys was pilot to the Argonautic expedition; and a type of Columbus.

All friends join in respects yours affect.
GIL. WHITE.

Sure your Fauna should sell outright for £100 clear of all deductions. Mr. Pennant gets that sum for his new edition of ' Brit. Zool. ;' and your work will contain much more new, original information. I want to see you the first of faunists. With regard to anecdote and real nat. hist. the less you borrow from books the better; you have a large fund of your own. Benj. will get very largely by Mr. P.'s Scotch tour.

LETTER XX.

Selborne, Oct. 4, 1775.

DEAR BROTHER,

FROM the hurry arising from a full house while the Lyndon family were with me; and by means of Mr. Thos. Mulso, who came as soon as they were gone to Fyfield, I find that your letter has lain unanswered for three weeks. It is proper therefore to sit down now I am alone, and answer your last before my friends return from Fyfield.

Mr. Barker sets out as this morning for Northamptonshire, and takes his leave of Hants at my Bro. Harry's house; but the ladies and Sam return hither on Friday; and Harry accompanies them and stays with me a few days. How long my sister &c. are to stay I cannot yet say. Your Fauna, to which I think myself at least a foster-father, is become, I hear with pleasure, a fine thriving child. I could be glad to examine its features, and to dandle it, and remark how it shoots up towards its $ἡλικια$; but the old difficulty of my church stands still in my way, and is like to prove as great a *remora* as usual: I am making enquiries concerning some assistance, but can hear of nothing yet to my satisfaction. Mr. Grimm has not yet appeared; the reason is because he has been detained so long in Nottinghamshire.

* * * * * *

Our people here, you know, call coppice-wood, or hedge-wood, *rice* or *rise*. Now Bro. Thos. has found that this word is pure Saxon; for *hris** signifies *frondes*. Thus has he vindicated this provincial word from contempt. I am lowering my bank in my garden, and throwing its border on an hanging slope: last winter I sank my walks so much, that this alteration became necessary. Where is Wollet the draughtsman to be found? Thos. Mulso, who draws sweetly, has taken hints concerning the Hawkley Slip, to be finished in town; bro. Ben has just purchased two freehold houses in S. Lambeth, one of which is to be used as his country house, into which he is to enter as soon as possible. He and Ben. are just gone from us. My sister Bet and Jane and Nanny are still at Newton; the latter is most marvellously recovered, and will now, I trust, do very well. Poor little Nanny Wood has been ill and has lost her colour. Bro. Harry has got another young man, a 50-pounder; he has now a fine income, and will soon, I hope, begin to lay by some money. Does your migrating clergyman visit you again this winter? Ring-ouzels came to us in September. Your snuff-pincers extinguish my candles in a very neat manner.

With respects to my sister, I remain
Your loving brother,
GIL. WHITE.

LETTER XXI.

London, Jan. 30, '76.

DEAR BROTHER,

As you have enjoined me to speak my sentiments with respect to your work, you must not think me didactic and forward in the following pages. It will be well to sweeten and diversify your tables of weather &c. with an alternate page of zool. ca-

---

* The top of a tree: "top and lop."

lendar, and interesting coincidences; for the generality of readers are apt to skip over whatever looks like figures. Your journal will be pretty long. An index perhaps has never entered into your head; yet such a thing may be expected in so large a work. You may no doubt, if you please, invent your system as well as Brown. You are not sworn to follow the arrangement of Linn. By that means the subject certainly rises on the reader. The Swedes admire Brown notwithstanding. *Faunæ Calpensis primitiæ* will no doubt be more modest; yet might your *full* history well deserve to be called a Fauna. In strictness Linn.'s *Fauna Suec.* is no more a *perfect* Fauna than your own, since some hundreds of animals must still have escaped his observation. Bro. Ben objects to a Latin title to an English book. Suppose you call it, 'Fauna Cal., or a Zool. Hist. of Gib.' &c.; for Natural Hist. it must not be called, since the plants are wanting. There is such a spirit gone forth against whatever is Linnæan, that I would not make the title page Linnæan. Your bookseller must be consulted a little in the title page and advertisements, as he knows best how to throw in little savoury and alluring circumstances to quicken the appetite of your buyer. By no means should you print, Bro. Tho. and I both think, 'til you have sold your copy: booksellers know how to subscribe off an impression to the trade, and to throw cold water on a work lying on the author's hand. We do by no means like your "sequimur patrem," &c.: you should have mottos relative to each class. Ovid, perhaps, somewhere among his monsters will furnish for the *Vermes*. Pray correspond with Padre Floroz, since Linn. will no longer write*. We can by no means see how you can be off from bringing up your work yourself: for no person will purchase what they have not seen; besides one hour's conversation will do more business than an hundred letters. Might not Benj. print and publish for you on the usual terms? We wish to see your papers, and to correct here and there, not out of vanity and a meddling temper, but because little errors un-

---

* [In May 1774 Linnæus had his first attack of apoplexy, from which he never wholly recovered.—T. B.]

avoidably befall and escape every author. Be sure to procure a good perspective *western* view of the harbor, town, and hill of Gib. to fold in as frontispiece, with references; it will contribute to explain many passages. You will have, I find, near 1000 pages, and 800 species.

As an electrician you should see Priestley's 'Hist. of Electricity:' he sets the whole in a pleasing light. Just as you wrote last my neighbours told me there were troops from Gib. at Alton; so I sent Thomas over with a note and invitation to your friend Cap. Shaw. He brought word that Mr. S. had passed through Alton, and was quartered at Farnham. I then wrote by the post to Farnham renewing my invitation; and received a letter of thanks, and excuses that they expected daily to be called for to march towards London, where the king would review them. However, the deep snow came and stopped their march; so that when I came to Farnham I found the soldiers still there : **I therefore called** on C. Shaw for five minutes in my postchaise **at the Bush-inn-gate**; and so ended the affair. He **expressed** his sense of my civility, and says he **will write to you very soon.** He does not expect to go to N. America.

As soon as Bro. Tho. is at liberty **he proposes laying in** materials for a history of Hants : he is in **possession of a fine fortune.**

I am **glad John (for now he is very** near six feet high I must no **longer call him Jack) behaves** so much to your satisfaction. He has lately **written to me;** and I have answered from hence, offering him a book of a guinea value, but desiring him to consult you and his master.

We condole with you on the loss of your excellent friend the Governor*. Perhaps by permission you may dedicate to the Archbishop, and, as the General is dead, may **be allowed to** speak with more warmth **of him than you could have done to**

* [The Hon. Edward Cornwallis, Lieutenant-General, and Governor of Gibraltar, was the son of Lord Cornwallis, uncle of the earl, and twin brother of the Archbishop of Canterbury. He died at Bird Place in Hertfordshire, on the 14th of January 1776, only about a fortnight before the date of this letter.—T. B.]

him. Shall I desire Mr. Lort to enquire whether such a dedication would be permitted, and well taken.

Poor Brown the artist! it is the fate of most ingenious foreigners: they have no manner of economy. Forster will be soon in the same condition: he and his son dress like noblemen, and give £60 per ann. for an house! They have published ' New Genera of Antarctic Plants.' Benj. has a share in this book. There is *Barringtonia*, a *Sheffieldia*, a *Skinneria*, &c. &c.

Their great work or ' Voyage ' is now under correction at Oxford. Have your churchyards in the N. any yew trees?

Pray send me Reaumur's *whole account* of the *Hippobosca hirundinis*. Pray write soon. London is now Petersburg; it freezes under our beds with shutters closed and curtains drawn. Bro. Ben.'s new house at S. Lambeth was last Sunday Archangel, with therm. at eleven, and every thing ice and snow.

Yrs. affect.
GIL. WHITE.

My love to my sister.

Look in Anacreon's Ode 43, and see if it affords any apt motto for insects in general. I have been to Mr. Grimm*, and am better pleased with his performances than I expected, and think I must send for him next summer. Bro. Th. talks of employing him some time hence. Excuse; we are called to supper.

* [Samuel Henry Grimm, the artist who was employed by Gilbert White to draw the landscape illustrations of his book, was a native of Berghorff, in the Canton of Berne, in Switzerland; but the greater part of his life was spent in England. He contributed to the 'History of Selborne' the vignette of the " Hermitage " in the title-page, both views of the church, the Temple, and the Pleystow. Whether the large folding frontispiece was drawn by him is uncertain, as no artist's name appears on it; but the style, both of the figures and the landscape, is much in the same character as his other drawings. He died in London, about 1794. —T. B.]

LETTER XXII.

Thames Street, Feb. 27.

Dear Brother,

Many thanks for your letter of the 18th, and for your extract from Reaumur. We all much approve of what you intend to *inscribe* to the Archbishop, thinking it neat and polite; but, like yourself, we do not much like your title page. Brother Ben says he thinks that "Hist. Nat.: Observations in Lat. 36°," should all be left out, and that it should begin with "An Essay," &c.: but it is not worth while to be solicitous about a title page. Swift says, "for a title page consult your bookseller." But the term "*Fauna Calp.*" they judged to be too quaint and pedantic for the beginning of a title; yet, I think, must by no means be sunk, for the following reason, because I believe you have always told Linnæus that you should call your book by that name; and therefore if he mentions your work in his last edition (as he certainly will) you will lose all the credit to be derived from such notice of you, if you mention no such title. Supposing Linn. to be dead, there can be no doubt that his son will put forth the new edition. By what we remember of the specimen of your work, we thought some articles too diffuse. It is natural for you to fall a little into this extreme from the regard you express for Reaumur, since all the French in Nat. Hist. are very circumstantial. Be so good as not to forestall my cobweb shower. I wish I had two or three dozen more of such anecdotes. An engraver has been with me; and I have been talking with him about his taking off 5 or 6 of my drawings: he says that my 4to drawings cannot be well executed under 8 guineas a piece; now 5 times eight is forty! Grimm is reducing my Hermitage-view in order to bring it to a proper size for a *vignette**: he is also to take it in a large scale for bro. Hen.

* [This forms the vignette in both the quarto editions.—T. B.]

You will see in the papers a remarkable cause in the commons between a patron and a rector who took two *distant* perpetual curacies; the matter was determined in favor of the rector: had it gone against him the rector of Fyfield would have had cause to quake. I propose staying in town 'til the 14th of March. Respects to my sister.

Your affect. brother,
GIL. WHITE.

If you think the mention of your degree of A.B. will occasion any inconvenience, you may easily drop it. Brother Tho. waits on the dean of Ely tomorrow at Lambeth: and will be sure to desire him to represent you and Harry in a favorable light to the new Bishop of Chester. Poor Nanny White declines very fast, and is in a very languishing state *.

LETTER XXIII.

Thames Street, March 5, 1776.

Dear Brother,

Brother Tho. and I both think that you should *yourself* write to the Archbishop one of your best letters, and beg to know of him whether you might dedicate to him, and tell him the reason why; and then you will act on sure grounds. If you are not permitted, you might mention the Gen. in your preface.

Brown, I think, is in gaol in St. George's Fields; but artists never work more steadily than when under confinement, Forster has just received a letter from Linnæus, who wants to publish a new *Mantissa* of plants in England. Brother Benj. declines meddling. Forster says that when you write to Linn. you should direct to him not as professor at Upsal, but as *academician*, since all such letters go free, because the academy is of royal institution. Forster's new genera of

---

* [After many fluctuations in the state of her health, she died in October 1777. See page 64.—T. B.]

Antarctic plants do not sell: so that the *Skinneria*, the *Sheffieldia*, the *Barringtonia* are like to sleep. Botanists think they shall never see the originals; and other readers care not a farthing about the matter. I marvel at the mildness of your weather in January. I told you, I think, that on the 31st my therm. was ½ below 0. There seems to have been a peculiarly severe current at Selborne. Mr. Y.* was so supine as never to put his therm. out! The therm. at S. Lambeth was at 6, at Fyfield 15, at Lyndon 19; in London areas at 20. We join in respects. I return home next week.

Yours affect.
GIL. WHITE.

Nanny White rides out at her father's country-house every day, and improves wonderfully. Molly White is at Cambridge.

Bro. Henry went away in January before the snow was melted and went through between high walls of that meteor. Bro. Tho. by no means approves of your title of " Zool. Anecdotes;" he thinks the latter too mean and unworthy a great book. He neither thinks that you should say, " The Nat. Hist. of the quadrup. birds, fishes and insects of Southern Spain," with &c. We wish also that you would throw something *savoury* into your title page concerning *migration*; for many readers pay attention to that *circumstance*, without regarding any other parts of Nat. Hist. Say what you can concerning *vegetation;* for the love of such knowledge increases. Even Bishops (your Bishop in particular), in order to recommend themselves, study botany. Mr. Curtis says, that men from the other end of the town call on him *in their coaches* to desire private lectures for grown gentlemen.

But your *bookseller, at last,* will be your *best* adviser respecting a title page; for such men best understand the pulse of the publick. Pray write to Selborne not long hence. Jack should send me an account of the therm. at Manchester. Mr. Lever has custom at his shop; but whether adequate to his boundless views, no man can guess. He is furnishing the

* [Mr. Yalden, Vicar of Newton.—T. B.]

whole *house* with specimens; still "Some Demon whispers, *Bubo*, have a taste" *.

Sir Tho. Gatehouse is ruined, and locked up in a garret here in town for fear of his creditors; and his lady, who brought a £1000 per ann., will for his life be reduced to poverty!!

LETTER XXIV.

Fyfield, May 15, 1776.

DEAR BROTHER,

BROTHER Thomas and his daughter have been with me for a week: yesterday we all three came down to this place, and found all well.

As I had got a frank for you, I thought it best to take it down with us, that all that had occasion might make use of it together.

Forster was presented to his doctor's degree at Oxford on account of his literary fame, and because he had hazarded his life in a circumnavigation in the pursuit of natural knowledge.

Pray write to Linn.; for if he only tells you of your new genera, &c., and affixes no names, he leaves you in the lurch; direct to him as an Academician, for reasons assigned in a former letter †.

We are glad you find your heavy duty so easy; for what is paid to curates is all neat money and occasions considerable deductions from a moderate living. Holdsworth I have procured; but I can't say the work gives me so much pleasure as it seems to have afforded you. I did not find so many genuine criticisms drawn from the face of the country and the modern practices in husbandry as I expected, but rather a collection of parallel passages from Cato and Columella. So much easier is it to compile, than to advance fresh remarks.

---

* "Some demon whispers, '*Visto* have a taste.'"—POPE'S *Essays*.

† [Linnæus's second and most severe attack of apoplexy occurred about this time.—T. B.]

Mr. Yalden will not probably set out for Spain 'til next spring: I shall exhort him by all means to take your recommendations in his pocket. He is a decent zoologist, and particularly an entomologist. He is returned, I hear, from Edinburgh to Winton.

Your quantity of drawings, I find, are considerable; no doubt they should be engraved in London. As to your botany it should be carefully overlooked by somebody; in the zoological part your powers are much more considerable and you want only a friend, as all men do, just to remark those small errors or slips which " *incuria fudit*."

You are the best judge whether you should address Mrs. Cornwallis; if you do, you may express your regard for her husband with more warmth than if he was living: *Quis desiderio sit pudor aut modus?* Send me some account of the *Hippobosca hirundinis* at your leisure.

Harry's little academy is in a flourishing way; he will, it is too probable, lose his £100 young gent. at Midsummer; but then at that time he is to have a fresh pupil of 14 years of age at £150 per annum. His building has been heavy on him; but without considerable additions he could not have stood on the present footing. So one must be set against the the other. We are much distressed in Hants by the long dry season; no grass, and a poor prospect for **spring corn**; butter 10*d*. per pound, and hay at £4 10*s*. per ton!

Mr. Chandler's stile and wording is very lame and defective indeed. Sir Tho. Gatehouse's effects are just sold off at both his seats. My respects to my sister and Jack; "John" I mean, now he is six feet high. You cannot take another living without becoming A.M. or LL.B., both which degrees will require time, attendance, and expense; **if you take a second living now, you render your first void** *ipso facto*.

The bloom on all sorts of trees is this year very extraordinary indeed!

At present I think of sending for Grimm about the beginning of July: I may employ him for perhaps a month. Mr. Yalden of Newton then talks of taking him for a week to draw his house and outlet; and then he is to go to Penruddock

Wyndham, Esq., at Warnford. So he will have a good stroke of work. His price is two guineas and an half per week. His buildings, human figures, quadrupeds, waters, perspective among trees are good; but his trees are not so pleasing: he has also a vein of humour; but that I shall not allow him to call forth, as all my plates must be serious. At the last exhibition he produced some very good drawings.

Harry's outlet is now very neat and beautiful. Capt. Shaw is but just gone from Farnham. I called on him in my return from town: he seemed inclined I thought to make me a visit; but he never came. Mrs. Etty has been very ill indeed since her lying-in, but is getting better; she has got another son, whose name is Simeon.

LETTER XXV.

Munstoke, Aug. 9, 1776.

DEAR BROTHER,

By your unusual silence I began to fear what has really been the case, ill health. You have perhaps by your attention to your book and other matters been too free with your constitution lately; you must therefore relax a little and allow yourself more time for riding and walking. Particularly, I think, you should avoid contention though in ever so good a cause; for any earnest agitation of the mind is bad for the stomach.

Lucomb's oak, we think, will at last probably turn out the Queen's *ægilops**: but this matter cannot well be determined 'til it comes to bear fruit. It carries its leaf all the winter in Devon, but casts it at Selborne, Essex, and elsewhere, and is probably a deciduous tree. Perhaps your *Homo sapiens* may be too close a copying of the Linn. system, and may appear pedantic to an anti-Linn. reader. I by no means want the

---

* [*Quercus lucombeana.* Of this fine species there are figures and a full description in Loudon's 'Arboretum,' vol. iii. p. 1852. Certainly distinct from *ægilops*.—T.B.]

Hippobosca hirund. just at any one particular day or week; only wish to see it at your leisure. Mr. Grimm was with me just twenty-eight days; twenty-four of which he worked very hard and shewed good specimens of his genius, assiduity and modest behaviour, much to my satisfaction. He finished for me twelve views. He first of all sketches his scapes with a lead pencil; then he pens them all over, as he calls it, with indian-ink, rubbing out the superfluous pencil strokes; then he gives a charming shading with a brush dipped in indian-ink, and last he throws a light tinge of water colour over the whole. The scapes, many of them at least, looked so lovely in their indian-ink shading, that it was with difficulty the artist could prevail on me to permit him to tinge them; as I feared those colours might puzzle the engravers; but he assured me to the contrary. From me Mr. Grimm went to Mr. Yalden to take a scape of his outlet from above the chalkpit. On Tuesday I brought my artist (at the desire of a gent. who was visiting there) to Lord Clanricarde's at Warnford, that he might take a drawing of an old building in his lordship's garden, now a barn: it is a curious piece of antiquity little known, and will prove an agreeable surprise to many as I am sure it was to me, who never heard the least of the matter before.

There is some reason to fear that Mr. Halliday's father may be taken by the American privateers in his passage home from Antigua.

Mulso has just got a second living near Winton; the name of it is Easton, it is worth £250 per annum. Our St. foin was finely made, then we had a dripping time that spoiled much clover, and some meadow-hay; and for the last fortnight in July we had glorious weather to finish off the meadow: now harvest is beginning and the weather dripping. Mr. and Mrs. Mulso join in respects. I saw one swift yesterday. At present I cannot say when I shall be at liberty to wait upon you and my sister; but you may be assured that I wish to have it in my power to see Blackburn. I conclude,

Your affectionate brother,

GIL. WHITE.

LETTER XXVI.

Oxford, October *.

DEAR BROTHER,

Your letter of October 2d arrived just as I was prepared to set out for this place, to which I was called a day or two sooner than I intended on account of the Univ. election. I left Bro. Thos. behind at my own house, and Bro. Ben. at Newton, intending to club for a post chaise in a day or two, and to return to town. Bro. Thos. has been bathing in the salt water at Lymington for rheumatic complaints. Poor Nanny White has been rather better for a day or two past, and has rested, and shewed a little appetite, and slept a little; so that her friends were willing to flatter themselves that her illness might take a better turn. She never had any cough.

I heartily wish it was as much in my power as in my inclination to assist you in the concern you mention. As to Mr. Hill, I never heard of him but at Fyfield, and therefore can only echo my Bro. Harry with regard to his business and reputation. He has, it seems, a partner, concerning whom it will be as needful to enquire as about the principal. There is also a Mr. Baverstock at Marlboro' (one of the Baverstocks of Alton), a man in a flourishing way, with whom Bro. Ben. is acquainted, who should be asked concerning the circumstances, temper, &c. of Mr. Hill; and the common trite observation, that there is somewhat of adventure and hazard when a man strikes out into many businesses, should not be totally disregarded. The variety and extent of the business must moreover occasion the absence of the Mr. and subject his people to be left pretty much to themselves. These matters I have thrown together as they occur, though no doubt they have all been considered well by you before.

As to the business of my journey I have carryed it con-

* [There is no date of the year in which this letter was written.— T. B.]

tinually in my mind, and have been still labouring the point.
As to my neigh. Robertson of East Tisted, he is very *willing
and desirous* to help me; but then he has it not in his power
without he can find somebody to take one of his churches off
his hands. He has met lately with a person that wavers about
it, and will send him a final answer soon. Upon this contingency at present does my Lan. visit seem to hang. Pray
write soon. I return hence on Wednesday, Oct. 19. Respects
to my sister.

Your affect. brother,
GIL. WHITE.

Fine weather for a week, after astonishing rains.

LETTER XXVII.

Fyfield, Nov. 12, 1776.

DEAR BROTHER,

As you have experienced so often how very necessary exercise
is for your health, you will no doubt be careful how any avocation or pursuit, how laudable soever, shall again interrupt
that regimen so essentially needful. Our bro. Thos. has found
vast benefit from his journey to Bath; the waters and the
bathing have quite quite removed for the present both his internal and his external ails. He advises, I find, if your
rheumatism returns, a journey to Buxton. Jack is very tall
indeed! but if he continues healthy, it will be esteemed an
advantage to be a well-grown man. You have never told me
whether he was bound for five or seven years.

With respect to your MS., you seem a cup too low, and do
not assume the importance of an author. If Mr. P.* had got
such a work ready, he would feel little diffidence, and would
expect it would produce some money. If you desire it, I shall
be willing to look it over, and perhaps Bro. Thos. will do the
same when at leisure. By what I saw, perhaps some articles

* [Doubtless " Pennant."—T. B.]

may be thought too long. The whale fishery is a fine new circumstance, and worthy of a national attention, especially as we may soon possibly have nothing to do with the N. American seas. But in such narrow limits, and so warm a climate, how can such an offensive occupation be carryed on without proving a vast nuisance to the garrison? Train-oil and whales' flesh must smell very vigorously in lat. 36. How wise have all the naturalists proved themselves to be by laying it down for granted that there were no whales in the Mediterranean*.

Last night my bro. received a letter from the attorney near Manchester, who wishes to be curate of Darwen†. He is urgent for matters to be brought to a bargain. Sure the injunctions and provisions against simony have never reached your part of the world. If disappointed, he will not, I hope, stir up a clamour against the southern non-resident.

D— is with me; he is good natured, but somewhat heady at times. It is well he is intended for trade, since he loves anything better than book: bodily labour he does not spare; for rolling, wheeling, water-drawing, grass-walk sweeping are his delight. I have taught him to ride; and perhaps a good seat on an horse may be more useful to him than Virgil or Horace. I tryed Phædrus, but my patience fail'd. However, he may procure health and strength and a little behaviour at my house. We all join in respects.

Yrs. affect.
GIL. WHITE.

My brother's outlet is still pleasing.

---

* [The occurrence of Whales in the Mediterranean can only have been fortuitous, and could not have led to the establishment of a regular trade as here alluded to.—T. B.]

† [Darwen, a township in the parish of Blackburn, of which parish John White was incumbent, and in whose hands the appointment rested. —T. B.]

LETTER XXVIII.

Selborne, May 4.

Dear Brother,

I SHOULD have wished that you had found your book more marketable, and that you could have sold it *outright*. Yet if Benj. offers to *join*, it looks as if he did not fear the want of success in the publication; besides booksellers have ways and means of subscribing off among the trade, in which authors cannot avail themselves.

My thanks are due for your calling on Edm. Woods, who will, I think, soon supply me with some windows. I wish I could prevail on you to come down and spend a little time with us, before you return northward.

As soon as I got to town I sent your *hortus siccus* by my bro. Thos.'s boy to Mr. Curtis's own house, and was in hopes he would have examined the plants.

No *swifts* appear yet, tho' we have soft weather. My left hand is full of gout; all my fingers look red and shoot and burn. If I have gout about me, it is best to come out. I hope you found and left Mrs. Snooke well.

The spirit of building prevails much in this district: Rich. Butler the thatcher is going to enlarge his house; John Bridger of Oakhanger builds a new one next spring; and Mr. P. of Rotherfield began pulling down yesterday.

" The child that is unborn may rue
The *pulling* of that day."

I am your loving brother,
GIL. WHITE.

Pray write often, and let me know what steps you take respecting your book.

LETTER XXIX.

Selborne, July 16, 1777.

DEAR BROTHER,

SOMEHOW or other I had persuaded myself that you were to write first; and having little to say as we had seen each other so lately, I thought I would stay 'till you gave the challenge, before I attacked you with an epistle.

As yet I have not seen your work, but shall peruse it with pleasure as soon as brother Thomas brings it. But he is going to bathe on the coast of Dorset for a few weeks. As I hoped and expected to see you derive some credit and emolument from your labours, I was sorry to hear that the whole pursuit is thrown aside for the present in some degree of disgust and chagrin. One thing I could never understand; and that is, you say in a former letter "that having so near a relation a bookseller, should you not agree with him about terms, no other publisher would meddle with your work, because your relation is one of the first editors in the natural history way." Now the force of this argument I could never see; for Cadell or any other man would be influenced alone by his own judgment, and, if he saw merit in the work and an interesting subject, would little regard, I should think, another person's sentiments. Unless you have experienced the inconvenience that you thought you foresaw, your suspicions were probably wrong.

The roof of my great parlor is finished; and my walls in a few days will be up to their proper pitch; so that we shall soon proceed to *rearing*. You do well in removing the earth that lies above your floors: I have taken away much for the same reason. I have not seen the Clergy Act, but am assured that it has nothing to do with *residence;* there is nothing compulsive in it, but it enables the clergy to borrow money on their livings, which they may lay out on the repairs of their houses, &c., and so exempt their representatives at their deaths from heavy delapidations. For the money borrowed the resident incumbent is to pay five per cent, and some small proportion of the principall off annually; a *non-resident* must pay *ten* per cent.: and when the borrower dies the residue remains a debt on the living 'till by degrees it is payed off. Mr. Etty, as far as he knows of the matter yet, for neither has he seen the act, approves much of the plan, and thinks he may avail himself of the matter so as to save himself from heavy demands on his family at his death. * * * *

We had wet weather all the month of May; but from the 10th of June to the 9th of July it was the strangest summer solstice I ever saw—nothing but wind and floods and clouds and wintry doings, so that we kept fires in the parlor most part of the time. We have now sweet weather.

Respects to my sister. Yours, &c.,
GIL. WHITE.

LETTER XXX.

Ringmer, Sept. 11, 1777.

DEAR BROTHER,

BEING informed that Mrs. Snooke was seized with the palsy, and had lost the use of one side, and that her speech was much impaired, and moreover that she was alone by herself without any friend; I set out at a day's warning, though surrounded with workmen, and arrived here late last Saturday evening. I found the poor old lady in a low languishing state, though better, the people about her told me, than she had been some days before. The next morning she was much mended, and has continued to mend so fast every day that she is become quite another woman; and Mr. Manning informed me this morning that he has now good hopes of a recovery.

Brother Harry brought your MS. to Selborne the first week in August; but, what between an hurry of business, company, and building, I have been able as yet to pay little attention to it. Yet, though I have not payed it that regard which I ought, a visitor of mine has read it through with great care, and, if I may judge from the many hours he bestowed upon it each day, should suppose he was well pleased. The person alluded to is Dr. Chandler the traveller in Greece, who being no naturalist has no partiality for the Linnæan system, but avers that it will prevent your book from becoming popular. He and I had much serious talk about the matter; and he asserts roundly that he is *sure* that if you could persuade yourself to divest it of its quaint garb (those were his words) that he is certain it would be worth £200 of anybody's money. He advises (no, he does not, for he spoke with great modesty on the occasion; he *hints*, I should say) that if you could prevail on yourself to exchange *Classes* and *Ordines* for Chapters, and to throw all your tables back into an appendix, that your book would be very much read. The generality of readers, he observes, are very lazy, and afraid of figures; though your tables, he thinks, may be pleasing and useful to some. He farther added that you might still refer to Linnæus, &c. at the bottom of each page. And I have observed myself that booksellers lately in new editions in natural works have added Linnæan names: and the reason is, because, though it is the fashion now to despise Linnæus, yet many languish privately to understand his method.

Pray weigh seriously what I have said, and consider about the Doctor's £200. You have not been informed, I think, that John Wells has at last consented to sell me the fields behind my house, that *angulus iste* which the family have so long desired. For this little farm I have laid down some money in part payment; so hope no untoward accident will now deprive me of it. With respects to my sister,

I remain
Your affect. brother,
GIL. WHITE.

Pray write to Selborne, where I hope to be soon.

LETTER XXXI.*

Selborne, Oct. 31, 1777.

Dear Brother,

Had I not been called the beginning of this month to Oxford, where I spent all my time either in college business, or inspecting and transcribing by means of an amanuensis many curious papers from the archives of Magdalen College, relative to the antiquities of Selborne, you had heard from me some time ago. In my pursuits as an antiquary Dr. Chandler has been wonderfully friendly, and communicative; and my discoveries about this place are very great: we examined 366 parchments.

I have now read your work, all but the entomology, once over, and am proceeding to read several parts twice over. In the whole I *much approve* of your book. Your preface is neat; your history is what I call true natural history, because it abounds with anecdote and circumstance; and I verily think your dissertations on the *Hirundines* are the best tracts I ever saw of the kind, as they throw much light on the dark but curious business of migration, and possess such merit as alone might keep any book from sinking. If consulted, I therefore *protest* loudly against the intention of throwing your papers aside; for I think in a thousand instances they will delight a good naturalist. I therefore pronounce, as the Vice-Chancellor of Oxon does on similar occasions, *imprimatur*. But then, to act as an impartial critic, I must also say that sometimes (and others think so as well as myself) your language is rather diffuse, and your sentences *too long*; and what I most wonder at is, that at times you not only use the same verb or its derivations 5 or 6 times in a paragraph, but sometimes twice or thrice in the same sentence. Being jealous of the

---

* [This appears to be the last letter to John White. On his decease the widow came to live with Gilbert, with whom she remained till his death.—T. B.]

honor of your work, I cannot admit of these inaccuracies, and have therefore presumed to amend some of them, but with what success I must leave you to judge; I must therefore desire you, who are so perfectly capable, to bestow a fresh and severe inspection on the language.

Brother Thomas is now in town; and I wish you would desire him to send me down your 'Entomology,' which I long to see. No wonder that you did not much relish Dr. Chandler's proposal of rejecting all *system:* the reason of sending you that advice was that I thought *then* that *system* was the stumbling-block between you and your chapman; but *now* I plainly perceive that warm words and some heats have arisen between you, which I hope will all soon be forgotten. Indeed I wonder that in *these days* any work should stick on hand of your sort, as I cannot but think that it might sell. Would it not therefore be best to make fresh advances in Fleet Street, and so set your work a-going in some way.

When you print, pray correct the press yourself; pray, before every class give an explanation of terms: Linnæus does so; and I think by this means the town might be led on gently to relish Linn. terms. But without a glossary how should men know what the *lorum* of a bird is! No wonder Linnæus does not answer your letters: poor man, he has grown childish*! Poor Nanny White was buried last Monday night in this churchyard; she dyed at S. Lambeth †. If you lend money on private security, pray be careful. Jack I hope will write to me about the earthquake. Brother Thomas has the best interest with Mr. Lort; I have none. Next week I put in my sashes, and proceed to ceiling and plastering my great parlor. Our weather is very tempestuous. The glass yesterday at 28·375. My best respects to my sister.

Your affect.
GIL. WHITE.

* [This was after his second attack of apoplexy.—T. B.]
† [She was the daughter of Benjamin White and was twenty-one years of age when she died.—T. B.]

LETTER FROM JOHN WHITE

TO

HIS BROTHER GILBERT*.

I HAVE sent brother Benj. word of what Linn. says about his new edition. This roundabout method will dispatch nothing. Brother B. must write his own proposals, if he means to deal with him at all. Surely you and I could manage to correct the press; at least in the Zoological part; the Botanical I must not pretend to.

Have you any queries to ask Linn. before I write again? You see he is willing to communicate, though busy enough.

This new enterprize of my friend Lever's disturbs me on many accounts. In the first place, I wish'd *you* to see the Museum in its native spot, Alkrington; in the next it will be gone from this country, of which it was one of the greatest ornaments; and *thirdly* it will rob me, I fear, of my friendly neighbour for a great part of the year. I heard from him immediately on his arrival in London. His plan is, he says, "to pursue Nat. Hist. and carry the exhibition of it to such a height as no one can imagine; and to make it the most wonderful sight in the world."

Upon this plan I think he is right to exhibit in London, where he will not only collect with more speed, but also make the thing defray its own expences, which no private fortune alone could possibly equal. If you can send the drawings to

---

* [This is the only letter from John White to his brother which I have ever seen, with the exception of one which relates exclusively to private family matters, and was written from Gibraltar, and is mentioned in the Memoir. The above letter was probably written in 1775.—T. B.]

town while Mr. Lever is there, he will bring them. I shall go to see him as he returns.

What leisure time I have I employ in collecting insects, which I have promised Mr. Barrington as a beginning of his 'Fauna Britannica.' I wish Jacky would pick up all the variety that he can, put them into spirits, and there let them remain till I can get them. Pray examine your sands for the *Myrmeleon*. If in England I know no likelier place. Why should not England have it as well as Sweden? * * * I now recollect that I promised some remarks on your Swift in my next. I have a few observations to make on that bird, but no criticism on your dissertation; and therefore I thought you would be better pleased to see Linnæus's letter.

I am drawing towards the conclusion of my insects; and shall then proceed to the quadrupeds, birds, and fishes. After all there must be a general correction and transcript of the whole, which will be no small undertaking.

We have had a sad, gloomy, wet, chilly season. We are now sitting over a fire. I have brush'd up my house as spruce as if it were for sale; but it is to give you as agreeable an idea of Lancashire as I can. * * *

Mrs. White is well, and joins in best wishes and respects with, dear brother,

Your most oblig'd and affect.
J. W.

[It was proposed at one time that a new edition of the 'Systema Naturæ' should be published in this country by Benjamin White. The discussion of this project will be found in the correspondence between John White and Linnæus, in the letters numbered from IV. to IX. inclusive. It was approved by John White, but positively declined by Benjamin upon commercial grounds. For similar reasons he refused to undertake a new edition of Linnæus's 'Mantissa Plantarum.' As this proposition was made in the year 1776 (the former edition, termed 'Mantissa altera,' having been published in 1771), it could scarcely have been done with the author's knowledge, as he was in that year suffering from a second attack of apoplexy, which had impaired his mental powers, rendering him a very distressing object. This melancholy circumstance is alluded to by Gilbert White in his letter to his brother John of the date of October 31, 1777, as the cause of Linnæus's not writing to him. —T. B.]

CORRESPONDENCE

OF THE

REV. JOHN WHITE AND LINNÆUS.

LETTER I.

FROM THE REV. JOHN WHITE TO LINNÆUS.

Gibraltar, June 30, 1771.

Sir,

Be pleased to permit an humble admirer of your works, and a lover of that study which your labours have rendered almost universal throughout Europe, to present you with a small specimen of his attempts to collect and class the animal productions of Southern Europe and Northern Africa. Having resided some years in this place, and been lately furnished with your admirable writings from my friends in England, and also with those of Ray, Scopoli, Geoffroy, Buffon, and others, I thought it might be some satisfaction to all real lovers of Natural Knowledge to see the several productions of this climate examined and displayed with some more accuracy than has yet been done by travellers, who generally treat on Natural History in a superficial way, and leave it the most defective part of their works. My researches have hitherto been confined to this fortress and its environs, as the duties of my function require my constant residence in the place. I hope to be able ere long to produce a tolerable 'Fauna Calpensis,' as an introductory essay, and, if it please God to grant me health and opportunity, to extend my plan by degrees. Your candour and humanity will pardon the errors and defects of an unexperienced adventurer, in consideration of his not uncommendable intentions; and if he may be so happy as to be honored with the instructions of so great a master, he humbly hopes to approve himself not altogether an unworthy disciple.

As Mr. Stenbeck, the gentleman who does me the favour to take charge of this letter, intends to travel by land, I could not burden him with anything of greater bulk than one small phial; wherein I have ventured to send a few of the most remarkable insects which I have collected this summer. The large Hymenopt. which I suppose to be the *Vespa crabroni congener* of Ray, seems also to answer to your *Sphex bidens*, except that it wants the *petiolus elongatus*. The four specimens which I send differ much from each other, and I judge them to be the two sexes of two species. They have a most remarkable difference in their sting (*aculeus*), those with the longest antennæ having the *aculeus tridentatus exsertus*, the others *aculeus simplex reconditus*. The *Panorpa coa* cannot abound more in that island than it does in this province. The *Gryllus turritus* is not less frequent: antennæ ensiformes in all. The other large insect without wings I am unable to class. It resembles the *Mantis* genus in form of the body and legs; but has not *caput nutans*. Nor can I reconcile it with any *Grylli*. *Sphex mauritanica* is common here; also *Sphex spirifer,—fissipes, clavipes, appendigaster*. Of the latter I send two. I send likewise two species of *Chrysis*: your *Chrysis bidentata* is frequent, but I have no specimens now; and several *Apes* (Bees), of which I cannot ascertain the species, except *Apis violacea*. *Mutillæ* are not uncommon here. I send one, which seems to differ from those in the 'Syst. Nat.' by the spot on the head and abdomen. The large Coleopt. is very common here, and resembles the *Lucanus cervus* in its general form; but it has not the antennæ of that genus, nor does it ever fly. A much smaller species of the same insect inhabits the sea-coast, where it devours the small *Cancer pulex*. I have sent a *Cancer brachyurus thorace lævi, lateribus 3-spinosis*, which I find not mentioned in your 'Syst. Nat.'

If any of these articles should be in the least worthy your notice and acceptance, I shall be happy in having communicated them, and shall be equally ready to supply you with any other of the productions of these climates which you may wish to see. I have made a considerable collection of the birds, amphibia, and fishes, and remarked the circumstances of their migrations. The *Hirundo melba* breeds in thousands on this rock. The *Hir. rupestris caudâ emarginatâ non forcipatâ* of Scopoli breeds in the inland mountains of Andalusia and Grenada, and in the winter, when those mountains are covered with snow, resides regularly on these coasts, and migrates for a short time only into Barbary. The *Hir. pratincola, Trachelia* of Scopoli, sometimes appears in this country*. *Alauda calandra* and *Turdus arundinaceus*, or *junco*, breed common in Spain and Barbary. *Turdus cyanus*, or *solitarius*, abounds on this rock. Also another species of *Turdus*, which I cannot find in any author; it is in all parts of a glossy black except the *uropygium* and *rectrices*, which are snow-white, tipped with black. *Upupa epops, Oriolus galbula, Merops apiaster, Junx torquilla, Phœnicopterus*, visit us annually in the spring; *Charadrius œdicnemus* in the winter. Among the fishes the most remarkable are the *Lepidopus* and *Lepadogaster*, two new genera of Dr. Gouan. The former is generally about six feet long, and comes from the ocean in summer in abundance. This species has the caudal fin forked, not subulate as described by Dr. Gouan. As for other parts of Nat. Hist., I have for some years kept a journal of the winds and weather, and variations of the thermometer and barometer, and measured the quantities of rain fallen this last year. I have also attempted something of a Flora, or state of the vegetable world during each month in the year; but I am at present not sufficiently conversant in Botany to make much progress in that branch.

But if from these loose hints you should be pleased to judge it to be in my power to furnish you with any satisfactory intelligence from this part of the world, you will give me great pleasure in honouring me with your commands. And whatever instructions you may choose to favour me with, be pleased to make use of the following address by any ships bound to London, "To the Rev. Mr. John White, to the care of Mr. White, Bookseller in Fleet Street, London."

* [*Glareola pratincola* of modern naturalists.]

This Mr. White in London is my brother, and will very punctually forward anything to Gibraltar.

I must now beg your pardon for the liberty I have thus taken to trouble you with intelligence which to a person of your extraordinary experience may be but trifling. However, should any part of it prove in the least degree acceptable, it cannot fail of giving much satisfaction to, good Sir,

Your sincere admirer,
And devoted humble servant,
JOHN WHITE.

Be pleased to write to me in any of the following languages, English, Latin, French, or Italian.

LETTER II.*

FROM LINNÆUS TO THE REV. JOHN WHITE.

Viro Reverendissimo Dno. Johann. White
S. pl. d.
Car. Linné.

Literas tuas V. R. die 30 Junii ante octiduum plane consternatus aperui, dum tu, cui nunquam mihi fortuna innotescere concessit, mihi offers tuam gratiam, tuasque divitias naturalium rerum. Mihi verba deficiunt explicandum affectum meum sincerum in virum tanto virtutis robore. Gratulor scientiæ quam ambo in deliciis habemus, quod qui fata rerum gubernat, te excitaverit in admirationem mundani operis Artificis. Nullum ego novi in regione quam inhabitas cui Deus antea concessit apertos oculos intueri naturalia, ubi concurrunt Hispanicæ, Lusitanicæ, Barbariæ plantæ, insecta, aves, reliquaque animalia; ad fretum penetrabunt pisces omnes qui ex oceano in M. Mediterraneum ire et redire debent.

* [This letter was printed in 'Contributions to Ornithology,' 1849, pp. 28, 29.—A. N.]

Tu, profecto, si in Europâ ullus, videbis plurima Creatoris miracula.

Piscium nominatorum nullum majori desiderio examinarem, quam *Lepadogastrum,* cujus ideam nequeo mihi a Gouani opere ritè formare, ut certus evadam, utrum *novum* format genus necne.

Hodie accipio lagenulam, a te generosissime mihi oblatam, in qua reperio rarissima tua insecta.

Sphex ista cum maculis 4 dorsalibus abdominis a me nunquam antea visa fuit. Addidisti et ejus varietates cum capite variegato, cum antennis luteis, cum maculis dorsalibus tantum duabus.

Sphex altera non minus rara et admodum singularis alis (laciniatis, s. erosis?) ferrugineis, apice nigris: neque illa a me visa fuit.

Mutilla an apud vos frequens? hic rarissima: an innotuerit ejus œconomia? habeo jam eam alatam.

Chrysis species varias vidi: sed quid in his sit sexus differentia non potui adhuc addiscere.

Gryllus turritus ad me antea tantum e Barbaria missus fuit. Adhuc hæsito de sexu. Alia mea individua habent antennas magnas ensiformes; alia antennas minutas setaceas: quæso inquiras in tuis *Gryllis turritis,* num uterque sexus habent similes antennas.

Tabanus iste forma muscæ ibidem mihi novus, et rarissimus fuit.

Panorpa coa, cum vobis vulgatissima, omnium in votis esset, ejus metamorphosin habere notissimam.

Gryllus turritus habet caput acuminatum, sed os versus terram, adeoq. nutans dici potest.

Nec *Sphex fissipes,* neque *clavipes* erat in vitro, quas inclusas scribis.

Chrysis tua viridis, ano cæruleo, videtur nova species.

Mutilla tua vix diversa est a meâ.

Lucanus tuus erat *Lucanus parallelepipedes.*

Cancer lateribus trispinosis mihi antea non visus fuit.

Si unquam capere posses, et me donare velles, *Pratincola Trachelia* esset mihi munus quod cum *Lepadogastro* præ reliquis maximè delectarer. *Tracheliam* aliquis mihi dixit debere amandari ad Hirundines: sed maximè adhuc dubito de veritate *.

Pennant a te dives factus fuit raris naturæ cimeliis.

Utinam possem aliquid tibi præstare pro tanto dono; anxius ero.

Upsaliæ, 1772, 20 Januarii.

LETTER III.†

FROM LINNÆUS TO THE REV. JOHN WHITE.

Viro Reverendissimo Do. Jo. White
S. pl. d. Carol. Linné.

Accepi nuper Thesaurum tuum verè aureum, missum d. 13 Maii; nec gratiorem unquam. Quibus verbis tuam in me prædicabo gratiam effari nequeo.

Aviculas tuas rarissimas antea non vidi: eas studebo diligenter, ubi museo s. bibliothecæ reditus, qui nunc ruri æstivo.

Hirundo melba, quam antea non vidi, affinis *Hirund. apod.*

Hirundo rupestris mihi antea ignota, verè distincta.

Coturnix tridactylus ‡ : an ex ordine Gallinarum aut Grallarum?

Motacilla Tithys § longè a meâ aliena.

---

* [In a letter to Pennant (March 19, 1772) I find the following allusion to this letter. "When I came to London I found a long letter from Linnæus to my Bro. John, lying in Fleet Street, occasioned by an epistle and some phials of insects sent by the latter to the former. The old arch-naturalist writes with spirit still; and is very open and communicative, acknowledging that several of the insects were new to him. He languishes to see a *pratincola*, being conscious that it belongs not to the genus of *Hirundo*."—T. B.]

† [Printed in 'Contributions to Ornithology,' 1829, pp. 31, 32.]

‡ [*Turnix sylvatica* of modern ornithologists.]

§ [*Ruticilla titys*.—A. N.]

1. *Zeus* an *Perca?* Proprii generis Piscis et novi: capite excoriato, reticulato, cælato.

Coryphænoides vix videtur convenire cum generibus notis. Doleo quod pinnæ dorsi, ani et caudæ erant mutilatæ, ut radios numerare non licuerit.

2. *Perca dipterygia* rubra ad *Percæ* genus forte pertinebit, caput licet muticum: ob pinnas duas dorsales vix *Sparus* aut *Labrus* erit.

Cancer arctos omnino.
Cancer carinatus est.
Cancer antennis longissimis.
Cancer rostro longissimo.

} Hæ *Squillæ* aut valde affines videntur verè species distinctas esse; cùm pedes didactyli differunt in diversis.

Cancer minutus est.
Cancer brachiis hirsutis, mihi antea non visus.

3. *Lacerta lemniscata* est.
Scarabæus hispanus est.
———— *typhoeus* est.
———— *laticollis* est, sed elytra non striata: an sexu?

4. *Scorpio australis* est. *Scorpio calpensis*.
Scolopendra *morsitans* **est.**
———— *forficata* est.
Meloe majalis **est.**
Asilus barbarus est.
Chrysomela sanguinea **est.**
Carabus granulatus **est.**
Tenebrio tibialis est.
Cottus gobio est.
Mantis gongylodes, an larva?
Cimex morio: qui copiosus erat.
Chrysomela goetingensis est.
———— *staphylea* est.
———— *marginata* est.
Curculio anguinus est.
———— *nebulosus* est.
———— *barbaro* similis sed triplo minor.
———— *Whitei!* brevirostris, ater, undique punctatus, novus.
Silpha littoralis est.
———— *rugosa* est.

Silpha oblongata est.
Scarabæus sabulosus est.
Hister ater, nitidus, elytris striis quinq. dimidiatis obliteratis, novus.

Upsaliæ, 1772, d. 7 Augusti.

LETTER IV.

FROM THE REV. JOHN WHITE TO LINNÆUS.

Sir,

Your first letter bearing the date 20th January met with some delay in England, and did not reach my hands till the first day of May; and on the 17th of the same month, when I sent a small collection of birds and insects, I was prevented from writing to you so long a letter as I intended by the sudden departure of the ship. The week following I was called away in haste from Gibraltar to take possession of preferment in England, and have, since that time, been too constantly engaged in my private affairs to afford that attention to my studies in Natural History which I would otherwise wish to do. Some time in December last I received your second favour in London, and was desirous of sending you some of my specimens of the most rare Calpensian animals; but I was informed that the frost had then shut up all navigation to the Baltic Sea, for the winter season. As soon as the communication opens again I will endeavour to send such as I think best worthy of your acceptance. I now propose to revise and correct my observations in Natural History made at Gibraltar, and to reduce the fauna of that district into a regular systematic form. Although I lived at that place sixteen years in the whole, yet, to my misfortune, it was only during the last four years that I became acquainted with this science, and with your admirable works. However, if I have leisure to model my materials, imperfect as they are, into any tolerable form, I shall some day beg leave to submit a copy of them to your inspection. Give me leave in the meantime to take some notice, in their regular order, of the several articles mentioned in both your letters.

Of two specimens of the *Lepadogaster* which I sent to England, one is lost, the other remains in my possession, and shall certainly be forwarded to you the first opportunity.

Sphex maculis quatuor dorsalibus, &c., which you say you had not seen before, seems to be *Vespa crabroni congener Raii*. Indeed I at first supposed it to be *Sphex bidens*, Syst. Nat., from which I think it differs nothing, except that it has no spines on the thorax. That which has yellow antennæ and only two spots on the abdomen is the male, the other female. I find no less than six varieties, which are probably the male, female, and neuter of two distinct species. In some the *aculeus*, or sting, is *tricuspid*, in others simple.

Sphex alis erosis, ferrugineis, apice nigris, was by me supposed to be *Sphex mauritanica*; but you will judge better on farther examination. I have two species of *Mutilla*; the largest inhabits the sandy parts of the isthmus, the other the high parts of the rocky mountain. I could not discover any particulars of their œconomy. The *Chrysis* which you remark is inserted in Mr. Forster's 'Nova Insectorum Centuria' as a new insect; he calls it *C. cyanura*, and another *C. cyanochrysa*. All my *Grylli turriti* have ensiform antennæ. I have not yet remarked their sexual differences. *Tabanus*, formâ muscæ, novus: be pleased to favour me with a specific distinction of this insect.

I took much pains last summer to discover the metamorphosis of *Panorpa coa*, but with little success. It inhabits sandy soils always, and its first appearance for three several summers was precisely on the 18th of May.

I believe both *Sphex fissipes* and *clavipes* were among the rest; perhaps they were lost by sticking close to other subjects.

If *Cancer* lateribus 3-spinosis be a new species, let me beg your specific title to that also.

The insect which you say is *Lucanus parallelepipedus*, Mr. Forster has also put among his *new* insects, by the name of *Tenebrio buparius*.

The only specimen that I have of *Pratincola Trachelia* is in bad preservation, but much at your service. It seems undoubtedly of the *Grallæ* Ordo. *Hirundo rupestris* was observed by me in the winter months as long ago as the year 1758, by Scopoli in the summer, about the year 1767. *Coturnix tridactylus* must without doubt belong to the Ordo of *Gallinæ;* possibly its legs were stretched too much in drying, and thereby made it resemble one of the Ordo of *Grallæ*. It differs from one in the 'Planches enluminées,' and, I hope, is a nondescript species; if so, be pleased to honour it with a specific character.

Motacilla tithys is the *Grey-redstart* of Edwards, and the *Ruticilla gibraltariensis*, No. 16, of Brisson.

Piscis novus, capite excoriato, reticulato, cælato; as you esteem it a new genus, demands likewise a generic, as well as a specific, name, from the great father of Natural History.

Coryphænoides rupestris not appearing in the 'Systema Naturæ,' Mr. Pennant gave it that name from Gunnerus. I have more specimens, of which I will send you the best. They are all found mutilated, being never taken alive in nets, but cut out of the stomach of *Squalus acanthias*. *Perca dipterygia rubra* appeared to me rare and doubtful. You will best ascertain its proper titles.

Cancer arctus * is, I suppose, *Squilla cælata*, Rondeletii.

C. carinatus †, vide N. 16, Brunnichii spolia maris Adriatici. *C. antennis longissimis* is certainly a distinct species. It's colours beautiful. *C. rostro longissimo* must also be a peculiar species. I have many specimens. *C. brachiis hirsutis* is found in vast abundance under loose stones on the sea shore. None larger than those which I sent you.

These four want Linnæan names.

Scarabæus hispanus is sometimes found inclosed in a hard oval ball of dung and sand mixed, through which, when moist, it works its passage with its horn. Does it undergo all its transformations in this prison? *Mantis gongylodes*

---

* [*Scyllarus arctus*, Edw. Crust. ii. p. 282, a well-known Mediterranean species. The *Cancer arctus* of Linn. Faun. Suec.—T. B.]

† [Most probably *Sicyonia sculpta*, Edw. Crust. ii. p. 409.—T. B.]

seems to be in its perfect state as you see it, for I never found any winged, or in a different form.

Mr. Forster mistakes your *Cimex morio* for a new insect, and calls it *Cimex aterrimus*.

On a review of my collection, I find about ten new species of birds, viz. four *Motacillæ*; one *Emberiza*; three *Alaudæ*; and two *Turdi*: also several fishes, besides many insects. As I hope to enlarge my collection still farther by the help of my friends at Gibraltar, I shall with the utmost pleasure endeavour to supply the most illustrious master of the science with every article that is valuable.

Mr. White, a bookseller in Fleet Street, London, (who is my brother, and to whose care I beg you to direct your future favours for me,) is desirous of knowing who is the person in Sweden, or elsewhere, that has the disposal of the last editions of your works; at what prices he may purchase many copies of them; and what new editions are now begun, or intended soon, either of your own, or any other valuable publications. If the proprietor will please to open a correspondence with him, he may draw on him for the amount of what he purchases, and depend upon immediate payment. My brother deals more particularly in the branch of Natural History than any other bookseller, and will probably have a large demand for books of that sort. I beg leave to return my most grateful thanks for your generous and instructive communications, and with my most sincere wishes for your health, and a prosperous progress in your most valuable labours, to subscribe myself with all due esteem,

Your obliged disciple, and most obedient servant,

JOHN WHITE.

London, January 1, 1773.

LETTER V.

FROM THE REV. JOHN WHITE TO LINNÆUS.

November 26, 1773.

Sir,

On the first day of this present year I had the honour to write to you a very long letter, in answer to your kind favour dated August 7, 1772, and also to inform you that I had left Gibraltar, and was come to reside in England, as well as to beg your farther sentiments concerning those birds which you had not thoroughly examined when you wrote.

As almost ten months have now elapsed, without my having any farther intelligence from you, I begin to fear that either my letter was not duly conveyed to you, or that you have not enjoyed that share of health which every lover of science must wish may be continued to you, by the goodness of providence, for many years. My letter was sent to the post in London, a few days after the date thereof, and should properly have reached your hands in the month of January last. Therefore to avoid, if possible the imputation of the least neglect of the honour conferred on me of being admitted among the number of your correspondents, I beg leave to communicate the above particulars, that you may be satisfied no neglect has happened, on my side. I venture, also, as before, to write in my own native language, supposing it equally obvious to you, and being in want of practice to express myself with equal readiness in the Latin tongue. However, if it happens to occasion to you any inconvenience in explaining an English letter, I will prevent it hereafter by making use of the Latin. The affairs of my new preferment engaged my attention the last summer, and prevented me from executing my intended 'Fauna Calpensis.' But I still hope to finish it, having a quantity of materials, and more specimens frequently sent by my friends at Gibraltar.

I mentioned in my last, that Mr. White, a bookseller, in Fleet Street, London (who is my brother), desires to know who is the person in Sweden, or elsewhere, who has the disposal of the last editions of your works, at what prices he may purchase a large quantity of them, and what new editions are now begun, or soon intended to be published, either of them or of any other valuable publications in your country. If either yourself or the proprietor will please to open a correspondence with him, you may always safely draw on him for the amount of what he purchases, and depend on punctual payment. My brother deals particularly in the branch of Natural History, and will probably have a larger demand for foreign books of that sort than any person who has hitherto imported them into England.

If it appears that my former letter has failed, I will send a copy of some particulars in it, because it contained many enquiries which I flatter myself your usual benevolence will condescend to resolve.

I have a *Pratincola*, *Lepadogaster*, and several other specimens, which I think worthy your observation; but my daily expectation of hearing from you prevented my sending them.

With most sincere prayers for your health and happiness and a prosperous perseverance in your studies, so universally beneficial to mankind, I am, illustrious Sir,

Your most obliged and devoted servant,

J. WHITE.

Please to direct,
To the Rev. John White,
Vicar of Blackburn, Lancashire.

I hear Mr. Logie, formerly Swedish Consul at Algiers, lives at Stockholm; if he be of your acquaintance, I beg my best respects to him and his family.

LETTER VI.

FROM LINNÆUS TO THE REV. JOHN WHITE.

Reverendissime Domine,

Literas tuas V. R. diei 26 Novembri nuper habui. Gratulor reditum in patriam. Lætor quod valeas.

Te non accepisse literas meas posteriores miror; forte iis non inscripsi nec dictam assignationem domûs, quod non recordor; me rescripsisse optimè recordor.

Inter tua erant multa quæ æternæ memoriæ mandari deberent, et ego in meis MSS. auri instar asservo propediem editurus, non sine inventoris honorificâ memoriâ.

Tetrao tridactylus est tam singularis in suo ordine, ut, nisi vidissem non credidissem. Quid de hâc ave dicit D. Pennant?

Piscis thoracicus novi generis est, cranio nudo suturis plurimis exarato, diaphano.

Motacilla antea mihi non cognita.

Spheges tres videntur valde affines, nec cædem.

Cancri squillæ 7 species, ni fallor, quamquam valde similes. Sic indicant partes, chelæ reliquaque distinctè descripta.

Hirundo rupestris, nescio an varietas *apus.*

Apis propria species, et reliqua omnia; pro quibus dum vixero, ero in tuo ære.

Exemplaria meorum operum omnia distracta sunt, ut nullus ea comparare queat in patria: novam darem eorum editionem, sed editor Salvius ante dimidium annum occubuit. Admodum multi a me expetiere exemplaria, sed comparare nullâ ratione ipse possum. Si aliquis in Angliâ ea edere vellet, possem præbere exemplar observationibus innumeris, et speciebus ultra mille auctum, cum ex omnibus Indiis gazophylaciis instructus fui ab eo tempore quo ultimam dedi editionem; ut taccam synonyma auctorum plurium recentissimorum. Op-

* [Printed by Jardine, Contr. Orn. 1849, pp. 37, 38.]

tarem imprimis Systema Naturæ, Genera et species Plantarum, nova Editione, me vivo, prodire.

Anglicam linguam loquentem satis intelligo, scriptam non æque facile; ipse Anglice scribere nequeo. Dum lego scripta, pleraque capio; si unum alterumve verbum deficiat, istud facile evolvo. Possum semper habere amicos qui optime linguam explicant. *Fauna* tua *Calpensis* esset et mihi et omnibus exoptatissima.

Pratincolam nunquam vidi; quæ de eâ habeant Scopoli, Pennant, Gmelin et recentiores alii, vidi. Ad *Grallas* eam referunt plurimi, licet rostrum videtur multum differre.

Lepadogaster neque a me visus fuit; videtur admodum singularis.

Logie, octogenarius, qui fuit consul Algirensis, vivit adhuc; et filius qui ibidem serius consul factus fuit, etiam mihi notus, sed de eo, ab adventu Algeriam, non audivi; scio tamen alium consulem Suecicum nunc esse Algeriæ.

Vale et fave tuo sincero cultori
Car. Linné.

Si novisti egregiam virginem Annam Blackburne, ipsam plurimum salutes. Floræ et Faunæ filia est in cujus amores ardeo.

Upsaliæ, 1774,
Jan. 2.

LETTER VII.

FROM THE REV. JOHN WHITE TO LINNÆUS.

Viro Illustrissimo Car. Linnæo, &c.
Literas tuas novissimas, Vir optime, diei 2 Januarii, accepi. Tuas quoque priores die 7 Augusti, 1772, datas accepi, pro quibus gratum meum animum ad Calendas Jan. 1773, rescripsi; quod te nunquam accepisse multum piget.

Historiæ Naturalis Patrem atque Decus adhuc valere plurimum gaudeo. Deum Opt. Max. plurimos felicesque daturum annos continuo exoro!

Verba tua de Syst. Nat. exemplari novo atque adaucto ad fratrem meum Benj. White, Bibliopolam Londinensem haud incelebrem, retuli. Ille quidem libros multos quotannis edit; eumque Illustrissimi Linnæi Operum Editionem ditiorem prælo lubentissimè commissurum certior factus sum, utcunque scire liceat quanti exemplar tuum, tantis observationibus auctum, emendum sit. Dic mihi igitur, Vir venerande, quot nummos aureos Anglicanos, (vulgò *Guineas* nuncupatos,) pro hisce Chartis tuis MS. tibi dandos exoptas, easque fratrem meum summo gaudio empturum nihil dubito.

Specimina jam habeo aliquot, et avium, pisciumque, & insectorum, quæ tibi mittenda retineo, donec navis aliquis ad patriam tuam ab his regnis solvat.

Sphex iste, cum maculis 4, abdominis flavis, anne *Sphex bidens*? an novus? sex ejus habeo varietates; forsan Marem, Fœminam Neutrumque duarum Specierum.

Marem esse, cui maculæ sunt duæ tantum dorsales, certè scio; majoremque, cui maculæ 4, cum capite variegato, antennisque brevioribus, esse *Fœminam*. Quibusdam aculeus est simplex, reconditus; aliis exsertus, tricuspis. *Sphegem* alteram, alis laciniatis, ferrugineis, apice nigris. *Sphegem* esse tuam *Mauritanicam* judicavi; sin alia sit, nomen specificum humillimè quæso.

Mutillæ species duæ apud nos (Calpenses) frequentissimæ. Earum œconomiam nondum observare licuit. Unam tantum habeo alatam.

Gryllus turritus in Andalusia vulgatissimus. Sexûs differentiam nescio: omnibus sunt antennæ ensiformes; setaceas nunquam vidi.

Tabani novi, de quo mihi scribis, nomen characteresque a te ediscere velim.

Anno præterito summo studio laboravi ad *Panorpæ coæ* metamorphosin eruendam. Annis 1770, 1771, 1772, *Panorpa coa* prodiit die 18° Maii; cum ante hanc diem ne unicam videre possim; ipso die 17° singulis his annis, omnes latebant, at die proximo passim occurrebant. Ex locis arenosis semper nascuntur. Dic mihi, rogo, *Cancri* novi lateribus tri-spinosis, et aliorum quos novos judicas, nomina Linnæana.

Hirundinem rupestrem antea, anno 1756, ad Calpem hyemare observavi: eam ad **Alpes aestatem** degere observavit D. Scopoli 1768.

Coturnix tridactylus ad ordinem Gallinarum procul dubio **censendus.** Ad Europam Africamque quotannis it, reditque, **cum** *Tetraone Coturnice.* Crura forsàn et femora in cadavere sicco nimis protensa fuerint, ex quâ causâ e Grallis videatur.

Piscis novi generis, cranio nudo diaphano, quaerere mihi liceat titulum Linnaeanum; et Generis, & Speciei. In Freti Gaditani aquis profundissimis raro admodum **reperitur.**

Coryphaenoidem in Syst. Nat. non video: **et Speciei, et** Generis ejus sum ignarus. *Percam dipterygiam*, rubram, novam aestimavi; **an rectè?** Nomina quoque adscribas, Vir benevole, rogo, *Squillis* meis **omnibus** novis, *Cancroque* novo brachiis hirsutis; **hic, ut vides,** summam attigit magnitudinem, nec **unquam major est.**

Apis speciem novam, cujus **meministi,** nec jam habeo, nec **recordor: characterem ejus specificum a** te requirere oportet; ne eam **Faunae** Calpensis **ex agmine omittam.**

Ad Faunulam meam Calpensem promovendam hodie **laboro:** at ejus omninò me, Faunam tuam Suecicam intuentem, **pudet!** In singulâ animalium Classe plurima desunt: Vermium **prorsus** sum ignarus. At tyrocinii **mei primitias benigno animo** accipere velint Naturae consultiores.

Viri *reverendissimi* **nomine** salutari, **non** meum est. Apud nos omnis Parochus atque Sacerdos, inter quos ego humillimus, *reverendus*; Episcopus *reverendus admodum*; Archiepiscopus solus *reverendissimus.*

Amicus quidam meus, D. Lever, provinciae hujusce Lancastriensis incola, rerum naturalium expertissimus indagator, ad Museum locupletissimum atque elegantissimum, Animalium, Lapidum, Conchyliorum, accumulandum summo opere sum**mis impensis ardet.** Is quoque **Aves** quasdam suo more bel**lissimè** conservatas, lapidesque quosdam schistosos, **ex** hujus regionis **carbonum** fossilium fodinis, figuris miris ornatos, tibi mittendos parat. Quandocunque navis aut a Londino, aut a Liverpool, Holmiam tuam navigatura sit, haec omnia imponenda curabo, **corumque** te certiorem fieri scribendo nequaquam negligero. Virginem egregiam quam nominas, nondum vidi; famam ejus antea audivi; temporibus æstivis ipsam tuo nomine salutare studebo. Loeflingii iter Hispanicum, ut ad meam quasi patriam pertineat, perlegere cupio; in Angliâ verò haud venumdatur. Iter quoque C. Alstroemer in Europam australem mihi forsan esset perutilis, at hic reperiri nequit. Quomodo *Lucanus* meus & *Lucanus* tuus *parallelipipedus* idem sit, parum intelligo; *Lucani* antennas non habet, at *Tenebrionis*. De *Motacillis* tribus novis tibi missis sententiam tuam spero.

Tenebrionem nisi femoribus anticis bispinosis; an novus est? *Scarabæum laticollem Scarabæi sacri* maritum esse mihi visum est ex variis observationibus.

Valeas, vir dignissime, et epistolarum tuarum exoptatissimarum deliciis me iterum exhilarare ne dedigneris!

Sum tui cultor amicissimus
JOHANNES WHITE.

Blackburn,
die 1mo Martii, 1774.

Squali glauci Calpensis dentes non granulati, sed acutissimi, serrati. Inter tua Addenda, *Lacertæ chalcidicæ* pedes tridactyli, minime 5-dactyli; in meo specimine pedes tridactyli. *Turdum* habeo novum, *pygargum*; veram speciem, non lusum.

Piscem habeo perpulchrum, Calpensem, *Bramam marinam* caudâ forcipatâ Raii Synopsis, p. 115. Hunc in Syst. Nat. haud invenio; ad *Chetodontis* genus pertinet.

Mantis phthisica Calpensis est; ut et *Gryllus umbraculatus*.
Artedi Opera hic rarissima; an venalia apud vos?

Turdus pygargus.	Parus cæruleus.
Turdus? an Motacilla?	Motacilla regulus.
Emberiza nova?	
Passer syrium Anglorum	Lepadogaster.
Pratincola.	Squilla nova.
Corvus corone.	
Junx torquilla.	Mus minimus, novus.

INSECTA.

Scarabæus excavatus, M. F.
———— lunaris? hispanus?
———— novus?
———— variabilis?
———— rugosus, Scopoli.
Tenebrio uncinus, novus.
Leptura bimaculata, nova.
Attelabus Calpensis, novus.
Apis catorhynchos, nova.
—— pyrrhopleura, nova?
—— ——, nova?
—— ——, nova?
—— ——, nova?

Sphex ——, aculeo tricuspidi.
Cancer ——, brachyurus, novus?

Esox sphyræna.
Cancer, e Pinnâ muricatâ.
Perca, lineis cœruleis.
Salmo Saurus.
Scomber? an Gasterosteus?
Sparus, Dentale della Corona, Brun.
Sparus ——, Cachucho Hispan.
Perca gigas, Bruennichii.
Chætodon.
Lepidopus.

LETTER VIII.

FROM THE REV. JOHN WHITE TO LINNÆUS.

Catalogus Animalium &c. ad Illust. D. Linnæum missorum die 19 Martii, 1774.

AVES CALPENSES.

Muscicapa (Linn. MS.).
Sturnus collaris, Scopoli.
Pratincola.
Turdus pygargus, **nova species.**
Emberiza, **n. s.**
Motacilla, caudâ albo nigroque maculatâ, n. s. [Defuit (Linn. M.S.)]
Motacilla, Passer sepium Anglor.
  an *Motac. curruca* Linnæi?
Corvus corone Anglor.
Junx torquilla.
Parus cæruleus.
Motacilla regulus.

———

Mus minimus, n.s.
Lapides quamplurimi schistosi e carbonum fossilium fodinis. Hæc

omnia e Museo Domini A. Lever, Lancastriensis.

IN LAGENULA.

Lepadogaster Gouani.
Squilla, nova?

INSECTA CALPENSIA.

Scarabæus excavatus, n. s. mas & fœm.
Scarabæus lunaris? hispanus?
Scarabæus variabilis?
Scarabæus rugosus, Scopoli.
Scarabæus novus?
Tenebrio femoribus uncinatis, novus?
Leptura bimaculata, nova?
Attelabus Calpensis, novus (Linn.)
  Apiano affinis (Linn.)
Apis catorhynchos, nova?

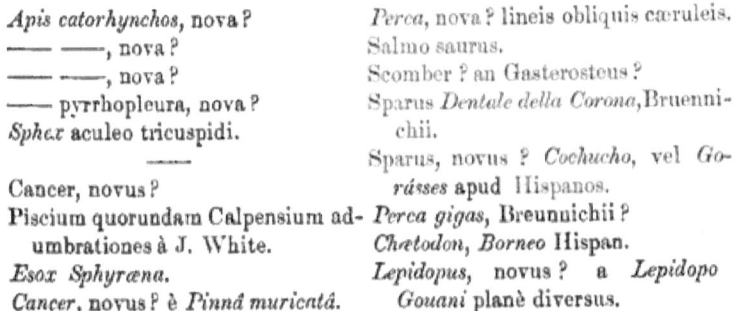

Apis catorhynchos, nova?
—— ——, nova?
—— ——, nova?
—— pyrrhopleura, nova?
Sphex aculeo tricuspidi.

Cancer, novus?
Piscium quorundam Calpensium adumbrationes à J. White.
Esox Sphyræna.
Cancer, novus? è *Pinnâ muricatâ.*

Perca, nova? lineis obliquis cæruleis.
Salmo saurus.
Scomber? an Gasterosteus?
Sparus *Dentale della Corona*, Bruennichii.
Sparus, novus? *Cochucho,* vel *Gorásses* apud Hispanos.
Perca gigas, Bruennichii?
Chætodon, Borneo Hispan.
Lepidopus, novus? a *Lepidopo Gouani* planè diversus.

Viro Illustrissimo Carolo Linnæo,
Equiti Aurato de Stella Polari, &c.
S.P.D. Johannes White.

Aviculas quasdam rariores, Insecta nonnulla Calpensia dubia, necnon & Piscium quorundum Adumbrationes meâ manu, rudi admodum atque imperitâ, delineatas, cum Avibus quoque paucis, communioribus, et Museo amici mei D. Lever, more suo perpulchro conservatis, Lapidibusq. figuris variis notatis, Londinum jampridem misi; ubi eas navi cuidam impositas esse exaudivi, cui nomen *Charlotta,* Navarchi autem nomen *Osterman*: Holmiam iste adnavigare paratus fuit, ubi hæc omnia (quorum supra Catalogus) mercatoribus ibidem commorantibus, quibus nomina *Dryer* & *Zelling,* se traditurum promisit. Cistâ ligneâ inclusa sunt: animo benigno accipias rogo.

Literas meas diei 28^{rt} Februarii te accepisse, & proposita tua de Systematis Naturæ Editione novâ imprimendâ brevi redditurum spero.

Quid de Avibus meis novis, quid de *Lepadogastro,* quid de Insectis hisce dubiis, quid de Lapidum figuris tam miris existimas, discipulo tuo humillimo interrogare liceat.

Piscium, (quorum en tibi Icones,) aliquos forsan esse novos mihi visum est; e. g. *Percam* lineis obliquis cæruleis; *Scombrum*; *Sparum* nuchâ tumidâ; *Sparum* cui nomen apud Hispanos *Cachucho*; *Percam gigantem,* an Bruennichii? *Lepido-*

pum caudâ forficatâ, a *Lepidopo Gouani,* cui caudâ rotundata, seu potius subulatâ, longè differt. *Cancer* quoque macrourus, quem in *Pinnâ muricatâ* habitantem inveni, novus mihi videtur.

Lanium Sengalum ab Algiriâ nuper accepi;
Cuculum glandarium a Monte Calpe.
Charadrius alexandrinus ibidem vulgatissimus.
Sturnum collarem D. Scopoli iisdem locis inveni. At revera *Sturnum* esse dubito; nonne potius *Fringilla*? Seminibus *Phalaridis* vescitur; vivum diu retinui.

Sunt qui *Motacillam* hanc meam rufescentem, cui cauda maculis albis nigrisque infra ad apicem notata est, *Turdum arundinaceum* esse, (seu *Junco* Raii) censeant. At rostrum habet minimè emarginatum, sed integerrimum; præterea et forma, et vita, moresque *Motacillam* indicant. Ad Hispaniam venit quotannis tempore vernali.

Tenebrio collaris, quem Africanum tu scribis, mihi missus est nuperrimè a Monte Calpensi.

Ichneumon quoq. *bicolorus* ab eodem loco venit, cui thorax est bispinosus, antennæ ferrugineæ, medio albidæ.

Myrmeleonis quiescentis alas non solum *deflexas* esse observavi, sed etiam utrinque *involutas*, totum abdomen tubulo quasi cylindrico amplectentes. *Myrmeleones* (i. e. perfecta imago) Diptera minora prædantur.

Valeas, Vir celeberrime! faveasque
cultori tuo amicissimo
J. WHITE.

Blackburn, 1774, die 22mo Aprilis.

Myrmeleon formicarium Calpense nec maculam habet alarem marginalem albam, ut in Syst. Nat. & Schœffero, nec maculas fuscas in limbo, ut apud Reaumurium et Geofroy; alas vero habet omninò immaculatas.

Ad quodnam piscium genus pertineat *Coryphænoides* meus *rupestris* adhuc hæsito. Pinnarum radios numerare nondum potui. Annon novi sit generis? Piscatorum retibus nunquam capitur. Omnes quos vidi in *Squali spinacis* stomacho inveniebantur.

Quid sibi vult verbum *Formycalyn*, scilicet nomen triviale quartæ speciei Myrmeleonis in Syst. Nat., haud ritè intelligo.

LETTER IX.

FROM LINNÆUS TO THE REV. JOHN WHITE.

Viro Reverendissimo et Venerando Dom° J. White.
S. pl. d. Car. Linné.

Accepi literas tuas ad Calend. Januarii datas, suo tempore et ad eas regessi. Accepi et datas d. 1 Martii, et 22 Aprilis. Accepi et ante duos dies merces tuas et dona vere aurea; pro quibus omnibus ac singulis grates immortales reddo, reddamq. dum vixero.

1. *Sturnus collaris*, Scop. An. i. p. 131. *Fringilla sordone* Manett. Orn. t. 338 f. 1.

    Avis Kyburgensis *Gesn. Orn. app.* 725. *Muscicapa* gulâ albâ fusco undulatâ, tectricibus alarum nigricantibus apiculo albo, *collaris* mihi dicenda. Rostrum admodùm parùm est emarginatum. Diversa a *Turdo arundinaceo*.

2. *Turdum pygargum* non antea vidi: erit equidem *Turdus*, apex rostri modicè incurvus.

3. *Pratincolam* antea non vidi; ad *Grallas* spectat, et proprii generis est, D^{no} Lever ne desinas grates meis verbis agere pro egregie et pulcherrime conservatis aviculis quibus me beare voluit.

Phytolithi filicum erant certe optimi.

Isti lapides qui referunt tænias non vidi; an radicum plantarum aquaticarum rudimenta?

Ista impressio in schisto ita refert *Sertulariam* quandam Ellisii, ut nisi magnitudo vetaret, dicerem eam *Sertulariam*. Alia foliis atris linearibus est *Zostera*.

Quadrati politi, *Quartzum coloratum*, Syst. Nat. 3, p. 65. *Fuci* rubri et pilosi impressiones rariores.

Lepadogaster Gouani in lagenulâ est certo *Cyclopterus nudus* meus, Syst. Nat. 414, 2.

Attelabus Calpensis. Hunc etiam ab aliis accepi.

Tenebrio femoribus uncinatis (bispinosis) *T. Calpensis* mihi dicendus.

4. *Motacilla* caudâ albo nigroq. undulatâ, a me antea non visa.

Myrmeleon formicarum rostrum habet, in alis stigma album, habeo jam insectum coram.

Artedi opera non prostant apud nos, sed Leidæ.

Gryllus umbraculatus, ubi habitat? Quid agit cum umbraculo? Te datore optimo multa animalia habeo.

5. *Tetrao tridactylus* pedibus nudis tridactylis.

6. *Hirundo rupestris* nigricans, rectricibus subæqualibus: 2. 3. maculâ albâ.

Piscis thoracicus capite excoriato, nondum nomen imposui.

Attelabus calpensis cærulescens, thorace piloso, elytris rubris punctis 3 nigris.

Sphex mutabilis atra, pedibus hirtis, abdomine maculis luteis 4.

Sphex erosa capite, thorace, alis, pedibusq. ferrugineis.

Apis calpensis labio superiore acuminato inflexo, abdominis segmentis punctis geminis nigris.

Cancer diæresis brachyurus, thorace lævi, lineâ transversâ insculptâ, marginibus serratis, chelis lævibus.

Cancer .... brachyurus subhirsutus manibus ciliatis.

Ex *Squillarum* prosapie 4 distinctæ, nondum posui differentias; et numero plura, præter ultima, te inventore alleganda.

Literæ excrescerent in infinitum si simul et semel omnia responso exponerem, nunc aliis negociis implicitus reservo reliqua proximæ epistolæ.

Scripsi multa addenda Vol. i. Syst. Nat. idq. quotidie: absolvi dimidium tomum. Si tuus frater edat, certus sum quod hoc prodest optimis typis, qui Anglis communes. Tam multa quæ quotidie prodiere, post priorem editionem operis, et quæ allegavi, multum laboris expostularunt. Si vixero, absolvam opus in Autumnum. Quid mihi offerat in sostrum? An poterit habere optimum correctorem typi?

Upsaliæ 1774, d. 3. Julii.

FROM THE REV. JOHN WHITE TO HIS BROTHER GILBERT
(with reference to Linnæus's last Letter.)

DEAR BRO.

ABOVE you have the old Professor's last epistle. You will see that *Sturnus collaris*, Scop., is not a new bird; that Linn. allows it not to be a *Sturnus* but a *Muscicapa*; and that he makes a strange mistake in supposing I could take it for *Turdus arund.* That which Mr. Pennant and you called *Turdus arund.* or *Junco* of Ray is mark'd in the margin 4; and Linn. agrees with me in calling it a *Motacilla*. He seems satisfied now about the *Pratinc.* Gouan's new genus *Lepadogaster* turns out to be nothing more than *Cyclopterus nudus*, Linn. Tanta est discordia Doctorum. Linn. seems now so fond of the specific *Calpensis*, that he will put that and *Whitei*, I suppose, to all my nondescripts. He is wrong in saying only 2, 3 *maculatis albis* in the tail of *Hirundo rupest*. It ought to be 2, 3, 4, 5.

LETTER X.

FROM THE REV. JOHN WHITE TO LINNÆUS.

VIRO ILLUSTRISSIMO CAROLO LINNÆO.
S. pl. dat Joannes White.

NULLA equidem ex re tantum et voluptatis et Scientiæ Naturalis veræ culturæ, quantum ex scriptis literisq. tuis, Vir clarissime, recipio. Verba tua novissima de Syst. Nat. novâ editione imprimendâ ad Fratrem meum Londinensem mandavi. At ille nummos prorsus ullos pro exemplari tuo offerre jam reformidat. Timet enim ne editio hæc reformata, Batavorum Germanorumq. typis furtivis vilioribusq., non sine damno suo, extemplò prodeat contaminata. Quicquid igitur in sostrum velles rogare, te prius nominare oportebit, ut ipse inde sciat an periculum sibi erit faciendum.

Ad Faunam meam Calpensem perficiendam quotidie adhuc

allaboro. Dubia tamen multa zoologica continuò mihi obviam accedunt. Ad hæc dimovenda nemo sanè valet, nisi magnus ille meus Apollo Succicus. Si mutationes aliquas singulares circa generum distributionem fecisti, *Syllabum Genericum* mihi 'mittere ne dedignere, ne methodus mea a methodo Linneanâ nimium discrepet.

Testudinum formas varias video. Sunt quibus testæ apertura est anterior, posteriorq. pro capite membrisq. recipiendis. Sunt quoq. quibus testa inferior valvis binis, quarum cardines transversi, clauditur, adeo ut animalis terrefacti caput atq. membra omnia penitùs abscondantur. Hujusmodi testas in Syst. Nat. memoratas non invenis. Anne igitur generis *Testudinum* * fieri possit divisio? exempli gratiâ, *testâ clausâ* seu *cardinatâ, testâ apertâ,* &c.

Avem Kyburgensem Gesneri examinavi; sed utrum hæc sit *Sturnus collaris* Scopoli, mihi jam videtur dubitandum. Gesneri figura est pessima; de gulâ maculatâ nihil dicit. *Sturnum collarem* Scop., *Turdum* esse *arundinaceum* nunquam suspicitur; at *Motacillam* meam *testaceam*, caudâ albo nigroq. maculatâ, esse *Turdum arundin.* quidam existimârunt. *Motacillam* Krameri, Elench. p. 375. n. s. eandem esse aviculam parum dubito, quum is a *Turdo* longè diversa sit. *Motacillæ* hujus nomen tuum specificum mihi desiderandum.

Quibus in locis *Gryllus umbraculatus* habitat, vel quid agit cum umbraculo, nondum mihi innotuit: unicum tantum inveni in viis arenosis, pedibus hominum conculcatum.

Hirundo rupestris Scop., mihi potius (pace tuâ) *hyemalis* dicenda; nam ipsa, sola forsan inter *Hirundines*, hyemes nobiscum degit. Hujus rectrices 2. 3. maculâ albâ dicis: at reverâ 2. 3. 4. 5. albo maculantur. *Piscis* thoracici, capite excoriato, &c. nomen Linnæanum, cum characteribus genericis valde desidero. Hujus specimen meum maximum longitudinem attigit undecim unciarum.

* [This distinction between the species of tortoises with the under portion of the shell entire and immovable, and those in which the sternum is movable on a hinge, was the discovery of Gilbert, and given to his brother to be communicated to Linnæus. This he did in this letter, but without any reference to his brother as the real discoverer! See Vol. I. p. 240, note.—T. B.]

Si *Attelabrum Calpensem* ab aliis accepisti, nonne nomen triviale a loco malè sumendum ?

Sphex iste, quem tu *mutabilem* vocas, quando habeat maculas quatuor abdominales, fœmina est ; hæc quoq. major : cæteri vel mares, vel forsan neutri. Maribus aculeus est tricuspis.

Sphex, cui nomen imposuisti *erosa*, mihi videtur parum discrepare a *Sphege Mauritanico* Syst. Nat.

Leptura bimaculata an nova ? *Scarabæus* thorace excavato, an novus ?

Œstrus est apud nos vulgatissimus, in Syst. Nat. nondum reperiendus. Hujus meminit D. Derhamus, Physico-Theol. p. 250. et Mouffletus, pag. 62, cui nomen dedit *Musca curvicauda*, sive σκολιουρος. Historia tamen apud Mouffletum a veritate multum aberrat. Nam ipsam (*curvicaudam*) equos aculeo suo pungere, omnino falsum est, quippe aculeum nullum habet. Nec stercora sua, ut quosdam putasse dicit, pilis equi affigit. Sed equos solummodo persequitur ut *ova* sua pilis eorum affigat, cujus rei testis non solum ipse D. Derhamus, sed etiam frater quidam meus, in agro Hantoniensi, rerum naturalium peritissimus. Ipse etiam paucis abhinc diebus *Muscam curvicaudam* ova sua pilis equinis affigentem, manibus meis captavi, curatissime observavi, verumq. esse *Œstrum* "*ore nullo, punctis tribus, absq. rostro*," certissime attestor. Hunc tibi mittendum conservo ; interea characterem ejus specificum accipe his verbis.

Œstrus - - - - - - alis maculatis, vultu albo, thorace nigro, pilis flavicantibus, abdomine elongato, acuminato, incurvato.

Omnis equi qui in pascuis paludosis hospitalitur, mensibus Septembri & Octobri, et in totâ Angliâ, & in Hispaniâ, venter crura, humeriq. hujus *Œstri* ovis scatent. Hæc ova juxta pilorum summitates tam fortiter adglutinantur, ut pilos ipsos prius eradicares quam ova a pilis divelleres ; ideoq. ova omnia simul cum pilis caducis ad terram cadere necesse est. En tibi igitur *Œstrum*, cujus larva non latet intra pecorum corpus ! at ubinam larvæ ejus nutriuntur per totam hyemem nondum novi. Nam *Eruca glabra caudata*, cujus meminit idem D. Derhamus, non est larva *Muscæ curricaudæ*, ut ipse falsò suspicatus fuit, sed larva *Muscæ Hydroleonis* Syst. Nat.

Ergo *Muscam* hanc *curvicaudam* nihil aliud esse quam verum *Œstrum*. Te certiorem fieri conatus sum, si forsan hoc tibi antea ignotum. *Cancri* macrouri iconem tibi misi, quem intra *Pinnam muricatam* inveni; an a te antea visus?

Cancer ursus Rondeletii, p. 564, ad Calpem perquam communis. Hunc in Syst. Nat. nondum invenio. Malum punicum valde refert, et colore, & figurâ, et magnitudine. Rondeletii figura mala est.

Cancer nutrix Scop., ut opinor, est *Cancer pisum* Syst. Nat., a *C. minuto* diversus. Intus Ostreas latitantem sæpius comperi.

Descriptio *Cancri varii* sive *marmorati*, apud Rondel. p. 566, cum Cancro meo lateribus tridentatis cui nomen dedisti *C. diæresis*, mirè convenit; at figura Rondeletiana nihil valet.

Apis abdominis maculis fulvis lateralibus, an nova? Forsan *A. marucatæ* mas, uti videatur ex descriptione apud Geoffroy, 2. p. 408. n. 3.

Emberizam quoq. misi novam, meâ sententiâ, an tuâ quoq. nova sit quærendum.

Mus minimus, quem tibi misit D. Lever pyxide vitreâ inclusum a fratre meo prædicto, Gilberto White, primò fuit inventus. Species certe non antea descripta, quamvis in Angliâ vulgatissima. Vide ejus descriptionem apud Pennant, Brit. Zool. Append. quam a fratre meo accipit. Omnium Quadrupedum facile minutissimus.

Amicus ille meus D. Lever Zoöphylacium suum elegantissimum Londinum deferendum jam parat, ubi omnibus gnavis ignavisq. eum conspiciendi dabitur facultas.

Deo optimo gratiæ meæ maximæ habendæ, quod mihi animalia hæc pauca colligendi copiam dederit, quæ vel sagacissimo Scrutatori Naturæ nondum innotuerunt. Quæcunq. sunt nova vel inaudita tua omnia summo jure censeo: Dentur dignissimo. Nulla mihi gratior voluptas quam tanto viro dandi libertas. De nomine meo scriptis tuis inserendo loqueris. Verbis tuis laudari, Fama est! Orna me, Vir celeberrime, si non Scriptis tuis, attamen Doctrinâ, Amicitiâ tuâ! Faxit Deus ut opus quod instituisti feliciter absolvas! Valeas! Sic optat, sic precatur, summo studio,

Tui cultor humillimus,
J. WHITE.

Blackburn, Lancashire,
  die 8 Octobri, 1774.

P.S. *Strix Scops* uberiore descriptione dignissima. Ut omnium Strigum minima, sic etiam pulcherrima est. *Jungis torquillæ* vel *Caprimulgi* perpulchris coloribus æmulatur. Aures, seu cornua, pennâ solitariâ constare non credo, nam certè plures pennæ surgunt gradatim ad aurium formam, quæ in cadavere parum percipiendæ. Aurium apertura in hâc ave modica est, ut in *Passeribus*.

Remiges primores serratos, pro charactere generico *Strigis* sumendos existimo, nam hos vidi in omni specie mihi cognitâ, nempe in *Bubone, Oto, Scope, Nycteâ, Alucone, flammeâ, Ululâ, passerinâ*.

Caprimulgi nomen aboleri optarem; anilem enim fabulam hanc avem carpere lactantia viscera rostro, credat Judæus Apella! *Hirundinis Melbæ rectrices decem* tantum (ut in *Hir. Apode*), digiti omnes 4 *antici*.

Dicitur in Syst. Nat. p. 343 *Hir. rusticam* una cum *urbicâ* autumno demergi, vereq. emergere: scire vellem an hæc opinio famâ tantum Veterum, an observationibus certioribus Hodiernorum, innititur. Ipse enim vidi, per plures annos, exercitus innumeros *Hirundinum* autumni tempore ad Africam transeuntes; eodem quoq. tempore *Caprimulgos* gregarios ad austrum migrantes vidi.

[The above letter closes the correspondence of John White with Linnæus. It is not improbable that it was never read by Linnæus, as it was in the previous May that he suffered an attack of apoplexy which "obliged him to close his literary labours."—T. B.]

CORRESPONDENCE WITH HIS FAMILY.

LETTER I.

TO THOMAS BARKER [*].

October 25, 1770.

Dear Sir,

By the register in my old bible it appears that

John White was bap. Feb. 12, 1601.
Richard White, June 10, 1605.
Henry White, Nov. 2, 1606.
Samson White, Knight, Nov. 30, 1607.
Eliz. White, Dec. 26, 1600.
    Marryed to Briscow.
Magdalen White, May 10, 1612.
    Marryed to Sedgewick; afterwards to Wood.

The children of Sir Samson White of Oxon.

John White born Nov. 30, 1636.
Richard White, Aug. 24, 1647.
    These two men possessed Swan Hall.
Henry White of Oxford, father of Dr. White, Dec. 28, 1648.
Gilbert White (vicar of Selborne), Feb. 15, 1650.
Francis White, Fellow of Baliol Coll., 1652.
Mary White, Nov. 14, 1650.

These are all the traces that remain of our family. If you had thought of it in time, it is pity you had not enquired farther of Mrs. Isaac and Mr. White of Bradley.

It does not appear why Swan Hall went into the female

[*] [His brother-in-law.—T. B.]

line; but most probably John White, born 1636, dyed single, and his Bro. Rich. born 1647, had a daughter who marryed Ashworth.

Hoping you will have as good a journey to London as I had to this place, I remain with due respects,

Yr affectionate humble servant,
GIL. WHITE.

P.S. I shall hope to hear from Sam.

LETTER II.

TO SAMUEL BARKER *.

Selborne, Jan. 1, 1771.

DEAR SAM,

I WAS much pleased to see so intelligent a letter from so young a writer, and shall be very glad to have you continue your correspondence.

The lines from the Odyssey are very *apropos* and will make a very suitable motto for the climate of Andalusia. My brother makes a very rapid progress in natural knowledge, and, considering he has no person to confer with or to advise him in his new study, does wonders. He sent me in October a fresh cargo of birds and insects which ought to have been here long ago; but as they came in a Levant ship, they are performing quarantine at Stangate Creek and will I fear be tumbled about and damaged.

When I opened your letter all the *Parnassia*-seed fell out, and I took it to be dust and dirt from the pocket of the person who brought it; but luckily it fell in my lap, so that I saved it all. I shall sow it soon in the sandy bogs, and see if I can succeed better.

The last winter migration that we have in these parts is the appearance of the *Œnas* sive *Vinago* Raii, the wild wood pigeon or stock dove, which comes in great flocks about the

---

* [His sister's only son.—T. B.]

end of November, and does not breed in these parts, perhaps not in the kingdom *. The pigeon that breeds in our woods and hedge-rows, and cooes all the summer is the *Palumbus* † or ring dove, the *palumbes* mentioned by Virgil in his eclogues:

"Nec tamen interea raucæ tua cura palumbes."

Your Un. Harry was with me towards the end of November. As we were walking in the evening we saw just after sunset a star of a moderate magnitude, just above the sun, which we concluded must be Mercury. My Bro. was much pleased to see what he thought to be that planet, as it was new to him; and I had never seen it before but once, and that was at Lyndon in 1760. You may let me know if Mercury was visible at that time.

With the compliments and good wishes of the season I conclude,

Yr affectionate Uncle,
GIL. WHITE.

The following is Mr. Sheffield's account of a visit to Mr. (afterwards Sir Joseph) Banks, sent to Gilbert White, and by him to Samuel Barker, Dec. 21, 1772. Banks returned from his well-known voyage in 1771 with the large collections described, augmented by his voyage to Iceland in July 1772.

"Dec. 2, 1772.

"My next scene of entertainment was in New Burlington Street at Mr. Banks's. Indeed it was an invitation from this gentleman that carried me to town. It would be absurd to attempt a particular description of what I saw here; it would be attempting to describe within the compass of a letter what can only be done in several folio volumes. His house is a perfect museum; every room contains an inestimable treasure. I passed almost a whole day here in the utmost astonishment,

---

* [*Columba œnas*. This species has for several years bred at Selborne, in the hollow of a large pollard ash, which had been for many years previously the haunt of owls. See note, Vol. I. pp. 96, 97.—T. B.]

† [*Columba palumbus*.—T. B.]

could scarce credit my senses. Had I not been an eye-witness of this immense magazine of curiosities, I could not have thought it possible for him to have made a twentieth part of the collection. I have excited your curiosity; I wish to gratify it; but the field is so vast and my knowledge so superficial that I dare not attempt particulars. I will endeavour to give you a general catalogue of the furniture of three large rooms. First the Armoury; this room contains all the warlike instruments, mechanical instruments and utensils of every kind, made use of by the Indians in the South Seas from Terra del Fuego to the Indian Ocean—such as bows and arrows, darts, spears of various sorts and lengths, some pointed with fish, some with human bones, pointed very finely and very sharp, scull-crackers of various forms and sizes, from 1 to 9 or 10 feet long, stone hatchets, chisels made of human bones, canoes, paddles, &c. It may be observed here that the Indians in the South Seas were entire strangers to the use of iron before our countrymen and Monsieur Bougainville arrived amongst them; of course these instruments of all sorts are made of wood, stone, and some few of bone. They are equally strangers to the other metals; nor did our adventurers find the natives of this part of the globe possessed of any one species of wealth which could tempt the polite Europæans to cut their throats and rob them. The second room contains the different habits and ornaments of the several Indian nations they discovered, together with the raw materials of which they are manufactured. All the garments of the Otaheite Indians and the adjacent islands are made of the inner bark of the *Morus papyrifera* * and of the bread tree *Chitodon altile* †; this cloth, if it may be so called, is very light and elegant and has much the appearance of writing paper, but is more soft and pliant; it seems excellently adapted to these climates. Indeed most of these tropical islands, if we can credit our friend's description of them, are terrestrial Paradises. The New-Zealanders, who live in much higher southern latitudes, are clad in very different manner. In the winter they wear a kind of mats made of a particular

* [*Broussonetia papyrifera.*—T.B.] † [*Artocarpus incisa.*—T.B.]

species of Cyperus grass. In the summer they generally go naked, except a broad belt about their loins made of the outer fibres of the cocoa nut, very neatly plaited; of these materials they make their fishing lines, both here and in the tropical isles. When they go upon an expedition or pay or receive visits of compliment, the chieftains appear in handsome cloaks ornamented with tufts of white dog's hair; the materials of which these cloaks are made are produced from a species of *Hexandria* plant very common in New Zealand, something resembling our hemp, but of a finer harl and much stronger, and when wrought into garments is as soft as silk: if the seeds of this plant thrive with us, as probably they will, this will be perhaps the most useful discovery they made in the whole voyage. But to return to our second room. Here is likewise a large collection of insects, several fine specimens of the bread and other fruits preserved in spirits; together with a compleat *hortus siccus* of all the plants collected in the course of the voyage. The number of plants is about 3000, 110 of which are new genera, and 1300 new species which were never seen or heard of before in Europe. What raptures must they have felt to land upon countries where every thing was new to them! whole forests of nondescript trees clothed with the most beautiful flowers and foliage, and these too inhabited by several curious species of birds equally strangers to them. I could be extravagant upon this topic; but it is time to pay our compliments to the third apartment. This room contains an almost numberless collection of animals; quadrupeds, birds, fish, amphibia, reptiles, insects and vermes, preserved in spirits, most of them new and nondescript. Here I was lost in amazement, and cannot attempt any particular description. Add to these the choicest collection of drawings in Natural History that perhaps ever enriched any cabinet, public or private:—987 plants drawn and coloured by Parkinson; and 1300 or 1400 more drawn with each of them a flower, a leaf, and a portion of the stalk, coloured by the same hand; beside a number of other drawings of animals, birds, fish, &c. And what is more extraordinary still, all the new genera and species contained in this vast collection are accurately described, the descriptions fairly transcribed and fit to be put to the press. Thus I have endeavoured to give you an imperfect sketch of what I saw in New Burlington Street; and a very imperfect one it is."

LETTER III.

GILBERT WHITE TO SAMUEL BARKER
(on the same sheet as the foregoing extract from Mr. Sheffield's letter).

Dec. 21, 1772.

DEAR SAM,

As I have promised for some time to write to you without fulfilling my promise; I shall, by way of making you some amends, send you the above written extract from my friend Mr. Sheffield's letter instead of something of my own composing. When you and I happen to meet, we will, if you like, read Virgil's Georgics together, together with Martin's translation and notes, and shall, I trust, find no small satisfaction from that most beautiful of all human compositions. Ben. White, while with me, read them thro' three several times; but he was at that time almost too young to relish so masterly a work.

Give my respects to your father, and tell him I owe him a letter which I intend to pay him soon; and inform him that hitherto our winter has been remarkably mild: within a fortnight I have cut grass for my horses; and nasturtiums abroad are still in bloom! Our mornings and evenings are full as mild now as they usually are at this season at Gibraltar: tho' at noon the therm^r is much raised at that place. My therm^r yesterday morning stood at 52! As I have some suspicions about the regularity of my barometer, pray send me a journal of your barometer for any month past; and let me know if the surface of the quicksilver in the receiver of y^r barometer be exactly 28 inches beneath the lowest mark on the plate.

My Bro. and sister John (who have been with me about a fortnight) are much favoured by this delicate weather, and will, I hope, be tolerably seasoned before severe frosts set in.

Bro. John is frequently incommoded by hoarseness, an infirmity that is very troublesome to a clergyman.

You will I hope write soon, and let me know how you succeed in y^r studies, and how much you and y^r sisters improve in drawing, and particularly in designing. Your sentiments on any subject will be very agreeable to me. All friends join in respects. I am

Y^r affectionate friend,
GIL. WHITE.

This autumn I had plenty of most delicate grapes, such as I have never seen since autumn 1762. The vines blowed very late; but the burning summer ripened the fruit at a vast rate, and made grapes and bunches of a vast size; and yet, what is very strange, the bearing wood for next year is very slender and poorly ripened.

LETTER IV.

TO THOMAS BARKER.

Selborne, Sept. 14, 1773.

DEAR SIR,

I CAN readily give you credit for the change of colour that befell the bulfinch, because when I first undertook the church of Faringdon, the person where I used to dine on a Sunday caught a cock bulfinch in the fields after it had arrived at its full colours[*]. In about a twelvemonth it began to grow dingy; and losing by degrees its gay apparel, it became leisurely, in I think about three years, as black or blacker than a blackbird, all save some of its wing feathers, which

---

[*] [This fact is particululy mentioned in the XVth letter to Pennant. See Vol. I. p. 45, and note.—T. B.]

continued white at least in part. This bird remained in this mourning garb to the day of its death, and lived, I perfectly remember, altogether on hempseed, a kind of food which, I have heard before, has a tendency to blacken those birds that live altogether upon it. The owner of the bulfinch had at the same time a skylark which was supported altogether in the same manner and became very dusky but not black.

Be pleased to remember that tho' I happened to have seen a similar case, yet I look upon the phenomenon as odd and extraordinary, and am much obliged to you for your information, and shall be for the future for any curious anecdote that falls in your way.

From the 9th of Aug. to the 14th inclusive, the heat was very severe night and day; and on the 13th, in the evening, arose from the S. that great tempest of thunder and lightning which did so much damage in and about London. The rain attending that storm was of signal service to the hops, which before began to languish. But in the night between the 18th and 19th of Aug. such a wind came from the N. that it well-nigh demolished all the plantations. In Sr S. Stuart's* garden, consisting of 20 acres, not one pole was left standing for many acres together; and as his crop was remarkably fine, he suffered the loss of many hundreds of pounds in that one night. Since the storm hops have never thriven, and are now picking, but are small and brown, and will be very dear and very poor and ordinary. My therm^r on the 13th of Aug. was at 78½ within doors.

In the beginning of wheat harvest we had some rain, which frightened some farmers, and made them house some of their wheat too soon; but, on the whole, wheat went in in most curious order. As to the spring corn, both here and on the downs it all lies abroad in a bad way; for we have had nothing but rain since Sep. 1. Apples fail in general: I have again, as I had last year, more than my share, but not one pear. My apricots were almost all cut off in bloom; but I have on my wall about 10 dozen of the best-ripened peaches

* [Sir Simeon Stuart, Bart., of Hartley Park, of whose family several monuments still remain in the church of that parish.—T. B.]

and nectarines that I ever saw, that are now in high perfection. My crop of grapes is very great, of which I shall begin gathering to-morrow; and they will supply my table constantly 'til the frosts strip the trees of their leaves. I wait much on my vines, and have them trained with great care and exactness.

My S^t foin was much damaged; but my meadow hay was got up in nice order. Hay has proved a prodigious crop in all parts. Bro. Tho. writes that some farmers in Essex offer to sell it at Xmass next at 25s. per ton out of the rick; and an year ago it was with us at £4 4s. 0d. I cannot think that with us the wheat is any thing of a crop.

Your affectionate brother and humble Servant,
GIL. WHITE.

LETTER V.

TO SAMUEL BARKER, FROM HIS COUSIN JOHN WHITE.

April 6, 1774.

DEAR COUSIN,

AT the request of my uncle I intend doing myself the pleasure of giving you some account of an extraordinary event which lately happened in the parish of Hawkley*. During the vast rains, a large fragment of the Hanger, late my grandfather's, slipped away for near two hundred yards in length, and fell down the step to the depth of forty feet, carrying with it the coppice-wood, hedge, and gate between the two fields, &c. The sinking of this gate is very strange, as it stands at present as upright as it used to do, and is as easy to be opened and shut.

The next thing to be observed is a little hop garden and pond, in the former of which there are two or three places that are sunk four or five feet; besides, many other parts of the garden are very full of large cracks and openings. The

* [For a full account of this remarkable landslip see Letter XLV. to Daines Barrington, Vol. I. p. 227, et seq.—T. B.]

bed of the pond is also very much sunk, and the place from whence the waste water used to run is now the highest part.

A lane which went down one side of this hill is sunk eight or ten feet, and very much pushed forward, so as to be rendered impassable.

There is situated in the same piece of ground with the pond (which is meadow-land) a small cottage, the inhabitants of which were greatly alarmed on the night in which this happened, by a gradual opening in their floor, till at last they perceived that part of the cottage nearest the hill begin to sever with very loud noises. The upper part of the cottage is since entirely fallen down.

A neighbouring farm-house is also so much sunk, and is so full of large cracks as to be rendered not habitable.

There is one field that was wheat last year, pretty well an acre, so much sunk that it is impossible to be ploughed. All the corn land which was affected by this event is full of large chasms and cracks, some two feet wide; the meadow land has very few of these cracks in it, but seems to be pushed forward, and is filled with large swellings of the turf, resembling waves: in some places where the ground met with any thing that resisted, it rose up many feet above its former surface.

In one place four or five trees are driven all together in a huddle. One tree is entirely bent down.

It is supposed eighty or an hundred acres of ground are damaged by this accident.

There has been a great concourse of people to see this event. It is computed that a Sunday or two after it happened, there were pretty near a thousand from different parts of the country. One of the persons to whom the cottage belonged has lately been about with a petition in order to attempt to rebuild it. Hoping that this account of mine will give you some idea of this wonderful accident; with duty to my Uncle and aunt, and love to my cousins,

I remain your affectionate Cousin,
JOHN WHITE.

LETTER VI.

TO THE SAME, FROM GIL. WHITE
(on the same sheet).

Dear Sam,

* * * * Jack and I are newly returned from London, where I caught a great cold. Tell your papa and mamma that I hope they will please to come and see me this summer, and will bring you and as many of y^r sisters as is convenient. Among other things you will be glad to see the strange sight described above. I have been prevented as yet by indisposition from seeing it myself.

Captn Cook and Mr. Forster, it is expected, will be at the Cape next Novem^r and home about next March. The S. and W. of England have suffered lately in a wonderful manner by floods; but I found by a gent. who arrived in town from N. Wales in the midst of all those bad doings that nothing extraordinary had happened in that way on the N.W. side of the kingdom; and so I find by my Bro. John's letters. The land springs or lavants are higher on the Hants and Wilts downs than ever they were known in the memory of man; and so they are at Faringdon.

Your affectionate Uncle,
GIL. WHITE.

Pray write soon.

LETTER VII.*

TO SAMUEL BARKER.

Selborne, Nov. 3, 1774.

Dear Sam,

When I sat down to write to you in verse, my whole design

* [A copy of this letter was given to me many years since by a near relative of Mr. Barker's.—T. B.]

was to show you how easy a thing it might be with a little care for a nephew to excell his uncle in the business of versification; but as you have so fully answered that intent by your late excellent lines, you must for the future excuse my replying in the same way, and make some allowance for the difference of ages.

However, when at any time you find your muse propitious, I shall always rejoice to see a copy of your performance, and shall be ready to commend, and, what is more rare and more sincere, even to object and criticise where there is occasion.

A little turn for English poetry is no doubt a pretty accomplishment for a young gentleman, and will not only enable him the better to read and relish our best poets, but will, like dancing to the body, have an happy influence even upon his prose compositions. Our best poets have been our best prose writers; of this assertion Dryden and Pope are notorious instances. It would be in vain to think of saying much here on the art of versification: instead of the narrow limits of a letter, such a subject would require a large volume. However, I may say in a few words that the way to excell is to copy only from our best writers. The great grace of poetry consists in a perpetual variation of your cadences: if possible no two lines following ought to have their pause at the same feet.

Another beauty should not be passed over; and that is, the art of throwing the sense and power into the third line, which adds a dignity and freedom to your expressions. Dryden introduced this practice, and carried it to great perfection; but his successor, Pope, by his over exactness, corrected away that noble liberty, and almost reduced every sentence within the narrow bounds of a couplet. Alliteration, or the art of introducing words beginning with the same letter in the same or following line, has also a fine effect when managed with discretion. Dryden and Pope practised this art with wonderful success. As, for example, where you say "the polished beetle," the epithet "burnished" would be better for the reason above. But then you must avoid affectation in this case, and let the alliteration slide in, as it were, without design; and this secret will make your lines bold and nervous. There are also in poetry allusions, similes, and a thousand nameless graces, the efficacy of which nothing can make you sensible of but the careful reading of our best poets, and a nice and judicious application of their beauties. I need not add that you should be careful to seem not to take any pains about your rhimes; they should fall in, as it were, of themselves. Our old poets laboured as much formerly to lug in two rhiming words as a butcher does to drag an ox to be slaughtered; but Pope has set such a pattern of ease in that way, that few composers now are faulty in the business of rhiming.

When I have the pleasure of meeting you, we will talk over these and many other matters too copious for an Epistle.

Yours affectionately,
GIL. WHITE.

LETTER VIII.

TO MRS. BARKER.

London, Nov. 26, 1774.

DEAR SISTER,

I HAVE been indebted to you for some time in the letter way; but as I have lately written to Sam, I was in hopes that a letter to one of the family would express my regard for the whole, and excuse my other obligations for a time. My business in town is to meet my Bro. John, and to bring up Jack, who is grown so tall and largo that it is full time that he was settled in the world.

Originally I intended to have met Bro. J. in town, and to have accompanied him to Blackburn, and so to have spent the winter between that place and Lyndon; but just as I thought I had at last procured help for my church, my assistant was called into Devon, to return he knows not when: " ibi omnis effusus labor." Sam will tell you the meaning of the Latin. Molly White thrives well at Selborne, and grows tall, fair and handsome, and is a fine girl; Nanny Woods also is very stout and hardy, and is a nut-brown maid. Poor Nanny White, who came to Newton in so deplorable a condition, has for these last five weeks mended in a most marvelous manner, so that her friends about her have good hopes—and, if she has no relapse, will be again soon in a comfortable state, tho' London, I fear, will be no ways fit for her for some time*. Berriman lies still in the same sad deplorable way, helpless and hopeless!

Winter comes on with hasty strides this year; and I begin to fear we shall have a severe one. Tell my niece Betty that I don't love snow now near so well as when I was of her age; I then thought it a very amusing pleasing meteor.

Jack is five feet 8 inches and $\frac{3}{4}$ high without shoes, and proportionably large. Pray tell Sam that I shall expect to hear from him in prose or in verse, in Latin or English, as he likes best. The insinuation that Mrs. Chapone † is a papist is a foolish slander, thrown out by somebody that envies her her literary reputation. I have been assured since that she is an Italian stage-dancer!

I am, with all due respect to all friends,

Your affectionate Brother,

GIL. WHITE.

* [This young lady was the daughter of Benjamin White. The hopes of her recovery were fallacious; she died at Newton in October 1777, at the age of 21, and was buried at Selborne.—T. B.]

† [This was the well-known authoress, to whom, when Miss Mulso, Gilbert White was attached, and of whom an account is given in the memoir.—T. B.]

LETTER IX.

TO MRS. BARKER

(with the following letter to Samuel Barker).

Selborne, March 30, 1775.

Dear Sister,

I could have much wished to have spent part of last winter with you; but just as I thought I had got a gent. to supply my church, he was called suddenly into Devon. Harry has got a large family indeed; Bro. Tho. and I were lately at the Xtening of his last boy, whose name is Edward. Our brother has lately much enlarged his house, which could no longer contain his numerous family: a new kitchen, and a new parlour over that, and garrets over that, all very large and roomy, make the house now very commodious; and nothing is to be regretted but the expence. As building is catching, I also talk of some addition to my house next summer; but I much suspect my resolution in setting about it*. Bro. John was disappointed in placing his son in London, and now thinks of placing him with a linen-draper at Manchester—a scheme, I think, much for the better in all respects; for in London they ask most enormous fees, and Bro. Ben has just given £250 with Edmund to Mr. Hounsom in Fleet Street. Alice Boxall, who removed after her husband's death to her daughter's, is lately dead, as is also John Neal. Poor Berriman lies in the same deplorable way still! Nanny Woods continues stout and well, and is a fine brown maid; her hair is remarkably fine. Molly White is very well, and is stout and large of her age, and a giant to Mrs. Etty. Your kind present to your native place I have disposed of in part; such gratuities in these hard times are very acceptable. Mrs. Isaac writes me word that her aunt Weston died intestate, and that by standing in her mother's shoes she shall come in for about

* [He, however, completed his drawing-room (24 ft. by 18, and 12 high) in 1777.—T. B.]

£5000. Altogether her children will be finely provided for. I am concerned to hear that Mrs. K. Isaac has such poor health. With respects to all the family, I conclude,

Dear Sister, your affectionate and obliged Brother,

GIL. WHITE.

Mr. and Mrs. Etty and niece join in respects. Friends are well at Newton. Bro. John is in pretty good forwardness with his Fauna Calpensis, or Natural Hist. of Gibraltar.

I forgot to tell my nephew in the proper place that Dryden's ode on St. Cecilia is nothing else, for an hundred lines together, but beautiful numbers, finely adapted to the sense.

He will, I hope, write soon.

Fierce frost at present, with snow. Woe to the wall-fruit!

LETTER X.

TO SAMUEL BARKER.

March 30, 1775.

DEAR SAM,

As I took no copy of my last hasty letter on Poetry, I am not very certain how far I went in that subject, and what I omitted. However, I think I said nothing concerning the *power* that masterly writers possess of adapting their numbers to their subjects, or rendering the sound an "echo to the sense."

Homer and Virgil no doubt enjoyed this faculty in great perfection, and have shewed wonderful instances of it; but then you must remember that fanciful commentators have over-refined on this power, and have found numberless beauties of this kind which the authors neither percieved nor intended.

The English language is very capable of being conducted to this perfection; and Pope in particular, in his translation of the Iliad, has frequently imitated the original most happily in this way. In his essay on criticism (which he published, as I remember, at 16 years of age) he has given several instances of this sort of power, as

"And the smooth stream in smoother numbers flows," &c.

But the finest instance that I remember in our own language for several lines together, is in old John Dryden's translation of a simile in Virgil, which, though I have not seen for these 20 years, I shall never forget on account of its singular elegance *.

> "As when a dove her rocky hold forsakes,
> Rous'd, in a fright her sounding wings she shakes;
> The cavern rings with chattering,—out she flies,
> And leaves her callow care, and cleaves the skies:
> At first she flutters; but at length she springs
> To smoother flight, and shoots upon her wings."
>
> " mox aëre lapsa quieto,
> Radit iter liquidum, celeres neque commovet alas."

In short, John Dryden is to me much the greatest master of numbers of any of our English bards; but then, contrary to most men, he never arrived at perfection 'til he was very old.

Rhime in itself is barbarous and Gothic, and unknown to the ancients, who would have despised such a jingle; but then it must be remembered that modern languages being destitute of the beauties derived from terminations and inflection, require some substitute. Besides, some of our best poets have conducted rhime with such address that it seems to fall in of its own accord, without their seeking; and if rhimes are shackles, yet these people move so gracefully in them, that we would not wish to see them divested of them.

Blank verse is, no doubt, when well conducted, full of dignity; but then perfection in that way is so rare that we never had but two or three poems that were worth reading. A desire of raising the diction above prose pushes men into fustian and bombast. Even the great Milton, the father of blank verse, is not always free from this vice, but ransacks the

* [This passage, with the original, appears afterwards at the close of letter XLIV. (the last) to Pennant, at p. 112 of the 1st volume.—T. B.]

whole circle of sciences for a set of hard words and rumbling terms that make his readers stare.

As to Thomson (not Tompson), his seasons are sweet poems, full of just description and fine moral reflections; but then this Scotch bard, thro' a desire of elevating his language above prose, falls also into fustian sometimes; and though he thinks much like a poet, is often faulty in his diction.

The 'Cyder' of John Philips, a didactic and Georgic poem in blank verse, is worthy your attention. This man dyed young; but had he survived 'till he had acquired a little more ease, and 'till time had somewhat mellowed his muse, he had been an excellent poet.

Somerville, quite in advanced life, wrote his 'Chace,' a poem full of warmth and spirit and all the enthusiasm of a young sportsman.

Thus have I given you my crude sentiments in a hasty way on the subject of English poetry. If my remarks afford any pleasure or information, my intention will be fully answered.

Venus, Jupiter, Mars, and Saturn appear now every clear night, as it were in a line; but how and when am I to find Mercury? Had it not been for your father, who shewed him to me at Lyndon in 1760 for near a fortnight together, I should never have seen him at all.

Yours affectionately,
GIL. WHITE.

LETTER XI.

TO SAMUEL BARKER.

Ringmer, Augst 12, 1775.

DEAR SAM,

SUSPECTING from the habits and shape that fern-owls might resemble the cuckow in its internal construction, I procured two, and found my suspicions not ill grounded; for upon dissecting the crop or craw *behind* the *sternum* immediately on the bowels, it was bulky and hard, and stuffed with *Phalænæ* of several sorts. Now, as it appears that this bird, which undoubtedly sits itself, is formed exactly as cuckows are, we may reasonably conclude that Mr. Herissant's conjecture that cuckows are incapable of incubation from the disposition of their intestines becomes groundless, and we are still to seek for the cause of that strange peculiarity.

G. W.

LETTER XII.

TO SAMUEL BARKER.

Sep. 6, 1775.

DEAR SAM,

As you desired, I procured a cuckow which was in some degree bare-breasted, yet showed no token of incubation from any scurfiness of the skin; besides, the bird had all the marks of being a young one. When we had cut open the breast-bone, and exposed the intestines to sight, we found that the crop or craw did not lie before the sternum at the bottom of the neck, as in the *Gallinæ* and others, but immediately over the bowels. This stomach was large and round, and stuffed very hard with food, which, upon examination, was found to consist of various insects, such as small *Scarabæi, Ptini, Elatri, Araneæ, Libellulæ,* &c., the last of which I have seen cuckows catching on the wing over Oakhanger pond more than once. The farrago also was made up of maggots and many seeds, which seemed to belong either to gooseberries, currants, cranberries, or some other berries; so that these birds apparently subsist on fruit and insects; nor was there the least appearance of bones, feathers or fur to support the idle notion of their being birds of prey. The sternum of this bird seemed to me to be remarkably short, between which and the anus lay the crop or craw, and immediately behind that the bowels; and close to the backbone the parts that distinguished the bird to be a male. Now it must be allowed, as the French anatomist observes, that the crop placed just upon the bowels must be in a very uneasy situation during the business of incubation; yet the way will be to examine whether some birds that do sit for certain are not formed in a similar manner, because then the notion of incapacity in the cuckow from formation falls to the ground. Now this enquiry I intend to make with a fern-owl, and as soon as opportunity offers.

G. W.

LETTER XIII.

TO SAMUEL BARKER.

Selborne, Nov. 15, 1775.

Dear Sam,

After some consideration I am in no manner of doubt but that murmur *electricum* is an error of the press; and that it should be murmur *elasticum*. For what in the world has electricity to do with hop-poles? Why, if it had, should the wind call it forth? Now as to an *elastic* murmur, or a deep *humming* sound, occasioned by the vibration of the *naked* poles when agitated by the wind, I have heard it twenty times in the months of March and April; and moreover, when I came to question my servant Thomas, he readily recollected to have heard such a *rushing* in hop-gardens in the spring months, and added, pertinently enough, that such a murmur might be observed every spring in gardens among kidney-bean-sticks, as I perfectly well remember. Therefore read (meo periculo) *elasticum*, instead of *electricum*. The only thing that sticks with me is that since this murmur may be so easily and naturally accounted for by *elastic* vibration, why Linnæus should express any wonder, or be in the least pother about so plain a matter, since it seems to me that it is as obvious why a pole should *hum* when put in brisk motion, as why the strings of an Æolian harp should, when brushed over by the wind, produce those delicate chimings and unisons—that is, by vibration. It is most probable, therefore, that there are no hop-gardens in Sweden, and that Linnæus never was witness himself to such a murmur, but takes his cue from some hasty and inaccurate correspondent.

I beg you would take two pieces of sponge of equal size, weight, and softness, and hang them by strings over an upland pond, in foggy weather, the one as *near* the *surface* as *possible* the other *several feet above* the water; then I desire you would squeeze the spunges in a morning and see which produces the most water. Then if the lower spunge should prove from repeated trials to be the moistest, I should hope the fact would in some measure corroborate my suspicions that ponds and pools do by *condensation* from the coolness of their surfaces, assimilate to themselves fogs and vapours by contact, and that is one reason why many very little upland ponds, tho' subject to a continual waste by cattle &c., yet never fail in the severest droughts, while larger ponds in *bottoms* frequently become dry. But as your father and you may probably hit upon a better experiment, I desire you would try such as you think most to the purpose *.

Moreover I desire that both of you would send me every hint in Nat. Hist. that occurs to your minds after your recent visit to these parts. My swallow monographies are printed off by the R. S. in vol. 69, p. 258: but the corrector of the press has made sad work with my unfortunate letters; for in one place he makes me say that " swallows eat grass," and in another uses *caves* instead of *eaves* ; moreover he has transposed my letters so as to misplace them, though I numbered them most exactly, and by that means has made a jumble of dates, besides putting two whens in one sentence and many more inaccuracies too numerous to mention ! O fie ! for so young a man to use glasses that magnify 200 times, when Linnæus planned and perfected his whole sexual system *nudis oculis.*

I wish you joy that Jupiter is restored to his liberty and

* [This subject is discussed in a very interesting manner in the XXIXth letter to Daines Barrington, Vol. I. pp. 192 to 195. It is probable that the experiments suggested above were carried out, as the more elaborate observations addressed to Barrington are dated three months later than this letter to his nephew.—T. B.]

dignity; for the Cornish man has seized on him and appropriated him to himself as a new discovered world.

Mr. Etty and I live here by ourselves, and, having no wives to controll us, do as we please: only we are deterred from going to London by the influenza. Pray return my best thanks to my sister for her agreeable present: and to your father and sisters for their company and conversation at Selborne. I acknowledge myself much in your debt, and shall endeavour to pay you in kind. Did you find *rushes* as much in use at Lyndon as Mrs. Rashleigh has done at   *? Many gent. at Oxford had never heard of rushes, perhaps because they were gent.

Yours affect.
GIL. WHITE.

LETTER XIV.

TO SAMUEL BARKER.

Jan. 5, 1776.

DEAR SAM,

GOSSAMER has from old times attracted the attention of the curious. Chaucer mentions it among the phenomena of nature not well understood or accounted for, such as thunder, &c.

The *Tabanus borinus*, I verily believe, has nothing in its tail, or blood-sucking rostrum, but a *Musca*-like proboscis. I have seen it suck the galled parts of Sir Sim. Stuart's working oxen, without giving them any pain or offence. It abounds most in moist places, and sultry weather. The *Œstrus curricauda* lays its nits, I know, but in the warm hours of the day; for my horses which are in stable all day, and out a-nights, are never covered with these eggs at home.

Pray examine those little dancing *Diptera* (*Tipulæ* I suppose they are) that sport the winter through, in fog, gentle rain, and even in frost and snow when the sun shines. Every

---

* [In the MS. the name of the place is quite illegible.—T. B.

sunny day when the sun shines they abound; and in warm lanes and under hedges the air swarms with them. Within doors woodlice, spiders, and *Lepismæ* are in motion, and many *Muscæ* in the stable; and earthworms come forth every mild evening; so that in mild weather insects are not so much layed up as is imagined. Some *Phalænæ* fly also all the winter. * * * *

G. W.

LETTER XV.

TO MRS. BARKER.

Thames Street, Feb. 7, 1776.

DEAR SISTER,

Mr. ETTY, Charles, and I came to town on Jan. the 22 and 23, and found the public roads better than we expected. Mr. E. brought up his son and has placed him at St. Paul's school, hoping that by means of good friends he may procure him some considerable exhibitions, that may help to support him in an university education.

As to Mr. W. you must not wonder or resent because he does not write; for when his daughter had a fever more than an year ago, Mrs. E. wrote to him *every* post for many weeks; yet he never returned one answer. However, when all was over he sent her a very handsome set of tea-china. And now during inoculation he never wrote once in the time or since, but is going to make a very handsome present of plate. Thus you see some men are of a very unwriting constitution, and yet neither want gratitude nor generosity.

Bro. Tho. talks of leaving off, and is letting down his stock in trade by degrees. Bro. Harry I found here: he was snowed in for a fortnight or more, and when he went away on Jan. 25 wrote word that it was with the utmost difficulty that he got along, and that if he had attempted a week sooner he would have been stopped by the way.

I have been spending some days at my Bro. Ben's new house at S. Lambeth, which is very commodious and very handsomely furnished. The rooms are rather small; but my Bro. has removed the partition between the two parlors, and so has made one good sitting room: he has besides an other parlor below and a drawing room above stairs of 27 feet in length; but it is narrow. This room my sister has furnished in a splendid manner. In short they, who have eleven children, shame me who have none and yet make a pother about building one room. Nanny recovers very fast by living in the country; and my sister looks much the better for being out of town. In short this house will probably lengthen all their days. Poor Berriman lies in the same sad state! Farmer Parsons has been near death with a fever; but is better. Abram Loe is dead and has left a widow and five small children. Farmer Turner has left his ale-house and is retired to his new house. He is before this, I trust, marryed to his House-keeper Rose Rawkins: the Bridegroom is 71, and the bride 69! I used to say that female beauty does not last above a century; but now I begin to retract.

(On the same sheet with the following to "Sam" and to Mr. Barker.)

LETTER XVI.

TO SAMUEL BARKER.

Thames Street, Feb. 7, 1776.

DEAR SAM,

I THANK you for your kind and intelligent letter; but you never told me whether the good people of Lyndon *burn rushes* or not, nor what you think of my amendment of *murmur electricum* of Linn. Dr. Hales, in Veget. Statics, settles the point from experiment that the *moister earth* is, the more *dew* it attracts, and that a surface of *water* attracts more moisture from the air than a surface of *moist earth*. I wish I could assist you in mosses: time and practice will render you more adroit; but some lessons would be better. Dr. Forster has already published a quarto volume of Antarctic genera, new genera with cuts. It is a splendid book, in Latin, and dedicated to the king. Bro. Ben. has a share. The Dr. has done honour to his friends, and has got a *Barringtonia*, a *Banksia*, a *Sheffieldia*, a *Skinneria**, &c. The *Barringtonia*† is a noble flower and is *polyandria monogynia*. The latin I think is good. His nautical work, in English, is now under correction, as to stile and idiom, at Oxford. Pray be more explicit about "the influence of the W. and S. exposure on our trees." We that see y^m daily do not so much observe. Write very soon, and direct to this house. Send me *all manner* of hints for Nat. Hist. I have made a visit to Grimm. Bro. John has finished his Fauna. The work will be large. Mr. Barr. wants me to join with him in a Nat. Hist. publication; but if I publish at all, I shall come forth by myself. Bro. Tho. is laying up materials for a History of Hants.· He will some day take an artist down.

LETTER XVII.

TO THOMAS BARKER.

Thames Street, Feb. 7, 1776.

DEAR SIR,

OUR snow, like yours, was not very great, but most marvelously drifted thro' the hedges, so as to fill all our lanes and cover the gates. I was forced to dig my way out of the village, and to ride for two Sundays following to Farr. attended by Pioneers. As long as I stayed, the therm^r continued abroad at 20. But on Jan. 28 (Thomas writes me word) it fell to 7, on 29 to 6; on the 30 it was at 10; and on the 31 it descended to half a degree below 0 !! a degree of cold beyond any instance that I have yet heard of! There

---

* [*Skinneria* was not finally removed from *Fuchsia*.—T. B.]

† [*B. speciosa*, Forst., Rumph. Herb. Amb. 3, 114.—T. B.]

was a rime. At S. Lambeth it was at 7. It froze under our beds in London!

Thanks for your information respecting Mercury. Pray throw out *all* sorts of *Nat. hints*. *I have employed the keeper of Domes-day Book to transcribe all relating to Selborne; and am to pay* 4*d. per line:* besides I have applyed for a transcript of all relating to the Priory in Magd. Coll. archives. Pray send me word what rivers were frozen in Italy; were they in Lombardy or in the more S. parts? Virgil in the Georg. mentions freezing rivers. Mr. Gibbon, a Hants Gent. publishes next week his 1st vol. in 4to of a Hist. of the latter Rom. Empire; there will be 4 vols. in all. I conclude respectively

Your affectionate Bro., Uncle, & Bro^r,
GIL. WHITE.

Respects to family.
Mr. Gibbon begins with Trajan *. Pray write soon.

LETTER XVIII.

FROM THOMAS BARKER TO GILBERT WHITE.

Lyndon, Feb. 13, 1776.

REV. SIR,

WE received your three letters in one; and as you desire to hear before you go out of town, I here sit down to write one. I find your cold was greater than ours. January 20 was remarkable: it was a cloudy morning, and as long as it continued so the cold was moderate; but as soon as it cleared up about noon it grew sharper, and at eight at night it got down to 11, after which it rose again. You asked Sam his opinion of the west and south exposure: he may tell you his opinion; and I will tell you mine. The south-west sides of trees do not suffer at all here, nor in most places where I go; but I

---

* [Gibbon resided near Petersfield, and appears to have been well known to Gilbert White. The first volume of his celebrated work was published on Feb. 17, 1776.—T. B.]

believe on such burning chalk and flint as the South Downs and Ambresbury* plains the scorching S.W. sun does more damage than the wind. This agrees with what your brother H. says, that wherever they can keep the ground moist the trees always thrive. So at Ringmer the trees and hedges toward the Downs are all cut; but as soon as you have passed Ringmer going towards Norlington you soon lose sight of any cutting by the sea-winds, which probably injure the plants as far as they blow the spray of the sea.

I do not know what rivers of Italy Mr. Heathcote spoke of as having been frozen this winter. I find his information came from Mr. Taylor, a clergyman whom I believe you formerly knew at Oriel College. He is now in Italy. His letter is dated at Rome, and says, "We have had colder weather here than in England. The river Arno at Florence has been frozen over, which it has not been these 13 years, and a pond 5 miles over, made by Augustus near Ostium, 14 miles from hence, which has not happened in the memory of man." The 13 years since the Arno was frozen will reach back just to the 5 weeks frost of January 1763, when there was that most remarkable rime, a most settled frost without breath of wind or glimpse of sun.

Your sister and nieces join in compliments to yourself and all friends, I being, dear brother,

Your humble servant,
T. BARKER.

LETTER XIX.

FROM SAMUEL BARKER TO GILBERT WHITE.

Lyndon, Feb. 13, 1776.

DEAR SIR,

IF Linnæus's murmur be nothing more than the rushing of the wind among the poles of a hop-garden, it is wonderful, as

* [An old, perhaps the more correct, way of spelling what is now Amesbury?]

you observe, that he should make any difficulty about it: on the other hand, there is no apparent connection between electricity and hops; so that probably it is some mistake of his correspondent.

During the late frost we observed that the cold was constantly most intense when the sky was clear. There was little or no rime here till the 31st of January, the day before the thaw. Does not a rime after a series of clear steady frost frequently precede a thaw? The rime in 1763 lasted the whole frost; but the sun had never appeared during the whole time.'

Since the breaking of the frost the weather has been in general wet and windy. On the night of the 5th there was a violent gust which lasted but few minutes, that blew down many hay-stacks, stripped houses, &c.; the windows of a gentleman's hot-house at Uppingham were shattered to pieces. Wo be to his exotics!

The influence of the S.W. exposure seems to consist in weakening vegetation so that the heads of trees in such a situation are thin of branches, and sometimes incline to the N.E. Of the four firs on Baker's-hill the easternmost is apparently the most thriving. Are the bodies of such trees prevented from growing to their full size, or are the leaves only and smaller boughs affected? Does grass and other vegetables suffer from this exposure?

The use of rushes as a substitute for candles is unknown in Rutland. Some of the poorest people, particularly manufacturers, use a kind of lamps that scarcely serve to make darkness visible; if they could be persuaded to try rushes the advantage would be considerable.

I should be glad to know how you like Mr. Grimm's performances. As your views consist principally of woods, an artist ought to be perfect in that difficult branch of drawing to give you satisfaction. The beautiful scenes of woods rising above one another, so pleasing to the eye, if not well expressed would on paper appear heavy and solid.

Aratus, in his 'Prognostics,' line 301, mentions $\dot{\alpha}\rho\alpha\chi\nu\iota\alpha$ "floating in the still air" as an indication of settled weather.

Are we to understand by this the spiders themselves, or gossamer?, as the word admits of both senses.

The same poet observes that cattle feed eagerly at the approach of storms—a circumstance that was taken notice of here the night the snow began. A naturalist acquainted with the plants and animals of Greece would receive much pleasure and information from perusing the whole poem.

My uncle Thos. desired me last year to observe whether the magnetic needle was affected during the appearance of bright northern lights: there has been no opportunity of remarking this, as during the whole winter there have been very few of them, and those inconsiderable. He also wanted to find an account of the ergot or horned rye, and the distemper it occasioned: this I have met with in the 55th vol. of the Phil. Trans. for the year 1765, no. 17, page 106 &c.

If during your stay in town you should happen to meet any of your botanical friends, I should be extremely obliged to you if you would ask which are the male and female flowers of mosses, and how they are distinguished, as I can discern no tokens of sexuality in the *antheræ*; and also what the receptacle is, and where situated.

I wonder Linnæus should not refer to Ray's 'Synopsis,' as Morrison, whom he quotes, takes whole descriptions from it.

With my sincerest respects to yourself, my uncle Thos., and uncle Benj.'s family, I conclude, Sir,

Yours affectionately,
SAMUEL BARKER.

LETTER XX.

TO THOMAS BARKER.

London, March 20, 1776.

DEAR SIR,

* * * * All our chalk barley was greatly damaged: we have none good but from the sands, where their harvest was earlier. The former sells for about 20s, and the latter for

about 26s. Farther west, where they have nothing but chalk downs, *all* their barley was pretty well spoiled; so that Harry complains he cannot, as yet, get any price at all for his crop.

What pigeons in a state of nature may do I cannot pretend to say; but this I know, that tame pigeons which are pampered by high feeding and lie perhaps under more frequent temptations from living together in crowds, are apt to forget the rules of strict chastity, and follow too often the example of people in high life. As to the smaller birds, it would be very difficult to ascertain the identity of the man and wife in different years.

Yours affect.
GIL. WHITE.

I thank you for this hint, and shall always be glad of more.

LETTER XXI.

TO SAMUEL BARKER.

London, March 20, 1776.

DEAR SAM,

You may comfort yourself that you are not the only person that finds himself under difficulties respecting the sexuality of mosses; for Mr. Curtis is by no means satisfyed concerning the distinctions made use of, but suspects very much that there are not the same obvious distinctions in them which in the more common plants so rationally support the Linnæan system. He is a very friendly man and always willing to communicate, and has therefore desired me to send you down the enclosed plate, containing representations of the fructification &c. of his mosses, such as he uses in his own lectures on the occasion. In the plate respecting the male and female *Vallisneria* you will see a wonderful instance of the wisdom of providence *.

* [The female flowers of *Vallisneria* are kept floating on the surface of the water by the tendril-like construction of the flexible stalk; the male

Mrs. Stebbing and I go down to S. together on Friday in a p. chaise. I shall not forget to take my sister's present.

Yours affect.,
GIL. WHITE.

The water-snails, two or three species now begin to be buoyant, and to crawl with their bellies upwards on or against the surface of the water. We have none **round** Seleburne *.

LETTER XXII.

TO SAMUEL BARKER.

Selborne, July 1, 1776.

DEAR SAM,

In the larger plants in general I found no difficulty at all, being assisted by Linn., Hudson, Ray's *Synopsis Stirpium*, &c.: but as to the mosses, I did not care to meddle, because they were become too minute for my eyes, before they begun to be employed in those enquiries. As to the genera of *Orchis*, *Ophrys*, and *Serapias*, there is great obscurity among them, as Linn. tacitly acknowledges, by calling in the distinction of their roots in his specific descriptions. In his system the distinctions should lie in the corolla, stalks, leaves. As to the different sorts of garden fruits, they are the production of cultivation, and belong only incidentally to the Linn. system, but are to be sought for in Miller's Dict. &c. As to the

---

flowers, when the pollen is ripe, become **suddenly detached from the plant, rise at once to the surface, burst open, and scatter the pollen over the female flowers** already open to receive it.—T. B.]

* [The buoyancy of the Limnæidæ, floating with the body and shell **hanging down below** the surface of the water, is caused not only by the **air within the** pulmonary cavity, but also by a certain degree of hollowing of the surface of the foot, the margin of which, by a sort of undulatory motion, conducts the animal slowly along the surface of the water.—T. B.]

Nymphæa alba, the white water-lily, there are none in this parish, but are to be found in Wishanger pond in the parish of Frinsham: if I knew when the seeds were ripe I would endeavour to procure some.

Dr. Forster assured me that he saw, some few times, appearances in the sky in the S. hemisphere, very similar to those we call *auroræ boreales.*

Our first young brood of swallows was marvellously early, appearing on June 15: the first week in July is the usual time. I have written to Grimm, and don't know but that I may see him next Monday: I expect also my nep. Rich. White, who is to stay with me some time. Nanny Woods is to dine with me to-day: she is tender and has got a cough.

We have built a new Hermitage, a plain cot; but it has none of the fancy and rude ornament that recommended the former to people of taste: this is strong and substantial, and will stand a long while, fire excepted.

Our solstice is cool and shady, but not very wet: I have ricked my St. foin in fine order; this day I begin to cut my meadow grass, which will prove a bigger crop by one 3rd than that of last year. Cucumbers do not succeed well in general this year. My bank, which was lowered when you were here, is now very gaudy and full of flowers. I have much wall-fruit, and a fine show for grapes; pears, plums, apples and cherries without number. As I was visiting last Tuesday at Bramshot I saw on the Portsmouth road Burgoyne's light horse marching down to embark for N. America. The horses were fine and the men fine young fellows; but they all look'd very grave, and did not seem much to admire their destination. The Atlantic is no small frith for cavalry to be transported over: the expence will be enormous! Brother and sister Harry have been in town and at Mrs. Snookes's. At Ringmer Ben. Woods caught the measles of John Mott, and fell with it before he left town; but his father sent him down to Fyfield after it came out! None of Bro. Harr.'s children nor Bro. Thos's has had this distemper; so there will be a sick house and much trouble; but the children can never fall at a better season of the year or time of life. Now, at Mids^r

Harry is to have a young gent. at the noble price of £150 pr ann. Harry and his wife (no small personages) and seven children, and two canary birds, and one aberdavine, and 10 parcels, a dormouse and a puppy-dog, all went down in two post-chaises.

Yours affect.
GIL. WHITE.

LETTER XXIII.

TO SAMUEL BARKER.

Ringmer, Aug. 19, 1776.

DEAR SAM,

A KNOWLEDGE of the grasses is the most desirable part of botany, because the most useful: but it is the most neglected; for graziers and farmers do not seem to distinguish any one sort of *Gramen* from the other—the annual from the perennial, the succulent from the dry, or the aquatic from the upland; whereas by attention their meadows and pastures might be much improved; and it is an old maxim, that he is an useful member of society, a good common-wealths man "who can procure two blades of grass where only one grew before."

I am not a little pleased to find that you have got the *Hirundo riparia* just at hand, because I shall expect from a man of your accuracy some circumstances of information which I cannot so well make myself master of at the distance of Wolmer forest. You will be pleased an other year to attend to the *exact* season of their coming and departure, time of nidification, and bringing out their first and second brood &c. &c. Pay attention also to the other three species; for I shall be glad of any *well attested* anecdotes, intending some time hence to publish a new edition of my '*Hirundines*' in some way or other*.

* [His two papers on this subject had been read at the Royal Society respectively in February 1774 and March 1775. He here evidently foreshadows his future book.—T. B.]

My artist Mr. Grimm stayed with me 27 days, 24 of which he worked very hard and displayed great tokens of genius and assiduity. He finished twelve drawings, one of which was a view of Hawkley hanger; but that scape I think did not succeed so well as some others. Bro. Harry made me a visit and was very much delighted with what was going on, and in particular with a view of the hermitage *, which G. is to copy for him in town. From me my artist went to Mr. Yalden †, and took a view of his house and outlet at the *edge of his chalk-pit*. The employer wanted and intended a view from the alcove; but the draughtsman, as well as myself, objected much to the uniformity of that scene: so I carried G. to the chalk-pit on the W. side of the house, from whence he took a charming view. From Newton I carryed G. to Ld Clanricarde's at Warnford, where in the gardens he took a perspective internal view, section, and elevation of a very curious old hall or church, unknown to the antiquaries, for a gent. visiting there, who will one day oblige the world with this neglected and obscure curiosity, now a barn. It is supposed to have been built by K^g John. The order is Saxon. From hence G. went to Wintŏn, to work there for a week or ten days on his own account, and is to call at Hartely on his return. I regret much that King John's Hall had not remained unnoticed a little longer, 'til my Bro. Tho. had been a little more at liberty; for when he has done with business he proposes to entertain himself with collecting materials for an history of the county of Southton: and I moreover marvel that I had never heard of this hall before.

Our people know nothing of the use of the rind or peel of the *Juncus effusus* for cordage.

I rejoice to hear that you learn French: you will very soon be able to read it.

The weather has been now very showery for just a fort-

---

* [This forms the vignette in the title-page of the first and several subsequent editions of the book; and the original drawing in Indian ink by Grimm is now before me, in a copy of the work belonging to the Rev. Edmund Field.—T. B.]

† [Vicar of Newton Valence.—T. B.]

night: our harvest is in a very bad way. When I arrived last Friday evening I was surprized to find Mrs. H. Isaacs and niece Becky at supper with my aunt. B. is grown beyond all knowledge. Nep. Richard, who has left school, is here with me.

Mr. Shadwell has left Stoneham Farm, which is raised from 250 to 400 pr ann. Thanks to Molly White for her agreeable letter. On the Friday you mention my therm^r rose up to 79 *within* doors—a pitch which I have scarce ever seen exceeded. Wheat grows in the sheaf. You have the *Stoparolæ*, I find; but say nothing of the white-throat, black-cap, *Reguli non-cristati* 3 species, the redstart. Respects to all.

Yours affect.
GIL. WHITE.

We have just weighed Timothy, who is encreased in weight just one ounce and an half since last August. *Stoparolæ* come to Selborne May 20, depart about Sept. 7.

LETTER XXIV.

TO SAMUEL BARKER.

Fyfield, Nov. 1, 1776.

DEAR SAM,

JUST as I thought you had been master of the manners and customs of the bank-martin, you write me word that you do not know it when you see it. The case is, you did not begin to look 'til the decline of summer, when all the *Hirundines* cease to frequent their nesting-places. If you will pay some attention to those holes in the spring, you will probably see the owners busyed in the matter of nidification: besides they are to be distinguished from their congeners by their *small size*, their *mouse-colour*, and their *wriggling desultory* manner of *flying*. Pray observe when they come first.

The instance you give of the swiftness of an hawk was somewhat extraordinary. But a very intelligent person assured me that he once saw a more extraordinary instance of command of wing in a daw, which is not very remarkable for feats of activity of that kind. As this person was riding on Salisbury Plain he saw a bird on the wing dropping something from its bill, and catching it again before it came to the ground, several times repeatedly: this unusual sight drew his attention, so that he rode nearer, and saw the same feat repeated to his great surprize. It appeared to him that the ball dropped and recovered was a wallnut. Now a wallnut, I should think, would fall much faster than a dead bird, whose feathers would meet with resistance from the air.

In 24 days Mr. Grimm finished for me 18 drawings, the most elegant of which are:—1. a view of the village and Hanger from the short Lithe*; 2. a view of the S.E. end of the Hanger and its cottages, taken from the upper end of the Street; 3. a side view of the *old* hermitage, with the hermit standing at the door; this piece he is to copy again for Un. Harry; 4. a sweet view of the short Lithe and Dorton from the lane beyond Peasecod's house. He took also two views of the Church, two views of my outlet, a view of the Temple farm, a view of the village from the inside of the present hermitage, Hawkley hanger (which does not prove very engaging), and a grotesque and romantic drawing of the waterfall in the hollow bed of the stream in Silkwood's vale to the N.E. of Berriman's house. You need not wonder that the drawings you saw by Grimm did not please you; for they were 3s. 6d. pieces done for a little ready money; so there was no room for softening his trees &c. He is a most elegant colourist; and, what is more, the use of these fine natural stainings are altogether his own: yet his pieces were so engaging in Indian-ink, that it was with regret that I submitted to have some of them coloured. Mr. Wyndham of Sarum has engaged G. next summer for 8 or 9 weeks in a tour round N. and S. Wales. I rejoice to hear you are so deep in French.

* [This forms the subject of the folded frontispiece to the first and to the subsequent 4to editions. The persons represented in the plate are:— 1. The Rev. Richard Yalden, the vicar of Newton; 2. Mrs. Yalden; 3. Mr. Etty, brother of the vicar of Selborne; 4. Mr. Thomas White, Gilbert's brother.—T. B.]

I am wonderfully delighted with the addition to my brother's little common parlor*; "nequeunt expleri corda tuendo;" it now altogether gives much ease to such a numerous family, and is very peculiarly light, roomy, and convenient, containing 400 square feet. Mr. Amyand is a very genteel pleasing youth. He puts me in mind of Mr. Brocket.

Yours affect.
GIL. WHITE.

Pray write soon to Selborne.

P.S. When the children are buzzing down at their spinnet, and we grave folks sit round the chimney, I am put in mind of the following couplet, which you will remember:—

> "All the distant din that world can keep
> Rolls o'er my grotto and improves my sleep."

LETTER XXV.

TO THOMAS WHITE, ESQ.†

Selborne, June 30, 1777.

Dear Brother,

The Dr.'s letter on the other side is very satisfactory and very edifying: for it not only proves that our Temple belonged to the *Knights Templars*, but that it was also a *Preceptory*, the Preceptory of Sudington, now called *Southington*, notwithstanding that B^p Tanner asserts that he never could find more than *two* preceptories in this county, viz. *Godesfield* and *S. Badeisley*. Hence we may be certain that the B^p did not get access to the Magd. Coll. archives.

Tho' the lands of the convent and the Templars abutted on

---

* [Where he was staying, and whence he dates this letter.—T. B.]

† [This letter and that of Dr. Chandler are in substance embodied in the XIth letter of the Antiquities (Vol. I. p. 316). In this department of his work the author's obligations to Dr. Chandler were very great; and a comparison of the present letter from him with the passage in the Antiquities referred to, will show this in a striking manner.—T. B.]

each other, and were intermixed, yet we see that those two societies of Religious lived on the best of terms, in an intercourse of mutual good offices, exchanging lands and permitting roads to be opened for each other's mutual convenience. We see also that Blackmere and Bradshott, names well known to modern ears, were also familiar to the neighbourhood four or five hundred years ago.

I expect Dr. Chandler soon, and regret much (and he assures me he does the same) that the statutes will not permit him to bring with him the Archive papers to Selborne, which contain much knowledge concerning the antiquities of this place—information that has never been pryed into, but has slumbered within the college walls ever since they were founded.

We have drowning weather and a dismal black solstice. Such rains make carriage very irksome, and the attendance on building very comfortless, and brick-burning very precarious; but the walls, I trust, will be the stronger, since the mortar is better blended into the chinks and crevices during so sloppy a season. Let me hear how you have sold your oak timber.

Yours, &c.
GIL. WHITE.

LETTER XXVI.

FROM DR. CHANDLER

(accompanying G. W.'s letter to his brother Thomas, June 30, 1777).

Oxford, June 14, 1777.

DEAR SIR,

I FIND five deeds with the seal of the Temple annexed to them. In the Index the first is No. 2. "Concessio Rob. Samford militis Templi cum assensu Capituli Priori et Conventui de Selborne totius tenementi cum omnibus pertinentiis hab. de dono Aymerici de Vasci" sine dato. No. 26 . "Concessio similis priori." Of these the first is tolerably easy to be read.

The Templars convey to John the Prior, and to the Convent for ever, "totum tenementum cum omnibus pertinentiis, sc. in terris et . . . . in pratis et pascuis et nemoribus et in omnibus aliis locis, quod habuimus de dono Aymerici de Vasci [so I read] in villâ de Seleburne," to be held "libere et integre et quiete ab omni seculari . . . . et exactione," as by the Templars, in consideration of 200 marcs sterl. paid by the convent to them for the purchase of other lands "in subsidium *Sanctæ terræ*." One of the witnesses is styled PRECEPTOR OF SUDINGTON. The three remaining deeds are in the Index:— No. 139. "Concessio fratris Rob^u de Samford &c. de uno *Cheminio* &c." sine dat. No. 140. "Concessio similis priori." No. 138. "Concessio fratris Rob^u militis &c. 10 sol. annuatim in perpetuum percipiend." sine dato. All these are likewise witnessed by Richard Carpenter, *Preceptor of Sudington*. Nos. 139 & 140 are grants from Rob. de Samford and the Templars of a *way* sufficient " ad ducendum carros et haretas, et ad fugandum *averia* a viâ que se extendit de *Sudington* versus *Blakemere* ultra terram Ricardi de la Strete usque ad terram dictorum Prioris et Conventûs quam habent in *Bradesete*." No. 138 is an engagement of Robert and the Templars to pay to the convent " decem solidos de camerâ nostrâ annuatim in perpetuum percipiendos ad domum nostram de *Sudington*, *per manum Preceptoris vel Ballivi nostri*, qui pro tempore fuerit," half-yearly until the Templars should purchase lands within a certain distance of the convent, and to be given as an equivalent.

Yrs. R. CHANDLER.

LETTER XXVII.

TO SAMUEL BARKER.

Selborne, Nov. 7, 1777.

DEAR SAM,

No event that I have met with for some time has given me more pleasure than the news of your being sent to the University, because, I trust, you will make the best use of this advantage, both in your literary pursuits, and by improvement in the knowledge of men and manners. As to a proper acquaintance, you have nothing to do but to lie by, and act a little on the reserve, and you will soon discern what young men are suitable to your purpose; and besides, young people of your own turn, when they know you a little, will naturally make some advances.

All the house-martins withdrew about the 7th of Oct., and seemed gone to a bird 'til Nov. 4th, when 21 were seen playing about under the Hanger all day, and for that day only. The circumstance seems the more odd and amusing to me, because I have known it befal more than once or twice. Where were they during the interval? and where are they now? This event militates strongly against emigration, and in favour of hiding. The bats do just the same all the winter and spring; they sleep at intervals, and then come forth, and feed, and retire again.

The order of *Polygamia frustranea* is constituted, you know, from having the *florets* of the *disk* hermaphrodite, and those of the *radius* neuter. Not knowing where to apply for a common knapweed * in bloom, I know not how to solve your difficulty. The district round Cambridge will furnish you in the summer with the great aquatics. When you are a little at leisure, I shall always be glad to hear from you.

I am your affectionate friend,
GIL. WHITE.

Don't fail to practise frequently in writing English.

* [*Centaurea scabiosa*.—T. B.]

LETTER XXVIII.

TO MRS. BARKER.

Selborne, Sep. 2, 1778.

DEAR SISTER,

My thanks are due for your kind letter. I have now the pleasure of seeing my house full of friends. My niece Anne Barker pleases me much, and is a sensible intelligent young woman. Mrs. H. Isaacs has not been here for 25 years, and, finding every thing much altered, hardly knows the place again. Molly White and y^r daughter seem well pleased to meet again; Jenny and Becky White are to come to Newton this week. Mrs. Yalden pressed their mother much to come; but she is in a very poor way, and chose to wave the journey. Mrs. Snooke has just written to me with her own hand; she did not complain much. Last post I had a letter from Blackburn: my brother's state of health and spirits is much the same; my poor sister makes sad complaints, and laments the state of their family; indeed they both merit the compassion of their friends. My great parlor * is now of singular service; but while it is so empty the echo is very troublesome. I have a new bed in my little red room, and have put my old white bed up in my late drawing-room, where I lie as you ordered me †. Bro. Harry's school thrives: he has just got three new pupils, and expects one more; his house is now quite full. My peaches ripen, but, the summer considered, are not so fine as might be expected. We have fine wheat and a vast crop of hops. Barley and oats are lean and poor. The failure of turnips is miserable!

Your loving brother,
GIL. WHITE.

* [Built the previous year.—T. B.]
† [In which room he died.—T. B.]

LETTER XXIX.

TO SAMUEL BARKER.

Selborne, Sept. 2, 1778.

Dear Sam,

I am much pleased to find that the University and your studies there give you so much satisfaction. There is no fear that you will neglect this opportunity of improvement, or spend your time amiss. I should rather wish that you were cautioned to remember that it is possible for a young man to apply too earnestly; and therefore I hope you will intermix daily exercise with y^r studies. To the generality of young men I am well aware that this caution would be needless; but to you, who, I know, apply yourself to all laudable pursuits with all y^r might, it might not be improper.

Dr. Chandler the traveller has been with me a month, and is just gone. He has furnished me with *more curious matter* respecting the antiquities of this place, and in particular with Will. of Wyckham's *Notabilis visitatio* of this Priory. From this long instrument, consisting of 36 injunctions and reprimands, it appears that this institution, which had then been founded one century, had deviated much from its original simplicity; for they had become mighty hunters, and used to attend junketings and feastings, had altered their mode of dress, and used to let *suspectæ* come into their cloisters after it was dark, had suffered their buildings to dilapidate, had pawned their plate, had administered the sacrament with such nasty cups and such nasty sour wine that men abhorred the sight (*ut sit hominibus horrori*), had let down their number of brethren from 14 (the original number) to 11, had suffered their friends and relations to hang on the convent and eat it up, &c. They also were got into a method of lying naked in bed without their breeches, for which they are much reprimanded. Moreover I find that the Knights Templars, by their statutes, were enjoined constantly to sleep in their breeches, and to have candles constantly burning in their dormitory. Should I ever be able to finish my work respecting this my native place, the old deeds and charters &c. will furnish a large appendix.

Your affectionate friend,
GIL. WHITE.

LETTER XXX.

TO MISS WHITE.

Selborne, Sept. 30, 1780.

DEAR MOLLY,

YOUR letters are always agreeable to me; but your last was particularly so, because it brought so good an account of the state of y^r father's health.

Finding that Larby alone would never finish his job, I hired a whole band of myrmidons, and set them to work on the Bostal, where they have made great dispatch, and have but half a day's work to come, which has been delayed by the rains. They ran through the upper part a day sooner than I expected, because as we advanced the soil grew shallower; but then we have been obliged to widen and raise all Larby's first attempt, because his path was so narrow, hollow, and clayey that it soon grew dirty and would have been impassable. By and with the advice of our privy council, we took a higher direction than was at first marked out, because it *much* shortened the path, and brings us out straight at the top of the *slidder* before you come to *shop slidder* at the corner of the Wadden. In our progress we found many pyrites in the clay as round as a ball, and some large *Cornua ammonis* in the chalk. All people agree, where party does not interpose, that it is a noble work; but there is a junto against it called *Zigzaggians*, of which Mrs. Etty is the head: but Mr. E. and Mr. Y. would be *Bostalians*, if they dared. The tall trees in the Hanger are very fine when you are among them, and the views thro' them romantic. My nep. Barker sets out for Fyfield on Monday, and regrets that he shall miss of you and y^r father. Bro. Ben. &c. came to Newton on Thursday.

The Bostal measures 400 yards, and the Zigzag, which is to be nicely cleaned out, 426.

Mrs. E. and her young people set out to-morrow for Oxford. Mr. E. is already in Oxfordshire.

All join in due respects and good wishes.

Your loving uncle,
GIL. WHITE.

Oct. 1. Pray write soon.
My barom^r is this evening at 28. 6. 10½!
Thomas's brother has his ague still; he has taken the roots of daffy-down-dillies.

LETTER XXXI.

TO SAMUEL BARKER, ESQ.

Selborne, Nov. 23, 1780.

DEAR SIR,

YOUR letter, tho' rather late, was very acceptable. I was glad to hear that you had a safe and pleasant journey back, and that you were so well pleased with y^r journey into Hants, as to be able on a retrospect to speak of it with some degree of satisfaction. The test will be whether you liked your late reception by expressing a willingness to come again. Pray give my respects to Mr. Brodrick, and tell him that I always esteem my friend's friends, and therefore if he will come over next summer, when you are here, from Pepperharrow, for a night or two, that I shall be glad to see him, and we will show him some such prospects in these parts as may not be unworthy his attention.

To say the truth, the lower part of the *Bostal* began to be dirty, so that the Zigzaggians (who have horns and hoofs)

began to triumph. Many of them, in the shape of horses and heifers, ran up and down it, doing it great damage with their feet; but to silence all clamour, I had all the bad part well bedded with a quantity of fern. Since this amendment, Mrs. Etty and her sister Stebbing and Mrs. Y. have been up and down it by night and by day, so that party feuds are likely to be at an end. You do not, I hope, flatter me about my Nat. Hist.; if you do not, I am much pleased to find that an intelligent person like yourself approves of it. Were it not for the want of a good amanuensis, I think I should make more progress; but much writing and transcribing always hurts me. All that I know about the sleep of fishes is, that at the Black Bear inn, in Reading, there is a stream in the garden which runs under the stables, and so under the road into the meadows; it is a branch of the Kennet. Now this water all the summer is full of carps, which roll about, and are fed by travellers, who divert themselves by tossing them crumbs of bread. When the cold weather comes, these fishes withdraw themselves under the *stables*, and are invisible for months, during which period I conclude they must sleep. Thus the inhabitants of the *water*, as well as of the *air* and the *earth* retire from the severity of winter. Timothy, your friend, retreated into his hybernaculum last week; he is laid up in the fruit border in a dry, wholesome, sunny spot; at Ringmer he was forced to lie in a swamp. My nep. Richard has been here; he was quite transported beyond himself with the pleasures of shooting, and, after walking more than 100 miles, killed *one woodcock*, which, ill-fated bird, took the pains to migrate from Scandinavia to be slain by a cockney who never shot a bird before!!! Pleasure is a most arbitrary matter! The pains my nephew took in his new pursuit would have been a great misery to many.

I conclude, your affectionate friend,
GIL. WHITE.

I made some remarks of moment on the house-martins just before they withdrew. They do not amount to proof; but the presumptions are very strong indeed.

Now the leaf is down, the Bostal discovers itself in a faint delicate line running up the Hanger, such as would require the hand of a Grimm to express it.

LETTER XXXII.

TO SAMUEL BARKER.

[Extract from Forster's 'Observations,' sent by G. W. to his nephew Samuel Barker, Mar. 26, 1781.]

" I NEVER heard or read of any one who had seen the southern lights (*Aurora australis*) before us; and tho' we spent three different seasons in or near the Arktic circle, we, however, observed them only the first time in the year 1773 for seven different nights. We were at that time from 58 to 60 S. latitude, and the therm. at 8 o'clock in the morning stood from 31 to 33 in the open air on deck. Their appearance was much the same as that of the N. lights: They were observed shooting up to the zenith in columns or streams of a pale light from a dark segment as a base near the horizon, and often spread over the whole S. hemisphere. Sometimes these lights were so transparent that stars could be observed thro' them; and at other times the stream seemed to be white, and more dense and opaque, and would not transmit the light of the stars. We saw these meteors on Feb. 18, 19, 20, 21, 22, 26, and on Mar. 15 and 16."—FORSTER'S *Observations in a Voyage round the World*, p. 120.

S. Lambeth, Mar. 26, 1781.

DEAR SAM,

RECOLLECTING that you enquired of me once with some earnestness whether our late circumnavigators had ever observed any auroras in the S. hemisphere, I have sent you the quotation above, which will put the matter beyond all doubt. My thanks are due for y^r entertaining account of the *Testudo aquarum dulcium* *.

You do very right, I think, in looking into history, which is a very gentlemanlike study. You, who have youth, health, and a strong retentive memory on y^r side, will soon make a vast progress.

Pray tell y^r mother that I thank her for her letter. Jack White's time will not be out 'til the 16 of next June, when he and his mother will come southward among his relations †. What mode of life that young man will take up I have not yet heard—whether he will walk the hospitals in town or become for a time a journeyman. Poor Joe Woods, son of Mr. Jos. Woods, a promising young man of 21, is just dead of a decline, to the great sorrow of his parents &c. With all due respects, I remain

Your affect. friend,
GIL. WHITE.

I propose to return home on Thursday.

Having had no rain, not once enough to measure, at this place since the last week in Feb., the degree of dustiness is horrible, and not to be described! As Bro. Th. and I walked out this morning, a gale rose from the N. which filled the whole atmosphere with such a cloud from road to road that the prospect was quite obscured!

On the 27 of Feb., Tuesday, the day I left Seleburne, we had such a terrible storm of wind that vast mischief was done in the S. and W. of England. I expected to hear of great damage, especially in Sussex; but was thankful to find that I had escaped with the overturning of my alcove into the hedge, the overthrow of my stone dial, and, what grieved me most, because it cannot be repaired, the ravage of my great wall and tree, which, they write word, is almost torn to pieces! The gale began at 11 A.M., wind W.; but the great damage

---

* [There is no indication to what species he refers.—T. B.]

† [About this time Mrs. John White, who had recently become a widow, came to reside with her brother-in-law, and continued with him until his death.—T. B.]

was done about 5 P.M., the wind N.W. Soon after, a calm succeeded. Derham remarks that most tempests from the W. vere a little at last to the N.W., and then the ravage and damage take place.

Pray write, and on *larger* paper.

LETTER XXXIII.

TO SAMUEL BARKER.
(From Mr. Field's copy.)

Selborne, Jan. 5, 1782.

DEAR SAM,

GOSSAMER has from old times attracted the attention of the curious. Chaucer mentions it amongst phenomena of nature not well understood or accounted for, such as thunder &c. The *Tabanus bovinus,* I verily think, has no sting in its tail or blood-sucking rostrum, but a *Musca*-like proboscis. I have seen it suck the galled parts of Sir Simeon Stuart's working horses without giving them any pain. It abounds most in moist places and sultry weather. The *Œstrus curvicauda* never lays its nits but in the warmer hours of the day; for my horses which are in stable all day and out all night are never covered with their eggs at home. Pray examine the little dancing *Diptera* (*Tipulæ* I suppose they are) that sport the winter through in fog, gentle rain, and even frost and snow, when the sun shines. Every sunny day insects abound, and in warm sunny lanes and under hedges the air swarms with them; within doors wood-lice, spiders, and *Lepisma* are in motion, and many *Muscæ* in the stable; and earth-worms come forth every mild evening; so that in mild weather insects are not so much laid up as is imagined. Some *Phalænæ* also fly all the winter.

Yʳ affect.
GIL. WHITE.

LETTER XXXIV.

TO HIS NEPHEW *.

A Meteorological Diary for December 1782, kept in a village 50 miles S.W. of London, in a woodland hilly district, and up at the head of rivulets that run into the Thames at Weybridge. The thermometer hangs within an open staircase.

Dec.	Thermom.	Barom.	Wind.	Rain.	Weather.
Day.		in.		in.	
1.	39	29·60	N.		Sun pleasant; red evening.
2.	36	29·60	E.		Frost, fog, and rime.
3.	36	29·75	E.		Frost, rime, sun; beautiful rimes on the hanging woods.
4.	35	29·70	N.E.		Frost, dark; lambs begin to fall.
5.	36½	29·50	E.S.E.		Frost, dark.
6.	37	29·40	S.E.		Dark, still, mild, moist.
7.	39	29·50	S.E.		Dark, mild, thaw.
8.	37	29·70	E.		Dark and still.
9.	36	29·50	S.E.		Dark and moist; rime on the hill.
10.	36	29·40	E.N.		Fog, dark, and moist.
11.	36	29·65	N.		Dark and still, like February; frost on hill.
12.	36	29·35	W.		Pleasant, spring-like.
13.	37	29·40	S.W.	0·44	Frost, thaw, rain.
14.	37	29·30	W.		Frost, sun, wind.
15.	37	29·40	W.		Frost, sun, wet.
16.	37	29·40	N.W.	0·47	Frost, thaw, rain.
17.	43	29·60	W.		Dark, wet, mild.
18.	47	29·80	S.W.		Blowing and wet; vast condensations on walls and wainscot; vast halo round the moon.
19.	43	30·25	S.W.		Sun, frost, gale.
20.	42	30·20	W.		Mild, with brisk gale.
21.	44	30·10	S.W.		Paths dry, grey, brisk air, pleasant.
22.	42	30·15	N.W.		Sun, cloudless; flies came forth.
23.	40	29·85	W.		Grey, brisk air.
24.	43	29·75	W.		Grey, beetles fly in the evening.
25.	45	30·00	N.W.		Dark and mild; boys play in their shirts, they did so on Xmas Day 1781.
26.	45	30·20	N.W.		Crocus's shoot; February weather.
27.	44	31·10	N.W.		Dark, still, mild; large flock of wood-pigeons.
28.	41	29·90	N.W.		Dark and still; boys play at taw in the dusty paths.
29.	43	29·80	N.W.		Do. sweet weather.
31.	42	29·90	N.W.		Frost, sun pleasant.

Total of rain in Dec. 1782.................. 0·91 inch.

Hares frequent the garden, and eat the celeri-tops, spinage, young cabbages, pinks, scabiouses, parsley, &c.

* [Son of ~~Benjamin~~ White.—T. B.]

The rain on the tower caught in a receiver since Nov. 3, 1782	1·42 inch.
On the ground at about 100 yards distance	1·97 „
More caught on the ground than tower	0·55 „

> "Grateful are these solar beams;
> And when the winds are hushed 'tis sweet to view
> The level ocean, earth with verdure deck'd,
> The plenteous waters of refreshing springs.
> And there are many beauteous objects more,
> Whose praise I might recount; yet none more welcome
> Than children, when they to the house of those
> Who long despaired of issue give a lustre."
>
> WOODHULL.

DEAR NEPHEW,

IF Mr. Nichols approves of my *diaries*, he may have more; they may serve to oppose to y^r father's, kept near town. I send you Mr. Woodhull's translation of the passage from Euripides, that you may compare it with mine*. Mr. W. has preserved the force of the word φαος very well. The ague-woman, Small, has been with me; she had two slight fits about a fortnight ago, but not since; she complains she is not stout.

Pray write to me, and let me hear what alterations y^r father is making; and I desire you would send me the *ichnography* of your father's house, above, below, with the *dimensions* of rooms. In this matter nephew Richard will help you; he drew my house in that way. Tell Miss White I thank her for the pound of tea. We had a good journey to and from Fyfield.

Your loving uncle,
GIL. WHITE.

Selborne, Nov. 29, 1783.

Sweet weather lately. I have moved my outer wicket towards the foot of the hill. I am in no manner of haste about the stockings. If they do but fit, I shall be pleased.

* [Vol. I. p. 507.—T. B.]

LETTER XXXV.

TO MARY WHITE.

Selborne, Jan. 22, 1783.

Dear Mary,

It is full time that I should acknowledge your late obliging letter, and return you and your mother and sister my best thanks for the agreeable visit that you made me in the autumn. I have only to regret that you could not, consistently with the respect that was due to other relations, extend it out to a much greater length.

As to music, your lessons and those of your sister gave me wonderful delight. I retain still a smattering of many passages on my memory, which I sing to myself when I am in spirits. Indeed I am often too much affected with musical harmony, especially of late years. The following curious quotation strikes me much by so well representing my own case; and by describing what I have so often felt, but never could so well express. " * * * Præhabebat porrò vocibus humanis, instrumentisque harmonicis, musicam illam avium : non quod aliâ quoque non delectaretur, sed quod ex musicâ humanâ relinqueretur in animo continens quædam, attentionemque, et somnum conturbans, agitatio ; dum ascensus, excensus, tenores et mutationes illæ sonorum et consonantium euntque redeuntque per phantasiam; cum nihil tale relinqui possit ex modulatione avium, quæ, quod non sunt perindè a nobis imitabiles, non possunt perindè internam facultatem commovere " *. When I hear fine music I am haunted with pas-

* [One might almost fancy that this passage from Gassendi must have been in Izaak Walton's mind when he wrote his exquisite description of the nightingale's song, which I cannot forbear quoting. "The Nightingale, another of my airy creatures, breathes such sweet loud musick out of her little instrumental throat, that it might make mankind to think miracles are not ceased. He that at midnight, when the very labourer sleeps securely, should hear, as I have very often, *the clear airs, the sweet descants, the natural rising and falling, the doubling and redoubling of her voice*, might well be lifted above earth, and say, 'Lord, what musick hast thou provided for the Saints in Heaven, when thou affordest bad men such musick on Earth.'" Such hold had the passage from Gassendi taken of Gilbert

sages therefrom night and day, and especially at first waking, which, by their importunity give me more uneasiness than pleasure, still teizing my imagination, and recurring irresistibly to my memory at seasons, and even when I am desirous of thinking of other matters: - - - - yet notwithstanding all these fine things, I would give six pence to hear you two maidens perform the *wopses*, the lesson with the jig, and that with the lovely minuet, &c. &c.*

The letter from *Nobody* puzzled the Mulso family for a long time. At first they suspected me; but the strange unknown hand, the London postmark, and some other circumstances threw them all out; so that, to put them out of doubt, I was forced to own the imposture, and to acknowledge that you were accessory. Mrs. Clement held her Xtening lately: I was godfather, and we named the child Isaac. Mr. Ch. Etty came in this morning from Spithead, where his ship, the 'Duke of Kingston' is lying at anchor in readiness for sailing soon. This young gent. says that peace is the general talk, so that he supposes they may possibly sail with a white flag, and without any convoy at all. We have had all this winter 26 Highlanders of the 77th regiment quartered in this village and at Oakhanger: where tho' they had nothing in the world to do, they have behaved in a very quiet and inoffensive manner, and were never known to steal even a turnip or a cabbage, tho' they lived much on vegetables, and were astonished at the dearness of southern provisions. Late last night came an express ordering these poor fellows down to Portsmouth; where they are to embark for India, near 100 of them aboard Ch. Etty's ship. Un. Harry writes word that he hopes his son Ch. will have a commission soon.

With all due respects I remain

Your affectionate uncle,

GIL. WHITE.

Several of our soldiers came from Caithness.

White's mind, that he quotes it verbatim three times in his correspondence.—T. B.]

* [See Letter LVI. to Daines Barrington, Vol. I. p. 251.—T. B.]

LETTER XXXVI.

TO MISS MARY WHITE.

Selborne, Feb. 7, 1783.

Dear Molly,

As the Spring begins to advance, and as we propose now being with you about the first week in March, we can hardly wish for half an hundred of salt fish so late; and Mrs. G. and Mr. Etty, I find, are of the same mind. We must therefore desire a note to his fishmonger to stop his hand.

Having expected the Rector of Faringdon for some time at my house, I could not so well say whenabout we should endeavour to get to Town; but as he has been here we shall hope to be at liberty as above mentioned, and we should be glad to know if that season would be convenient.

"Look upon the rainbow, and praise him that made it: very beautiful is it in the brightness thereof." Eccles. xliii. 11.

"On morning or on evening cloud impressed
Bent in vast curve, the wat'ry meteor shines
Delightfully, to th' level sun opposed.
Smit with the gaudy scene th' unconscious swain
With vacant eye gazes on the divine
Phœnomenon, gleaming o'er th' illumined fields,
Or runs to catch the treasure which it sheds.
 Not so the sage: inspired with pious awe
He hails the federal arch [*], and looking up
Adores the God whose fingers formed this bow
Magnificent, compassing heaven about
With a resplendent verge:—'Thou mad'st the cloud,
Maker omnipotent, and thou the bow,
And by that covenant graciously hast vow'd
Never to drown the world again: henceforth
Till time shall be no more, in beauteous train
Season shall follow season, day to night
Succeed:' inspired so sung the Hebrew bard [†]."

Mimo-Milton [‡].

[*] Gen. ix. 12-17. [†] Moses.
[‡] [Vol. I. p. 502.—T. B.]

The end of Jan. and this month have been very wet; so that I fear wheat will get very high, and that the season for our spring-crops will be bad, especially if harsh weather succeeds at once. How will your cellars come off? When do the young men go to college?

Your affect^{te} uncle,
GIL. WHITE.

Mr. Denison is chosen to Holiburn school * in the room of Mr. Willis: poor Mrs. Robinson, who has 10 children, made what interest she could for her husband, who is at present a navy chaplain in the W. Indies: she got two votes, her opponent three. There are but five feofees, one of them a broken blacksmith.

LETTER XXXVII.

FROM MISS MARY WHITE.

Feb. 10, 1783.

* * * The Monthly Reviewers produce whole passages, which Mr. Cookson has copied from their criticism on Mr. Madan's work †.

Be so kind as to bring with you the account of the poplar that we left at Selborne.

Since I began this, which was some days ago, I have had the pleasure of receiving a letter from you, for which I am

---

* [An endowed school at Holyburn, near Alton, for the education of the children of the parish itself, and of 12 from Alton. The master was formerly required to be a clergyman of the Church of England, which is not now necessary.—T. B.]

† [The work here alluded to was 'Thelyphthora,' published in 1780, which was very generally read, and almost as generally reprobated. Madan, although attached to the evangelical party in the Church, offended the feelings and principles of the religious public by his bold advocacy of polygamy and some other doctrines obnoxious to the views of Christians in general.—T. B.]

much obliged to you. We shall depend on seeing you and Mrs. J. White the beginning of March; and I hope the weather will continue mild and favourable for your journey.

We are much obliged to you Sir for your rainbow; and as we are no poets I beg leave to send you in return two ready made. "The fancy is infinitely more struck with the view of the open air and sky that passes through an arch than what comes through a square or any other figure. The figure of the Rainbow does not contribute less to its magnificence than the colours to its beauty, as it is very poetically described by the son of Sirach: "Look upon the Rainbow and praise him that made it; very beautiful it is in its brightness: it encompasses the heavens with a glorious circle, and the hands of the most High have bended it."

> "* * * * Refracted from yon eastern cloud,
> Bestriding earth, the grand etherial bow
> Shoots up immense; and every hue unfolds
> In fair proportion, running from the red
> To where the violet fades into the sky.
> Here, awful Newton, the dissolving clouds
> Form, fronting on the sun, thy showery prism;
> And to the sage-instructed eye unfold
> The various twine of light by thee disclosed
> From the white mingling maze. Not so the boy;
> He wondering views the bright enchantment bend
> Delightful o'er the radiant fields; and runs
> To catch the fading glory: but amazed
> Beholds th' amusive arch before him fly,
> Then vanish quite away." *

---

* [The following charming lines from James Montgomery, embody perhaps the most beautiful and touching figure suggested by the subject, to be found in our language :—

> " But, see, on Death's bewildering wave,
>   The rainbow Hope arise;
> A bridge of glory o'er the grave
>   That bends beyond the skies.

You will probably see my brothers here before they go to college, as I believe they will not leave home till the second week in March. Mr. Grimble has sent your wig*.

Please to remember me to Mrs. J. White and thank her for her kind letter by Mr. Etty. My father and brother desire best respects to yourself and all friends.

With almost constant pumping we have hitherto kept the water out of the cellar; but a few more wet days we fear will get the better of us.

I am, dear Sir,
Your obliged and affectionate niece,
M. WHITE.

LETTER XXXVIII.

TO THE REV. EDMUND WHITE †.

Selborne, Feb. 21, 1783.

DEAR NEPHEW,

I COULD wish that you would make it a rule to read aloud to yourself every day some portion of S. or the Common Prayer, tho' ever so short, and that you would also sometimes read before a judicious friend—but at the same time plainly and unaffectedly; and do not aim at anything theatrical or fine,

---

> "From earth to heaven it swells, and shines
> The pledge of bliss to man;
> Time with eternity combines,
> And grasps them in a span."   T. B.]

* [The following humorous lines formed the order sent by Gilbert White to his wig-maker in London:—

> "Ye worthy friends in Abchurch Lane,
> Who do our noddles thatch,
> Send me a wig, but not too big,
> With care and with dispatch."   T. B.]

† [Son of Benjamin White, and afterwards rector of Newton Valence. —T. B.]

but only attend well to what you read; and your own good sense and ear will tell you at the time how to modulate your voice, and lay your accents justly according as you are affected by what is before you.

Mr. and Mrs. W. Y. who are just gone, and Mr. and Mrs. Clements in the room, join with Mrs. J. Wh. in respects. Remember me to Whites 3^{tius}, 4^{tus}, and 5^{tus}. I am, dear White 2^{ndus},

Your loving friend,
WHITE 1^{mus}.

LETTER XXXIX.

FROM SAMUEL BARKER.

Lyndon, Oct. 8, 1783.

DEAR SIR,

You received, I imagine, some days ago a letter from my father informing you of our return to Rutland and expressing our acknowledgements for the very agreeable entertainment we received at Selborne. The time I spent there I remember with extreme pleasure, and have been told several times since my return that I am grown much fatter in my excursion. Great indeed must be the efficacy of the *three things* that could produce a visible effect on a person who has in that respect been hitherto quite incorrigible.

At leaving Fyfield I went to London by the Bath coach; and as you know my propensity for seeing, you will not wonder that I prefered a seat on the box to one within the carriage on a fine day: the road from Andover as far as Hampshire reaches I think very pleasant; and in crossing the dreary heath near Blackwater, a distant view of Hindhead, Crooksbury Hill, Guildford Downs, &c. excited very agreeable associations. Mr. and Mrs. Brown are expected in Rutland this week; and I have the satisfaction of informing you that, when my sister wrote last, she thought herself *entirely* free from her cough, and was grown so hardy by bathing, riding, and walking as to bear the air during the late windy weather without inconvenience. Still I cannot help being rather sollicitous on her account; for winter in the 53ᵈ degree of latitude, you know, must be tedious and may be severe.

I have consulted Le Clerc's comment on the passages in the books of Judges and Samuel that mention the deriving presages or omens from accidental events and words spoken without premeditation. He takes notice of the custom in both places, and refers to the 24ᵗʰ chapter of Genesis, where Abraham's servant finds Rebecca to be the person he is in search of, by her drawing water for him and his camels—and mentions as parallel passages the omen given to Priam (Iliad, 24. 308 &c.), and the prayer of Anchises (Æneid, 2. 689), which I think are rather signs requested and obtained immediately from heaven than presages drawn from incidental events, of which nevertheless the Greek and Roman writers are full. The following story, which, whether true or false, is taken from oriental authors, shews that the same ideas have been prevalent in Persia and Tartary. Scheik Sefi, the prophet here mention'd, lived near Ardebil in Media, at the time that Tamerlane (Timour) overran Asia; he was celebrated for his sanctity and miracles, and was an ancestor of Ismael Sophi, the first prince of the family that possess'd the throne of Persia from about 1500 to 1722, when that country was conquer'd by Maghmoud the Afghan.

Tamerlane, after his victory over Bajazet, was passing thro' Media, and was much persuaded to pay a visit to this Scheik, who lived the life of a hermit in a desert.

"Omnium autem cum esset rituum religionum, nationumq. tolerans, ac superstitionibus astrologicis maximè addictus, miraculis tamen ægrè tribuisse fidem, vel ex hoc liquet; quod a familiaribus suis vix induci potuerit: ut ad visendum sæculi oraculum paucis parasangis a via deflecteret; quoniam ipsum impostorem esse, qui imperitiam vulgi luderet, firmiter sibi persuasum erat. Ad explorandam veritatem dum viam ingreditur, animo tacitus proponit, crediturum se pietati hominis, si is sibi satisfaceret in tribus quas tunc excogitabat, conditionibus: quarum prima erat si multum humanitatis, minus reverentiæ, nihil submissionis sibi exhibuerit; altera, si quid sibi, tunc admodum famelico, vescendum obtulerit insoliti quod per vitam nunquam comedisset; tertia, si quid stupendi visendum ostenderit. His præmunitus, religiosum adoritur; qui a discipulis, **adesse orbis** domitorem, audiens; nihil mutato vultu, nec intermissa, quæ oculos distinebat, lectione, introduci eum jubet; & intranti assurgens, locoq. cedens, sessum **ut** ad sinistram capiat familiariter rogat; **est** enim ea sedes in hac gente honoratior. Tum blandis verbis **salutato**, de victoria gratulatur; eam non humanis viribus, **sed Dei** beneficio & Providentiæ tribuendam, gravi Laconismo monens; **ut** cætera taceam. Obtutu longo Imperator **senis** gravitatem miratus, **tandem, quod** esuriret, jentaculum ab eodem poscit. Scheik **desiderio satisfacturus,** lac et caseum promi e penu jubet, **cum eremita aliud cibi** genus non haberet. Obsonium cum **heros acri** appetitu manducasset, Deum testatur nunquam se satiatum cibo gratioris succi, & loci sterilitatem contemplatus, quærit, ubi sua pascua, ubi pecora habeat. Ad quæ Scheik, jugum indigitans montium, vides illic fruticeta, inquit, hæc pascua sunt: videbis etiam pecora; & vibrato in altum candido linteo, assue**factus hoc** signo capricervas, ex summis culminibus in Timuri conspectum provocat, ibi mulgenda præbentes ubera, more mansueti pecoris. Quo viso, heros, conditionum recordatus, eremitam verè pium & Dei O. M. amicum agnoscit, prioris quoq. pœnitens odii, quod in caput ejus juraverat, si impostorem deprehenderet, nunc reverenter habet & ab **eo se** prius discessurum negat donec Scheik **a se documentum** petiisset conciliatæ gratiæ."—*Kæmpfer, Amœnitates Exoticæ, Fascic.* **1.**

This interview, but without these particulars, is mentioned by D'Herbelot, article Scheik Safi or Sefi: how milk and cheese could be a new species of food to a Tartar prince I do not understand; that it was uncommonly excellent **we are** to conclude from Tamerlane's asseveration.

In London I examined Dobson's translation of 'Paradise Lost,' **and find he** has named Sin *Ate,* and Death *Hades.* The Hades of the Greeks is I think a different person from Milton's Death. Should not you have followed Mr. Warton's advice and used the name *Thanatos?* The difference of these two persons is I think well illustrated by a very striking passage in the book of Revelations, Chap. 6, where Death is seen riding on a pale horse and *Hades* follows to swallow up the dead.

All here join in respects to yourself and Mrs. White; and I remain

Your obliged and affectionate nephew,
SAMUEL BARKER.

LETTER XL.

TO MRS. BARKER.

Selborne, Oct. 19, 1784.

DEAR SISTER,

FROM the fineness of the weather and the steadiness of the wind to the N.E. I began to be possessed with a notion last Friday that we should see Mr. Blanchard in his balloon the day following; and therefore I called on many of my neighbours in the street, and told them my suspicions. The next day proving also bright, and the wind continuing as before, I became more sanguine than ever; and issuing forth in the morning, exhorted all those that had any curiosity to look sharp about one o' the clock to three towards London, as they would stand a good chance of being entertained with a very extraordinary sight. That day I was not content to call at the houses only; but I went out to the plowmen and labourers in the fields and advised them to keep an eye to the N. and and N.E. at times. I wrote also to Mr. Pink* of Faringdon, to desire him to look about him. But about one o'clock there came up such a haze that I could not see the Hanger. However, not long after, the mist cleared away in some degree, and people began to mount the hill. I was busy in and out 'till a

---

* [See note by Rev. Edmund White, p. 156.—T. B.]

quarter after two, and took my last walk along the top of the pound-field, from whence I could discern a long cloud of London smoke, hanging to the N. and N.N.E. This appearance, for obvious reasons, encreased my expectation; yet I came home to dinner, knowing how many were on the watch, but laid my hat and surtout ready on a chair in case of an alarm. At twenty minutes before three there was a cry in the street that the balloon was come. We ran into the orchard, where we found 20 or 30 neighbours assembled, and from the green bank at the S.W. end of my house saw a dark blue speck at a most prodigious height, dropping as it were from the sky, and hanging amidst the regions of the upper air, between the weather-cock of the tower and the top of the may-pole. At first, coming towards us, it did not seem to make any way; but we soon discovered that its velocity was very considerable; for in a few minutes it was over the maypole, and then over the Fox on my great parlor-chimney, and in ten minutes more behind my great wall-nut tree. The machine looked mostly of a dark blue colour, but sometimes reflected the rays of the sun and appeared of a bright yellow. With a telescope I could discern the boat, and the ropes that supported it. To my eye this vast balloon appeared no bigger than a large tea-urn. When we saw it first it was north of Farnham, over Farnham heath—and never came, I believe, on this side the Farnham road, but continued to pass on the other side of Bentley, Froyle, Alton, and so for Medstead, Lord Northington's at the Grange, and to ye right of Alresford and Winton, and to Rumsey, where the aerial philosopher came safe to the ground near the church, at about five in the evening. I was wonderfully struck at first with the phænomenon, and, like Milton's "belated peasant," felt my heart bound with fear and joy at the same time. After a while I surveyed the machine with more composure, without that awe and concern for two of my fellow creatures lost, in appearance, in the boundless depths of the atmosphere! for we supposed *then* that two were embarked in this astonishing voyage. At last, seeing with what steady composure they moved, I began to consider them as secure as a group of storks or cranes intent on the business of emigration, and who had

> "Set forth
> Their airy caravan, high over seas
> Flying, and over lands, with mutual wing
> Easing their flight."

Mr. Taylor, our new vicar, has taken possession of S. living; and I have reassumed the curacy, after an intermission of 26 years! Mrs. Etty rents the V. house; but has been gone 8 or 9 weeks, and does not return till winter. Mr. Yalden is gone to Bath in company with Mr. Budd. Bro. Ben and family are at Newton, but go next week. Bro. Tho. has been expected here all the autumn, but is not yet come. Mrs. H. White brought Lucy to my house lately for change of air: the poor young woman is languid and has over-grown her strength; but I perceive no bad symptoms. We have apples and pears innumerable, and very fine grapes. Mrs. Clement is in a fair way, I suspect, to encrease her family. I wish you joy of y^r late grand-daughter, which makes my 41 nephew and niece! I have very dutiful nieces, who seem disposed to make me as *great* an uncle as they can. Mrs. J. White joins in respects. I am with all due affection and regard,

Your loving brother,
GIL. WHITE.

Sweet autumnal weather! We have had no rain since Sept. 27th, not enough to measure. I miss poor Mr. Etty every day: he was a blameless man, without guile. His son Charles is in London making interest for an appointment to India. His escape off Ceylon was wonderful!

[The letter (to Mr. Pink) was the occasion of a very ludicrous circumstance. Mr. Pink, a very respectable yeoman, was on his way to Alton market, the day after he received the letter, when he overtook a neighbour who was going to the same place, and, after the first salutation, asked him if he had seen or heard of Mr. White of Selborne lately. Being answered in the negative, he said, "Ah! poor man, he is very far gone indeed," pointing to his head: "I had a letter from him yesterday; and what do you think he said to me, and desired me to do? he told me to look out sharp to the

N.E. between one and three o'clock to-day, and perhaps I should see two men riding in the air in a balloon;" to which his neighbour replied, "Then he must be pretty far gone indeed." Mr. Pink expressed great sorrow, as he very much respected him. When they came to Alton Butts, a small open common just as you enter Alton, a large concourse of people were assembled together looking earnestly upwards. Mr. Pink addressed the multitude, and asked them what they were about; to which they replied that if he would look over the church he would see, as well as themselves, two men riding in a balloon. After satisfying themselves of the truth of this, Mr. Pink jogged his companion, saying, "Neighbour, I think Mr. White is not so far gone as you and I thought him!"]

LETTER XLI.

MARY WHITE TO HER UNCLE GILBERT.

South Lambeth, May 17, 1785.

DEAR SIR,

By the kind letter I received from you last Friday*, we were very sorry to hear that you have been so much affected by the late cold weather, which indeed has been unusually severe. Within these few days it has been rather milder with us; and I hope you likewise may have found it better than it was; but till the wind changes to a warmer quarter, I fear we shall not have any soft fine weather.

Piers Plowman (printed in 1550) says, " by some who were more acquainted with antiquity than myself, I have learned that the autour was name Roberte Langelande, a Shropshere man, born in Cleybirie, about eight myles from Malverne Hilles." All that Mr. Warton says, in his observations on the Faerie Queene of Spencer, which he refers to in his Hist. of Poetry, is, "the author of Pierce Plowman is Robert Longlande, or Langelande, according to Bale, and Wood, who likewise calls him Malverne." It is probable neither Bale, Wood, nor Warton had any other authority than that which I have quoted above. From whence Mr. Warton calls him a Fellow of Oriel my father cannot say.

* [The letter here referred to I have not found.—T. B.]

We hope it will not be a long time before you and Mrs. White favour us with your company at South Lambeth. My father would be obliged to you to bring him some roots of the *Arundo donax* with you*.

Mr. B. White told me he had answered your query about Dugdale. I am glad to hear Mr. Dusueloy has been so successful in his trial with the farmer, who, by all accounts, behaved in a most unpardonable manner to him. The enclosed card relating to " Sic " my father found in his drawer the other day, and sends you. The following passages are from Pezron's 'Antiquities of Nations:'—" The Spartans called a swine *sic*, in Greek σικα ; and the Celtæ and their posterity even now when they hunt that animal use no other word than *sic, sic*." " SICATOR. This anciently signified a small hog, and is taken from *sica*, in old times a hog; and all of them came from the Celtick *sic*, that denotes the same thing; and hence the Romans rightly enough called those stars *sucula* which now-a-days are placed in the head of Taurus, and were named ʽυαδες (*porcelli*) by the Grecians; for you must observe that the word is derived from ʽυες, *sues, porci*, and not from ʽυειν, *pluere*, to rain, as the Greeks would have it, and as 'tis generally taken to be derived at this day. 'Tis very likely that that knot of stars that are about the other part of Taurus had formed another name in the Northern barbarian sphear, which was the first and ancientest of any; for I shall shew in another place that the Grecians borrowed it of them, but added to and made great alterations in it."

My father and mother desire to be remembered to you.

I am, dear Uncle,

Your affectionate Niece,

MARY WHITE.

* [The plant here alluded to was sent to Gilbert White by his brother John from Gibraltar. The original is still flourishing on my lawn.— T. B.]

LETTER XLII.

FROM SAMUEL BARKER TO G. W.

Lyndon, Nov. 1, 1785.

DEAR SIR,

My best acknowledgements are due for the very friendly treatment I received at Selborne, and the agreeable time I passed there. You know, I presume, how large a party we form'd at Fyfield. I stay'd there near a fortnight, and left it on Monday sennight. From Fyfield my uncle H. and myself paid a visit to the venerable remains at Abury. The apparent effects of time and weather, and the rude figure of the stones, called one's ideas back to the remotest antiquity, and to those primitive days when, as we read, the patriarchs used to set up *great stones* in commemoration of any remarkable event.

Silbury hill is a wonderful performance. A hill whose perpendicular height is 170 feet, the diameter of its base 500, and of its top 100 (for such, according to Dr. Stukely, are its dimensions), is not the work of man in a state of barbarism, of man the hunter nor man the herdsman, but of men collected into towns and directed by governors. Surely such remains prove that kingdoms have been erected and arts cultivated in our island of which we have little suspicion. As I stood on this wonderful tumulus I felt myself inclined to hope I had seen a performance as extraordinary as the Egyptian pyramids; but on examining the accounts of their magnitude, I find the works of our Druidical ancestors will bear no comparison with those of the Egyptian monarchs.

How much we walked at Fyfield, how much we laughed, and how we play'd trios in five parts, I imagine you have heard; so that I have only to tell you of my western expedition on my return. To keep up my character of *explorator*, it was incumbent on me not to travel a road with which I was acquainted; on which account I crossed Wiltshire in a N.W. direction, over the Marlborough downs by Chippenham and Malmesbury, and concluded my first day's journey at Minchinampton, by which means the vale of the Severn and the Malvern hills were brought into my reach. The day had favour'd me much; but in the dusk of the evening clouds arose from the S.W., and scuds of small rain came on, which, had they continued the next day, would have effectually prevented my sight of the prospects I had promised myself the next morning. I was seized with a terrible qualm, and could not help thinking of our friend Ajax's prayer

Δος δ' οφθαλμοισιν εδεσθαι
Εν δε φαει και ολεσσον.

My fears, however, were vain; and the first object I saw on Tuesday morning was Venus shining very bright thro' a hole in the window-shutter. My ride this day was delightful, by Stroud and Painswick to Gloucester. Exquisite indeed is the prospect from the hills above the Severn, of the river, the city of Gloucester, the Worcestershire hills, and the Welsh mountains. In the afternoon I set out for Malvern, and made Lidbury in my road, to visit the county of Hereford: that evening I crossed the hills, but in the dusk; so that the prospect was undistinguishable. On the Wednesday morning the weather again favour'd me, and from my chamber window at Great Malvern I saw the sun rise behind Bredon hill. I then ascended the hill, and saw all that part of the island in one great map beneath me, from Clifton hill above Bristol to the Wrekin near Shrewsbury, and from the S.W. parts of Northamptonshire to Radnorshire mountains. My satisfaction was much increased by having with me a very intelligent director, whom I met with at Malvern, and who pointed out to me the objects in view, and told me their names. Whether these views, however, are superior to those from Black-down and Leith-hill I am by no means certain. From Malvern I went homewards thro' Worcester, Birmingham, Coventry, and Leicester—but saw nothing remarkable except the view from Lickey, a high ridge above Bromsgrove, from whence an immense extent of country is visible, and think myself very fortunate in having had weather clear enough to afford a sight of such distant objects so late in the year. On my return I found all the family well. Your journey to Oxford, I hope, has been of no disservice to you; I think I heard at Fyfield you were there. With best respects to yourself and all friends with you, I remain,

Your obliged and affect.
SAM. BARKER.

LETTER XLIII.

TO SAMUEL BARKER.

Selborne, April 17, 1786.

DEAR SIR,

PARTLY thro' idleness and partly thro' infirmity, I have too long neglected your late letter. My thanks are due for y^r curious account of the climate of Zarizyn*: and I feel myself the more obliged, because you know I love to study climates. Whether you translate or abridge Dr. Pallas I do not know, but should be glad to see the remaining part of that year, if the subject does not give you too much trouble. I believe all fervid regions afford instances of undulating vapours, that at a distance appear like water: Arabia I know does; and the phenomenon is finely alluded to in the Koran. In what language does Pallas write?

The summer-like weather of last Friday fetched out *Timothy*. There is something very forlorn and abject in that creature's first appearance after a profound slumber of five months. When a man first rouses himself from a deep sleep he does not look very wise; but nothing can be more squalid and stupid than our friend, when he first comes crawling out of his hibernacula; so that some farther lines of Dryden's ode

---

* [This is to be found at pp. 641–646 of the third volume of the original edition of Pallas's 'Travels' (*Reise*, u. s. w. St. Petersburg: 1776).—A. N.]

(written, he supposes, on purpose to ridicule tortoises) may well be applyed to him

> "He has raised up his head
> As awaked from the dead,
> And amazed he stares around."

There was, as I remember, one Abdon a judge of Israel, of whom there is nothing memorial, but that he had 40 sons and 30 nephews. As a father this chieftain, I must acknowledge, exceeded me much: but as to the matter of *nepotism*, I go much beyond him; for I had 42 neps. and nieces before, and now Mrs. Brown's little daughter makes the 43rd; and I have more at hand, if I do not reckon my chickens before they are hatched. Nep. John of Alton, now Dr. White, has met with an ugly accident: as he was descending from his hayloft, the ladder turned and gave him a bad fall on the stones; by which he bruised his side and dislocated his *left* wrist: but he was not confined one day, and is getting well. This young man has found employ and much riding about; but he must have time to approve himself before he can expect much prime business*. On March 26th Mrs. and Miss Etty left us for some weeks: and on the 30th by permission came Mr. Taylor our vicar and his bride Miss Lisle of Moyle's Court near Ringwood, Hants. This lady is of a very good family in this county, and niece to Mr. Lisle of Crookes-easton—the gent. who stood and carried the grand contested election for this county in 1733; but it cost him £10000. The lady was desirous of spending part of her honeymoon at her husband's parish. Charles Etty is expected home in June. Nep. Edm^d †, for which I highly commend him, is parting with all kinds of farming whatsoever: he lets all his tithes, and all his glebe; reserving only to himself 3 or 4 fields for his horses and cows. He will now know what he has to depend on, whereas both his late uncles were much imposed on, and were subject to all the rabble and hurry of common renters. Ed. I trust, some time hence will make an excellent neighbour, but has

---

* [He afterwards removed to Salisbury, and became surgeon to the Infirmary.—T. B.]

† [Vicar of Newton Valence.—T. B.]

been as yet a very bad one; for his time has been so taken up with various courtships that he has never been at home yet for 10 days together. He marries, I think, in June, but first keeps another term at Oxford.

All my apricots were cut off by that violent weather in the middle of March! So deep was the snow, and so starved the birds, that the poor ring-doves came into our garden to crop the leaves and sprouts of the cabbages! Hay is become very scarce and dear indeed! My rick is now almost as slender as the waste of a virgin: and it would have been much for the reputation of the two last brides that I have married, had their wastes been as slender. We have just covered the dirty part of the bostal with small flints. The first *swallow* that I heard of was on April 6th, the first nightingale on Ap. 13th. The great straddle-bob Orion, that in the winter seems to bestride my brewhouse, is seen now descending of an evening, one side foremost, behind the hanger. The almanack announces Venus to be an evening star; but I have not seen her yet.

Miss Etty is not so well as could be wished: she is low and languid, and often short-breathed. Miss Layton of Alton, Mr. Charles Etty's niece, is lately dead. Mrs. J. Wh. and I thank your mother for her kind letters: the former will write soon. We think Mrs. Taylor an agreeable woman. I am, with all due respects,

Your affect. uncle,
GIL. WHITE.

LETTER XLIV.

TO SAMUEL BARKER.

Selsburne, Aug. 1, 1786.

DEAR SIR,

As you know I am fond of the history of various countries, and in particular love to study and compare climates; it was very kind of you to take so much pains to compleat the history of Zarizyn for a year.

I return you my thanks for your making me your confidant in a matter of so much moment as that of your taking a wife*. You no doubt will make a prudent choice; and then there will be a good prospect of your being happy in a state where both parties must concur, to render the change agreeable. As it is much the fashion now for the man and his wife to set out on a visit as soon as the ceremony is over, we shall be glad to see the lady and you here, where our new niece will receive all proper respect and every attention from myself and Mrs. J. White. Edm^d's wife made my nephews and nieces 45; and we expect every day to hear that Mrs. Ben. White has added one more to the number; so that according to appearances the lady we are talking of will be the 47th.

We have experienced a very dry and hot summer; most part of June was sultry: yet we had a good crop of hay, and have a fine prospect for wheat, which is very tall and even: the hops also look well; but of late the pastures and meadows burn, and the gardens suffer greatly. My grapes are very forward, and the crop large. Plums we have none, and no wasps yet.

When I see you, you must tell me all the circumstances of your long tour, which cannot fail to entertain. I only fear that after your eyes have been stretched with the sight of Skiddaw &c. you will despise the mole-hills of this district, which once used to delight you so much. My intended niece will I trust be pleased with our hanger and prospects. Whitwell, I think, is a pretty situation. In the year 1742 I spent a very pleasant vacation there. Tell your mother that on the 10th of this month she and I shall have a new sister. Verses have been written on ladies' *eye brows*; but you talk of the beauty of y^r Mrs.'s *eye-lashes*: in that matter, as far as I remember, you speak like a Turk.

Now you talk of ladies, can you repeat " pretty, pretty Peggy Haggitt " three times in a breath ?

* [Mr. Samuel Barker married Miss Haggitt, daughter of a gentleman of Northamptonshire.—T. B.]

We expect Mrs. Etty from Beaconsfield every day. Her son Charles, it is to be hoped, will soon return from Bombay.

Your loving uncle,
GIL. WHITE.

· Little Tom Clement is visiting at Petersfield, where he plays much at cricket: Tom bats; his grandmother bowls; and his great grandmother watches out!!

LETTER XLV.

TO MRS. MARY BARKER.

Selborne, Oct. 25, 1786.

DEAR NIECE,

I RECEIVED your favour of Oct. 12, and rejoice to hear that my nephew Mr. Barker has made so prudent a choice, and has so fair a prospect of happiness in the matrimonial state. He is to live, I find, at the parsonage house at Whitwell, where I spent three very agreeable months as long ago as the year 1742, when I was a very young man.

Present my respects to y^r father, and tell him that the caterpillars of *Phalænæ* devoured all the foliage of our oaks in the bud, and therefore of course there could be no acorns, but that the beeches were loaded with mast, and that I was not unmindful of his injunctions, but have employed people to pick up a quantity of seeds from those trees, which I intend shall be cast into the bushes on the down. We had a wet, cold August and September after a dry spring and hot summer. We have grapes in vast abundance, that were very forward in July; but they are not so delicately ripened as in some more favourable autumns, tho' now good. The beginning of this month deluged all the country, and had like to have blown us all away: the tempests and torrents were dreadful! From the 4th to the 11th of this month inclusive the quantity of rain was 5·04! but now we have delicate weather, and a fine wheat season.

The late election at Salisbury has done my nep. John much honour; but neither he nor his mother is elated on the occasion, because he quits a little certain business in hopes of greater. He certainly was getting ground at Alton. Should he succeed at Sarum, there will be more field-room for getting money than in our poor rough district; and so there had need; for the infirmary brings neither salary nor emolument, but only credit, from the supposition that the surgeon is a man of skill and merit in his profession.

Bro. Tho. is here, and Bro. and sister Ben. and Mary at Newton: they join in respects. I am glad to hear that Mr. and Mrs. Brown have left Uppingham. I am, with all due respects,

Your affectionate uncle,
GIL. WHITE.

Our hop-planters returned from Weyhill fair with cheerful faces, and full purses, having sold a large crop of hops for a good price. The reason was because the Kentish hops, which were a fortnight behind, were blown away by the tempests. The parish of Selborne will be much benefitted by the hop plantations, to the amount, some say, of near £2000. The women had a fine picking, and earned 2s. 6d. pr day. Uncle Harry has built him a hermitage at Fyfield, on which Sam White has written a good copy of verses. Mr. Twopeny is just married.

LETTER XLVI.

TO THOMAS BARKER, ESQ.

Selborne, Jan. 10, 1787.

DEAR SIR,

I HAVE herewith sent you the Selborne rain, an account of which, I think, has been kept very exactly, but know nothing of the Fyfield and S. Lambeth rain. There fell such a glut of rain in the beginning of Oct. that men were in some pain about the wheat season: however such lovely weather followed quite into Nov. that the sowing time was unusually good. Again during the first 14 days of Dec. there fell 5 inch. of rain: this deluge washed our malm grounds sadly.

Rain at Selborne in 1786.

Jan.	6·58	Aug.	4
Feb.	1·27	Sept.	4·5
Mar.	1·53	Oct.	5·04
Apr.	1·63	Nov.	4·38
May	2·16	Dec.	5·62
June	1·05		
July	1·81		39·57

As to strong beer at Mr. Yalden's, I can say nothing about the management of it, because John Pullinger, who had the sole conducting of it, has left Edm^d White: I only know that my strong beer is much admired by those that love pale beer, made of malt that is dryed with billet. My method is to make it very *strong*, and to hop very *moderately* at first; and then to put in, at two or three times, half a pound at a time, of scalded hops, before I tap it. This is the Wilts method, and makes the beer as fine as rock-water. As my family is small, I never brew more than *half hogsh.* at a time; but then I put malt at the rate of 13 bush. to the hogshead, and only 3 pounds and half of hops at a brewing. I tap my half hogsheads at about 12 months old, and always brew with rain water when I can. The tank at Newton is made of brick: their beer was, and is often good; but their water when drank by itself, has a filthy taste of lime and moss. Their table beer does not keep in summer.

Please to present my best thanks to my sister for her kind charity, which will be very acceptable to our numerous poor. Mrs. Etty is here, but will leave us soon, perhaps 'till midsum^r.

Your affectionate servant,
G. WHITE.

The crop of beech mast was prodigious, and of great

service to men's hogs, which were half fat before they were shut up. Between mast and potatoes, poor men killed very large hogs at little expence. Tom Berriman's hog weighed 16 scores, yet ate only *seven* bush. of barley-meal; whereas without the help above mentioned, he would have required 20 bush^r.

Dame Berriman is much disordered in her mind, and very violent. I sent a woman to scatter some beech seed in every bush on the down.

Mrs. J. White joins in respects.

Barom^r has been very high for some days; on Monday it was 30·3.

LETTER XLVII.

TO SAMUEL BARKER.

Seleburne, Jan. 8, 1788.

DEAR SIR,

It is to be hoped that you are not so punctual a man as to register all the letters that you write to your friends, because the distant date of y^r last epistle to me would reproach me with neglect and negligence towards one of my near relations. I have been very busy of late, and have at length put my last hand to my Nat. Hist. and Antiquities of this parish. However, I am still employed in making an Index—an occupation full as entertaining as that of darning of stockings, tho' by no means so advantageous to society. My work will be well got up, with a good type and on good paper, and will be embellished with several engravings. It has been in the press some time, and is to come out in the spring. It pleases me much to find that you still pursue y^r botany. I had reason to suspect that y^r noble neighbour had a propensity to the same enquiries, because I have sometimes met him at Curtis's garden. Bro. Tho. thinks it may be best to cover the Gingko* a little in severe weather. We have had a very deep snow, which began on Sunday, Decr 23, and lasted for

* [*Salisburia adiantifolia.*—T. B.]

two or three nights and days, so that several of our hollow lanes became impassable. The turnpike thro' your village must be a very pleasant circumstance, and prevent such inconveniences to which, I remember, in old days it was very liable. I recollect to have heard Mr. Isaac say that they had often been snowed up, and that he had shot woodcocks and snipes from his bed-chamber window as they came to feed at the fine perennial spring from whence y^r parish * takes its name.

Mr. Charles Etty left us last Friday, and went to his ship, the 'Duke of Montrose,' now lying at Gravesend, in which he is soon to sail for Madras and China as third mate. The wicked wood-cutters entered our hanger this day for the second time in order to fell some more of our beautiful beeches. Last year they cleared as far as the *shop-slidder*, and will strip now as far as Hercules! If my niece does not come and see the remains of that sweet pendulous covert next summer, she will never be able to conceive how lovely and romantic it once had been. Sam White is a very fortunate lad; for not long since the provost and fellows of Oriel elected him to a good exhibition, founded by Dr. Robinson, B^p of London, which he is to enjoy for three years. I have just sent y^r father an account of the Selborne rain during last year: it will again greatly exceed that of Rutland.

S. White † has undertaken to translate the 'Prognostics' of the Greek poet Aratus into English verse; it has never, it seems, been rendered into our language, but was so admired by the Romans, that Cicero and others thought it worth their pains to give a Latin version of it for the amusement of their countrymen. Virgil, I fear, that notorious poacher of every thing that was elegant in the Greek tongue, has gleaned up every fine image, and transplanted them into his 'Georgics.' It is remarkable enough that there is now sitting at my elbow an Oxford gent.‡, who is deeply employed in making an *Index*

---

* [Whitwell.—T. B.]

† [Samuel, Son of G. W.'s brother Harry at Fyfield.—T. B.]

‡ [The Rev. Mr. Churton, an intimate friend and correspondent of G. W. Many of the letters which passed between them will be found further on in this volume.—T. B.]

also; so that my old parlor is become quite an *Index-manufactory*. Mrs. J. White joins in best respects, and the good wishes of the season to you and lady; and I am, with all due affection,

Your loving uncle,
GIL. WHITE.

LETTER XLVIII.

TO HIS NEPHEW BENJAMIN.

Selburne, Feb. [1788?]

DEAR SIR,

I RECEIVED your letter concerning Mr. Pegge, but cannot, as you well know, promise anything. At the same time, also, I received by Molly six more sheets of clean proofs, so well corrected that I have not met with one error; and indeed the errata are so few, that at present they will go into a small compass, and are as follow:—

P. 31. line 15. For *teems* read *teams* *.

P. 91, line 7. d. comma, and for *or* read *of* *.

P. 219, line 15. For *no tbe* read *not be* *.

As I find you advance apace, I have by bearer sent up my 'Antiquities,' because I do not find myself able to correct or improve them any further. You will be pleased not to be offended at the vague spelling of the names of *men* and *places*, but to take them as you find them in their places, because centuries ago men had no criterion to go by, but spelt just as it happened, even their own names often not twice alike. Should not the quotations from the documents be printed in *italics*? You will, I conclude, have a title-page to the 'Antiquities,' to which the Priory seal will make a proper vignette. The great N. view of Selborne is engraving, I understand, and will be opposite the first title page; the view of the Hermitage will then best perhaps appear opposite p. 62, in which mention is made of it. That the documents may be kept safe

* [These misprints were not corrected.]

together, I have numbered them, and put them in a proper bag.

As fast as I receive **my proofs,** I continue to enlarge my Index. The title-page to the 'Nat. Hist.' is furnished with apt mottos. My thanks are due for all your **good offices,** & **for your** late trouble in purchasing me £200 stock.

Your loving uncle,
GIL. WHITE.

P.S. I take the liberty **to return the book of Royal Forests,** &c., from which I have extracted some information. **You** will also receive my Preface **or** Advertisement. Concerning the disposition of the Hermitage **print please to consult** y^r **father** and father-in-law.

Might **not** the Hermitage print come in well at the back of the first title-page, or as a tail-piece to the 'Natural History'*?

Please to observe that all *æ* diphthongs, as *musæ, phalænæ,* &c. **are** always written *muse, phalene,* &c. in old records. When there is any very bad Latin in the evidences, please **to** put in the margin, "*sic.*"

LETTER XLIX.

TO THOMAS BARKER, ESQ.

Jan. 8, 1789.

DEAR SIR,

You must have heard no doubt before now, of the sad and afflicting news from Fyfield, of the sudden **and unexpected** event that has plunged a numerous family **in the** deepest sorrow and trouble. How the **poor man has left his** concerns, and how the widow and children are to proceed, I have not yet heard; however, as money will probably be wanted, my two brothers and nephew Ben and self have each began with a present. When the news arrived here I wrote away immediately to Lady Young, entreating her to apply to

* [See note at p. 128.]

the Chancellor for the living of Fyfield for Sam*; but she returned for answer that she had kept up no acquaintance with Lord Thurlow, tho' a near relation, for many years. Bro. Ben wrote immediately to the Chan^r, and Bro. Tho. applyed by means of Dr. Lort, who prevailed on the B^p of Bangor, Dr. Warren, to press the matter home, and to move the compassion of the great man by representing the afflicted situation of the family. For a short time we were almost ready to flatter ourselves with some hopes of success: the great bar seemed to be that Sam was not in orders; however, two or three days ago a note came to Bro. B. from the Chan. informing him that Fyfield was disposed of, but that Uphaven was at his service. Now you must remember that Uphaven was a very small vicarage indeed; however, Bro. H., I hear, had improved it not a little.

I now see more and more reason to be thankful to providence for enabling me to procure so many friends to assist me in getting Sam* elected fellow. That young man, whom all speak well of, may become the stay and support of the family. By the statutes of his coll. he will not be able, I fear, to take orders till June, when he may take possession also of a fine curacy, now held for him. Charles also is intended for orders, and has kept some terms at Oxford.

It is needless to tell you that we experience a long and severe frost, which commenced Novr 23, and has never been out of the ground since. The snow in this district has been very little. After a very dry spring and summer and autumn, about ten days in Septem^r excepted, the failure of water is remarkable. The ponds are all dry, and most of the wells in the village, and among the rest my own. As to Edm^d White's tank, it has failed for these seven weeks, and he is obliged to fetch his water from the S. side of Nore hill. My column on the other side makes a very small figure in respect to what I used to send you.

Mrs. J. White returns my sister thanks for her late letter. I am disposing of her guinea among the poor. Never were gratuities of that sort more acceptable than now.

* [The son of Henry White.—T. B.]

Rain in Selborne. 1788.

	in.	h.		in.	h.
Jan.	1	60	Aug.	3	22
Feb.	3	37	Sept.	5	71
Mar.	1	31	Oct.	0	0
Apr.	0	61	Nov.	0	86
May	0	76	Dec.	0	21
June	1	27			
July	3	58		22	50

We hear now from all quarters that nep. John the surgeon gets business very fast, and is allowed to be in a way to become the first medical man in Salisbury. Little Ben thrives, and grows very fast.

Mrs. J. Wh. joins in best respects and wishes. I am

Y^r affectionate brother,

GIL. WHITE.

LETTER L.

TO SAMUEL BARKER.

Selborne, May 6, 1790.

DEAR SIR,

We had heard that Mr. Haggitt* had been very ill, but were not aware, till your letter came, that his disorder was of a dangerous and alarming nature. On his own account, and for the sake of his numerous family, we hope it will please God to restore him to his former health, and preserve his life for many years.

The Major Jardine that you mention was well known to my Bro. John—an active, lively, intelligent Scotchman, that had been a private in the artillery, but, having had some education, was ready to enter into any pursuit where knowledge was to be acquired. He showed a great facility in modern languages, had a taste for music, and a smattering in Astronomy, &c., was good-natured, clever, ready to assist, commu-

* [The father of Mrs. Samuel Barker.—T. B.]

nicative and pleasant, but exceedingly poor, having married a Spanish girl without a farthing, who brought him a housefull of children and all her happy relations to live on him when he was only lieutenant. He was supposed to be the son of a Knight of Malta, whom he called his uncle.

What can be the meaning of the following advertisement, which I have seen in the papers? "The life of the Hon. Thomas Chambers Cecil, late Knight of the Shire for Rutland, father of the present member for Stamford, and brother to the Earl of Exeter." What makes me wonder because this man was always represented formerly as little better than an idiot! Now you talk of biography, have you seen the life of Mr. Elwes*, late member for Berkshire?

Dr. Chandler and lady, who have been abroad almost four years, and who returned from the Continent only last Feb., have borrowed Selborne parsonage-house for the summer, and came to reside last week. The Dr., who is an unsettled man, likes this method of procuring an habitation, because it looks so like *not* settling. Roaming about becomes a habit with gentry as well as mendicants, who, when they have once taken up a strolling life, can never be persuaded to stay at their own parishes. The lady is very big with child, and sent for her midwife this morning; so they reached Selborne just in time. They brought a little son with them, a pretty boy, who was born at Rolle in Switzerland, as it were by accident, while posting home to England. Rome is the place that the Dr. admires, where he can have his fill of virtù; he has, I find, secret languishing to return to that capital, to study in the Vatican, and to dine with cardinals. In his passage to Italy, they hired a ship at Marseilles, which was to land them at Cività Vecchia; for some time they had such prosperous gales that the master told them they would be at their destination presently. But as they approached Italy such squalls came off from the Apennines that, after beating about for some days, and fearing that they must run for some harbour in Sardinia, they with difficulty made Porto Longone, in the Isle

* [The celebrated miser, who died in 1789, leaving a fortune of £500,000.—T. B.]

of Elba. Their return from Rolle in Nover last was singular enough. Not daring to venture thro' France, they set out for Basle: here they went 50 miles to the right to see the falls of Schaffhausen!! When the Dr. came to enquire of the watermen at Basle what small craft they had on the Rhine, and whether any house-boat, they said there was nothing but some very small flat-bottomed wherries, but that they could tack two of these together. On two such wallnut shells tyed together embarked the Dr. and lady, the nurse and child, and the French valet, without oar or sail, or any awning that could be kept up, and thus ran at the rate of near 80 miles a day to Dusseldorf, amidst the damps and fogs of Nover, on the expanded face of the Rhine, which was very full and very rapid!! Here they turned off for Brussels, not being aware of what was to befall them, but soon found themselves in a city that expected every day to be cannonaded with hot balls. Here they stayed till they saw the streets barricaded and intersected with deep intrenchments, and at last escaped to Lisle, which was not without its difficulties and embarrassments. The Dr. and lady went twice by water down the Rhosne from Lyons; the scenery on its banks is grand and beautiful. I have just received a letter from the Rev. James Anderson, LL.D., F.R.S., F.A.S., of the Academy of Arts &c. of Dijon, &c.* He directs from Edinburg, and, having seen my book, desires my assistance towards his 'Bee,' a weekly work which he proposes to send forth as soon as he can settle a correspondence to his mind. His prospectus to his work is curious, and promises information.

Nep. John White of Sarum has got him an house and two pupils. Nothing but want of health will hinder that young

* [James Anderson was an influential agricultural writer, and for some time cultivated a large tract of barren land in Aberdeenshire for the purpose of carrying on his agricultural experiments and improvements. He returned to the neighbourhood of Edinburgh, where he had originally resided, and afterwards conducted two periodical publications, 'Recreations in Agriculture' and the 'Bee.' I do not find that Gilbert White ever practically responded to the request mentioned. In 1780 the University of Aberdeen conferred on him the degree of LL.D.; the title of Rev. is, I believe, unauthorized. He died in 1808.—T. B.]

man from being successful and prosperous. His business encreases. Mrs. J. Wh. joins in best respects to yourself and Mrs. Barker.

Your affectionate uncle,
GIL. WHITE.

We expect bro. Tho. next week.

Mrs. Chandler is a pleasant woman, with a good person. While I was writing she was brought to bed of a daughter. Respects at Lyndon.

LETTER LI.

TO MISS MARY BARKER.

Feb. 18, 1792.

DEAR NIECE,

I HEREWITH send you an account of the last year's rain, which was very great, and in particular in Nov., when there fell from the 13th to the 19th, both inclusive, about 5·10. We were surprized to hear of the vast snows and severe weather that you experienced in Dec^r, because all the while we had little snow, and no frost of any continuance.

Rain at Selborne in 1791.

Jan.	6·73	Aug.	1·73
Feb.	4·64	Sept.	1·73
Mar.	1·59	Oct.	6·49
Apr.	1·13	Nov.	8·16
May	1·33	Dec.	4·93
June	·91		
July	5·56		44·93

We condole with you on the loss of old Mrs. Barker, who yet seems to have been a happy woman; for after a blameless life, spent in affluence and comfort among affectionate relations, she departed this life in peace at the good old age of 90 and upwards. I have disposed of your mother's guinea with much satisfaction among such old people as seemed to want it most. Old Dewye and wife are alive, but almost childish—and old George Tanner; but he has been confined to his bed for three months. Charles Etty did not come home in his own ship (in which he was second mate), because, it was said, he broke his leg at Madras the very evening before the ship was to have sailed. Poor dear Caroline Bingham was a most amiable girl, and a fine figure; but she dyed suddenly as soon as she left this place, to the great sorrow of her parents! They have several more children.

Dr. Chandler is in London settling the concerns of his brother; he was a clergyman in Surrey, and has left a daughter grown up. Mrs. Chandler looks a little as if she intended to encrease her family not long hence. The death of my good friend Mr. Mulso is a sad loss to his children; where his daughters are to live we have not heard. My brother Benj., we hear, begins to think seriously of relinquishing his business to his sons; and meditates a retreat into Hants for the remainder of his life, intending to leave S. Lambeth. Perhaps he may settle at Marelands *, a beautiful seat between Alton and Farnham, late the residence of Mr. Sainesbury, uncle to Mrs. Edmund White, and agent to Lord Stawell, Ld Salisbury, the Marquis of Downshire, &c. &c. This gent. dropped suddenly out of his chair and was dead in a moment on the eve of his birthday, while his wife was preparing an elegant entertainment for his friends the day following. Mr. S. was a man of an excellent character, and beloved by everybody. Mr. Clement, very fortunately, is to succeed his friend in his agencies for Lord Stawell and Mr. Beckford; these employs will make a very handsome addition to Mr. Clement's income, and will give him credit and reputation in the neighbourhood. Mrs. J. White begs to join in best respects to all your family and to friends at Whitwell and Stamford.

I remain y^r loving uncle,
GIL. WHITE.

* [Benjamin White died at Marelands, in the 69th year of his age. He was buried at Selborne, March 15, 1794.—T. B.]

Feb. 18, 1792. We have enjoyed lately sweet summer weather; but last night a most severe frost came on, with snow, and therm^r at 21! Newton friends lay here last night.

Marelands house and farm belong to Lord Stawell.

LETTER LII.

TO MRS. BARKER.

Selborne, Jan. 2, 1793.

DEAR SISTER,

WHILE Mrs. J. White is employed in knitting, and Mr. Churton in reading and writing, I sit down, as I have usually done at this season of ye year, to send Mr. Barker the quantity of rain, and you some account of our welfare.

Rain in 1792.

	in.		in.
Jan.	6·07	Aug.	4·25
Feb.	1·68	Sept.	5·53
Mar.	6·70	Oct.	5·55
Apr.	4·08	Nov.	1·65
May	3·00	Dec.	2·11
June	2·78		
July	5·16		48·56

Ned White, you may have heard, is settled with a Banker in London, where he gives satisfaction, and is allowed £50 p^r annum. Gil. White has been so unfortunate as to lose his master, an attorney at Bath, by death, after he had served three years; and what was worse, the man dyed insolvent. By this untoward accident, the poor young man has been thrown out of employ for three or four months, but, by the interest of friends, was reinstated in business yesterday with a gent. at Petersfield, where he is to stay three years more without a premium, but must pay for his board. The first premium, £200, is all lost! Mr. and Mrs. B. White have lately been with us for a few days; and both seemed very well. Poor Nanny Woods's new husband is in a dangerous decline. Much used to be said of his bad health; and therefore it is a pity that the match took place! Dr. Chandler keeps improving his parsonage house, and therefore, I conclude, has no thought of moving. He has taken off an entry from the Hall, and has made the rest of that room into a good parlor. Much was the damage that we sustained by the late sad wet summer and autumn in our hay, our fallows, our corn, and our forest fuel, which lies rotting in the moors of Wolmer. Our brick burner, after he had paid duty for a large cargo of bricks and tiles, never could get them dry enough for burning. My fruit never ripened, and especially my grapes. The year 1782, part of which you spent here, was somehow less distressing, tho' the rain was then upward of 50 in., as you may see by my book. Y^r grandson, I hope, will thrive, and become as honest and good a man as his grandf^r and father. Mrs. J. Wh. thanks you for your late kind present.

Mr. Churton was lately presented by Braze-nose Coll. to one of their best livings, the rectory of Middleton Cheney in Northamptonshire but near Banbury, which he hopes will neat him £400 per ann. He is obliged to rebuild part of the house. Mr. Churton joins with us in all the good wishes of the season.

I remain yours affectionately,
GIL. WHITE.

Old George Tanner is still in bed. The widow of James Carpenter was buried yesterday, aged 93.

I will bestow y^r charity in a proper manner, and return you thanks for it.

LETTER LIII.

TO SAMUEL BARKER.

Selborne.

Dear Sam,

I THINK Mr. Dobson would have done better to have followed Mr. Warton's advice. Have you seen Mr. Colman's translation of Horace's Art of Poetry? In his comment the translator objects to Mr. Hurd's exposition of that epistle, and, I think, with great reason. Mr. Hurd says the Epistle to the Pisos was intended to illustrate the usages of the Roman stage, whereas Mr. C. avers that it was purely a dissuasive letter to the elder Piso not to be in too much haste to publish some poem, probably a domestic one, which that writer, as a nobleman, might have submitted to his friend Horace. I would wish you to see the publication. I have just bought Somerville, & am surprized to find, not having read it these 20 years, that his 'Chase' exceeds most of our poets in its cadences and the sweetness of its numbers. Mr. Warton highly extols his 'Hobbinal,' which does not strike me so much, though its numbers are elegant.

Your affect.
GIL. WHITE.

LETTER LIV.

FROM THOMAS WHITE TO HIS BROTHER GILBERT.

London, Nov. 9, 1775.

Dear Brother,

I SHALL be glad to see you in town, but know not what to say concerning the disorder that is very general here. I believe most people that have it felt ill some time ago; but I am not conversant enough amongst sick people to say positively there is no fear of your taking it now. Molly and the whole family have had colds, coughs, &c., but are now nearly well; as to myself, I have escaped, like John Woods's old horses, by old age and other infirmities. Thank you for the elegant quotation from Middleton*. Is not the ridicule some of our wise governors would have thrown on America applicable to Cicero's on Britain? and may not America be to England ere long what England is now to Rome? I cannot allow that the Romans acquired their riches by virtuous industry; the infamous oppression these people exercised over mankind has been handled too tenderly.

Illinc is pure Saxon, a bank cast up for boundary; hence our "linch" and "linchot" between fields. As you seem to allow me to frolick in conjecture (as Johnson says), I will examine the fields.

Molly goes to-morrow with Dr. Thomas to Cambridge; she has had no return of her complaint, and is to use the cold bath there. I want you to read Plot's treatise 'De origine Fontium,' in which he states what has been advanced on all

---

* [The following is undoubtedly the passage sent by Gilbert White to his brother, referred to in this letter. The intensity of Middleton's antipathy to modern Rome and Romanism is manifested in more than one of his works. The 'Life of Cicero,' from which the present passage is taken, had appeared in 1741. It was published by subscription; and there were no less than six thousand subscribers to the first edition.

After quoting from letters to Atticus, to Cicero's brother Quintus, to Trebatius, &c., Middleton proceeds in the following strain.

"From their railleries on the barbarity and misery of our island, one cannot help reflecting on the surprising fate and revolutions of kingdoms:—how Rome, once the mistress of the world, the seat of arts, empire, and glory, now lies sunk in sloth, ignorance, and poverty, enslaved to the most cruel as well as the most contemptible of tyrants, superstition and religious imposture; while this remote country, anciently the jest and contempt of the polite Romans, is become the happy seat of liberty, plenty, and letters, flourishing in all the arts and refinements of civil life—yet running perhaps the same course which Rome itself had run before it, from virtuous industry to wealth, from wealth to luxury, from luxury to an impatience of discipline and corruption of morals, till, by a total degeneracy and loss of virtue, being grown ripe for destruction, it falls a prey at last to some hardy oppressor, and, with the loss of liberty losing every thing else that is valuable, sinks gradually again into its original barbarism."—T. B.]

hands by former writers and favorers, the assertion of subterranean connections with the sea, against Ray and others. I cannot help looking on these communications as imaginary, and am inclined to join with Ray, who asserts that rain and dew are sufficient to supply all springs. When you describe the perennity of the Selburn spring, it does not seem foreign to the purpose for you to sum up the evidence on both sides, remarking the peculiarity of upland ponds being supplied when those in the vallies fail*, which I believe will prove a new observation. Certainly hills and mountains are condensers, and convert by their coldness the ascending vapours into water; but more of this when we meet.

I am, yours aff^y,
THOS. WHITE.

TIMOTHY THE TORTOISE TO MISS HECKY MULSO.

From the border under the fruit wall,
Aug. 31, 1784.

Most respectable Lady,

Your letter gave me great satisfaction, being the first that ever I was honor'd with. It is my wish to answer you in your own way; but I never could make a verse in my life, so you must be contented with plain prose †. Having seen but little of this great world, conversed but little and read less, I feel myself much at a loss how to entertain so intelligent a correspondent. Unless you will let me write about myself, my answer will be very short indeed. Know then that I am an American, and was born in the year 1734 in the Province of Virginia in the midst of a Savanna that lay between a large

---

* [This subject is treated of fully and in a most interesting manner in the XXIXth letter to Barrington (Vol. I. p. 192).—T. B.]

† [It is evident from this allusion that Gilbert White's amusing *jeu d'esprit* was occasioned by some verses addressed by Miss Mulso to Timothy the Tortoise. These, however, I regret to say, I have not succeeded in finding.—T. B.]

tobacco plantation and a creek of the sea*. Here I spent my youthful days among my relations with much satisfaction, and saw around me many venerable kinsmen, who had attained to great ages without any interruption from distempers. Longevity is so general among our species that a funeral is quite a strange occurrence. I can just remember the death of my great-great-grandfather, who departed this life in the 160th year of his age. Happy should I have been in the enjoyment of my native climate and the society of my friends had not a sea-boy, who was wandering about to see what he could pick up, surprized me as I was sunning myself under a bush; and whipping me into his wallet, carryed me aboard his ship. The circumstances of our voyage are not worthy a recital; I only remember that the rippling of the water against the sides of our vessel as we sailed along was a very lulling and composing sound, which served to sooth my slumbers as I lay in the hold. We had a short voyage, and came to anchor on the coast of England in the harbour of Chichester. In that city my kidnapper sold me for half-a-crown to a country gentleman, who came up to attend an election. I was immediately packed in an hand-basket, and carryed, slung by the servant's side, to their place of abode. As they rode very hard for forty miles, and I had never been on horseback before, I found myself somewhat giddy from my airy jaunt. My purchaser, who was a great humorist, after shewing me to some of his neighbours and giving me the name of TIMOTHY, took little further notice of me; so I fell under the care of his lady, a benevolent woman, whose humane attention extended to the meanest of her retainers. With this gentlewoman I remained almost 40 years, living in a little walled-in court in the front of her house, and enjoying much quiet and as much satisfaction as I could expect without society. At last this good old lady dyed in a very advanced age, such as a tortoise would call a good old age; and I then became the property of her

---

* [I have already stated that Timothy belonged to a North-African species; and I now add that there is only one species of the genus *Testudo* inhabiting the United States, *T. polyphemus*, which is very different from Timothy in appearance and zoological character.—T. B.]

nephew. This man, my present master, dug me out of my winter retreat, and, packing me in a deal box, jumbled me 80 miles in post-chaises to my present place of abode. I was sore shaken by this expedition, which was the worst journey I ever experienced. In my present situation I enjoy many advantages—such as the range of an extensive garden, affording a variety of sun and shade, and abounding in lettuces, poppies, kidney beans, and many other salubrious and delectable herbs and plants, and especially with a great choice of delicate gooseberries! But still at times I miss my good old mistress, whose grave and regular deportment suited best with my disposition. For you must know that my master is what they call a *naturalist*, and much visited by people of that turn, who often put him on whimsical experiments, such as feeling my pulse, putting me in a tub of water to try if I can swim, &c.; and twice in the year I am carried to the grocer's to be weighed, that it may be seen how much I am wasted during the months of my abstinence, and how much I gain by feasting in the summer. Upon these occasions I am placed in the scale on my back, where I sprawl about to the great diversion of the shop-keeper's children. These matters displease me; but there is another that much hurts my pride: I mean that contempt shown for my understanding which these *Lords* of the *Creation* are very apt to discover, thinking that nobody knows anything but themselves. I heard my master say that he expected that I should some day tumble down the ha-ha; whereas I would have him to know that I can discern a precipice from plain ground as well as himself. Sometimes my master repeats with much seeming triumph the following lines, which occasion a loud laugh.

> "Timotheus placed on high
> "Amidst the tuneful choir,
> "With flying fingers touched the lyre."

For my part I see no wit in the application; nor know whence the verses are quoted; perhaps from some prophet of his own, who, if he penned them for the sake of ridiculing tortoises, bestowed his pains, I think, to poor purposes. These are some of my grievances; but they sit very light on me in comparison of what remains behind. Know then, tender-hearted lady, that my greatest misfortune, and what I have never divulged to any one before, is—the want of society of my own kind. This reflection is always uppermost in my own mind, but comes upon me with irresistible force every spring. It was in the month of May last that I resolved to elope from my place of confinement; for my fancy had represented to me that probably many agreeable tortoises of both sexes might inhabit the heights of Baker's Hill or the extensive plains of the neighbouring meadow, both of which I could discern from the terrass. One sunny morning, therefore, I watched my opportunity, found the wicket open, eluded the vigilance of Thomas Hoar, and escaped into the saint-foin, which began to be in bloom, and thence into the beans. I was missing eight days, wandering in this wilderness of sweets, and exploring the meadow at times. But my pains were all to no purpose; I could find no society such as I wished and sought for. I began to grow hungry, and to wish myself at home. I therefore came forth in sight, and surrendered myself up to Thomas, who had been inconsolable in my absence. Thus, Madam, have I given you a faithful account of my satisfactions and sorrows, the latter of which are mostly uppermost. You are a lady, I understand, of much sensibility. Let me, therefore, make my case your own in the following manner; and then you will judge of my feelings. Suppose you were to be kidnapped away *to-morrow*, in the bloom of your life, to a land of Tortoises, and were never to see again for fifty years a human face!!! Think on this, dear lady, and pity

Your sorrowful Reptile,
TIMOTHY.

CORRESPONDENCE

OF THE

REV. R. CHURTON* AND GILBERT WHITE.

LETTER I.

TO THE REV. R. CHURTON.

Selborne, Nov. 17, 1779.

DEAR SIR,

On opening your favour, I was much pleased to see your name at the bottom; because you are a gentleman to whom I am much obliged, and to whom I wished for an occasion to express my acknowledgements.

You are a fellow of a college as well as myself, and therefore must be well aware that with regard to elections it is not in my power to enter into any promises: but you may be well assured that I shall have the better opinion of Mr. Smith for

---

* [The Rev. Ralph Churton was born in the year 1754 at Bickley, a township of the parish of Malpas, in Cheshire. He was educated at Oxford, and became a fellow of Brazen-nose College. He was the author of sermons, letters, and other works, and was highly esteemed by the literary and religious society of his time. When his correspondence with Gilbert White commenced, he could not have been more than about 24 or 25 years of age.—T. B.]

what you say of him, and, if I am able to attend at Easter, shall mention your recommendation to the society.

When the summer is established, if you find within yourself an inclination to visit Hants, I shall be very glad to see you at my house, and to show you our prospects, which are romantic enough. Your company and conversation, provided you can bear with the infirmities of a deaf man, will be very agreeable to me. Dr. Chandler is now sitting at my elbow, and is deeply engaged in Bp. Waynflete's Registers, two vol. fol. which I obtained to be sent to my house from Winton by permission from the Bp. of that diocese: last summer we had Bp. Wyckhame's registry of the same bulk and number of vol. I am, Sir,

Your obliged servant,
GIL. WHITE.

LETTER II.

TO THE SAME.

Selborne, near Alton, Hants,
July 3, 1780.

DEAR SIR,

As I have always wished to express my gratitude for the many good offices you have conferred on me, I must desire that you would furnish me with an opportunity, by taking the trouble to come to my house, where I shall rejoice to see you in the course of this summer.

At present my beds are all like to be full for two or three weeks to come; but by the end of July at farthest I shall be glad to see you for 4 or 5 weeks. It will probably be in my power to shew you a new country, and a district not unpleasing in fine weather. If you can bear with the infirmities of a deaf man, your company and conversation will be very agreeable to me: and in yr answer I bar all proposals respecting some future summer, because at my time of life there is little dependence to be made on distant engagements. Pray take me, in the very words of Creech, "just as I am, very much disposed to receive you, and ready to shew you all civilities."

If you are a botanist, we have a very good *Flora*, to whom I am willing to introduce you. You are, I find, learned in *yew-trees*: we have at hand several noble ones.

We have just found a large *stone-urn* down at the Priory [*]; for what use it was made it remains for you to inform us.

We will examine *The Temple, King John's hill*, &c. &c.

I am, with great esteem,
Yr obliged, and humble servant,
GIL. WHITE.

Dr. Chandler, who is going to be very busy with Bp. Beaufort's Register, fr Winchester, joins in respects. When my beds are at liberty I will write: pray let me hear soon.

LETTER III.

TO THE SAME.

Fyfield, near Andover, Hants,
Aug. 31, 1780.

DEAR SIR,

YOUR favour of July 10th carried with it a very obliging air, because it seemed to imply that you will endeavour to pay me a visit.

Now let me (as old men love to be didactic) enjoin you to leave the N. as soon as you conveniently can, and to get to Selborne by the last week in Sepr at farthest; for it seems to me to be very unreasonable to desire you to come so far

---

[*] [The discovery of this urn and its destruction are mentioned in the 'Antiquities' (Vol. I. p. 370). An antiquarian friend, probably Dr. Chandler, suggested that it might have been a standard measure for the Priory.—T. B.]

only for a week or a fortnight. About the time that term begins I should be glad also to go to Oxford, and, provided health permits, will give you a cast in a post-chaise about the 12th or 13th of Octob^r all the way to Coll.

Dr. Chandler left me the week before last. After much delay we got one vol. of Bp. Beaufort's Register, the only one that can be found : but it contained only 13 years of a long episcopate of above 40. It did not afford much concerning Selborne, but would, it seems, furnish much matter concerning the Lollards, who were cruelly harassed in the reign of Hen. 4.

The way to Selborne is *Dorchester, Wallingford, Pangborn*; here leave the Reading-road, and go down the new turn-pike for *Aldermaston*-wharf, *Aldermaston; Basingstoke, Tunworth-down* under *Hackwood*-park pales, the *Golden-pot* ale-house, *Alton, Faringdon, Horse-and-Jockey, Selborne*.

Please to direct to me as before at Selborne near *Alton* Hants. If you know anybody in the N. whom it may concern, you may assure them that the crop of hops in the S. is prodigious ; and that they are very fine in quality. I conclude

Your most humble servant,
GIL. WHITE.

Pray write soon.

LETTER IV.

TO THE SAME.

Seleburne, near Alton, Hants,
Dec. 7, 1780.

DEAR SIR,

IF you have no more fears about a winter-journey than I had at your time of life, you might, I should hope, favour me with a visit during the approaching vacation. The country indeed

is now shorn of its tresses, and much in dishabille; but we
have still pleasant foot-paths, wild views, and chearful neighbours. I will give you some roast-beef, plum-pudding, and
other Xstmass-cheer. We do not, I believe now keep the
good season that is advancing so jollily as you do in the N.;
but you will, I hope, be pleased with visiting Sr Adam de
Gurdon's hall, where that old baron probably entertained his
tenants with an ox roasted whole, and floods of brown ale.
What I want is for you to try your hand at this place at this
disadvantageous season; and then I shall not doubt but you
will like it better in the summer. We have just finished a
walk† of 400 yards in length thro' an hanging wood just
above my house; which we are apt to think will please
strangers, because we like it ourselves. From hence we look
on the village in a very pleasing light. If you are a draughtsman, I can show you some stained views taken from nature by
an artist that came down to me from London.

My progress in Nat. Hist. is very slow indeed: I now and ‡
* * * * * * * * * * *
advertised, I see, and will be out in Feb. I heartily wish he
may give no reason for complaint with respect to religious
matters: in other respects he will be secure of fame.

If I was to meet Gen. Arnold I should address him thus:—

> "But wherefore thou alone? wherefore with thee
> Came not all? * * * * *
> * * * "had'st thou alledg'd
> To thy deserted host this cause of flight
> Thou surely had'st not come sole fugitive."

     I am, with due respect,
      You most humble servant,
        GIL. WHITE.

Mr. G., I understand, will draw a comparison between
Xstianity papal, and Mohammedism; and indeed I am at a

---

† The Bostal.
‡ [A portion of this letter is lost.]

loss to say which will make the most hideous picture. I mean the popery of the darker ages *.

LETTER V.

TO THE SAME.

Selborne, Dec. 10, 1780.

Dear Sir,

By your letter of the 14th to Dr. Chandler, which the Dr. has communicated to me, I am glad to find that you are so well disposed to make me a visit, and hope you will meet with no interruption. You will not, I hope, over-stay this unprecedented run of fine weather, that has befallen us now for more than three weeks, without rain, wind, or frost!

If you have a friend in London to whom you can send y^r portmanteau, then you need only desire him to direct it for you "at ye Rev^d Mr. W. at Selborne, to be left at the Swan-Inn at Alton, by the Southampton coach," which comes from the Belle Savage-Inn on Ludgate hill; but if you have no such person, then direct it to Mr. Edm^d White at Mr. Hounsom's mercer in Fleet-street London, to be forwarded to Mr. White &c. by the Southampton coach.

If you call at Caversham pray present my most respectful compliments to Mr. Loveday, and the ladies. I have not the pleasure to be known to Dr. Loveday.

Your most humble servant,
GIL. WHITE.

* [At page 120, in a letter to Mr. Barker, the forthcoming work of Gibbon is mentioned; this referred to the first volume only. The allusion in the above letter to Mr. Churton is to that further portion of the history which, accordingly, made its appearance, in the second and third volumes, in February 1781.—T. B.]

LETTER VI.

TO THE SAME.

Selborne, May 9, 1781.

Dear Sir,

When I called at Brazen-nose Coll. in the Easter week, I was sorry but not disappointed in not finding you, because Mr. Loveday had intimated that probably you would be gone on a visit to his son.

As you have seen Selborne, and the nakedness of the land at Xtmas, you will not do it justice if you do not come and visit it in all its glory, in its full foliage, and verdure.

I therefore exhort you and enjoin you to come and spend the Whitsun vacation here, where your company and conversation will be very acceptable; and, if I mistake not, my neighbours will be glad to see you also.

If you come by Caversham, be pleased to ask for a parcel of papers which I left with Mr. Loveday.

I am, with due respect,
Your most affectionate servant,
GILL. WHITE.

If you will direct y^r portmanteau to be left at the Bell Savage on Ludgate hill London, to be forwarded to the Swan at Alton by the Southampton coach, it will, I trust, come safe.

LETTER VII.

TO THE SAME.

Seleburne, Jan. 4, 1783.

Dear Sir,

Your long and communicative letter of Dec. 16 gave me much satisfaction. After you went away my family became very large for the rest of the summer. I had with me my bro. Th. White, and daughter and two sons, my sister Barker from Rutland and her two youngest daughters, and at times my nep. J. White son of Mrs. J. White, who is just settled at Salisbury as a surgeon, being invited by some friends who seemed perswaded that there was an opening. My nieces, Barkers, especially the eldest of the two who is 22 years of age, have (I speak as a foolish uncle) very fine fingers, and play elegantly on the harpsichord. These maidens entertained us day after day with very lovely lessons from Niccolai, Giordani, and several other modern masters, in a very agreeable manner. But I find, as I grow old, that music, tho' very sweet and engaging at the time, yet occasions very unpleasing sensations afterwards. When I hear fine lessons I am haunted with passages therefrom night and day, and especially at first waking, which by their importunity give me more pain than pleasure: airs and jigs rush upon my imagination, and recur irresistably to my memory at seasons, and even when I am desirous of thinking of other matters. The following curious quotation strikes me much by so well representing my own case, and by describing what I have so often felt, but never could so well express. "Præhabebat porro vocibus humanis, instrumentisque harmonicis, musicam illam avium: non quod aliâ quoque non delectaretur; sed quod ex musicâ humanâ relinqueretur in animo continens quædam attentionemque & somnum conturbans agitatio; dum ascensus, excensus, tenores, ac mutationes illæ sonorum, & consonantiarum euntque redeuntque per phantasiam: cum nihil tale relinqui possit ex modulationibus avium, quæ, quod non sunt perinde internam facultatem commovere." *—*De vitâ Peireskii per Gassendum.*

I am glad that you met with the Star-sluch in Cheshire, after you had examined the *Tremella nostoc* in Hants. Not that I had any doubt myself that the former was a vegetable, but because I met with intelligent people who are still per-

* [This is the third time this passage is quoted by Gilbert White: first in the LVIth letter to Barrington, and again in a letter to his niece Mary White.—T. B.]

swaded that this substance is a mass of indigested food cast-up out of the stomachs of crows! and some have told me that they have distinguished the limbs of frogs among it! As to a star-sluch growing on the bough of an oak; this must have been a matter of accident. The seeds of all *Fungi*, you know, are lighter than air, and therefore float about in it; and vegetate only when they happen to fall on a proper *nidus*.

Dr. Ch. seemed a good deal chagrined about the behaviour of his prime minister. If he had not come home just in time, a *bern* would have been born unto him in the vicarage. Sim Etty, tutored by the Dr., runs about the village, and repeats to every one he meets, with great vehemence;—" Mulieri ne credas, ne mortuæ quidem." Ch. Etty is at the Nore aboard the Duke of Kingston, and is expected every day at Spithead; from whence he is to make a visit here for a day or two before he sails for India.

I thank you much for procuring Mr. Hampton's pamphlet, which you will please to leave at my brother's. You will, I hope, make yrself known to him; I have mentioned you to him. You will see a roomy shop, well furnished, with old gent. in leathern doublets. Timothy the tortoise would make but a poor king: he would be so slow in his motions as to be but a king Log at best; and an alert enemy would deprive him of half his dominions, before he could awake from his profound slumbers.

I will take care of your *Rex Platonicus*, and hope I shall bring it you at Exeter. My bro. Th. opened several of the barrows on our down in the summer, but found nothing. Now you talk of last summer, it was a strange summer indeed! Nothing like it, I believe, has befallen since the year 1725, when it rained every day, except about 10 in July, from March 29th to Septem^r 29th; but then the first part of said year was very dry. In 1782 the rain that fell at Selborne was 50 inc. 26 hund.! and of this the greatest part came in the first 9 months; for Oct^r, Nov^r, and Decr were comparatively dry; Dec. afforded only 0 inc. 91 h. I would have you dine with my bro. Ben in Fleet street: he dines always about three o'clock. If you would call some morning at my bro. Tho. White's at South Lambeth, just beyond Vauxhall turnpike, he would be glad to see you. It is a pretty walk from town to S. Lambeth! If you will go there and dine* (next?) Sunday, you will meet both families; for they both live* (there?).

[Here followed the pleasing lines "On the early and late blowing of the Vernal and Autumnal Crocus," which will be found among the Poems at the end of the first volume; they were first written in this letter to Mr. Churton.—T. B.]

I am, with all due esteem,
Your most humble servant,
GIL. WHITE.

Neighbours are all well. Mrs. J. White joins in the good wishes of the season.

LETTER VIII.

TO THE SAME.

Seleburne, Aug. 20, 1783.

DEAR SIR,

Tho' my house is full of company, yet I must no longer delay to answer your agreeable and intelligent letter from Williamscot. Poor Mrs. Etty has been a great sufferer both in mind and body, having paid a long attendance on her son Andrew, who languished from spring to midsummer, and then dyed of a slow decay. What added to the affliction was, that Miss C. Etty was lying all the while under the same circumstances at Winchester, and dying first, was brought to this place; so that I had the sorrowful office of burying these two young people, the one on one Saturday, and the other on the following. Ch. Etty has not been heard of since he sailed for India in March; but the papers mention

* [These words, or some of similar meaning, have been torn from the edge of the letter.—T. B.]

the Duke of Kingston (his ship) having called at the Cape Verds in April, all well.

We have experienced a long summer, with intense heats, little rain, and no storms. But what has been very extraordinary, was the *long-continued haze*, extending thro' this island, and, I think, thro' Europe, attended with vast honeydews, which destroyed all our hops, and lasted more than a month. Thro' this *rusty coloured* air, the sun, "shorn of his beams," appeared like the moon, even at noonday. The country people looked with a kind of superstitious awe on the red lowering aspect of the great luminary, "Cum caput *obscurâ* nitidum *ferrugine* texit." And I have no doubt, but that the unusual look of the sky at Cæsar's death, mentioned both by historians, and poets, was somewhat of the same kind. As I love to trace natural appearances, I desire to know if you saw a very large luminous meteor traversing the sky from N.W. to S.W. on Monday even Aug. 18 about 9 o'clock. Pray hunt for star-sluch, because several intelligent people, one at present in this house, stare and wonder when I advance that the matter is vegetable; and Dr. Chandler in particular shakes his head, and asserts that the mass is frogs thrown up indigested. But I beg to know why crows are not sometimes crop-sick, and have not weak digestions in Hants (yet we have no such appearance) as well as in Cheshire. Apply a magnifying glass to the substance, and try to discover the seeds.

I return you thanks for Hampton's pamphlet, and am indebted to you whatever it cost. The notices concerning Wolmer-forest in Gent. Mag. came, I conclude, from Dr. Chandler, whose extracts from the Worldham Register are genuine. We have this year a most lovely harvest, much corn—but no hops. Our fruit is well ripened, and grapes very forward.

You pay an high compliment to my crocuses, but were not aware that it will bring more lines on your back. Read them, as little exercises, made last autumn for the use of my nephews (for such they really were), and then you will give them all reasonable allowances. Some weeks ago Dr. Chandler was at Portsmouth; but we have not seen him. The Dr. does not seem disposed to settle. May I presume to send my humble respects to Dr. Townson, whom I have sometimes seen, a long time ago, at Magd. Coll. Sportsmen expect a vast breed of game this season. Pray be so good as to favour me with a letter at your leisure. Mrs. J. White joins in respects. I am

Your obliged servant,
GIL. WHITE.

I am glad that you are pleased with the passage from the life of Peireskius, and that you, as well as myself, have been haunted with passages in music.

If you will look in Gent. Mag. for June 1783, you will find, under article "Metamorphosis," a copy of verses written by a poor dear Oxford friend long since dead, who was pleased, about 35 years ago, to make himself merry with my attachment to gardening.

A HARVEST-SCENE *:

AFTER THE MANNER OF THOMSON.

    Wak'd by the gentle gleamings of the morn,
Soon clad, the Reaper, provident of want,
Hies, chearful-hearted, to the ripen'd field:
Nor hastes alone, attendant by his side
His faithful wife, sole partner of his cares,
Bears on her breast the sleeping babe; behind
With steps unequal trips the infant train †.
Thrice happy pair, in love and labour joined!
    All day they ply their task; with mutual chat
Beguiling each the sultry, tedious hours:
Around them falls in rows the sever'd corn;
Or the shocks rise in regular array.

---

* [These lines were inserted in the second and subsequent editions of the work.—T. B.]

† [. . . sequitur patrem non passibus æquis,
    Pone subit conjux.   Æn. ii. 724.]

But when high noon invites to short repast,
Beneath the shade of shelt'ring thorn they sit,
Divide the simple meal, and drain the cask :
The swinging cradle lulls the whimp'ring babe
Meantime ; while growling round, if at the tread
Of hasty passenger alarm'd, as of their store
Protective, stalks the cur with bristling back,
To guard the scanty scrip and russet garb.

LETTER IX.

TO THE SAME.

South Lambeth, Mar. 30, 1784.

Dear Sir,

I take it very kind that you should remember me, when probably I owed you a letter all the while. As I propose to return to Selborne on Friday next, and to set out for Oxford on Easter Tuesday, it does not seem very probable that we shall meet. If you are in London on a Thursday, I would advise you by all means to attend on the R. S. and Antiquary-meetings in their new splendid rooms at Somerset-house. Dr. Chandler can probably put you in a method of being introduced ; if you do not see him, attend in the outer room, between the two rooms, at a *quarter* before *seven* in the evening, and enquire for Dr. Lort, who, I trust, on your using my name, will introduce you to both the meetings, where perhaps you may hear somewhat worth your trouble. The Antiq. Society, I find, is growing very fashionable ; for I observed that many Right Honourables were balloted for on Thursday se'nnight. The weather has been dismal and winter-like ever since I left home ; however, I have great advantages in these parts, having a bed at command both in town and country and a carriage to take me to town. Tho. Davis, the bookseller, has just published his memoirs on plays and players, a pleasant book. He has a good stile, and language that no man need be ashamed of, and abounds in curious and pleasant anecdotes. Mr. Etty has heard twice from his son at the Cape of Good Hope; his ship was burnt in the Indian seas, from which he had a miraculous escape, and was carried naked aboard another ship in company; he lost every thing. Molly White's rhimes were Norwegian. If you see any lines in **Gent. Mag.** on such soft weather as I have languished for in vain the spring thro', treat them with what lenity you may.

Mrs. J. White joins in respects. If you hear nothing curious at the R. S. or Antiq. meetings, at least you will see two grand rooms and many respectable people, besides Somerset House, a national building as big as three or four colleges!

I am, with due respect,

Your most obedient servant,

GIL. WHITE.

LETTER X.

FROM MR. CHURTON TO GILBERT WHITE.

Brazen-Nose, Jan. 22, 1786.

DEAR SIR,

EPIC poets, with the approbation of Horace, "in medias ruunt res;" but a letter-writer, a much humbler being, commonly begins at one end, though it may happen to be the wrong end. Let me inform you then, first of all, that on Monday last I got to College safe and well, and found my portmanteau in my room waiting my arrival. Of some parts of my travels since I left Selborne you may possibly have heard from your neighbours. This, however, you probably will not have heard; and I know it will give you pleasure to hear, that I found Mr. Loveday, excepting some slight remains of a cough, very well, his hearing better than usual, and his memory, in spite of all that he says, just as good as it has ever been since I have had the happiness of his acquaintance. Mrs. Loveday was confined, in consequence, I believe, of her great attention to Mr. L. in his late illness. The rest of the family were well. Dr. and Mrs. Loveday returned to Williamscot, whence a letter says a bundle of anecdotes, &c., respecting the spectators &c., was sent to London a year or two ago. This is a little episode. Now for Caversham again, whither I went to tea after dining in Reading; and as I was going in the dusk I was accosted in a manner that amused me not a little—" Why, it looks very *ghastly*; all these meadows are *quite* flooded entirely." From Caversham on Wednesday I proceeded to Windsor, and thence next day as far as Kensington, where I met Miss Chase in the street, and accepted an invitation to dinner. I found the family full of joy with the very agreeable news which they had received the day before, as you have probably heard, from the two Mr. Chases in India. Next day I went on to London, had the pleasure of seeing your brother very well in Fleet Street, and, after making several other visits, dined with Mr. Lewis in Frederick's Place, where I had the pleasure of finding him and Mrs. Lewis and abundance of nephews and nieces (for they call me Uncle Churton) very well, and a prospect of an addition to the number very soon. Mr. L. had seen a letter from Mrs. Chandler a few days before; all well. Having finished my business in town, which was to learn whether Mrs. Winchester was at H. Wycombe, I returned to sleep in the purer air of Kensington, and next day set forward for Wycombe; but I had not gone far when I perceived a solitary flake of snow approaching the ground. " Oh!" quoth I, " is this the sport I am to have?" and another and another feather, either from Wales or somewhere else, soon succeeded, and I was as white and fair in my snowy plumes as you please. After riding about ten or a dozen miles, a bit of bread and a glass of brandy, "decus vitæ," were no uncomfortable things; and I got on to Wycombe, the snow still continuing, neither wet nor fatigued.

I see Whitney's 'Emblems' are in the Bodleian. Bellendenus, who published the work which I mentioned, " De tribus luminibus Romanorum," from which Middleton is said to have translated whole pages in his ' Life of Cicero,' published before a small 12° tract which is called ' Ciceronis Princeps;' and this, like the ' Lumina,' is drawn up in the words of Cicero, and contains the scattered maxims &c. relating to government from the different parts of his works; it is addressed to Prince Henry; and in the preface he mentions having drawn up from the same author what he had said on the History and Antiquities of Rome, and digested in several books which he intended to publish. He no doubt means the 'De tribus lum. R.;' but he does not there call it by that name; and why he did so call it, no account, as far as appears, can be given. I have shewn the inscription on the ostrich shell at the vicarage to a linguist. It is Dutch; but the word on the flag of the ship, which, if I copied it right, has no *vowel*, is as yet a puzzle. I observed a circumstance in the late frost which was new to me; but I daresay you are well acquainted with it. Having pulled off, as I was going to bed, my silk stockings and those I wore under them together, as I was separating them I heard a great crackling, upon which I carried the other into the dark, to see as well as hear the effect; and during the separation the sparks were so vivid and plenteous that a person unacquainted with electricity would have thought the stockings would be burnt. After this, holding the silk stocking in one hand, I passed the other down it several times, and as often as I did it a blaze, but without any noise, followed my hand; I think the stockings have been washed only once. The next day, having an older pair on, the frost still continuing, there was no noise or fire during the separation, nor could I elicit the smallest spark with my hand. It seems by this as if silk lost in some degree its electrical as well as wearable properties by time. I dined yesterday in company with Dr. Parr, late of Norwich, but now going to a living in Warwickshire, where he means to take a few boarders. He is a Cambridge man; and a sermon of his is reviewed in the last Mag. He himself reviews sometimes; the Oxford Cicero was reviewed by him, where I had a little rap, having in the account of MSS. said "*licet fert*" instead of "*ferat.*" I suppose he does not know who drew up the account. He seems a very sensible and learned man; but, *pace tanti viri dixerim*, dogmatical and overbearing. * * * I began this two or three days ago; but one business or other prevented my finishing it. I have written to Dr. Chandler. Give my best respects to Mrs. J. White, and comp^ts to the surgeon, who I hope will get on well in his new situation. I hope Mrs. Etty and the ladies are well, and beg to be remembered to them. I owe you many thanks for your kind hospitality, and, hoping to hear from you at your leisure, I am,

Yours, &c.,
R. CHURTON.

LETTER XI.

FROM MR. CHURTON TO GILBERT WHITE.

Selborne, June 6, 1787.

Dear Sir,

I am just arrived from Waverley, and very sorry not to find the master of this hospitable mansion at home. I did not know that I should be at Waverley these holidays till just before I set out thither; and when my plan was fixt I purposed at several times to write to enquire whether you were at Selborne; but one or other avocation prevented me. So here I am; and your bread and butter, and cream and tea and sugar, will shortly suffer great depredations. However, in some respects I hope you will be the better, aye, and the richer, for my visit. In the first place I bring you an Anglesey penny from the fair hands of Miss Loveday, who, I hope, by this time is in perfect health. When I called at Caversham on Whit Tuesday a bad fever was just gone off, but she still kept her bed. Of her friends, however, she was not unmindful, and she sent me down this coin with a commission to bring it hither. I never saw Mr. L. in better health or spirits, though his leg, which he bruised some time ago and neglected, is not well, as it would be soon if he would rest it before him; but he prefers a wounded leg with activity to sound limbs and idleness. This incomparable friend of ours, who knows every thing, presently showed me the 'Annals of Waverley' in print, among some other tracts published by Gale. Dr. Adee, M.D., whom you knew probably, collected a Hist. of Waverley Abbey; and my friend Dr. Bostock has a transcript of it. He has made considerable use of the annals, and appears to have put together all, or nearly all, that is to be met with on the subject. I left a paper for you at Fleet Street, which said that the heart of Peter de Rupibus was buried at Waverley, and his body at Winchester. The Hist. of Waverley mentions this; and Dr. Adee adds "that when Mr. Child first came to the place, a heart was dug up in a leaden pot, and preserved in some liquor." Simon de Montfort is also mentioned; but this, I think, I extracted on the said paper.

No Mr. White, no Mrs. J. White, no Mr. Edm. White, no Mrs. Etty! Alas poor Selborne! thy grotesque lanes, thy romantic vales, thy delightful walks, thy verdant hills, thy extensive prospects deserve to be honoured by other inhabitants than the philosophic Timothy in the beginning of June! Here, however (for I have almost done mischief enough to the loaf), here " Let me wander all unseen, By hedgerow elms and hillocks green," in fields somewhat more fertile than the Surrey hills, where the largest of the trees first planted by O. Hunter is about 3 feet in girt, after growing, I believe, more years than I have been growing; but then in height they have far outstript me, to say nothing of my friend the archer of Rolle[*], who honoured me with a letter yesterday after a half year's silence. He says not a syllable about returning to England; but if he has left Rolle, as perhaps he may before a letter arrives, it will be forwarded. He says the English literature and nation enjoy in Switzerland a degree of esteem which is very flattering to a lover of his country, and that it is surprizing to see the number of English authors to be met with in the libraries of gentlemen in the delicious little town where he was when he wrote to me.

I enclose you a letter from the 'Wanderer' ("Thickness the traveller"); how instructive it may prove I know not. Mr. Burby tells me he saw a letter from C. Etty which was forwarded to Mrs. Etty, and that he apprehends he is on the

[*] [Dr. Chandler.—T. B.]

English coast, if he is not landed. I was much indebted to the hospitality and conversation of S. Lambeth during my visit to the metropolis at Easter, which was not so long as it would have been if the smoke had not given me a wretched cough, which the air of Oxford and the country removed some time ago. I am afraid I shall not see Selborne again this summer, as I am bound for Cheshire towards the end of the Term, which begins to-day. I came across the country from Waverley by the Holte, through Kingsley, and along the edge of Wolmer, and never was much out of my way I believe. Some of the hills hereabout I knew as I approached them; but there was a clump of trees on a promontory to the left of the Temple nearer Empsholt which disturbed me a good deal. I thought I must have seen and remembered such a prominent feature (if you allow fashionable expressions) in the landscape. I am much obliged to you for the kind letter which I found in my room on my return to college after Easter. And now let me enquire after friend Timothy. He looks very well, and says not a syllable of a late elopement. Perhaps he is ashamed of it; and yet who knows whether he was not going in quest of his master; and if he had not speedily been brought back he might possibly have surprized you by an unexpected visit at S. Lambeth. Thomas tells me that C. Etty *is* arrived in England, which I am very glad to hear. I saw Mrs. Etty for five minutes at Beaconsfield on my way to London. The rain, which is just set in, will, I hope, be of service to the country; but I could gladly have excused it for three hours longer—one to walk about here, and two to ride back to Waverley. My great coat I very wisely left at Reading. I *might* make that in my way to Waverley; but then I should run a risk of losing my dinner, which, at a proper interval after breakfast, is an object of some importance. It still rains, and I am still, dear Sir,

Your most obedient and much obliged servant,
R. CHURTON.

LETTER XII.

FROM MR. CHURTON TO GILBERT WHITE.

Brasen Nose, Oct. 14, 1787.

DEAR SIR,

I OUGHT to have written to you sooner; but, besides other reasons, my cold was rather worse, either from change of weather or travelling, or both, and I was not willing to send you an unfavourable account. I hope I can now truly say that I am still better than when I left Hants, though my cough is not yet entirely gone. I lost my way to Waverley as usual; but I did not much regret it. I endeavoured to cut off angles upon entering the Holt; and keeping a good look out for the great oak, I found myself under it before I was aware. I rode round it, and must confess it the largest by far I ever saw. The nearest to it, but "longo proximus intervallo," grows at Marbury in Cheshire. Going on from the oak I came to the Lodge, no very splendid house for a nobleman. Here I got instructions from one of the servants, and proceeded without any more deviation to Waverley. I sheltered once or twice for a few minutes in the Holt while a slight shower passed over; and the next day I stopt at Hartford bridge (where I breakfasted) about two hours on a similar occasion, and then got on safely to Caversham. Mr. Loveday's cold, which had been better, was that day increased; but from losing some blood twice since that, he is stronger, and his cold much better. The next day was rather stormy; but by quickening or retarding my pace, I slipt through the clouds without getting wet, and got to Oxford in good time. The next day, which was Saturday, not feeling very bold, I went in a post-chaise to Williamscot; and good nursing and gentle rides, though we could not procure a milch ass, soon made me better.

Oct. 15. On my road from Reading hither I saw martins

and swallows, perhaps half a score of each. On the 6th, going to Williamscot, I saw two swallows; and last Friday (12th) I saw about half a dozen martins flitting about over the village of Williamscot; I have seen none since, though I had some hopes of seeing some to day as I was riding at noon about Headington; for it was particularly fine. I thank you for forwarding the letter, and will repay you with pleasure whatever you may have advanced for me on that or any other account when I have the happiness of seeing you again; and I do hope, please God, to live to see the day when my health shall be established in such a degree that I may not be a burden and plague to my friends wherever I am. I looked in the 'De Senectute,' where a country life is celebrated, but do not meet with any passage that I think quite applicable as a motto. I saw your Provost at church to day, and thought he looked very well; his wig improves him much. At Williamscot I cast my eye over the account of Alien Priories; and I see a great part of the account consists of extracts in Latin, titles of deeds, or references to them, &c.; so that if there is Latin in the Selborne 'Antiquities,' it will be agreeable to good authorities. However, for my own single opinion (and I speak with the frankness of sincere friendship), I should like it never the worse if in one or two of the letters Latin was less introduced, provided the sense could without much difficulty be given in honest English. I hope Mr. B. White, who I suppose is still your neighbour or your guest, finds his health before this time perfectly re-established. I beg my best respects to him, and to Mr. T. White, and, in one word, to all at Newton and Selborne. * * * I owe you indeed many, many thanks for your most obliging friendship and hospitality, which you will permit me to present with every good wish for your welfare.

I am, dear Sir,

  Your very sincere and faithful servant,

    R. CHURTON.

LETTER XIII.

FROM MR. CHURTON TO GILBERT WHITE.

Williamscot, Banbury, July 31, 1788.

Dear Sir,

You were kind enough in your last letter not to require an immediate answer; yet I made a discovery about a week ago which I did intend to communicate earlier. Do not be alarmed; it is not the *hibernacula* of the *Hirundines* that I have found out, nor even the longitude, though I did indeed meet with a person at Higham Ferrars who told me he had discovered that, and the perpetual motion, and to square the circle. My discoveries are of a much more humble nature, and what any other travelled gentleman, even if he did not ride a black horse but a pale *white one*, might have made. In the course of my travels I came to Bourn, a small market town in Lincolnshire. Inquiring for curiosities, "You have heard, I dare say," said a decent man in the street, "of *Bourn well head*, a spring that turns three mills in the space of a mile," I think he said, but certainly in the parish. I went to see it; and I will extract the account of it from my as yet *inedited* journal. "You might take it at first for a stagnant pool; but there are no runners (as a man called them) into it, and the water is most clear and beautiful, in extent perhaps 30 yards by 20; and one if not two copious streams run out of it (I believe they mostly run into one; but the streams are divided in some places for the convenience of the town): yet it is in the midst of a flat country, and I question whether there is any land higher than this as much even as three feet within as many miles. Indeed the sides of the pool are some of them higher than the adjacent land, and seem to have been raised either to give the streams issuing hence the direction wished or greater force, or for both purposes. There are 'trenches,' as they call them, close by, which perhaps surrounded this noble spring. The 'castle-yard' is adjoining on the side next the town. The largest extent of the intrenchments in a quadrangular form is beyond. An elderly man told me there are many very fine springs in the parish; the town doubtless has its name from this spring. The mills are 'undershot;' and one of them is not above a hundred yards from the well-head, though by the stream (that winds about) it may be more. There is higher land (perhaps it may be called a hill) about three miles off, perhaps not quite so much, and in appearance a wood upon it." I send you this account, as it confirms your etymology of Selborne, if it needs confirmation; and if you think so you may perhaps mention this in a note, if the work is not entirely finished. I have not looked to see whether Camden says any thing about Bourn, but it is likely he does. * * *

Your obliged servant,
R. CHURTON.

LETTER XIV.

FROM GILBERT WHITE TO MR. CHURTON.

Selborne, Oct. 14, 1788.

DEAR SIR,

I SNATCH this opportunity, by means of Mr. Ventris, who is going to leave us, to return you thanks for your kind enquiries, and to inform you that my brother was mending very fast of his first complaint, but was seized last night with a sharp fit of the gout, which we trust in the end may do him good. The new Rector talks of coming to Faringdon to reside immediately, tho' he is not yet in possession. We are glad to hear that you got well to Coll.

Y^r very humble servant,
GIL. WHITE.

LETTER XV.

FROM GILBERT WHITE TO MR. CHURTON.

Selborne, Dec. 3, 1788.

DEAR SIR,

THERE is an old maxim, which poor dear Mrs. Etty now and then made use of, that when once "Stir up we beseech thee, O Lord, the wills of thy faithful people," &c. had been read and passed over, the festival of Xtmass came creeping upon us before we could be aware. Being reminded by this wise saw, I began to think that I would write to neighbour Churton, and invite him to S., when your agreeable letter came in.

It is a very flattering account that you give of the reception which my book met with at Caversham and your lodgings. There is reason to wish that the work may find many more such candid readers: if not, what is to become of the Editors, who have spared no expense in *getting* it *up*, and who have printed off a large impression?

I am now reading every day yr friend Dr. Townson's discourses, which give me, as you engaged that they would, singular satisfaction: there is an acumen, and nicety of critical discernment, not often to be met with. In his sermon, p. 282, I am particularly charmed with the author's remarks upon the use Xt made of his parables, and the reasons why they were so nicely adapted to the taste of his hearers!*

We have just heard that Miss and Reb. Chase were on the wing for India. Their motive must be, no doubt, a view of settling in the married state. Celibacy has something in it so abhorrent to the sex, that they will flie from pole to pole to

---

* [The reference is to Dr. Townson's 'Discourses on the Four Gospels,' which were at that time much celebrated. Dr. Townson was a Fellow of Magdalen College, Oxford, and Rector of Malpas, in Cheshire, Mr. Churton's native place. He became Archdeacon of Richmond, and died in 1792.—T. B.]

avoid it. However, let their fate be what it may, I wish them happy.

Pray bring what you transcribe respecting the κορωνη and χελιδων; some use may possibly be made of it. I rejoice to hear that Dr. Chandler is well. I most readily condole with you on the sad calamity that has befallen at Windsor; and pray to God that He will be pleased speedily to restore the King to a right use of his faculties. Should the nation be long deprived of one of its states, so necessary to the constitution, such a spirit of party, it is to be feared, will break forth, as may make what we remember of political struggles a mere *civil game* to what may ensue.

Mr. Loveday has just written me a letter, in which he says, "If in the perusal any things should occur worthy of remark, such observations shall be transmitted to Selborne." Now pray tell that gent. that any strictures from such a quarter will be most gratefully received; and be sure to add, that could such have been obtained before publication, they would have been deemed inestimable. Pray come on the 24th; for if you cannot be as regular in your migrations as a ring-ousel or a swallow, where is the use of all your *knowledge*? since it may be outdone by *instinct*. When Ld Botetourt was Governor of Virginia, a slave, meeting him, pulled off his cap, and made him a bow, which the benevolent peer returned. Good God! says a by-stander, does your L^{d}ship pay any regard to such a wretch? By all means, says the good nobleman: would you have me outdone in common civility by a negroe? Mrs. J. Wh. joins in respects to you and J. Etty; and to Mr. Ventris, when you see him.

Yr most humble servant,
GIL. WHITE.

LETTER XVI.

FROM MR. CHURTON TO GILBERT WHITE.

Malpas, July 31, 1789.

Dear Sir,

* * * Since my last I have heard of many instances of the great havoc which the long frost of last winter made with fish in ponds. My brother says he has observed them in former frosts when a hole was made in the ice, appear at it almost dead, and after continuing there a short space, swim away very alertly. But last winter was far worse. I should have been glad to have seen your Goossander and Dun-diver, if they were as beautiful in plumage or as curious in their formation as the speckled diver which I did see; and more beautiful or more curious I think they hardly could be. At Whitsuntide I went to Cambridge to examine old manuscripts; but when I was there I saw some other curiosities; and amongst the rest I was pleased to see the skeleton of a speckled diver in the anatomy school. Dr. Harwood*, the Professor of Anatomy, shewed me this among his collections; and I think it was done by himself. The feet with their web were entire. * * *

Mr. Gough's 'Camden' I have only had leisure just to look into, but it seems a truly Herculean opus. Mistakes are unavoidable in much shorter works; so that if this have some, as it is said to have, it is far from being wonderful. He was of Bene't College, Cambridge, and I am not certain whether the master did not tell me that he was a pupil of his. His father died when he was young, and his mother was a rigid presbyterian, and he was brought up among persons of that stamp.

* [Sir Busick Harwood, M.D., of Christ's College, Cambridge, was Professor of Anatomy in the University from 1785 to 1814. On his death his private collections were purchased by the University, and with them originated its present Anatomical Museums. His osteological specimens were not numerous, and that spoken of above no longer exists.— A. N.]

When he was entered at Cambridge, and had been at prayers, he turned to his Guardian who went to fix him there, and said with some emphasis, "This is a very rational form of worship," or words to that effect; and I hope his approbation of what so highly deserves it continues unabated. When I was in town at Easter I saw Mr. Gough twice and had great reason to be pleased with him. I had been told he had a plate of our founder's monument. This was not true; but, though I had heard an account of him rather different, I found him extremely civil and communicative. He came to the coffee house and sat with me half an hour.

I was much obliged to Mr. B. White, Jun., for a seat for myself and a friend to see the procession to St. Paul's; but I will not attempt to describe that truly magnificent spectacle, of which you have had a better account by word of mouth from those who saw it†. * * * *

I am, with comp^{ts} to Mrs. J. White, to the family at Newton, &c. &c., Dear Sir,

Your sincere humble servant,
R. CHURTON.

P.S. I believe Dr. Loveday desired me to say with his comp^{ts} you should have any notes Mr. L. had made, or himself, on the History of Selborne.

LETTER XVII.

FROM GILBERT WHITE TO MR. CHURTON.

Seleburne, Sept. 1, 1789.

DEAR SIR,

YOUR letter of July 31st lies before me, and informs me that you are now breathing your native air, which, I hope, will agree with you: Malpas will moreover, I trust, prove a

---

† [This was on the occasion of the King, George III., going to St. Paul's to return thanks for his recovery, April 23, 1789.—T. B.]

mother to you, and **not a step-mother**. The reason that Edm^d White delayed **his journey to Oxford was** the badness of the weather, which broke-up the party; however he went himself on the last day of term but one, and took his degree on **the last** day. I rejoice to hear that y^r good friend Dr. Townson continues so well at his advanced time of life; and **desire my** respects to him. As to Dr. Chandler I have heard from him twice in the course of this summer, and **have** looked him out an house, the best in Alton: he seemed in his last to pay some attention to my information; but I have doubts about his settling, and do not depend on him as **a** neighbour. **He at** present **is much embarrassed by the** troubles in France, which would render **a journey through** that kingdom truely dangerous. He **talked in his** last of going up to Basil, and so down the Rhine to Holland. While I was in town I turned over Mr. Gough's 'Camden': it is truely a Herculean labour: no wonder that there should be some mistakes. In the map of Hants I saw *Wetmer* Forest instead of *Wolmer*. Were I to live near you I verily believe I should make an ornithologist of you. **I have just** found out that the country people **have a notion that the** *Fern-owl,* or *Eve-jarr,* which they also call a *Puckeridge,* is very injurious to weanling calves by inflicting, as it strikes them, the fatal distemper known to cow-leeches by the name of puckeridge*. Thus **does this harmless,** ill-fated **bird fall under a** double imputation, **which** it by no means deserves,—in Italy, of sucking the teats of goats, where it is called *Caprimulgus*; and with us of communicating a deadly disorder to cattle. But the truth of the matter is, the malady above mentioned is occasioned by the *Œstrus bovis,* a dipterous insect, which lays its eggs along the backs of kine, where **the** maggots, when hatched, eat their way through the **hide of the beast into the flesh, and** grow **to a large size. I have just talked with a man who says he has been called in, more than once, to** strip **the calves that had died of the puckeridge; that the** ail or complaint **lay along the chine, where the** flesh was full of

---

* [These observations on the *puckeridge* will be found almost verbatim in the "Observations on Birds," Vol. I. p. 439.—T. B.]

purulent matter. Once I myself saw a large rough maggot of this sort taken out of the back of a cow. These maggots in Essex are called *wornils*. The least attention would convince men that these birds, weak and unarmed as they are, cannot inflict any harm on kine, unless they possess the powers of animal magnetism, and can affect them by fluttering over them. Pray ask y^r brother whether he knows the bird and the distemper, and whether Cheshire men are persuaded that the latter is occasioned by the former. We had experienced a most lovely wheat-harvest; but now there is rain, which will respite the partridges for one day at least. As soon as we came from town my house became full of visitors; we have had Mr. and Mrs. Sam Barker from Rutland, and Miss Eliz. Barker, a fine young woman, who is allowed to be a very good lesson-player on the harpsichord. They left us last Tuesday. We now expect my Bro. Tho. White and family. My brother, I hear, is very well. Pray present my respects to Dr. Loveday, and tell him I should be very glad to see any notes or remarks made by him or his venerable father on the history of Selborne: could they have been procured before publication, they would have been more valuable, because I might then have availed myself of their corrections. My book is still asked for in Fleet Street. A gent. came the other day, and said he understood that there was a Mr. White who had lately published two books, a good one and a bad one; the bad one was concerning Botany Bay, the better respecting some parish. The bookseller recommended the parochial work; and told the enquirer that he did not believe the author ever had been at Botany Bay, or had ever written about it.

Mrs. J. White joins in respects. Mr. and Mrs. Ed. White are gone to Ramsgate in Kent, a watering-place on the coast. Mr. and Mrs Taylor are here. We have again a very fine crop of hops.

Yr most humble servant,
GIL. WHITE.

LETTER XVIII.

FROM MR. CHURTON TO GILBERT WHITE.

Brasen-Nose, Oct. 25, 1789.

Dear Sir,

The date of your last and still unanswered letter I am ashamed to mention. However, though I have not written to you, I am glad to hear my friend Miss Reeve has been seeing you. Very learned and, I hope you think, very civil, a knight's eldest daughter with perhaps a thousand pound for every year of her age, or at least half as many. Hendon House near Maidenhead is in a most charming country, and as yet perhaps a *non-descript*. As you are perfectly acquainted with every quadruped and bird and insect and flower near Selborne and have introduced them to the public and to immortality, it will be a pleasant circumstance to vary the scene, and add celebrity to Windsor and its neighbourhood.

> "Methinks I see thee straying on the 'thicket
> And asking every' bird that roves the sky
> 'If ever it have' seen fair Selborne's down.''

I cannot say but I am interested in this expected *migration*. I can then whip over to see you often and take a dinner or a bed for a single night and return to college. But Selborne is a long way off. And yet it is worth going a long way to see, if it agrees at all with the account which a very curious and interesting book in my room gives of it. You must know that I am reading this work with great avidity in the very few leisure moments that I can find or steal, and I am only sorry that the Index to a volume containing such a variety of useful and authentic information is not much more copious. If you are acquainted with the writer of this " good book,'' you may tell him, with my humble service, that I hope to be able to give him some papers that may help in the second edition to remedy this single defect. But it is time to answer your queries in regard to the distemper called "*Puckeridge*." I consulted my brother and other persons on this subject and minuted down the particulars he gave me, in which others also concurred. The name of *Puckeridge* is unknown in Cheshire. The disease along the chine, or rather the maggots that cause it, they call "worrybrees"* and a single one "worrybree." But they are so far from thinking these maggots prejudicial, that, on the contrary, they judge the calf that has these "worrybrees" in the back less likely to be *struck* (as they call it) with the *hyant*, which is or is considered a distinct disorder. When they are affected with this it is perceivable by the hand; for the skin is hard, and rustles (if you know that word) under the hand when rubbed by it. Sometimes there is one or more spots of this nature, and sometimes the body is almost covered with them. When the skin is taken off, the flesh in those parts is like jelly. It is deemed almost incurable, and they die in a few hours. My brother never knew or heard of more than one instance of a calf thus stricken recovering. That was but slightly affected, perhaps in a single spot; and the owner took the skin off the part and put in a rowel, or something of the sort. This disorder prevails most in Spring and Autumn, and commonly in calves of the first or second year, seldom in older cattle. Quid existimas de hac questione, an Puckerigium sit Hyantium? and whence comes this remarkable word? Are the Hyades supposed to cause it? I have heard the expression planet-struck, but whether of this disease I am not sure. In Cheshire they call calves the first winter *twinters*, in the second year *sterks*. The last is common, the other growing obsolete. I take it to be a contraction of *two winters*; for it is applied to them not as soon as calved, but when, if they were calved in winter, they are two winters old.

Dr. Loveday had a letter, about six weeks ago, from Dr.

---

* [The *Œstrus bovis* is commonly known in many parts of England by the name "breeze." This is derived from the A.-S. "briose," which had originally a similar signification. The additional term "worry" refers, of course, to its effect upon cattle when attacked by it. Of the word "hyant" I can find no trace.—T. B.]

Chandler, still at Rolle, but talking of moving, but yet, if possible, more unsettled in his plans than ever. You mention jack-daws building in **rabbit-burrows**. It is not equally extraordinary, but perhaps you may not know that they build in Elden hole, a **perpendicular** aperture in a rock, about 90 yards deep, in Derbyshire. I did not take any of their nests, nor, indeed, did I see any; but I heard them chattering most loquaciously, and perhaps "disturbed their ancient solitary reign," by throwing stones into their little **kingdom, when I was in** Derbyshire about 5 years ago. I go to town on Saturday and return the Monday se'nnight. I shall probably hear of you in Fleet Street, and in **a short time, I hope** (though I am unreasonable to expect it), be favoured with a letter. You will be so good **as** to remember me with **my best wishes and** respects to Mr. T. White, who, I understand, is now with you, as also to Mr. Edm. White &c.

I am, dear Sir,
Your sincere and much obliged humble servant,
R. CHURTON.

Dr. Bostock has gained a Chancery suit and another son. Remember me to Miss Reeve when she calls next.

LETTER XIX.

FROM GILBERT WHITE TO MR. CHURTON.

Selborne, Dec. 4, 1789.

DEAR SIR,

Tho' Oxford appears to my timid apprehensions to recede every year farther and farther from Selborne; yet to you, who are in the prime and vigour of life, Selborne ought not to be one inch more removed from Oxford than when I first knew you: therefore we shall depend much on seeing you at Xtmass as usual. I have much to say to you: for surely we live in a most eventful and portentous period; when wars, devastations, revolutions, and insurrections crowd so fast upon the back of one another, that a thinking mind cannot but suppose that providence has some great work in hand! But of all these strange commotions, the sudden overthrow of the French despotic monarchy is the most wonderful—a fabrick which has been now erecting for near two centuries, and whose foundations were laid so deep, that one would have supposed it might have lasted for ages to come: yet it is gone, as it were, in a moment!!

These troubles naturally put me in mind of Dr. Chandler, who, the last time we heard of him, was at Brussels, in a most uncomfortable situation, having his baggage seized and his papers tumbled about, for which he was in great concern. A man of his resolution and address, and who, by his long voyage to the Levant, has, as it were, been inured to dangers and difficulties, might by himself make his way thro' all the misrule and uproar that prevail in all the provinces of the Netherlands: but the case is very different where a man has a wife and infant to protect and take care of; and therefore I heartily wish that he and family were safe at home. My account of our visit from Miss Reeve, who paid us a great compliment and did us much honour, I knew would make you and Mrs. Ventris smile: I could tell you also, if I had a mind, of a great honour received from Lady Coterel Dormer. You are very kind in taking the trouble, amidst all yr busy hours, of enlarging my index: when I had carryed it to its present bulk, I desisted out of pure modesty, thinking I should swell the vol. unreasonably; but, to say the truth, when I showed it to my Bro. he expressed a wish that it had been fuller: it was then too late.

Your *worry bree* is undoubtedly a corruption of *breeze* or *breese*, a synonymous word with the *gad-fly*, well known to naturalists: as to *hyant*, we know nothing of the term, or of the distemper intended thereby. When I was at Elden hole I remember to have seen daws flying from out that horrible and tremendous chasm. These birds, thought I, are wise in their generation: for here they may breed uninterrupted from age to age, since the most roguish boys dare not interrupt their ancient inaccessible kingdom.

Are you a *Whiteist*; or a Badcockist? for I hear every man in Oxford must be one or the other. I can tell you how you may do Edm^d White a good office. When he and wife were in Oxford, last summer, they quartered at the Bear-inn, where they left behind them the first vol. of the first edition of *Dilly's prose elegant extracts*: it is a very odd-shaped vol. in 4to, somewhat like a music book. If you could recover this book, it would be received with thanks.

Mrs. J. Wh. and I join in respects to you and James Etty; and in best wishes to Mr. Ventris, who, we hope, is recovering his health and strength very fast. When does Bp. W. Smith, yr founder, appear? We long to see you a biographer, and to read the result of your painful and curious enquiries.

Yr obliged and humble servant,
GIL. WHITE.

When you write, present my respects to Dr. Loveday and Dr. Townson. How I wish that we had such a man as either of them living at Selborne!

LETTER XX.

FROM MR. CHURTON TO GILBERT WHITE.

Brasen-Nose, Dec. 13, 1789.

DEAR SIR,

Your excellent letter deserves a much better answer than I have time or ability to honour it with. But I can assure you of one thing, which you, in your kindness to your friends, will be glad to hear of. I depended upon having the pleasure, V.D., of spending my Christmas at Selborne before your obliging invitation arrived, and on that account declined Dr. Loveday's invitation to pass the holidays at Williamscot, where, however, I hope to be for two nights towards the latter part of this week, and then, after speaking twenty pounds worth of Latin on St. Thomas's day, and eating mince pies with the Principal, to set off for Reading, Tuesday the 22nd, and proceed for Selborne next day. So far so good. But this is not all. I inquired for the volume left at the Bear; and it is no discredit to the house that the book was found safe in a drawer in the bar, and is now safe in my room waiting to be put up in my portmanteau. Dr. Chandler, wife and son arrived at Clapham about a week ago safe and well, as you will probably have heard by some means or other before this reaches you. Alas! I have only found time to read, and with much satisfaction, the History of Selborne, but not to do much in enlarging the Index. However the loss is less material as Dr. Loveday has already or will soon undertake it, and do it effectually. Marvellous indeed is the state of things on the Continent, and when and how good order and good government will be restored is far beyond my ken. But an all-wise Providence, which can controul the madness of the people, superintends the whole, and seems, as you justly remark, to have some great work in hand. I did not know till you told me that the "fatherlanders," as the papers call them, seized Dr. Chandler's portmanteaus; and I was afraid they were lost through negligence. I hope they were restored; but I have not positively heard so. I shall be glad to learn the particulars of the honour received from Lady Coterel Dormer, and other matters, *ex ore tuo*. And among these I am curious to hear more about *worry-breese* and *hyant*; for if the distemper known in Cheshire by the latter name never visits Hampshire, the reason is well worth enquiring after. I scarcely know whether to call myself a "Whiteist" or "Badcockist." The pamphlet of Dr. Gabriel I think clearly shews that considerable assistance was received, but by no means ascertains the degree. In my own notion the Professor* would do well to state fairly and explicitly what was composed by Mr. Badcock, and what by himself; and there are also some circumstances in his behaviour respecting the note which should be stated in a more

* [White was Professor of Chemistry at Oxford. He was no relation of Gilbert White's.—T. B.]

favourable way to his character, if they can consistently with truth.

Bishop Smith sends his compliments and thanks you for your kind enquiries; but he says he shall not " walk the town numbering good intellects " till next winter. His biographer has lately had so much unavoidable business on his hands respecting the living that he has had no time to talk with the dead. I am, dear Sir,

Your very sincere and obliged humble servant,

R. CHURTON.

LETTER XXI.

FROM MR. CHURTON TO GILBERT WHITE.

Brasen-Nose, April 1, 1790.

DEAR SIR,

I AM just returned from a short visit at Williamscot, whence I fully purposed writing to you; but yesterday, which was to have been the day for that friendly office, I was totally disabled by a bad headach, and the effects of it are far from being gone at present. But expected business made my return indispensable; and, now I am here, lest this memorable day should lose its *honour*, the previous arrival of another fellow made my presence unnecessary. However, let me discharge my debt to you as well as I can; for if I wait longer, you will perhaps be on your way hither before this can reach Selborne. Dr. Loveday and all his family are very well. He desires his best respects to you, and had a hearty laugh at the excellent parody of the " young idea," which I had forgot to mention when I was there before for two nights. The presents were wrapped and directed at Fletcher's shop; but yours, it seems, was spelt by some " unlettered muse." I gave them a list of names with proper orthography. Your little niece had a happy escape from a perilous situation. I remember being astonished at Mr. Warton's remark which you quote, where he says " Milton had a very bad ear." As to such lines as that you cite (" Shoots invisible virtues ") I think they were studiously rough, slow, or redundant, though I do not pretend to determine the exact reason of each, or undertake to justify them. But, as you justly observe, " his manly melodies cannot but charm the judicious reader." And if smoothness is required, Pope himself, with all his polishing, has no lines more smooth and flowing than the inimitable passage where he describes " smooth Adonis from his native rock run[ning] purple to the sea." And the numbers and pauses are so charmingly varied that they " bring no satiety." I have not heard who is the author of the ' Village Curate.' I think Mr. Crabbe wrote on some such subject; but of him I know but little, only I have heard his poetry commended. I thank you for your intelligence about Dr. Chandler, from whom Dr. Loveday and myself hear *almost* as often as when he was at Rolle or at Rome. I am the more surprised at his not writing to me as I sent him some papers to Fleet Street about W. of Wainfleet, which he should have told me he had received safe. I am glad you are likely to have him for your neighbour during the summer; and I hope your fine views will make him cease to languish for Switzerland or Italy. I hope I shall have the pleasure of seeing you here next week. My motions are a little uncertain. My immediate senior is going on Monday to look at Stoke Bruern near Towcester, which his senior has declined accepting, and he wants me to go with him; but it is cold sport looking at a living one is not sure of; and, to say the truth, I do not at present wish for the option, as I wish to finish the lives of our Founders before I accept a living from their society; and I have at present only written about four score quarto pages of the bishop's life, and not yet translated him to his second Bishopric. Excuse a shabby letter. Present my best respects to Mrs. J. White and to the family at Newton. I am, Dear Sir,

Your very sincere and most obliged servant,

R. CHURTON.

LETTER XXII.

FROM MR. CHURTON TO GILBERT WHITE.

Brasen-Nose, Oct. 5, 1792.

Dear Sir,

I take the opportunity of enclosing, in a packet to Dr. Chandler, the two papers which I promised you, one of them the epitaph of Mr. Ray, the other the extract from Aristotle about the *Caprimulgus*, to which I have added a passage about swallows in Italy that I thought you would like to see. Mr. Armetriding, Rector of Steeple Aston, is a naturalist, and as I called there, driven by stress of weather, on my way from Williamscot, we were talking about the said *Caprimulgus*, and he took down Mr. Pennant and seemed to think that *Dor-hawk* was one of the best names there given to this bird. For other news of no great moment, I refer you to Dr. Chandler's letter. I hope you are quite well, and beg my best regards to Mrs. J. White.

Do you agree with Mr. A[rthur] Young about Lunar years? that every nineteenth is in its general features of wet, dry, &c. very similar? This Mr. Armetriding shewed me in Mr. Young's annals, where, from some minutes of the nineteenth year backward from the present, it appears that that also was extremely rainy. I have heard the same remark of the Lunar Cycle before. I am, Dear Sir,

Your sincere humble servant,

R. CHURTON.

The following are the passages referred to in the above letter enclosed to Dr. Chandler:—

[Ray was born at Black-Notley, in the county of Essex, in the year 1628, and died in the same place early in the year 1705. "He was buried (according to his own desire) in the church of that parish, where a monument is erected to him." The epitaph is too long for insertion here *in extenso*. It commences with the following words:—

'Eruditissimi viri Johannis Raij, A.M.
Quicquid mortale fuit,
Hoc in angusto tumulo reconditum est.
At Scripta
Non una continet Regio :
Et Fama undequaque celeberrima
Vetat mori."

It concludes

"Sic benè latuit, benè vixit Vir beatus,
Quem Præsens Ætas colit, Postera mirabitur."

See the 'Memorials of Ray,' edited by the late Dr. Lankester, including Dr. Derham's 'Remains and Life of Ray.' Printed for the Ray Society, 1846.—T. B.]

Extract from Dr. Townson's Journal of his Tour into Italy, &c.
1768, 1769.

"May 27 (1769), to Frescati [from Rome] 14 m.; about half way is Pontano, famous for a good dairy and belonging to the Borghese family. Here it was that Mr. Morison, once dining in the farmhouse in the large room swarming with swallows, was desired not to disturb them because they cut the air and rendered it wholesome, as the people of the family alledged to him."

ὁ δὲ καλουμενος αιγοθηλης εστι μεν ορεινος, το δὲ μεγεθος κοττυφου μεν μικρῳ μειζων, κοκκυγος δ᾽ ελαττων. τικτει μεν ουν ωα δυο η τρια το πλειστον, το δὲ ηθος εστι βλακικος*. θηλαζει δὲ τας αιγας προσπετομενος· ὁθεν και τοὔνομ᾽ ειληφε. φασι δ᾽, ὅταν θηλαση τον μασθον αποσβεννυσθαι τε, και την αιγα αποτυφλουσθαι· εστι δ᾽ ουκ οξυωπος της ἡμερας, αλλα της νυκτος βλεπει.

ARISTOT. Hist. Animal. l. ix. cap. xxx.

Quem caprimulgum appellant, avis montana est, magnitudine paulo major quam merula, minor quam cuculus, moribus mollior. Parit ova duo, aut tria cum plurima. Sugit caprarum ubera advolans, unde nomen accepit. Cum suxerit, uber extingui, capramque excæcari aiunt. Parum clare interdiu videt, sed noctu perspicax est.

---

* The Latin translator, meaning, I suppose, to express this clause, has "moribus mollior," and introduces it as if it followed " ελαττων," "paulo major quam merula, minor quam cuculus, moribus mollior," which may be true: but besides the deranging of the text, which is the same in other editions, I fear this is not the sense of the Greek ; for βλακικος seems rather an impeachment of the *understanding* than an encomium on the gentleness of our friend the *Caprimulgus*. And yet ηθος, again, belongs

P.S. Mr. Lewis has often seen the *Caprimulgus*; and behold he said "It was a *foolish* bird." Here is your ηθος βλακικος again; and it is a curious coincidence of opinion with our friend the Stagyrite, whose works certainly our friend the Bank Director never read. The ground of this notion I leave to your better discernment to account for. I will only propose one query. Does it appear foolish to English eyes, as it did anciently to Grecian, because it hovers about, and if put up, soon lights again, and does not wisely consult for its own safety by distant flight?*

LETTER XXIII.

FROM GILBERT WHITE TO MR. CHURTON.

Selborne, Nov. 15, 1792.

Dear Sir,

As your own account of the bad state of your health, written to Dr. Chandler, gave us much concern, so in proportion your late cheerful letter to Mrs. Chandler afforded us no small satisfaction. I sit down now to invite you to spend *part* of your Xtmass holidays with us. But as yr usual time of vacation, when divided into two parts, will be little or nothing, we hope you will be able to extend yr furlow. You have of late years paid me a compliment for varying my

---

rather to the qualities of the heart than those of the head. *Judicent eruditi*†. For the rest, exclusive of the fabulous account of sucking goats and drying up their milk, &c., the author seems to give in a few words some very characteristic traits of the bird described. But here I am the rhetorician teaching Hannibal the art of war.

* [It entirely depends upon the time of day when it is observed— stolid and stupid in the day time, bright and active in the evening, as stated above by Aristotle. See Letter XXII. to Pennant and note (Vol. I, p. 65).—T. B.]

† [Aubert and Wimmer translate the expression "und hat ein schoues Wesen."—A. N.]

phrases of invitation: but all those terms of words are exhausted, and I have now nothing left but the plain, honest assertion of wishing to see you, as often and as long as you can make it agreeable and convenient to yourself.

I return you my best thanks for your quotation from Aristotle, of which I hope to avail myself soon; and for a *correct* copy of the inscription on the tomb of the great Mr. Ray. It is pleasant to hear that friends to Genius are still to be found, who, at periods, are ready to repair and beautify the monument of departed worth, nor suffering it to be effaced with weeds and filth. However his *works* will be, as the inscription says, the most lasting monument of his fame. Every time you come, I have been provided with a new book for your inspection. In some respects you will think Mr. Arthur Young's Journey in France reprehensible; and will not always subscribe to his politics. However the writer is a man of observation, and has a curious chapter on Climate. In three summers he threaded every corner of that vast kingdom, and made an excursion thro' the Pyrenees to Barcelona, and another over the Alps and Apennine to Turin, Venice, Florence, &c. Mr. Y., I fear, is no friend to us parsons. Mr. Marsham has just sent me a long letter; but he complains of infirmities. Mrs. J. Wh. joins in good wishes; and desires respects to the provost, when you see him; and to the Cox family, Dr. Nowell, &c. &c. With all due regard I remain,

Yours affectionately,
GIL. WHITE.

Take care of your health, and don't study too hard. When the shell of yr House is compleat, insure it. A friend of mine at Salisbury has just had a house, not quite finished, burnt to the ground. It was to have cost 4000!

LETTER XXIV.

FROM MR. CHURTON TO GILBERT WHITE.

Brasen-Nose, **Jan.** 23, 1793.

SUCCESS to matrimony! and *Caprimulgus*. My friend and tutor Dr. Radcliffe is married. Mr. John White is married: and I cordially congratulate Mrs. J. White on the occasion, as well as yourself on having another agreeable addition to the *small* number you before had of nephews and nieces. My friend Mr. Banner, I think I perceive, will certainly take Dudcote, if no better living falls during his option. Powerful are female attractions and engagements! However, the living is more desirable than he expected. I wished to write sooner but could not; and now have scarcely a moment to spare; and tomorrow I must go about my buildings and enclosures at Middleton. Dr. Loveday's family were well recovered from the measles. The Provost of Oriel and Mrs. Everleigh and daughter were very well when I drank tea there on Sunday. Mrs. Cox is very well. Mr. Cox when I called was in bed with a cold and gout, but not an unkindly fit. Mr. Ventris somewhat better, but not perfectly well. You perhaps have heard of me in London from Fleet Street. I slipt into the pit to see his Majesty &c. in the Theatre, where I never had seen them before. We were all loyalty. "God save the King" twice after the play and twice after the entertainment. "Rule Britannia" twice. The Queen sang, the King beat time, &c.

The alien bill gives great content in London. There was lately a report that poor Mr. Page was dying, and a canvass out of the university began for the Speaker and Sir W. Scott, Dr. Wenman having declined. Should there be a vacancy I hope you will think of one who, besides having been my brother pupil and class fellow—potent recommendations—is universally esteemed as the best Speaker the H. of Commons ever had.

I have seen or dreamt (I hope not the latter) that Ld Malmsbury is descended from a daughter of Robt Townson, B^p of Salisbury. But I cannot find it in any peerage here; and I wrote to Fleet Street; neither can they find it. If it is in your peerage I shall be very glad if you will inform me of it. I want to have it in a note which is or should be now set for the first proof. When I saw it I neglected it, not knowing I should want it, or thinking I could turn to it again; but it is gone. Such a treacherous thing is memory, or mine at least. I hope your cold is entirely gone and you are in perfect health, of which I earnestly wish you long enjoyment, and of every other blessing, and am with comp^{ts} at the vicarage, Dear Sir,

Your ever obliged servant,
R. CHURTON.

LETTER XXV.

FROM GILBERT WHITE TO MR. CHURTON.
(Endorsed by Mr. Churton, "The last from my dear Friend.")

Selborne, Jan. 26, 1793.

DEAR SIR,

HAD you staid only one day longer with us, you would have seen J. White and his bride, late Miss Louisa Neave, who, having been married at Downton near Sarum by Mr. Lear, set off immediately for this place. We have good reason to be pleased with our new relation, who is sensible, intelligent, and in her carriage much of a gentlewoman. She is a nice needlewoman and also a proficient in music, and can shoulder a violin, out of which she brings a good tone, but could find no one to accompany her. Tho' her husband is in stature one of the sons of Anak, yet he has made choice of a little wife, who, we all agree, in her profile resembles Miss Reb. Chace, but exceeds her in her make and turn of person.

I am much obliged to you for the latin translation of the *Caprimulgus*, which will be useful, but have lost my advocate with the R.S.; for on my applying to Mr. Barrington, who used to present my papers, he writes me word that he has no longer any interest with that society, but that he will endeavour to find a member that shall present my dissertation. This circumstance, as you may imagine, is not so pleasant as when I had a friend who was often one of the Council, and ready to abet my compositions.

There is, indeed, a curious coincidence of opinions between Mr. Lewis and the Stagyrite! for which I cannot advance a better reason than what you have mentioned yourself. Yet can I not call that a *foolish bird* which knows the times and the seasons, and conducts its migrations over seas and continents with such accuracy and success, and, impelled by all the feelings of στοργη and affection, is ready to repel intruders, and by menaces to defend to the best of its power its callow and helpless young!

I have told you sometimes of an old physician at Southtŏn, Dr. Speed, who used to go over once every year, in May, to the Isle of Wight, for which period the people used to reserve their ails. For these last two winters my coughs have been kept till y^r arrival, and then became so bad that without your kind assistance I could not have continued my duty. When you left me I had some dread about the ensuing Sunday; but, thanks be to God, my infirmity ceased on the Saturday, and has not been bad since. As soon as y^r letter came we turned to my peerage book, but could find no traces respecting Lord Malmsbury; so I conclude that his creation was subsequent[*]. Possibly before now you may have recovered y^r stray idea, that has wandered away, or lay snug in some corner of y^r memory.

Mrs. J. Wh. joins in best respects and wishes to you and all friends.

Yours sincerely,
GIL. WHITE.

Sad work in France!!

[*] ["The Earl's ancestor, James Harris, Esq., of the Close, in Salisbury, married Gertrude, d^r of Robert Townson, Bishop of Salisbury, and died 1679, aged 74."—*Debrett*. The creation dates only from 1788.—T. B.]

LETTER XXVI.

FROM MR. CHURTON TO GILBERT WHITE.

Brasen-Nose, Mar. 15, 1793.

Dear Sir,

Dr. Loveday has robbed me of the pleasure of making you a present of a book lately published here, to which we are jointly in different ways contributors. I hope you will have received your copy from Fleet Street, attended with one from Dr. Chandler, before this reaches you. And now let me canvass you for the author of the Village Curate. Mount your steed—not immediately though, but next Michaelmas—and assist in putting the Professorship of Poetry in hands worthy to be employed where Lowth and Warton have appeared before. At the same time, please to inform Dr. Chandler that he owes me a letter, and that he must get Dr. Bingham and every vote he can for a gentleman of his own college. The Trinity gentlemen, Mr. Clarke and Kett, have each secured some votes in our college and elsewhere by starting so early; but we are at least two to one in Br.-Nose friends to Mr. Hurdis (or his merits rather, for we were not acquainted with him), and several active in his cause.

I am very glad you are so well pleased with your neice. Mr. Armetriding is just married to a Lancashire lady, about the size of her you mention; but there is not one of our Northamptonshire rectors married, nor, I fear, going to be. The house at Middleton has begun, or is about to begin, to rise, after having stood still during the winter.

Best respects to all friends.

I am ever, with truest esteem, dear Sir,

Your most obliged servant,

R. CHURTON.

MISCELLANEOUS LETTERS.

LETTER I.

FROM THE REV. JOHN LIGHTFOOT[*] TO GILBERT WHITE.

Uxbridge, Jan. 27, 1773.

DEAR SIR,

I KNOW not how to excuse myself for not answering your kind letter before, when I tell you that I returned to Uxbridge from my northern tour the 24th of Octob., now a quarter of a year ago. I had a most agreeable journey, and experienced all the varieties from venison down to barley bannocks, and from claret down to whisky, and from a good feather bed to one of heath with a plaid for a covering. We visited sixteen of the Western Islands, and the greatest part of the continent on the western coast from Annandale to the borders of Strathnavern in Sutherland, which is 58′ 20″ north, where the snow was lying on the mountains in August. The red deer inhabited the summits of these mountains, and the roebucks the birch

---

[*] [The Rev. John Lightfoot was a well-known botanist. He accompanied Pennant in his second tour in Scotland in 1772, and afterwards published his 'Flora Scotica,' in 2 volumes 8vo, in 1785. He was a Fellow of the Royal Society and one of the founders of the Linnean Society. He officiated at Uxbridge for many years, and died there in 1788.—T. B.

Lightfoot is also known as the first who clearly distinguished the Reed-Wren, which he described (Phil. Trans. lxxv. p. 11) by the name of *Motacilla arundinacea*. This epithet, having been already applied by Linnæus to a species strictly congeneric, has had to be dropped, and the bird now bears the name of *Acrocephalus streperus*.—A. N.]

woods at their base. The ptarmigans are seen as tame as pigeons among the grey barren rocks, and the black and red game swarm upon the heaths, and the eagles descend from the precipices and prey upon them all. The *Saxifraga nivalis, stellaris, aizoides,* and *oppositifolia,* with the *Arbutus alpina, Hieracum alpinum, Cucubalus acaulis, Sibbaldia procumbens,* and *Azalea procumbens, Cherleria,* and some others are the herbage of the Scottish Alps. The *Arbutus uva-ursi* covers the inferior rocks, and the *Narthecium ossifragum* with the *Juncus* and heath tribe cover the low grounds. This may serve to give you a faint idea of the country of Scotland towards the northern extremity. In many parts of the Lowlands, especially near Edinburgh, great improvements are made in agriculture, and in many places, as in the Lothians and the Carse of Gowrie, the country is as fertile as in England. In other places, where the soil will permit, the inhabitants are making large strides towards improvements. The people every where, from the duke to the peasant, are extremely hospitable and kind to strangers; so that a recommendation to one gentleman will frank a traveller all through Scotland. I am now employed in making out a Scotch Flora, to be annexed to a Fauna of the country by my companion, Mr. Pennant. I shall be glad to have it in my power to comply wth y^r obliging invitation to Selborne; but I cannot now say when I shall be able to enjoy that happiness.

The bee which frequents the *Stachys,* from the account Mr. Yalden has given me of it, must be the *Apis manicata,* from the spines at its tail.

I am S^r wth great respect,

Your most obed^t hble serv^t,
JOHN LIGHTFOOT.

LETTER II.

FROM THE REV. JOHN LIGHTFOOT TO GILBERT WHITE.

Uxbridge, Sept. 13, 1773.

Dear Sir,

I have this summer, in company with Mr. Banks, been making the tour of North and South Wales. I set out in June, and am but lately returned; this will apologize for my not acknowledging your obliging letter sooner. I owe you many thanks for your repeated and most friendly invitations; but I know not how we have affronted the Fates that they will not suffer us to have an interview. This summer I have no chance of seeing Hampshire, having enough to tye me by the leg for many months to come. I flatter myself, however, that I shall yet have it in my power to visit Selborne again, and bilk these troublesome Fates, that have so often come between us, which I shall be heartily glad to do, as I hate to be cheated by such jilts. I hope you are of the same mind as myself, and will endeavour to return them the compliment by trying your luck at Uxbridge. I met with our friend Skinner at Brecnock in the beginning of August. He talked of paying a visit to his brother at Purley near Reading, about Michaelmas. He uses little exercise, and suffers much from the gout.

The *Dodecatheon meadia* is an elegant plant, and singular in its appearance; it is a native of Virginia and Carolina, and was first named *meadia* by Mr. Catesby in compliment to Dr. Mead; but Linnæus, finding afterwards the old name of *Dodecatheon* made use of by Pliny for a plant agreeing in description very nearly with this, chose to adopt the ancient name for the *generic*, and retain the known received name for the *trivial*, according to a rule laid down in the 'Critica Botanica.'

Wales in general behaved to us with great politeness. We had fine weather through the whole journey; we found the greatest hospitality, a multitude of plants, and five or six not before discovered in South Britain, though I had before seen them in Scotland. Snowdon was very complaisant; three times we scaled his highest top, once enveloped so in clouds that we could not discern each other at twenty yards' distance; but no sooner had we refreshed ourselves with our necessary *viaticum* than the clouds withdrew, and gradually discovered to our wondering eyes the most glorious prospects we ever beheld. The clouds all settled about the midway on one side of the hill, appearing like great volumes of snow in various grotesque figures, one behind another. The sun tinged their edges with silver, and darting his rays now and then between them discovered the rugged precipices, the limpid lakes, the trembling cascades, and distant vallies beneath us. Over them appeared the British Alps, the Irish Sea, and coast of Ireland, almost all North Wales; the coasts of Lancashire and Cumberland, with the Islands of Anglesea and Man, appeared at one view, like a great map spread beneath us. In short, we seemed as if we had been snatched up into the clouds, and were taking a peep on the little world below.

I am, with great respect,

Y^r most obliged and h^{ble} serv^t,

JOHN LIGHTFOOT.

LETTER III.

FROM MR. SKINNER TO GILBERT WHITE.

(Extract.)

Purley, Berks, Oct. 17, 1773.

DEAR SIR,

* * * In July last I spent an evening with Mr. Banks[*] and Mr. Lightfoot at Brecknock. They had been botanizing from Bristol through the counties of Glamorgan, Carmarthen,

[*] [This was a year after Banks's visit to Iceland with Solander, Lind, and Von Troil.—T. B.]

and Pembroke, and had been very successful. In the environs of St. Vincent's Rock only (visited by every botanist) they found three new British plants (one of these the *Arbutus uva-ursi*), and afterwards several others that were either new or very dubious, as not having been found by the botanists of the present age. Among the former *Sison verticillatum*, a common plant in the meadows of Carmarthenshire; among the latter *Cheiranthus sinuatus, Adiantum capillus-veneris,* and a species of *Festuca* unknown to Linnæus, but figured in Ray's 'Synopsis,' tab. 17. fig. 2, vide p. 403, with several others I do not immediately recollect. They were bound to Snowdon, in the neighbourhood of which they proposed to spend five or six weeks. I have not heard of their success; but as Lightfoot had with great accuracy collected the names and places of the curious plants they hoped to find from Ray and others, I presume the journey, which was new to both of them, has not been thrown away. You have, I believe, seen Lightfoot since his Scotch tour with Mr. Pennant, and of course have heard that he discovered many plants that had escaped the Scottish botanists. * * *

The last advice I had of Linnæus was from Mr. Banks, to whom he had written but a little before, with a good deal of chagrin, for not having sent him the specimens of the South Sea plants he had promised him. He said " He was an old man, and that if it was intended he should ever see them, the sooner they were sent the better." Mr. Banks thought he was well.

I am, with great esteem,

Your obliged friend, &c.,

R. SKINNER.

LETTER IV.

FROM LIEUT.-COL. MONTAGU [*] TO GILBERT WHITE.

Easton Grey, near Tedbury,
Gloucestershire, May 21, 1789.

Sir,

Although I have not the pleasure of being personally acquainted with you, yet I flatter myself you will pardon this intrusion of an enthusiastic naturalist.

I have been greatly entertained by your 'Natural History of Selborne,' in the ornithological part of which I find mention made of three distinct species of willow-wren. Can you inform me if they are (besides the common) the larger and lesser pettychaps of Latham, neither of which is described by Pennant in his 'Brit. Zool.'? He describes a species with the inside of the mouth red, which I cannot make out in this country; those two of Latham's I believe I have got, as far as I can judge from the description that gentleman favoured me with; but his sedge-wren I am at a loss for, as he describes the sedge-bird besides of the 'Brit. Zool.' I should esteem it a particular favour, if you have it in your power, if you will favour me with the weight and description of the two uncommon willow-wrens.

I was induced to take this liberty as you say you are a field-naturalist, and perhaps may have it in your power to assist me in my present pursuit. I am collecting and preserving the birds and their eggs of these parts, a provincial

---

[*] [George Montagu was born in 1755, and died June 20, 1815. At the time of his writing this letter he must have been collecting the information which he afterwards published in his 'Ornithological Dictionary.' The Lady Jane Courtney (or Courtenay) subsequently mentioned in the letter was his mother-in-law, whose daughter he married when he had completed his eighteenth year. Lady Jane was sister to Lord Bute, First Lord of the Treasury on the accession of King George III. See the memoir of Montagu, by Mr. Cunnington, in the 'Wiltshire Magazine' for 1857 (vol. iii. pp. 87-94).—A. N.]

undertaking, in which I am got forward; and as those of Hampshire and Wiltshire are nearly congenial (the coast excepted), some species, I presume, are more frequently met with about you than with us: will you excuse my mentioning a few that, should they fall in your way, you will confer a considerable obligation on me by favouring me with them? The hawks and owls are difficult to get: of the former I want all except the sparrow, kestrel, and common buzzard; of the latter all the eared and the little owl. The great butcher-bird and wood-chat, goat-sucker, cross-bill, aberdevine or siskin, and spotted gallinule, with many cloven and web-footed water-birds, together with any of their eggs; and as you mention snipes and teals having bred near you, their eggs would be highly acceptable, with others not common which you may be able to obtain. And in return, Sir, if there is anything in my former or future researches that can afford you any satisfaction, I shall with the greatest pleasure communicate.

That amiable and excellent naturalist, Mr. Pennant, has done me the honour to say I have discovered some things to him he was not before acquainted with; and I flatter myself I have other notes in store when I have more time to write to him more largely upon the subject: this you know is the busy season for a naturalist, and the days are not half long enough for me.

A fine morning called me from this, and in my walk my ears discovered a note I had never before heard. I pursued it into the thick of a wood, and after much difficulty killed the bird as it was delivering its song (if I may so call it) from the branch of an oak tree. It proved to be a willow-wren; its note was very different from any I had ever heard before, somewhat resembling a note of the blue titmouse. It was continued without variety, like the grasshopper-lark, but not quite so quick or shrill, nor of so long duration; between each song the pause was considerable. The note I confess has staggered me; but its appearance, size, &c. discover nothing new. The common willow-wren, I well know, has two very distinct songs. The first after their arrival, before they are paired, I considered as their love-call; the other their soft courting or amatory song. As to shades of colour or size, this species varies considerably: that of the male is much brighter and stronger than the female, and is considerably larger, and even in the same sex there is frequently a visible difference. I last year killed a male and female together when the former was in pursuit of the latter, on her first arrival in the spring (as I suppose you know all our male migrating birds precede the female in their vernal visit): in these the great disparity in weight and difference in colour would have puzzled exceedingly, had I not, some time before the barbarous act was committed, paid attention to the addresses of the male. I confess I am not acquainted with the one you describe with the primaries and secondaries tip't with white; and if you are still of opinion that it is a distinct species, I should be obliged to you for it. If you should favour me with any small bird at this season, it will be advisable to wrap it up in soft paper sprinkled or damp'd with vinegar, first laying the feathers smooth, and then covered with thicker paper wetted with the same; this will preserve the bird moist, and defy putrifaction. Larger birds should be carefully opened with a sharp knife from the vent upwards, laying the feathers back with damp paper to prevent their being blooded in taking out the intestines; a little alum or nitre should be thrown in, and the incision stopped with tow; and if a little of the alum and tow were put into the mouth it would ensure its coming to me in good order. If you have any conveyance to Bath, and you will take the trouble of directing either a box or basket for me to the care of the Right Hon. Lady Jane Courtney, Milsom Street, Bath, I shall get it the day after it arrives there. Notwithstanding my post town is in Gloucestershire, I live in Wiltshire, where I shall be happy to obey any commands from you, and remain, Sir,

Your most obedient humble servant,
G. MONTAGU.

LETTER V.

FROM LIEUT.-COL. MONTAGU TO GILBERT WHITE.

Easton Grey, June 29, 1789.

Dear Sir,

I am exceedingly obliged to you for y^r polite favor, and hope you will excuse the mistake in my address.

I am not able to boast of being an ornithologist so long as you, tho' I have delighted in it from infancy, and, was I not bound by conjugal attachment, should like to ride my hobby to distant parts; yet I agree with you that naturalists in general attempt to explore too wide a field, their researches are too extensive; whereas if persons well qualified were to confine themselves to particular districts, the natural history compiled from provincial authors would no doubt throw much light on the subject.

I confess myself greatly obliged to your work for the discovery of the *third* species of *willow-wren*, and for the first determined separation of the other two species, with whom I was perfectly well acquainted as to their notes, but suspected that the same bird might produce both notes promiscuously. Your work produced in me fresh ardour, and with that degree of enthusiasm necessary to such investigations; I pervaded the interior recesses of the thickest woods, and spread my researches to every place within my reach that seemed likely. I was soon convinced of two distinct species, not only in their song, but in size, colour, eggs, and materials which w^h they build their nests. The third species, which you seem to think peculiar to your beech-wood, I flatter myself I have at last discovered to be an inhabitant of this part; but they are very scarce and partial. Three only have I discovered; two of which I brought down with my gun from the top of tall oak-trees in a thick grove interspersed with brambles. From the reiterated note, somewhat resembling the blue titmouse, and their colour being more vivid than the other species, I do not hesitate to pronounce it that discovered by you, tho' mine did not possess any white on the tips of the quills or secondary feathers; but the belly was of a pure white, and the action of its wings agrees with your description: besides the note it commonly uses, which is somewhat grasshopper-like, it produces a shrill note five or six times repeated, something like the marsh titmouse. One pair of these birds I only know of about this neighbourhood now, the nest of which I have not been fortunate enough to discover; if one should come across you it would be an acquisition to me. You are perfectly right in saying the name of *willow wren* is very inadequate. I wish you had given them distinct names, as I believe you have the merit of the original discovery. I am surprized Pennant makes no mention of these acquisitions to ornithology, as your letter of the 17th of Augt 1768 long preceded his last edition. Do you know if Latham has adopted them in his 'Systema Ornithologiæ,' which is to come before the publick next winter? I am at a loss for your *blue pigeon-hawk*, especially as you say its female is brown; from its place of resort I should conceive it to be the hen harrier, and that you had not corrected the mistake of other ornithologists, and which Pennant fell into in his first ed^n, where he gave the *ring tail* for its female. Their habits and manners are nearly the same, only the latter perch on trees occasionally; its white rump at once distinguishes it from all others when skimming over the surface of the earth like the hen harrier: it makes its nest on the ground. Both these species we have, but not preserved, not having been able to procure them, being scarce and shy. Perhaps I may be favoured with them from you, as well as their eggs, another season, if not this. If y^r *pigeon-hawk* should be different, I should be obliged to you for further explanation, as I am not acquainted with it by that name.

The *Hobby* which I want has been called the blue hawk by some: its eggs I should be glad of, and are no doubt to be found in y^r extensive woodlands; they are scarce with us.

You were surprized at my requesting of you the Goatsucker. 'Tis true many parts of this county produce them, but they are not to be commanded; and one bird in the spring or before Augt is worth twenty after that time, as most birds are then out of feather, and the young ones are seldom in full or proper plumage till the winter, and many till the ensuing spring. In the latter end of October birds have mostly done moulting and are again fit for preservation; however, scarce birds are at all times acceptable, till a better supplies its place. Since I wrote I have killed the male Goatsucker; and as I have seen a female, it is probable I may get it, but the egg I despair of in this part.

I remain, d^r Sir,

Your much obliged and faithful humble servant,

G. MONTAGU.

LETTER VI.

FROM GILBERT WHITE TO JOSEPH BANKS, ESQ.

Selborne, April 21, 1768.

SIR,

LEST you should suspect that I forget my promise, I take the liberty to acquaint you that either the unusual dryness of last month, or some unknown cause, has retarded the blowing of the *Lathræa squammaria**; it does not yet appear above ground as usual. When it had appeared I should not have failed to have sent you a specimen in a pot, with the *Coleoptera* its constant attendants; but now I find last night, by a letter of Mr. Pennant, dated from Chester, that you are going to leave the kingdom again in pursuit of natural knowledge.

I was greatly in hopes once that both you gentlemen would have honoured me with your company this spring; but now it seems that unless Mr. Skinner of C.C.C. should happen to come (as he has partly promised), I must plod on by myself, with few books and no soul to communicate my doubts or discoveries to.

* [This plant has grown in a garden in the village within the last few years, and appears to have been parasitic upon the roots of plum-trees.— T. B.]

The district round this village is, I believe, a fine field for botany; we have great variety of aspects and soils, and many rocky lanes for capillaries; not to mention chalky hills, sands, bogs, clays, and vast woods. Here are moors that have hardly been trodden by the foot of a real botanist, where I should suspect some rare matters may be discovered. As to summer birds of passage, we have a good variety. I think I can shew 16 or 17 species round the village, among which are three species of the *Motacillæ trochili*. The vast large bats are beginning to appear, some of which I shall endeavour to procure.

After wishing you all health and a great deal of success and satisfaction in your laudable pursuits, a prosperous voyage and safe return,

I remain, &c., &c.

[This letter is printed from a copy in Gilbert's writing, but without signature.—T. B.]

CORRESPONDENCE OF ROBERT MARSHAM,

OF STRATTON-STRAWLESS, IN THE COUNTY OF NORFOLK,

AND GILBERT WHITE.

[AMONG the numerous letters to and from Gilbert White kindly communicated to me by Algernon Holt White, Esq., were ten from Mr. Marsham; and it happened that exactly the same number of autograph letters from Gilbert White to Marsham, constituting together very nearly the complete correspondence, were in the possession of the Rev. H. P. Marsham, of Rippon Hall, near Norwich, the great-grandson of White's correspondent. The interchange of copies of the respective letters enabled the Council of an excellent local natural-history society at Norwich * to publish the correspondence entire. I have selected the following brief notice of Mr. Marsham from some account of his life by Thomas Southwell, Esq., the secretary of the society.—T. B.

"Though far less celebrated than his contemporary and correspondent, Robert Marsham is already known to most readers of White's posthumously published writings as one to whose opinions the latter often referred in terms of respect. Born the 27th of January, 1708, Marsham began to show early in life a fondness for arboriculture. On the 8th of February, 1728, he entered as Fellow-commoner of Clare Hall in the University of Cambridge, but it does not appear that he ever proceeded to a degree. He subsequently went abroad (in 1737 and 1738) and travelled through France, Switzerland, and Italy, amassing much knowledge, which

* [The Norfolk and Norwich Naturalists' Society.]

he was able to apply in various ways in after time. He succeeded to his father's estate of Stratton-Strawless, some seven miles north of Norwich, in 1751, and from that period he seems to have travelled much in England, particularly where any remarkable trees were to be seen, and, as these letters prove, he became acquainted with many of the most eminent men of his day. Arboriculture was evidently his ruling passion, and he delighted in making experiments in the growth of trees, the results of which he communicated from time to time to the 'Philosophical Transactions' of the Royal Society, of which he was elected a Fellow on the 9th of June, 1780, and admitted on the 31st of May, 1781. He died on September 4th, 1797.

"The 'Indications of Spring,' of which he left such a remarkable register, afforded him annually recurring topics for remark; and the value of his observations on rural subjects may be well estimated by White's exclamation:—'O, that I had known you forty years ago!'"*]

LETTER I.

MARSHAM TO WHITE.

Stratton, near Norwich, July 24, 1790.

Sir,

I HAVE received so much pleasure and information from your ingenious Nat. Hist. of Selborne, that i cannot deny myself the honest satisfaction of offering you my thanks: & i hope you will excuse the liberty that i have taken.—I have kept a poor imperfect journal above 50 years; but it has been chiefly confined to the leafing and growth of Trees; & was undertaken by the advice of my most estimable friend the late Dr Hales. By that i find that Linnæus's Disciples, & their followers, are mistaken in their supposed rule of Nature, *that all plants must follow in order.* For you see by the Indica-

---

* [With the permission of Professor Newton, I have selected many of his notes from the copy published by the Society.—T. B.]

tions of Spring in the last Vol. of the Phil. Trans. which, very imperfect as it is, the R. S. did me the honour to print, there are reverses of many days.

Sir, i was much pleased with your Poetry in the Sum^r Evening walk.—I hope you will excuse my asking you some questions for my information. The copulation of Frogs as you describe*, is the manner of Toads with us: & i never saw Frogs so engaged.

By your account of the Swallows on the 29 of Sep. 1768, i presume that you believe in their migrating: & there are very strong reasons to believe so of some other Birds. Many Woodcocks are found by the Light-houses in Norfolke in the Autumn, that are kill'd by flying against the Lights: and the Earl of Orford † informed me, that the Landgrave of Hesse sent him a ring taken from the leg of an Heron, with Ld. O. name upon it. This is certain proof of the Heron's going from England: & myself have seen (coming from Holland) a Wagtail (Motacilla alba) flying about the Ship, seemingly at ease, when out of sight of Land. These, without Admiral Wager's ‡, Adanson's §, & Smith's ‖ (the earliest account that i can recollect in print), are sufficient for migration: & the proofs for torpidity are also undoubted. So we may conclude

---

* [See Letter XVII. to Pennant, Vol. I. p. 50, and note.]

† [George Walpole, grandson of the great Sir Robert, succeeded his father as third Earl of Orford in 1751, and died in 1791. He was a celebrated falconer, but is perhaps better remembered from having sold the valuable collection of pictures at Houghton to the Czarina. At his death the title passed to his uncle, the well-known Horace Walpole.—A. N.]

‡ [The evidence of Admiral Sir Charles Wager, some time First Lord of the Admiralty, was first published by Collinson in 1760 (Phil. Trans. li. p. 461), and has been often reprinted.—A. N.]

§ ['Histoire Naturelle de Sénégal &c.' Par M. Adanson. Paris: 1757, pp. 67 and 90. Reference is again made to his observations further on. They have been frequently quoted.—A. N.]

‖ [The reference here is probably to a passage in 'A Natural History of Nevis, and the rest of the English Leeward Charibee Islands in America, &c. In Eleven Letters from the Rev^d Mr. [William] Smith, &c. Cambridge: 1745.' Writing of Nevis and St. Christopher's, the author says (p. 51) "at the Sun's declension towards the Tropick of Capricorn from the Equator, we are visited by a few Swallows."—A. N.]

they are both true. But the annual increase in the Swallow tribe, which are lost in Winter, affords unaccountable difficulties to be cleared. I have had 4 pair attending my house as many years as i can remember. If these produce two broods of 5 young, you see, Sir, one pair only will in 7 years produce above half a million, 559870 birds: yet the number every Spring appears the same. If both broods are destroyed, surely the old birds would be lessened by accidents, so as to be perceptible. If the early or the latter brood is preserved, you see the next Spring Birds will be as 5 to 2, if all the old Birds are lost: and i never heard that Swallows are increased in any part of the Globe. We know that all the carnivorous Birds drive off their young as soon as they are able to provide for themselves; & i conclude that fish-eating Birds do the same: for when i was on the charming Lake of Killarny, i was told that was the case of a pair of Ospreys*, that yearly nested on an Island of Rock in that Lake. But we cannot suppose the Swallow tribe can fear the want of provision. S^r, you know the Fern Owl is one of the Spring Birds, and appears here as the latest comer. I used to have many in my Woods; but since the long and severe Winter of 88 i have had very few. Is not this a presumptive proof of their torpidity? & that they were destroyed by the severity of that Season?—Your account of the 26 & 27 of March in 1777 was felt here in Lat. 52·45°, but no Swallows appeared. The 27th was insufferably hot, with a S.W. Wind; which changed in the afternoon to N.E. with a thick Sea-hase, and my Therm^r sunk above 20 degrees in 3 or 4 hours. The greatest change I have ever observed.—I find in 1776 Jan. 31. your Therm^r sunk to 0. mine of Farenh^t was at 16. & in 1784 Dec. 10. when your Dollands was 1. below 0, mine was but at 10. The coldest Air I have measured was Jan. 19. in 1767. when it

* [The name "Osprey" seems to have been formerly applied to the Sea-Eagle (*Haliaetus albicilla*) as well as to what is now known as the Osprey (*Pandion haliaetus*). Thompson states (Nat. Hist. Ireland, i. p. 29, note) that no proof of the latter's building either at Killarney or elsewhere in Ireland had to his knowledge yet been recorded, and it is therefore likely that the species spoken of in the text was the former.— A. N.]

was down to 1. I take the liberty to tell you this, as it possibly may be entertaining to you to see the difference of less than 2 Degrees of Lat.

Sir, when you print a 2^d Edition, (which the merit of your Book will certainly soon demand) i hope in your description of the Holt Forest, you will pay a compliment, justly due, to the Oak by Ld Stawel's Lodge: as I suppose it is the largest in this Island. I went from London on purpose to see it in 1759, and again occasionally in 1778. 'Tis at 7 feet full 34 feet in circumf. & had not gained half an inch in 19 years; yet i could not see it was hollow. If i measure right i make 14 feet length of the Holt Oak to contain above 1000 feet, viz. above 320 feet more than the Cowthorpe Oak, which Dr Hunter, in his Edition of Evelyn's Silva*, calls the largest in England. I early begun planting, & an Oake† which i planted in 1720 is at one foot from the earth 12 feet. 6. inches. 0 round; and at 14 feet (the half of the timber length) is 8.2.0. So measuring the bark as timber, gives 116F.$\frac{1}{2}$, buyers measure. Perhaps you never heard of a larger Oake & the planter living. I flatter myself, that i increased the growth by washing the stem, & digging a circle as far as i supposed the roots to extend, & spreading saw-dust, &c. as related in the Phil. Trans‡.—I wish I had begun planting with beeches (my favourite Trees as well as your's), & i might have seen large trees of my own raising. But i did not begin Beeches 'till 1741, & then by seed; & my largest is now, at 5 feet, 6.3.0 round, & spreads a circle of + 20 yards diam^r. But this has been digged round & washed, &c.——The last Winter was so very mild with us, that the leaves of many of my very young Oaks preserved their green into April, & a large Hawthorn (headed the preceeding year) has its old leaves now: which i never observed before, in any deciduous trees: tho'

* ['Silva: or, a Discourse of Forest-trees, &c. By John Evelyn. With notes by A. Hunter.' New Ed., 2 vols. 4to, York: 1786; vol. ii. p. 197. The Cowthorpe Oak grew on an estate belonging to Lady Stourton, and an engraving of it is given by Hunter, who introduces his notice of it by a reference to "My ingenious friend Mr. Marsham."—A. N.]

† [See Vol. I. p. 467.]

‡ [Vol. lxvii. p. 12.—A. N.]

I once had a second leafing of a Hawthorn about Xmass. But those leaves faded before Spring. I sent the account to Sʳ J. Pringle when P.R.S.*, but he thought it not strange. Sir, if you do not take the Ph. Trans. if you please i will send you a copy of my Indicaᵐˢ of Spring, as it may be an amusement to you, to see how much later we are in Norfolk than you are in Hampshire. I am, with great esteem,

    Sir, your most obedient,
        humble servant,
           R: MARSHAM.

P.S. I have now in a Stack of Blocks a young Cuckow fed by a water-Wagtail.

LETTER II.

WHITE TO MARSHAM.

        Selborne: near Alton: Hants,
                Aug: 13th: 1790.

GOOD SIR,

As an author I have derived much satisfaction from your kind & communicative letter; and am glad to hear that my book has found it's way into Norfolk, & that it has fallen into the hands of so intelligent and candid a reader as Yourself, whose good word may contribute to make it better known in those parts. I am glad that You happened to mention your most estimable friend the late Dr. Steven Hales; because he was also my most valuable friend, and in former days near neighbour during the summer months. For tho' his usual abode was at Teddington; yet did he for many years reside for about two months at his rectory of Faringdon, which is only two miles from hence; & was well known to my Grandfather and Father, as well as to myself. If I might presume to say that what you see respecting the copulation of toads is, I think, a mistake, you will pardon my boldness: because the

* [Sir John Pringle, President of the Royal Society, 1772–1778.—A. N.]

amours carryed on in pools and wet ditches in the spring time are performed by *frogs*, which are more black and bloated at that season than afterwards. As to toads they seem to be more reserved in their intrigues.

With regard to the annual encrease of swallows, & that those that return bear no manner of proportion to those that depart; it is a subject so strange, that it will be best for me to say little. I suppose that nature, ever provident, intends the vast encrease as a balance to some great devastations to which they may be liable either in their emigrations or winter retreats. Our swifts have been gone about a week! but the other hirundines have sent forth their first broods in vast abundance; & are now busied in the rearing of a second family. Myself & visitors have often paid due attention to the oak in the Holt, which ought indeed to have been noticed in my book, and especially as it contains some account of that forest. You have been an early planter indeed! & may safely say, I should think, that no man living can boast of so large an oak of his own planting! As I had reason to suppose that actual measurement would give me the best Idea of y^r tree, I first took the girth of my biggest oak, a single tree, age not known, in the midst of my meadow: when tho' it carries a head that measures 24 yards three ways in diameter, yet is the circumference of the stem only 10 ft. 6 in. I then measured an oak, standing singly in a Gent's outlet at about two miles distance, & found it exactly the dimensions of your's. After such success you may well say with Virgil,

"Et dubitant homines serere, atque impendere curas?"

In an humble way I have been an early planter myself. The time of planting, and growth of my trees are as follows. Oak in 1731—4 ft. 5 in. Ash in 1731—4 ft. $6\frac{1}{2}$ in. Spruce fir in 1751—5 ft. 0 in. Beech in 1751—4 ft. 0 in. Elm in 1750—5 ft. 3 in. Lime in 1756, 5 ft. 5 in.* Beeches with

---

* [A more particular account of these trees, with a note on their present condition, will be found at p. 468 of Vol. I. I am sorry to have to add that the fine spruce was, on the 20th of February of this year (1877), blown down, being uprooted in consequence of the softening of the soil by the long-continued rains.—T. B.]

us, the most lovely of all forest trees, thrive wonderfully on steep, sloping grounds, whether they be chalk, or free stone. I am in possession myself of a beechen steep grove on the free stone, that I am persuaded would please your judicious eye; in which there is a tree that measures 50 feet without bough or fork, and 24 feet beyond the fork: there are many as tall. I speak from long observation when I assert, that beechen groves to a warm aspect grow one-third faster than those that face to the N. & N.E., and the bark is much more clean and smooth. About thirty or forty years ago the oaks in this neighbourhood were much admired, viz., in Hartley wood, at Temple, & Blackmoor *. At the last place, the owner, a very ancient Yeoman, thro' a blameable partiality, let his trees stand till they were *red-hearted* & *white-hearted* 3 or 4 feet up the stem. We have some old edible chest-nut-trees in this neighbourhood; but they make vile timber, being always *shakey*, & sometimes *cup-shakey* †.

As you seem to know the *Fern-owl*, or *Churn-owl*, or *Eve-jar*; I shall send you, for your amusement, the following account of that curious, nocturnal, migratory bird ‡. The country people here have a notion that the *Fern-owl*, which they also call *Puckeridge*, is very injurious to weanling calves by inflicting, as it strikes at them, the fatal distemper known to cow-leeches by the name of *puckeridge*. Thus does this harmless, illfated bird fall under a double imputation, which it by no means deserves;—in Italy of sucking the teats of goats, where it is called *Caprimulgus*; & with us, of communicating a deadly disorder to cattle. But the truth of the matter is, the malady above mentioned is occasioned by a dipterous insect called the *œstrus bovis*, which lays it's eggs along the backs of kine, where the maggots, when hatched, eat their way thro' the hide of the beast into it's flesh, & grow to a large size. I have just talked with a man, who says, he has been employed, more than once, in stripping calves that had dyed

---

* [See Letter I. to Pennant, Vol. I. p. 4.]
† [See the observations on chestnut timber, Vol. I. p. 471.—T. B.]
‡ [This subject is fully treated of in the "Observations on Birds," Vol. I. p. 439, and in a letter to Mr. Churton, Vol. II. p. 213.—T. B.]

of the *puckeridge*: that the ail, or complaint, lay along the chine, where the flesh was much swelled, & filled with purulent matter. Once myself I saw a large, rough maggot of this sort squeezed out of the back of a cow. An intelligent friend informs me that the disease along the chines of calves, or rather the maggots that cause them, are called by the graziers in Cheshire *worry brees*, & a single one *worry bree*. No doubt they mean a *breese*, or *breeze*, the name for the *gad-fly*, or *œstrus*, the parent of these maggots, which lays it's eggs along the backs of kine.

But to return to the fern-owl. The least attention & observation would convince men that these poor birds neither injure the goat-herd nor the grazier; but that they are perfectly harmless, & subsist alone on night-moths & beetles; & thro' the month of July mostly on the *scarabæus solstitialis*, the small *tree-beetle*, which in many districts flies and abounds at that season. Those that we have opened have always had their craws stuffed with large night-moths & pieces of chafers: nor does it any wise appear, how they can, weak & unarmed as they are, inflict any malady on kine, unless they possess the powers of animal magnetism, & can affect them by fluttering over them. Upon recollection it must have been at your house that the amiable Mr. Stillingfleet kept his *Calendar of Flora* in 1755. Similar pursuits make intimate & lasting friendship. As I do not take in the R. S. T. I will with pleasure accept of your present of a copy of y^r *Indications of Spring*. Hoping that your benevolence will pardon the unreasonable length of this letter, on which I look back with some contrition, I remain, with true esteem, Your most humble servant,

GIL. WHITE.

Any farther correspondence will be deemed an honour.

LETTER III.

MARSHAM TO WHITE

Stratton near Norwich.
Aug. 31.-90.

Sir,

I am much obliged to you for your entertaining & instructing letter; & pleased to find that you was acquainted with Dr Hales: and i believe all men that knew him esteemed him. I have had the good fortune to know most of his family.

Sir, i conclude that you are right, & that i was mistaken about the amours of the toad: but so are my acquaintance also. Frogs, you know, generally leap or jump; now the people we talk of, only walk or creep; and i thought that i had particularly observed their swelled bellies. But if i should live to another Spring, i will examine them with more care.—With respect to the measures of your Trees, i hope we take them at the same height from the Earth, viz. 5 feet, and then your's and my Trees are nearly equal. Your Oak, I see, gains about 9 tenths of an inch yearly for 58 years, and mine the same in the Grove: but one transplanted from that Grove (which was sowed Acorns in 1719,) gains above 14 tenths, as it was last Autumn 8 F. 3 I. when the largest in y^r Grove is but 5 F. 3 I. Such is the benefit of transplanting! or perhaps, to speak honestly, the giving as much room as the Tree requires.—I am surprised that your Trees can increase so fast in chalky or stony soil. But perhaps your charming Beech of 50 feet to the head was not of your own planting. I wish i could get a peep at it, & make my bow to you; but all the pleasure of rambling is ended with me; I having been lame now near two years, & not once out of the Village in that time. For i have a stony complaint also, which keeps me from a carriage.—Mr. Drake has a charming Grove of

Beech in Buckinghamshire*, where the handsomest Tree (as i was informed by a friend to be depended on) runs 75 feet clear, & then about 35 feet more in the head. I went on purpose to see it. 'Tis only 6 F. 6 I. round, but straight as possible. Some Beeches in my late worthy friend Mr. Naylor's† Park of Hurstmonceaux in Sussex, ran taller & much larger; but none so handsome.—Norfolk is too flat a Country to try the difference of the growth of Trees on ye cold or warm sides of hills; but i entirely agree with you in the great advantage of warmth. This County is very ungenial to Elms, which are generally hollow before they are a foot square, & Ash does not thrive with me. I have left off planting Chesnuts; but they grow quick, and, i conclude, to the largest size of any Tree in this Island. I have one i raised from the nut, which was 2 feet round at 55 high in 1781. 'Tis a very handsome plant, & holds clear above eleven yards, with a fair head. I have seen several Chesnut-trees above ten yards round; & Lord Ducie's‡ i measured above 15 yards; which i conclude is the greatest. But i find they

* [Probably at Shardeloes, near Amersham.—A. N.]

† [Francis Hare (son of a Bishop of Chichester) was born in 1713, and assumed the name of Naylor in 1734, on succeeding to the estate of his uncle George Naylor, who had bought Hurstmonceaux. In his youth he is said to have been guilty of extravagance and dissipation of every description, joining the notorious "Medmenham Brotherhood." He died in 1775, when the estates passed to his half-brother, Robert Hare, whose grandsons were the accomplished Francis, Augustus, Julius, and Marcus Hare. Hurstmonceaux Castle was destroyed by Wyatt in 1777, and now remains a ruin.—A. N.]

‡ [This magnificent Spanish chestnut at Tortworth, in Gloucestershire, has been mentioned by nearly all writers on trees from Evelyn's time to our own. The particulars of it given in the text a few lines lower down seem to be taken from Ducarel's paper ('Phil. Trans.' 1771, p. 168), where they are quoted from the 'London Magazine' for 1758 (p. 482). A very fair representation of it, taken in 1824, is given by Strutt ('Sylva Britannica,' pl. xxix.), and Loudon says ('Arboretum Britannicum,' p. 1038) that "it may, indeed, possibly have been one of those planted by the Romans." I saw it in August, 1875, and Lord Ducie kindly informs me that its "present girth is about 17 yards; but each measurement will vary, as the trunk is covered with ligneous warts, and a tape may either cover or miss one of these, thus altering its dimensions."—A. N.]

cannot bear the severe frosts. I had one of this sort, in the severe Winter of 39–40, split very near half an inch wide, where i could run a table-knife it's length into the crack: but this is quite closed; & covered with bark. To show you the growth of this kind of Tree, i have a memorandum of a former Rector of an adjoining Village, "that he planted a Chesnut Tree by his Church in 1610," which was in Autumn 1788, 19 F. 4 I, or 184 inches in 178 years. I suppose Ld Ducie's Tree may be 1100 years old, if it increased in the proportion reasonable for such a vast Tree; & might be about eleven yards round in King John's time, as tradition calls it the great Chesnut at that time.—Stillingfleet was a very estimable man. I knew him from his first leaving College. Fortune frowned on him from his birth, 'till near his end. He used for many years to visit me. His father, after the Bishop's displeasure, lived on his little Rectory in Norfolk.

Sir, in your 39th letter to Pennant you ask where the Stock-dove breeds? In Norfolk in hollow Trees*. The Fern-Owl lays its eggs on the plain Land. I think your Countrymen should be punished for laying so heavy a charge against an innocent Bird. I find a memorandum of mine of so old a date as Sep. 14. 1722. *i shot a ring-Ouzel*. This was the first my father had seen. This shows they are strangers in Norfolk. But i have seen of them twice since, in severe frost. You do me honour to accept my Indications of Spring. To explain to you, i mark leaf, as soon as the smallest leaf appears; and i name the County (if not in Norfolk), as i have observed so near as Hertfordshire, they are sometimes a week earlier than here. You see 'tis shamefully imperfect.—The equal number of the returning Swallows seems the greatest Mystery, amongst the many Mysteries that attend them.—Sir, as i live in hopes of sometimes having the favour of hearing from you, pray never again make an apology for length; every Article is pleasing to me: but I

---

* [Its breeding at Selborne is fully stated in a note on the passage referred to, Vol. I. p. 96.—T. B.]

am unreasonable to wish for so much of your time. I am, with true esteem, Sir,

    your most humble
      & obliged servant,
        R: MARSHAM.

P.S. I have had the pleasure of recommending your Work to all my correspondents.—I know no man in your County, but Mr Chute, the father of your new Member. I congratulate you that Election bustle is over; as i suppose, during the contest, ye were as inimical as young Cuckows. I presume you have read Mr Jenner's account of the Cuckow in the Ph. Trans. Vol. 78*; he handsomely disculpates the Cuckow of the want of στοργὴ.—There is a gentleman in this County of the name of Gurdon of good fortune†. The family, i suppose for some centuries, has been owners of a Village called Letton. They have lately changed the name for Dillingham.—We have the greatest flight of Swallows i think i have ever seen at this time. I heard the *flying note* of the Fern-Owl on Aug. 20.

 * [See note to Letter IV. to Barrington, Vol. I. p. 123.—T. B.]
 † [This remark doubtless has reference to the notice of Sir Adam Gurdon in the 'Antiquities of Selborne' (Letters VIII. and IX.). Mr. Gurdon of Letton, High Sheriff of Norfolk in 1789, added to his own surname that of his mother, daughter and heiress of Theophilus Dillingham, of Shelton, Beds., and died in 1820. He was succeeded by his son, who dropped the second surname. According to Sir Bernard Burke ('Landed Gentry'), the Gurdons of Letton are descended from Robert Gurdon (who died in 1343), the second and disinherited son of the above-named Sir Adam by his second wife Almeria or Ameria.—A. N.
 Gilbert White states positively and repeatedly that Gurdon had no son, and that Ameria's sons were by her second husband (Vol. I. p. 308).—T. B.]

LETTER IV.

MARSHAM TO WHITE.

Stratton near Norwich. Dec. 29. 90.

Dear Sir,

It was not for want of inclination, but want of matter, that i did not offer you my hearty thanks for the favour of your very entertaining letter of the 12th of October*. I have very lately met with some intelligence that may afford you some amusement, so wish to lay it before you.

As i knew nothing of Mr Jennor's character, & as some of his history of the Cuckow is extraordinary, i desired my very estimable friend Lord Suffield† to enquire that of Mr Hunter; he is perfectly satisfied of Jennor's accuracy. He was his Pupil & lived in his house upwards of four years. Jennor sent parts of the account of the Cuckow to Mr Hunter 18 months, or more, before they were published. Hunter has himself repeated some of the experiments, & found them correct: & this last Summer, he put a Blackbird's egg into a hedge Sparrow's nest, & left three of her own eggs; & the Sparrow hatched them & brought them all up. Mr Hunter was not perfectly satisfied, that the ejecting the young sparrows from the nest was the act of the young Cuckow only, but suspected some aid of the foster-mother: however she & the Blackbird let the young Sparrows enjoy their nest quietly. —Hunter told his Ldp. that he was now making repeated observations upon a species of the Nightingale sent to him from Germany, as a song Bird. Accident led him to suspect that this Bird could (if one may so speak) see clearly in the dark. His time of frolic is after midnight: he then hops about the Cage from perch to perch, & from the wires of one

---

* [This letter is missing.—T. S.]
† [Sir Harbord Harbord, created Lord Suffield 1786, died 1810.—N.]

side to the other side. Hunter has changed the Cage, & altered the places of the perches, & taken every precaution to exclude every particle of Light; & being shut up in the closet with the Bird, says, he hears him hop from perch to perch, & so on without ever seeming to blunder or mistake. He is almost certain of the fact*. I have transcribed Lord Suffield's words that he wrote.—From my own knowledge i can say but little, only, that on the tenth of last November, a Swallow laid dead just under the window of the room i live in; so we must see it the day it fell: & as the last of my Swallows appearing, was on the 30 of Sep. this Bird was most likely in it's torpid state, when some accident removed it. The tail was short, so i conclude it was of the latter brood. But although i have had the eaves & roof of my house searched, no bird can be found. Yet it seems unlikely that a single Swallow should hide for the winter when they are so companionable in the Summer, that you very seldom then see a single bird. So i must conclude others are hid near it. On the 17th of this month i had Turnip-flowers; which i find are earlier than i had seen before. Violets have been in flower weeks ago. But i have not marked them in my Indications of Spring. You see, Sir, that i began my work very lazily with very few articles. I believe the Elm leaves that you saw at Sunbury on the 20 of Feb. in 1750, were earlier than any i had seen. I find in my journal in 1738. the Elms had leaves on the 23 of March N.S. at Genoa; & on my landing at Antibes the 3d of April, the Rye was in ear.—If it had been my good fortune to know you 50 years ago, i am sure i should have been a wiser, & better man: & i hope 'tis not too late now.—On ye 24th i found a dark Butterfly in my keeping-room, which led me to my Indications: & find the earliest (yellow) Jan. 14 last year. The Season points to me

---

* [I am not aware of any record of these observations (though doubtless made at the time, according to Hunter's practice) having been published. From the expression used in the text the bird seems not to have been the common species of Nightingale (*Daulias luscinia*); and if not, it was doubtless the "Sprosser" (*D. philomela*), which is common in Eastern Germany.—A. N.]

to wish you many more years of health, to enjoy the honest pleasure resulting from your instructing mankind.

I remain, with great esteem, dear Sir, your obedient
& obliged servant,
R: MARSHAM.

P.S. I think you was poorly paid in 100 shillings for 100 feet of good Elm. The Beeches you mention (tho' hollow) of 30 feet round, are above ten feet larger than i have ever seen.—I had last week an account that there is now in Stonleigh Park* (amongst abundance of fine Oaks) an Oak 23 F. 11 Inches round at 5 feet. The Tree is sound & in health.

[Franked by "W. Fellowes;" endorsed by White, "Mr Marsham."]

LETTER V.

WHITE TO MARSHAM.

Selborne: Jan. 18th. 1791.

Dear Sir,

As your long silence gave me some uneasiness lest it should have been occasioned by indisposition; so the sight of your last obliging letter afforded me much satisfaction in proportion.

I was not a little pleased to find that your friend Lord Suffield corroborated the account of the Cuckoo given by Mr. Jennor, whose relation of the proceedings of that peculiar bird is very curious, new, & extraordinary.—It does not appear from y^r letter that you endeavoured to revive the Swallow, which fell down before y^r parlor-window.—I have not yet done with trees, & shall therefore add, that my tall 74 f. beech measures 6 feet in the girth at two feet above the ground. Beeches seem to me to thrive best on stoney, or chalkey cliffs, where there seems to be little or no soil. Thus about a mile

---

* [Stoneleigh near Kenilworth, now the seat of Lord Leigh.—A. N.]

& an half from me to the S.E. in an abrupt field, stand four noble beech-trees on the edge of a steep, rocky ravin, or water-gulley, the biggest of which measures 9 feet 5 inches at four feet from the ground. Their noble branching heads & smooth rind show that they are in the highest vigour & preservation. Again the vast bloated, pollard, hollow beeches, mentioned before, stood on the bare, naked end of a chalky promontory, many of which measured from 20 to 30 feet in circumference! they were the admiration of all strangers. How has prevailed the notion that all old London was built with chestnut? It is with us now vile timber, porous, shakey, and fragil, & only fit for the meanest coopery purposes. Yet have I known it smuggled into Portsmouth dock as good ship-building oak!*

The more I observe & take notice of the best oaks now remaining in this neighbourhood, the more I am astonished at the oak which you planted yourself. For there is amost noble tree of that kind near Hartely house, which I caused to be measured last week; when behold, at four feet above the ground the girth proved to be only 14 feet, when yours measured 12 ft. 6 in.! Why this fine shafted tree, with it's majestic head escaped the ax (*sic*) thirty years ago, when Sr. Simeon Stuart felled all it's contemporaries, I cannot pretend to say. If you ever happen to see the *Hamadryad* of y^r favourite Oak, pray give my respects to her. She must be a fine venerable old lady. For a diverting story respecting an Hamadryad, see the Spectator, vol. 8, p. 128.

Behind my house I have got an outlet of seven acres laid out in walks by my father. As the soil is strong, the hedges, which are cut-up, are prodigious. The maples about 35 feet in height, & the hasles & whitethorns 20, which, when feathered to the ground, were beautiful: but they now, being 50 years old, have rather over-stood their time; & besides, the severity of Decem^r 1784 has occasioned irreparable damages among the branches. Thus much for trees. Lord Stawell †

* See note, p. 266.
† [Henry **Stawell** Bilson Legge, Lord Stawell, succeeded in 1780 to the barony conferred upon his mother, and died in 1820.—A. N.]

has lately sent me such a bird, sprung & shot in his coverts, as I never saw before, or shall again. I pronounced it to be a mule, bred between a cock pheasant & a pea-hen*.

You say wood-cocks in their passage strike against light-houses on y^r coast: a Gent. tells me, that at Penzance sea-fowls frequently dash in the night against windows where they see a light.—My well is 63 feet in depth; yet in very dry seasons, as last autumn, it is nearly exhausted: yet you would be surprised to see how few inches of rain falling will replenish it again. How do rains insinuate themselves to such depths? The rains this winter have been prodigious! In Novem^r last 7 inches; in December 6 inches. The whole rain at Selborne in 1790 was 32 inches. Sure such thunder, & lightening & winds have never fallen out within your observation in one winter! Had I known You 30 years ago, I should have been much pleased; because I would have gone to have seen you; and perhaps You might have been prevailed on, when all our timber was standing, to have returned the visit. In the year 1746 I lived for six months at Thorney in the Isle of Ely, to settle an executorship, & dispose of live stock: there I lost nine oxen by their eating yew, as mentioned in my book †. I hope you will write not long hence. With the truest respect & esteem I remain,

Your most humble servant,
GIL. WHITE.

The dark butterfly which you saw was the *papilio urticæ*: it is often more early than the yellow *papilio rhamni*. At this moment the Barometer stands somewhat below 28 inches 5 tens! the rain this day has been very great from the S.E.!

---

* [See "Observations on Birds," Vol. I. p. 430 and note.—T. B.]
† [Vol. I. p. 292 and note.—T. B.]

LETTER VI.

WHITE TO MARSHAM.

Selborne: Feb. 25th: 1791.

Dear Sir,

It was elegantly remarked on our common friend, & my quondam neighbour Doctor Stephen Hales, by one who has written his character in Latin, that—"*scientiam* **philosophicam** usibus humanis *famulari* jussit." The observation was just, & the assertion no inconsiderable compliment: for undoubtedly speculative enquiries can bear no competition with practical ones, where the latter profess never to lose sight of utility.

As I perceive You loved the good old man, I do not know how I can amuse You better, than by sending you the following anecdotes respecting him, some of which may not have fallen within your observation. His attention to the inside of Ladies tea-kettles, to observe how far they were incrusted with stone (*tophus lebetinus* Linnæi) that from thence he might judge of the salubrity of the water of their wells:— his advising water to be showered down suspicious wells from the nozle of a garden watering-pot in order to discharge damps, before men ventured to descend;—his directing airholes to be left in the out-walls of ground rooms, to prevent the rotting of floors & joists;—his earnest dissuasive to young people, not to drink their tea scalding hot; his advice to water-men at a ferry, how they might best preserve & keep sound the bottoms or floors of their boats;—his teaching the house-wife to place an inverted tea-cup at the bottom of her pies & tarts to prevent the syrop from boiling over, & to preserve the juice;—his many tho' unsuccessful attempts to find an adequate succedaneum for yeast or barm, so difficult to be procured in severe winters, & in many lonely situations;—his endeavour to destroy insects on wall-fruit-trees by quick-silver poured into holes bored in their stems;—& his experiments to dissolve the stone in human bodies, by, as I think, the juice of onions;—are a few, among many, of those benevolent & useful pursuits on which his mind was constantly bent. Tho' a man of a Baronet's family, & of one of the best houses in Kent, yet was his Humility so prevalent, that he did not disdain the lowest offices, provided they tended to the good of his fellow creatures. The last act of benevolence in which I saw him employed was, at his rectory of Faringdon, the next parish to this, where I found him in the street with his paint-pot before him, & much busied in painting white with his own hands the tops of the foot-path posts, that his neighbours might not be injured by running against them in the dark. His whole mind seemed replete with experiment, which of course gave a tincture & turn to his conversation, often somewhat peculiar, but always interesting. He used to lament to my Father, how tedious a task it was to convince men, that sweet air was better than foul, alluding to his ventilators: and once told him, with some degree of emotion, that the first time he went on board a ship in harbour at Portsmouth, the officers were rude to him; & that he verily believed he should never have prevailed to have seen his ventilators in use in the royal navy, had not Lord Sandwich*, then first Lord of the Admiralty, abetted his pursuits in a liberal manner, and sent him down to the Commissioners of the dock with letters of recommendation. It should not be forgotten that our friend, under the patronage of Sir Joseph Jekyll †, was instrumental in procuring the Gin-act, & stop-

---

* [John Montagu, Earl of Sandwich, born 1718, three times First Lord of the Admiralty, and holder of that office during the very eventful period of Lord North's administration. In his lifetime he was popularly known by the nickname of "Jemmy Twitcher," from a character in Gray's 'Beggar's Opera,' but is now best remembered by the group of islands which Cook (whom he greatly encouraged) named after him. He died in 1792.—A. N.]

† [Sir **Joseph Jekyll**, born 1664. An eminent Whig statesman, and Master of the Rolls to George I. Died 1738.—A. N.]

ping that profusion of spirituous liquors **which threat'ned** to ruin the morals & **constitutions of our common** people at once. He used to say, that the hogs of distillers were more brutal than the hogs of other men; & that, when drunk they used to bite pieces out of each other's backs & sides! With due respects I remain,

Your most humble servant,
GIL. WHITE.

I did myself the honour of writing to you very lately about trees, & other matters. **This** winter **continues wet &** mild: wet springs are bad **for Selborne.** My crocus's make a fine show.

LETTER VII.

MARSHAM TO WHITE.

Stratton, March 1, 1791.

DEAR SIR,

I WAS intending to write you my thanks for the favour **of** your pleasing letter of the 18th of Jan: but waited for something to arise that might afford you some pleasure; when this day's post brought me the honour of your letter of the 25 of Feb. Every article relating to that excellent man the late Dr. Hales, cannot fail of being pleasing to me. I never saw him towards being angry, but when he talked against Gin. I think it was first from him that i heard Onions were good for people suffering with the **Stone.** I then thought **but** little about it: **but as** i have, **for two years past,** felt some painful symptoms of that malady, i often sup **on roasted** Portugal **Onions,** and hope i receive benefit from them.—My good Friend, when you touch upon Trees, you touch my mad string. My favourite Oak is 12 F. 6 I., but this is at one foot from the Earth, and Sr Simeon Stuart's* **Oak** is 14 feet at 4 feet from the Earth. The best Oak i have, is **14 F. 2 I.$\frac{1}{2}$**

* [That Sir Simeon Stuart, who owned and occupied the parish of Hartley Maudit, and who at one time represented the county in Parliament, was closely associated with the contiguous parish of Selborne, is shown by the following letter, which was addressed by him " To Mr. White, at Selebourn ;" to which is added, in another hand, " To be given to the next vicar." It is remarkable that Gilbert White, the vicar, the grandfather of the naturalist, had died in February of the same year; and, although the letter is dated eight months later, Sir Simeon could not even then have been aware that he had lost his neighbour.—T. B.

"Harteley, Nov. 22, 1727.

"S$_{IR}$,

"In the last will of my Lady Stuart my Grandmother, there is a clause *hisce verbis*. 'I give & devise to y^e L^d of y^e mann^r & the Church Wardens & Overseers of y^e poor of Harteley Maudytt Com. Southton, fifty pounds to be laid out by them on the purchase of some land or house for y^e use & intent following, that is to say y^t they the then L^d of ye Mann^r Ch Ward^{ns} & Overseers of ye poor shall procure **an able minister out of the neighbourhood of** ye s^d Parish of Harteley every year on ye day of my Death, to preach a Sermon in y^t parish Church on Death, future Judgement **or on the Resurrection from Death**. And for the Ministers pains in so doing to give unto ye s^d Minister for so doing 20^s, & y^t they, ye s^d L^d of the Mann^r Ch War & Overseers of ye Poor shall distribute amongst ye poor people of ye parish of Selebourn and ye poor people of Harteley that shall then & there be present at Divine Service ye residue of ye Rent of ye s^d Land &c. without any mann^r of Favour & Affection.' My Lady died Sep. 1699 & there has been an annuall Sermon, & ye Interest of ye s^d money, y^t is 50^s yearly, distributed according to ye s^d Will. This present year some considerable time before ye s^d Day of my s^d Lady's obit I, as L^d of ye mann^r of Harteley, ye Ch: W & Over. did, by writing under our hands, appoint Mr Long Curate of Greatham to preach ye s^d Sermon on one of ye above texts—wch when he acquainted Mr Avery therewith, he (Avery) did with some warmth refuse him, that he, nor no other w^t ever should preach in his pulpitt, and y^t he would doe it notwithstanding any appointment of any one—upon wch notice being given me by ye s^d Mr Long I caused ye poor to be made acquainted that there would be no such Sermon on y^t day in Harteley Church as appointed by ye Testatrix & of the true reason thereof, as well to save ye poor people coming so far in vain as also to preserve my poor Grandmother's intention as far as may be—but they were then acquainted that ye s^d money should be distributed in ye s^d 2 parishes nevertheless—I was from home at ye time but on consideration of ye size of ye parishes and of ye proportions y^t used to be had in giving ye s^d money, I think it may be as

at 5 feet, which is above **19 feet at one foot, and 16 F. 9 I.**
at 3 feet. But i **lately** was told that Mr Archer of Hale near
Downton in Wiltshire has eight Oakes in his park or pastures,
for which he has been offered eight hundred pounds. This
account is so **extraordinary that** i wish i knew any man that
lived **near the** place, that i might enquire the measures **of
them.** I forget whether i told you of Mr Leigh's Oakes at
Stonleigh Abbey in Warwickshire? The largest is at 5 feet,
23 F. 11 I. in circumfer^e.

As the following relates to our favourite Trees (Beech) i
will intrude on your patience with **a memorandum of** mine
dated May 26. 1752, when i was with **my worthy friend M^r**
Naylor at his Castle of **Hurstmonceux in Sussex,** viz.:—" The
" finest Grove of Beeches in the park that i ever saw. One
" felled two years ago ran 81 feet before it headed. I felled
" one an underling very small in the Grove merely to guess
" the height of its neighbours, which was +62 feet to the
" head. I believe some are above 100 f. high, and run 80, or
" very near, before they head, and i think some are **70 without**
" **a branch.** Some are large & spreading. I measured one
" +16 F. round at 5 f. a very handsome one +13 f. & an
" extreme handsome one 11 F. 5 I. & ¼. the handsomest is
" but 10 F. 6 I. an Arm of one standing single extended
" +20 paces from the trunk." Again in 1767. Some
" Beeches laid felled in the park, one was +72 feet long as
" cut for timber, squared above 2 feet at 24 f. length; &
" marked 222 feet: a Grove of tall Chesnuts near the
" Beeches from 10 to 12 feet in circumf. at 5 feet." I do not
love the Chestnuts no more than you: they have nothing of
the obedience towards their masters which Beeches show: if

---

near to Truth and Justice as can be found out, to allott 20^s to ye poor of
Selebourn & 10^s to ye poor of Harteley, and y^t is ye reason y^t herewith I
send y^o 20^s begging ye favour it may be distributed to such & so many
of y^r poor as y^o shall think fitt & y^t were capable & likely to have
edified by ye Sermon had such been preached. * * * I beg y^r pardon
for y^r trouble and am S^r

"Y^r obedient Servt.
"SIMEON STUART."]

you cut off an Arm of Beech, they seldom produce another; but an Oak will give you 2 for one, & a Chesnut (in defyance) 5 or more for one. I have this winter had several favourite Beeches digged round, two spades deep, as far as the roots extend, in hopes it may promote their growth. But i do not recommend this as œconomy. If i can thus gain half an inch extra, i reckon myself paid the 3 half crowns expended on the Tree.

My eyes water so much that i am forced to write by instalments, as Bankrupts pay their debts.—The Swallow was dead, & a wing torn off.—I certainly never remember so much thunder in a winter as in this, & perhaps not so much wind & rain. But as i do not measure the rain, i am not certain.— Tho' the Season has been uncommonly mild, i do not find the Indications of Spring so early. e.g Snowdrop F. Jan. 16. Thrush sings Feb. 14. Rooks build Mar. 2 & i have not heard a Ring-dove coo yet; but stockdoves on the 23 of Feb.

In my favourite Book, the Nat. Hist. of Selborne, i am perplexed to find C. Taylor Vicar in 1784, as i thought you had the Vicarage: and i suppose that your namesake, in 1691, the charitable Vicar was an Ancestor of your's.

I should have gone on with last Winter, & as a strong proof of its mildness have told you that i have a Hawthorn & a Hornbeam both headed last year, ye first full leafed & green, the last, some leaves green.—I forget the authority, but i am confident i have heard that old London was built of Chestnut [*]. Tho' 'tis apt to be split with frost, 'tis certainly lasting Timber, although it grows quick. Perhaps i may have

---

[*] [The statement is made by Ducarel (Phil. Trans. lxi. p. 137, for 1771), but, as appears by Marsham's next letter, he had not seen it there.— —A. N.]

[The question to what extent chestnut timber formerly took the place of oak, and how far the material of the roofs of churches, &c., long supposed to have been constructed of the latter, proves upon more careful inspection to be of chestnut, has of late years excited considerable interest. One of the oldest remaining churches in this country, that of Greenstead in Essex, still retains its wooden walls entire, and is constructed, if I am rightly informed, of this timber. It is believed on good grounds that it was originally erected as a shrine or resting-place for the

told you before now, that a Chestnut which i **raised from** the nut, measures **Timber at** 55 f. high, & is a very handsome Tree. I **wish** i **could** view your Beech of 74 feet, & your pleasing outlet: alas! all round me is as flat **as round Thor**ney. I am, with true esteem, my dear Sir, your most humble,
& obliged servant,
R: MARSHAM.

Ld Stawell's bird must be a great curiosity. Mar. 4.

P.S. In 1748 i enclosed above 20 acres of my Waste, & planted it. The poorest Land with Scotch Firs, & the best with Beeches, & another part chiefly with Oaks. I wish i could walk with you **about this Wood, as** i **believe you** would find more variety than you expected. One part of the Beech are tall Grove, & near that they are short and spreading. The Oaks also are part tall & part pollards &c. Although i walk in it **most** days, yet i am never weary of it; but when alone can **look**, & admire the different beauties of ye different shapes of y^e **trees.** One Beech already extends its Branches ten **yards from** the trunk. I have a Lingstack in it for rest & shelter, (not half **so pretty** as your Hermitage), but it takes the **Cathedral of Norwich & 2** Country Churches **into view.** —Mar. 5. i have just heard a **Ringdove coo, & seen a Haw**thorn l. my first Crocus F. was **Feb. 10.**

[This letter is endorsed by White:—"Did you see any beeches in Italy? Lombardy Poplars? Chestnuts? Clapham Common."—Memoranda of his answer, which is missing, as will be seen by Marsham's reply.—T. S.]

---

body of St Edmund, the King of the East Angles, on its transportation from the scene **of** his murder **to the place of** his sepulture **at** Bury St. Edmunds **in the year** 870.—T. B.]

LETTER VIII.

MARSHAM TO WHITE.

Stratton: July 8. 91.
1791.

DEAR SIR,

My thanks are justly due to you for the favour of your pleasing letter of the 8th of June[*]. If i am not the wiser for every letter of yours, 'tis my own fault, or want of memory. In not seeing Hurstmonceux, you lost not only the sight of the tall Beeches &c. in the park, but also one of the most entire old Castles in England. I find by my notes, 'tis 77 of my steps (suppose yards) long, & 72 deep. & the moat 20 yards broad. The great staircase 40 feet square, and 22 back stairs, so like each other, that i chalked my door, to prevent my going into rooms that i should not; they being 48 on a floor as my friend told me. Your letter made me look over my old journal, which i believe i had not done of 50 years, & i find no mention of Beeches in Italy; nor does my memory supply me with any. I remember some in Switzerland near Bern, that were mixed with Firs, that i think were very tall but not large. The poplars in Lombardy, are lost to my memory, & are not mentioned in my journal: but in the public walks by Florence a part was felled, & i find some were above 100 feet long, & very slender. I greatly dislike the Tree in England. I noticed a wood of Oakes betwixt Rome & Naples, being very tall but not large, and the leaf more indented than ours. So i send you a leaf.

I am obliged to you for engaging your Nephew at Salisbury to gain intelligence of Mr Archer's Oakes: but i believe 'tis unnecessary. A friend was with me lately, to whom i told the account. He said he had been at Mr Archer's, & " remembers some Trees by his house, which appeared nothing " extraordinary; like some of your best." Now my best was

[*] [This letter is missing.—T. B.]

but 25 guineas.—I got a peep at Mr Rook's sketches of the Duke of Portland's Oaks*. But i fear he is a bad calculator of the age of Trees from their size. I have not seen Daines Barrington's controversy with Dr Ducarrel †. But although I respect Mr Barrington, yet i must see he is too partial to any opinion that he has adopted, to allow the weight of any evidence that makes against him. You may remember his zeal against birds migrating ‡. The latest bird that i have noticed appearing here, I mean its first appearance, is the Fern Owle. I saw one this Spring, May 2. but did not hear one sing 'till June 14th. I wonder Willoughby says nothing of their migrating.—I have been much entertained with Mr Townsend's travels in Spain §. But i must conclude that he was misinformed when he says that "Nightingales sing all the year," Vol. 3. p. 45. Your friend that lived in Andalusia, i doubt not, knew it is not so. With us the song of that bird is confined to as short a time as any. By the bye, i was as careful as in my power towards the love-making of the

* [A plate giving "A North West View of the Green Dale Oak near Welbeck," no doubt one of those to which reference is intended, is given in Hunter's edition of Evelyn's work (vol. ii. to face p. 200) and bears in the corner "A. Rooker Sculpsit."—A. N.]

† [In the 'Philosophical Transactions' for 1769 (vol. lix.) is a communication from Barrington "On Trees which are supposed to be indigenous to Great Britain," in the course of which he maintained that the Spanish Chestnut was not one of them, and controverted the opinion of Ducarel previously published (*Anglo-Norman Antiquities*, p. 96) that not only was old London built of Chestnut-timber, but that there still existed a large tract of Chestnut Woods near Sittingbourne in Kent. The controversy was continued by Ducarel and others in 1771 (Phil. Trans. vol. lxi. pp. 136-166), and Barrington replied on the whole case (*tom. cit.* pp. 167-169). Barrington seems on the whole to have been right (see Loudon, Arb. Brit. p. 1987).—A. N.]

‡ [Barrington contributed to the 'Philosophical Transactions' for 1772 (vol. lxii. pp. 265-326), "An Essay on the periodical Appearance and Disappearance of certain Birds at different times of the year."—A. N.]

§ ['A Journey through Spain in the years 1786 and 1787.' By Joseph Townsend, A.M., Rector of Pewsey, Wilts; and late of Clare-Hall, Cambridge. Second Edition, 3 vols. London: 1792. The author being of the same college as Marsham was very likely personally known to him.—A. N.]

frogs last Spring, and the gentlewoman seemed to be a toad. She *walked* not *jumped*, her belly was the ash colour with black spots, & the colour of her back like the toad. I am ignorant of the characteristic marks of either of y^r gentry. I was pleased long ago with the rows of Oakes by Odiham, as growing well upon unpromising Land. But i have seen great Oakes upon absolute sand. viz Ld Thanet's in Westmoreland * was 31 F. 9 I. round in 1765 & Mr Lemon's at Northaw Herts, whose top was the largest i ever saw: some arms extended full 60 feet from the trunk, which was 19. feet 7 In. round: i could not omit this in ye paper on ye increase of Trees in ye Ph. Trans. 1759. We have only the Oak with the long stalk to the acorn, & the leaf without stalk. I thought the Oaks in Sussex, & many other Counties more pleasing trees than in Norfolk; but i did not observe the leaves. I remember near Ucfield, in the road from London to Herstmonceux, an Oak with yellow leaves; which struck me as very curious, & my good friend Naylor got me some of the acorns, but none grew. I presume you have noticed this Oak, as i have heard of another with leaves as yellow as the Elm in autumn.

In answer to your last Article, i was a young fellow in 1733 when many Counties were inflamed with contested Elections (when Sr S. Stuart lost his Election by 2 in your County) & engaged warmly in that new amusement: & drank & smoked for the Cause, although i relished neither. But old age, that blunts the edge of all passions & my seeing, according to Pope———"how like, Whig ministers to Tory," has cooled my party zeal: & i feel myself satisfied with giving my vote for a friend, without enquiring about his party. So if you had asked me my party, i can hardly tell you. But i will add, that i love the King, & the Constitution, & am disliked by both parties.

Two articles of your letter vex me, viz. that your infirmities deprive me of the pleasure of seeing you in Norfolk; the other, that in naming me, you have struck out the word *friend*, & put *correspondent*. I should have been proud, to be called

* [At Whinfield Park (Loudon, *ut suprà*, p. 1771).—A. N.]

friend by the Author of the Hist. of Selborne: for i am with great esteem, dear Sir, your most humble
& obliged servant,
R: MARSHAM.

P.S. Although last Winter & the fore-part of Spring were (i think) the mildest that i remember (except the Earthquake year 1750), yet I find many articles of Spring later than in several colder Seasons. I find snow on ye 5th of May. We have had some drying E. wind, but hardly to be called hot. The begining of June 2 or 3 days the air was thick, in small degree like what you noticed in 1783. Letter 64. On the **last of June** i found my best Oak & best Beech **had** each increased an inch, which i find is more than my Trees had done in the two years measurement, which are in the Ph. Tr. in 1758. so i hope for a good year's growth: as they have two months **more** to grow. The lateral shoots of healthy Beeches are 2 feet; & one of the Copper coloured Beech is near 21 inches.

I am with great esteem
Dear Sir your most humble
& obliged servant
R: MARSHAM.

P.S. when i wrote this i hoped for a friend to direct it; but no neighbours are come down: & i am ashamed to make you pay for a leaf. I did not see i had concluded my letter before, but am too lazy to write it over again; & hope you will pardon this, & the many other blunders in an old fellow of 84.

LETTER IX.

WHITE TO MARSHAM.

Selborne near Alton:
Decr. 19. 1791.

DEAR SIR,
Your letter, which met me so punctually in London, was so

intelligent, & so entertaining, as to have merited a better treatment, & not to have been permitted to have lain so long unnoticed!

That there is no rule without an exception is an observation that holds good in Nat. History: for tho' you & I have often remarked that *Swifts* leave us in general by the first week in August: yet I see by my journal of this year, that a relation of mine had under the eaves of his dwelling house in a nest a young squab swift, which the dam attended with great assiduity till September 6th*,—& on Octob^r 22. I discovered here at Selborne three *young martins* in a nest, which the dams fed & attended with great affection on to Novem^r 1st, a severe frosty day; when they disappeared; & one was found dead in a neighbour's garden. The middle of last Septem^r was a sweet season! during this lovely weather the congregating flocks of house martins on the Church & tower were very beautiful & amusing! When they flew off all together from the roof, on any alarm, they quite swarmed in the air. But they soon settled again in heaps on the shingles; where preening their feathers, & lifting up their wings to admit the rays of the sun, they seemed highly to enjoy the warm situation. Thus did they spend the heat of the day, preparing for their Migration, & as it were consulting when & where they are to go! The flight about the church consisted chiefly of h. martins, about 400 in number: but there were other places of rendezvous about the village, frequented at the same time. The swallows seem to delight more in holding their assemblies on trees. Such sights as these fill me with enthusiasm! & make me cry out involuntarily,

> "Amusive birds! say where your hid retreat,
> When the frost rages, & the tempests beat!"

We have very great oaks here also on absolute sand. For over Wolmer forest, at Bramshot place where I visit, I measur'd last summer three great hollow oaks, which made a very

---

* [Occasional instances are recorded of the retarded departure of the swift, such as that mentioned by Gilbert White in this letter; but they are quite exceptional. See Vol. I. pp. 94, 175, 417.—T. B.]

grotesque appearance at the entrance of the avenue, & found the largest 21 feet in girth at five feet from the ground. The largest Sycamore in my friend's court measures 13 feet. His edible chestnuts grow amazingly, but make (for some have been felled) vile *shaky*, *cupshaky* timber. I think the oak on sands is shaky, as it is also on our rocks, as I know by sad experience the last time I built.—The indented oaken leaf which you gather'd between Rome & Naples was the *quercus cerris* of Linnæus. The yellow oak which you saw in Sussex escaped my notice.

Richard Muliman Trench Chiswell Esq. of Portland Place, & M.P. tells a friend of mine in town that he has an *Elm* in Essex for which he has been bid £100. It is long enough, he says, to make a keel ungrafted for a man-of-war of the largest dimensions. As he expressed a desire of corresponding with me, I have written to him, & desired some particulars respecting this amazing tree.

You seem to wonder that Mr. Willughby should not be aware that the Fern-owl is a summer bird of passage. But you must remember that those excellent men, *Willughby & Ray*, wrote when the ornithology of England, & indeed the Nat: History was quite in it's infancy. But their efforts were prodigious; & indeed they were the Fathers of that delightful study in this kingdom. I have thoughts of sending a paper to the R. S. respecting the fern-owl; & seem to think that I can advance some particulars concerning that peculiar, migratory, nocturnal bird, that have never been noticed before. The rain of Octo^r last was great, but of Novr still more. The former month produced 6 in. 49 hund. but the latter upwards of 8 in.: five & $\frac{1}{2}$ of which fell in one week, viz. from Nov. 13th to the 19th both inclusive! You will, I hope, pardon my neglect, & write soon. O, that I had known you forty years ago!

I remain, with great esteem,

Y^r most humble servant,

GIL. WHITE.

My tortoise was very backward this year in preparing his Hybernaculum; & did not retire till towards the beginning of Decem^r. The late great snow hardly reached us, & was gone at once.

LETTER X.

MARSHAM TO WHITE.

Stratton, Feb. 12, 1792.

DEAR SIR,

MANY thanks are due to you for your very pleasing & instructing letter of the 19th of Decr but procrastination has prevented your receiving them. This failing which afflicted me in my younger days, increases in æt. 85; & as i have nothing worth communicating to you, it might safely have continued longer. Our Winter began early, & was uncommonly severe before Xmass. From the 8 of Dec^r, to the 23^d was constant frost, with little snow. The 12th was the coldest, viz. near 10 below friezing point. We here, like you in Hampshire, had but little snow. I had a Woodcock in my house the first of October.

Your new correspondent's Elm seems to me extraordinary. You know the keel of a first-rate ship of War is 147 feet long. This cannot be less than 8 feet round. As Elm is generally slender in proportion to the height, Mr. Chiswell's Elm should be at least 200 feet high: viz. near double the height of the tall Trees of this Island; credat &c. The tallest Elms i can recollect are by St John's Coll. Camb. which i should think are not much above 100 feet. You know i traced Mr. Archer's Oakes near Downton, 'till they contracted into sticks. You may remember, that Dr Hunter in his notes in his edition of Evelyn's Silva, says that an hundred of Sr Rowland Wynn's Oakes sold for 5000£ *. This i investigated, by

---

* [Hunter (*op. cit.* ii, p. 288), however, says *fifty* tons for £2500.— A. N.]

my good friend Lord Suffield, & find it is true. Two of the Trees called the Lord & the Lady were valued at 70 Guineas each. In another note, he says without good authority, that the Earl of Hertford* fell'd a Wych Elm in his park in Lisburn (Ireland) that contained 99 tun of timber†. Being known to his Lordship when abroad, i wrote to him; and his Ldp tells me, it was an *Oak* not *Elm*, that he did not *fell* it, but it *fell of itself*, in a calm summer day, to his sorrow. It was sound, the trunk or body was 29 feet long, & 36 in circumference. which sold for 48£. one piece of the head for 5£. 10£. for Bark, and 58£. for the rest of the head. Tot. 121£. As we do not know where the circ. was taken, you see we are left in ignorance: if at 14 f. ½ which should be, then his Ldp was abominably cheated. Hunter also mentions an ash at Leg or Leix in Queens County in Ireland 39 f. round near the ground, and 28 f. at six f. I try'd for an account of this Tree from my great neighbour the Earl of Bucks ‡ when he was Lieu^t, which not receiving so early as i wished, i wrote to my old friend Dr Man Bp of Corke. But all i have gained is, that a print of it was engraving in London. This i have not seen: & a print without a scale would certainly not satisfy my curiosity.—Your friends Sycamore is a little larger than I have seen, and his pollard Oaks are respectable.

I observed nothing remarkable in this Winter but a greater number of the red-wing Thrush than usual, & have as yet but Two articles for my Indications of Spring for 92. viz. Snowdrop F. Jan. 25. & yellow Butterfly this day. Your Relations Swifts delay was extraordinary. My Swallows left me Sep. 27. but one was seen within 5 miles on ye last of October.—I shall long for your account of the fern Owl in the Ph. Trans., as i conclude you can give a better account of that

* [Francis Seymour succeeded his father as Lord Conway in 1732, was created Earl of Hertford in 1750, and Marquess in 1793. Died in 1796.—A. N.]

† [I have not been able to find Hunter's reference to this tree or to the Ash presently mentioned.—A. N.]

‡ [John Hobart, succeeded his father as Earl of Buckinghamshire and owner of Blickling in Norfolk, in 1756, Ambassador at St. Petersburgh in 1762, Lord Lieutenant of Ireland in 1777, died in 1793.—A. N.]

harmless pleasing bird than i have seen. We used to have more of them formerly than of late years. I have never heard one sing on the wing. I love the Swallows and H. Martins so well, that i lament the want of their company in Autumn as heartily & as much as i do the warm weather. I should have concluded from your Tortoise's late hiding that the winter would be mild.

I conclude that you have read Boswell's life of Dr Johnson. A friend of Dr Horne's (late Bp of Norwich) told me, that his Ldp had read it twice, & was going the 3^d time thro' it; & said it was the most entertaining Book he ever read. It made me laugh several times; but the banter upon it, in the new Lady's Magazine for Sepr last, made me laugh more heartily. If you love a laugh (which you must do, as you are a wise man) you cannot fail of it by that sketch. 'Tis supposed to be by the Author of the Bath guide*. I took the trouble of transcribing it, in order to bind it with Boswell, as a Supplement. I presume you have seen Gilpin's Book of the views in the new Forest†, & noticed his false quotation of Bryden's letter‡: where he says the Chesnut on M. Ætna is 204 f. in *circumf.* which he unluckily writes *Diameter*: as if the Tree was not large enough! Townsend says in his travels in Spain, at Valez, Nightingales sing all the year. I wish you would ask your Friend in Spain, if that is true?

I know that you do not love Chesnut-trees, but as a good man you are not averse to hearing of some merit in them. The great Land-stuard Mr. Kent §, told me 'tother day, that

---

* [This piece, however, is not included among the poetical works of Anstey, who wrote 'The New Bath Guide,' as collected and published by his son in 1808.—A. N.]

† ['Remarks on Forest Scenery, &c.,' by William Gilpin,' 2 vols. London: 1791 (vol. i. p. 130).—A. N.]

‡ ['A Tour through Sicily and Malta. In a series of letters to W. Beckford, Esq., from P. Brydone, F.R.S.' New Edition. 2 vols. London: 1790 (vol. i. p. 119).—A. N.]

§ [Nathaniel Kent, "A well-known and highly respectable land and timber surveyor" (Loudon, *op. cit.* p. 1993). The details given in the text are included by him in a paper (Trans. Soc. Arts, vol. x. p. 31).—A. N.]

at Mr. Windham's*, removing the place of a gateway, one post was Oak, the other Chesnut only a foot square, & by the date on it had stood 50 years. This was sound, & set down again; & the Oak was quite rotten. & some years ago, some railing was done at Mr. Windham's with posts of Oak & Chesnut (the same size); these being moved this year, all those of Oak were rotten, & all of Chesnut served again. But this Tree certainly splits more with frost, than Oak; but must be excellent for paling. Had Fortune given me your acquaintance 40 years ago, i should have been a great gainer, & you but little. Be assured dear Sir, that your letters are always a Feast to me, & that i remain with true esteem your most humble servant

R: MARSHAM.

P.S. As long as i have measured Trees, by way of calculating their age by their size, i did not attend to the height from the earth, when i took the circumference: & i find my friends have been as careless as myself. Whereas an Oak mostly increases one third more at one foot from the earth, than it does at 5 feet. Thus, e. g. the Oak i planted in 1720, is at 5 f. 9 F. 5 I. 7 10'. & at 1 f. is 13 f. & my best Oak at 5 f. is but 14 F. 3 I., which at 1 f. is 19 F. 3 I. Now, tho' i saw my Trees were larger near the earth, i never considered that they must increase more yearly to make that bulk: & yet i think when Willoughby was writing on the fern-Owl, he should have recollected that he did not see that bird in Winter. But i acknowledge he has done a great deal; & I am often obliged to him, for the trouble he has taken.

[This letter is franked by "H. Hobart," and is endorsed by White, "Mr. Marsham, Feb. 17, 1792."]

* [William Windham of Felbrigg (born 1750, died 1810), for many years M.P. for Norwich and subsequently for Higham Ferrers, Chief Secretary for Ireland (1783), Secretary at War (1794–1801), and Secretary of State for War and the Colonies (1806–1807). The evidence afforded by the next of Marsham's letters shows that he was recommended to White's book by Windham, who possibly became acquainted with it through Daines Barrington, like himself a member of "The Club." In connexion with the text may also be mentioned Loudon's statement (*op. cit.* p. 1990) that one of Windham's ancestors was a considerable planter of Chestnuts.—A. N.]

LETTER XI.

WHITE TO MARSHAM.

Selborne: Mar. 20th, 1792.

DEAR SIR,

You, in a mild way, complain a little of *Procrastination*: but I, who have suffered all my life long by that evil power, call her the *Dæmon* of *Procrastination*; & wish that *Fuseli*, the grotesque painter in London, who excells in drawing witches, dæmons, incubus's & incantations, was employed in delineating this ugly hag, which fascinates in some measure the most determined & resolute of men.

You do not, I find, seem to assent to my story respecting Mr. Chiswell's elm. There may be probably some misapprehension on my side. I will therefore allow Mr. Ch. that priviledge which every Englishman demands as his right, the liberty of speaking for himself. "In regard to my tree," says he, "it is a *Wych Elm*, perfectly strait, & fit for the keel of the largest man of war. The purveyor of the navy offered my late Uncle £50 for it, altho' it would have cost as much more to have conveyed it to Portsmouth; & he would have run all risque of soundness. It grows about eleven miles from Safron Walden, in a deep soil, & near 30 from Cambridge, the nearest place for water-carriage. I will measure it next summer."—He adds, "I have been, & am a considerable planter; & have been honoured with three gold medals from the Society of Arts," &c. Thus far Mr. Ch.

As I begin to look upon You as a Selborne man, at least as one somewhat interested in the concerns of this place; I wish that You could see "The sixth Report of the Commissioners appointed to enquire into the state & condition of the Woods, Forests, &c. of the Crown," &c. This Report was printed February, 1790; tho' never published: but distributed among the members of the house of commons from some of whom

You may borrow it, as I have done. This curious survey will inform you, from the best authority, of all the circumstances respecting the advantages, usages, abuses, &c. of our Forest of Alice Holt, & Wolmer. Here you will see, that the Forest now consists of 8694 acres, 107 of which are in ponds; that the present timber is estimated at £60,000; that it is almost all of a size, & about 100 years old; that it is shamefully abused by the neighbouring poor, who lop it, & top it as they please; that there is no succession because all the bushes are destroyed by the commoners around; that y^r old favourite Oak, the *Grindstone Oak*, is estimated at 27 loads of timber; that the peat cut in Wolmer is prodigious; in the year 1788 in one walk 942 loads; & in another walk the same year 423 loads, besides heath, & fern; & in the same year 935,000 turves; &c. &c. &c. Lord Stawell is the Lieutenant, or Grantee, whose lease expires in 1811, as I have said in my book. That Nobleman did me the honour to call on me a morning or two ago, & sat with me two hours: he brought me a white wood-cock, milk white all over except a few spots.

My friend at Bramshot place, where I measured the great pollard oaks, & Sycamore last summer, has got a great range of chesnut-paling; I shall tell him what Mr. Kent says respecting timber of that sort. The rain with us in 1791 was 44 in. 93 hund.: upwards of 8 inches of which fell in November! the rain of the present year has been considerable. Our indications of spring this year are thus: Jan. 19. *winter-aconite* blows: Jan. 21. *Hepaticas* blow. Jan. 29. *Snowdrop* blows: 31. Hasels: Feb. 4. *Crocus* b.: 13. *brimstone butter-fly*; 21. *yellow wagtail* appears. 26. *Humble bee*: March 16. *daffodil blows*, and *Apricot*: 19. *peaches*, & *nectarines*. I have read **Boswell's** *Johnson* with pleasure. As to Bishop Horne I knew him well for near 40 years: he has often been at my House. Stillingfleet, I see, wrote his *Calendar* of *Flora* at your house: He speaks in high terms of the hospitable treatment that he experienced at Stratton.

Wonderful is the regularity observed by nature! I have often remarked that the smallest *willow wren*, (see my Book) called here the *Chif-chaf* from it's two loud sharp notes, is always the *first spring bird* of passage, & that it is heard usually on March 20: when behold, as I was writing this very page, my servant looked in at the parlour door, & said that a neighbour had heard the *Chif-chaf* this morning!! These are incidents that must make the most indifferent look on the works of the Creation with wonder!

My old tortoise lies under my laurel-hedge, & seems as yet to be sunk in profound slumbers. You surprise me, when You mention y^r age: y^r neat hand, & accurate language would make one suppose you were not 50. I remain, with true esteem,

Y^r most obliged servant,

GIL. WHITE.

When Mr. Townsend avers that the Nightingales at *Valez* sing the winter thro', I should conclude that he took up that notion on meer report; because I had a brother who lived 18 years at Gibraltar, & who has written an accurate Nat. Hist. of that rock & it's environs. Now he says, that Nightingales leave Andalusia as regularly towards autumn as other Summer birds of passage. A pair always breeds in the Govern^{rs} garden at the Convent. This Hist. has never been published, & probably now never will, because the poor author has been dead some years. There is in his journals such ocular demonstration of *swallow emigration* to & from Barbary at Spring and fall, as, I know, would delight you much. There is an *Hirundo hiberna*, that comes to Gibraltar in Oct^r, & departs in March; and abounds in & about the Garrison the winter thro'.

LETTER XII.

MARSHAM TO WHITE.

Stratton: July 14. 92.

My dear Sir,

After many attempts on my part, at length our inveterate enemy, Madam Procrastination, has permitted me to offer my thanks to you for your very pleasing letter of the 20th of March. As one of 85 years i acknowledge her haggard form; but half a century ago, she sometimes appeared as a Siren. So Fuseli may be puzzled, whether he should paint her young or old.

You oblige me, & i heartily thank you, for looking on me as a Selborne man. I am certainly a well-wisher wherever your interest or pleasure is concerned. All the compliment i can make you in return, is to call a favourite Beech by the name of Mr White's Beech. You know Linnæus complimented his friends, by calling new plants after their names. This is not in my power to do, as i know but few old ones. But you should know some particulars of your Tree. 'Tis about 50 years old, & runs clear about 25 feet, then about as much in handsome head, preserving its stem straight to the top, & spreads a circle of about 50 feet diameter. This i reckon the handsomest proportion for an out-side Grove Tree. For an inside Grove Tree, i should wish the stem longer, about 2 thirds of the height, & the spread of the head less: & for the Lawn or single pasture Tree, i wish the branches should hang so low as only to suffer a man to ride on horseback under them; & the Tree to appear at a little distance like a green hill. These are my proportions for the beauty of Trees in different situations. But i will quarrel with no man, if he likes other proportions better. I presume that Grove of Oaks called Losels, mentioned in my favourite Book, p. 5. ran

clear stems 4, 5^{ths} of their height: which runs them too like to
hop-poles. And perhaps the venerable Oak which stood in
the Plestor, was the very shape i wish a single Tree to be! I
remember an Oak of Mr Leman's at North hall in Hertfordshire, that spread a circle of about 130 feet diameter. And
the Bp of Bath & Wells* informed me, that the Bp of
Salisbury's Oak spread 115 feet in the longest diameter, &
112 in the shortest; & appeared at a distance a perfect semi-
globe. Although i am much pleas'd with your view of
Selborne, & the description you give of it, yet the great
quantity of rain that falls there, is a strong drawback to the
pleasure of living. above 50 inches in 1782, & last year
almost 45, seems to me very extraordinary; as 'tis above
double what Dr Arbuthnot supposes falls upon the Globe viz.
22 inches. Essay on Air. p. 88. where you find but 19 inches
at Paris. Indeed, when i was last in Scotland (about 6
weeks) it was every day rain, more or less. We had a good
deal of rain last Winter, tho' little laying snow, whilst the
papers spoke of much, both in the North & West.—The
Spring has been very watery, and still continues, to the grief
of the Farmers, for their Hay: & notwithstanding these rains,
i find the season has not been kind to my Trees. All sorts
appear not in good health. My favourite Beeches appear
brown rather than green, from the abundance of Mast, &
very few have as yet increased an inch in circumf. A Cedar
had gained an inch & half on ye 5th but my best Oaks not
above half an inch. For Indications of Spring. Jan. 25
Snowdrop F. ye 29th at Selburne. Jan. 30th Hepatica F. 21st
at Selburne,—Feb. 11 Crocus F. at Selburne. Feb. 4 Crocus
b. Feb. 12 brimston Butterfly. at Selburne Feb. 13. Mar. 21.
Daffodil F. at Selburne Mar. 16. Perhaps my deafness
might deprive my hearing of Spring Birds, but i have heard
hardly any Thrushes this year; & i heard not the Fern Owl,
'till June 26. Here i must observe with mortification that

* [Charles Moss, Bishop of St. David's, 1766, Bishop of Bath and
Wells, 1776, died 1802. Marsham's communication, before mentioned,
to the Royal Society, on washing trees was in the form of a letter to him.
—A. N.]

my Phil. Trans. brought me no account of the fern-Owl, which i expected from a former letter of your's.—Beech l. Ap. 11.—Oak l. Ap. 13. Swallow Ap. 13. Cuckow Ap. 22. I put down articles in my Indications of Spring, only from my own knowledge. But i have often accounts that i fully believe, e. g. a Swallow this Spring on the first of April. I should have been glad to have seen the white Woodcock Ld Stawell gave you; & i will try to borrow the sixth report of the Com" for enquiry &c. I can easily believe great abuses are practised upon them. I have an old Park (long disparked) formerly belonging to the Crown, & after to the Bp. of Norwich, & the neighbours steal as much wood from it, as i gain.—I never heard of a Winter Swallow until you named it. I should rejoice to read your Brothers Nat. Hist. of the Rock &c. Pray Sir why do you not publish it? I should think it would sell well, as curiosity seems to increase amongst mankind.—I do not know the Bird you call the Chif-chaf. But i am filled with wonder by the Harmony and Beauty of all the Works in the Creation. I remain with true esteem dear Sir your obedient

& obliged servant,
R: MARSHAM.

A gentleman of my acquaintance in this County had a tortoise of above 100 years old, from the family account, which was unluckilly killed by the Gardener. As i find by your Book, you was formerly a Sportsman, i conclude you love dogs, so i may tell you an history of a favourite bitch of mine. I destroyed her first litter of whelps; her 2^d litter she laid in a secret place. These i also destroyed; her 3^d she layed in a large cony-burrow over a furlong from the house, & quite out of sight: could human wisdom do more?—She went a hunting with a partner dog, & i chastised them, the partner first: for every lash i gave it, she cried, as if suffering herself. When i whipped her, she did not cry once. Was not this feeling more for her friend than herself? & is not this a proof of more exalted friendship than you have ever known in the human race? Dr Leigh says he knew a dog starved himself on the death of his Master. See his History of Cheshire*.

P.S. my friend who recommended to me the Nat. Hist. of Selborne calld on me this morning & directed my letter.

[Franked by " W. Windham."]

LETTER XIII.

WHITE TO MARSHAM.

Selborne: Augst 7. 1792.

Dear Sir,

WHILE all the young people of this neighbourhood are gone madding this morning to the great last day's review at Bagshot†; I am sitting soberly down to write to my friend in Norfolk; almost forgetting, now I am old, the impulse that young men feel to run after new sights; & that I myself, in the year 1756, set-off with a party at two o' the clock in the morning to see the Hessian troops reviewed on a down near Winchester‡. While I was writing the sentence above, my

---

* ['The Natural History of Lancashire, Cheshire, &c.' By Charles Leigh. Oxford: 1700. Folio. Book ii. pp. 8, 9.—A. N.]

† ['The Diary or Woodfall's Register' for Wednesday, August 8th, 1792, contains the following paragraphs:—

" Bagshot Camp. Tuesday, Four o'Clock—P.M.

" The spectacle of this day exceeded any public exhibition in this kingdom. At six at least *a hundred thousand* persons were upon the ground. At eight the King and Queen, with the Prince, the Dukes of York, Richmond, [Commander-in-Chief], &c., and their attendants. At nine the Review began in the hollow, below Cæsar's Camp. * * * At one the concourse was so immense, that at least *one hundred and fifty thousand* horsemen, (exclusive of the army) were upon the field. The Pedestrians were innumerable."

* * * * * * * *

" Yesterday being the grand Review of the troops encamped on Bagshot Heath, the King went from Windsor in his Post-chaise soon after Eight o'Clock. * * The manœuvres began soon after the King's arrival, at half-past nine."—A. N.]

‡ [These were doubtless the forces who have left so ill a name in the

servant, & some neighbours came down from the hill, & told me that they could not only hear the discharges of the ordnance & small arms, & see the volumes of smoke from the guns; but that they could also, they thought, smell the scent of the gun-powder, the wind being N.E. & blowing directly from the scene of action at Wickham bushes, tho' they are in a direct line more than twenty miles from hence.

As I had written to you as long ago as March, I began to fear that our correspondence was interrupted by indisposition; —when your agreeable letter of July 14th came in, & relieved me from my suspence. You do me much honour by calling one of your beeches after my name. Linnæus himself was complimented with the *Linnæa borealis* by one of his friends, a mean, trailing, humble plant, growing in the steril, mossy, shady wilds of Siberia, Sweden, & Russia; while I am dignified by the title of a stately Beech, the most beautiful & ornamental of all forest trees. The reason, I should suppose, why your trees have not encreased in growth & girth this summer is the want of heat to expand them. I have not this year measured my firs in circumference; but they have, I see, many of them, made surprising leading shoots. My account of the *Fern-owl*, or *Eve-jarr* was prevented by *Madam Procrastination*, who, a jade, lulled me in security all the spring, & told me I had time enough, & to spare, till at last I found that the R. S. meetings were prorogued till the autumn; against which I hope to be ready: & as I have got my materials, trust that when I do set about the business " verba haud invita sequentur." By *all means* get a sight of the

---

United States of America. They landed at Southampton on the 15th May, 1756 (Gentleman's Magazine, 1756, p. 259), and went under canvas. Towards autumn, when it was time to move them into winter quarters, there was a strong feeling on the part of the licensed victuallers against receiving them into their houses, and it was doubtful how far the law allowed the billetting of foreign troops. Accordingly on the 5th November huts were ordered for them (*tom. cit.* p. 544), but an Act of Parliament being passed compelling the same treatment to be shown to them as to British troops, the Hessian camp began to break up on the 23rd December, and officers and men were distributed amongst the various towns in the south of England (*tom. cit.* p. 592).—A. N.]

sixth Report of the *Commiss^rs* &c., it will entertain You, & furnish You with much matter, & many anecdotes respecting Selborne, of which I could have availed myself greatly had they been printed before I published my work. My book is gone to Madras, & several to France, & one to Switzerland, & one copy is going to China with Lord Macartney: but whether some Mandareen will read it, I know not. We have a young Gent. here now on a visit, the son of our late Vicar Etty, who assures me, that at Canton he has seen the Chinese reading English books; & has heard them converse sensibly on the manners & police of this kingdom. The *Chif-Chaf* of this village is the smallest *willow wren* of my History. Once I had a spaniel that was pupped in a rabbit burrough on the verge of Wolmer forest. Tho' I have long ceased to be a sportsman, yet I still love a dog; & am attended daily by a beautiful spaniel with long ears & a spotted nose & legs, who amuses me in my walks by sometimes springing a pheasant, or partridge, & seldom by flushing a woodcock, of late become with us a very rare bird. Remember the story of Pylades & Orestes; & do not say that exalted friendship never existed among men. *Chif-Chaf*, the first bird of passage, was heard here March 20 :—*swallow* was seen March 26 :— *nightingale* and *cuckoo* Apr. 9 :—*House-martins* April 12 :— *Redstart* April 19:—*Swift* April 14:—*Fern owl* heard May 19: —*Fly-catcher*, the latest summer bird, May 20. We have experienced a very black wet summer & solstice; but none of those floods & devastations mentioned in the newspapers! Indeed we know no floods here, but frequent rains. Yet in warm summers we have as fine melons, & grapes, & wall-fruit as I have ever seen. July at an average produces the most rain of any English month. This last measured 5 in. & 15 h. —Pray, good Sir, procure better ink: your's is so pale, that it often renders y^r neat hand scarcely legible! I am now offering my intelligent young neighbours *sixpence* for every authentic anecdote that they can bring me respecting *Fern-owls;* & will give you the same *sum* for the same information. As I was coming over our down after sun-set lately, a cock bird amused us much by flying round & settling often on the turf. As he passed us, he often gave a short squeak, or rather whistle. We were near his nest. These, like other birds of passage, frequent the same spots. There are always three pairs on our hill every year. Did you know Sr John Cullum* of your part of the world? He was an agreeable, worthy man, & a good antiquary. I was also well acquainted with your late good Bishop Horne†: he has often been at my house. I concur with you most heartily in y^r admiration of the harmony and beauty of the works of the creation! Physico-theology is a noble study, worthy the attention of the wisest man! Pray write. Our swifts have behaved strangely this summer: for the most part there were but three round the church, except now and then of a fine evening, when there were 13. They seem to be all gone. House-martins leave Gibraltar by the end of July! I conclude with all due regard.

Y^r Humble S.
GIL. WHITE.

* [Sir John Cullum, born 1733, Fellow of St. Catharine's Hall, Cambridge; Rector of Hawstead (1762) and Vicar of Great Thurlow (1774), both in Suffolk. His History of the former parish and of Hardwick Hall forms No. xxiii. of the 'Bibliographia Topographica Britannica,' and was republished in 1813. He wrote also 'Observations on Cedars' and on Yew-trees in churchyards. Died 1785. (Rose, 'Biographical Dictionary,' vi. pp. 507, 508.)—A. N.]

† [George Horne, born 1730, at Otham, near Maidstone, scholar of University, Fellow and afterwards (1768) President of Magdalen College, Oxford; Dean of Canterbury, 1781; Bishop of Norwich, 1790 (Le Neve, Fasti Eccles. Angl. Ed. Hardy, ii. p. 474); died 17th Jan. 1792. A distinguished Hebraist, author of many critical and controversial works, but chiefly known for his 'Commentary on the Book of Psalms.' His life was written by his friend Jones of Nayland. (Rose, *ut supra*, viii. p. 372.)—A. N.]

LETTER XIV.

MARSHAM TO WHITE.

Stratton: Octr 20. 1792.

My dear Sir,

Ever since i received your very entertaining letter of the 7th of August, i have had intentions of offering my thanks; but added to *the Demon*, i have suffered other delays from infirmities of old age, such as Rheumatism, &c &c, which make me abhor the sight of a pen & paper. But i am resolved to tell you a piece of Stratton history, viz. my wife has a Turkey that layed 15 eggs, & reared her brood; then she layed 63 eggs, & ceased; & then layed 20, then ceased, & has now laid 8, one on this day. She was of Spring twelvemonth. The old women round us think this extraordinary. Of the Swallows i can only say they left us on ye 18^h of Sep^r & on ye 25th we had a large flight appeared & off then a large flight on ye 14 & 15 of Oct^r & one Bird on ye 16. One of my men told me yesterday, that he saw a young Cuckow. This for torpidity! Perhaps it was a fern Owl: but that will answer the same purpose, only, you should owe me sixpence for it. I long for your account of that pleasing & harmless bird.— Except the first ten days of August, our Summer has seemed to me very cold & watery.

Sir, as my old friend (for as such i esteem you) you must have been troubled with my Tryals to increase the common ordinary growth of Trees. I have plagued the R. S. more than once on this subject. so i will hope for your pardon for this my half madness. My last tryal has been digging round my Trees. This is a circle as far as the small roots extend from the trunk; & this is done two spades deep. In Beeches about 50 years old, this circle will be about 20 yards diameter. Last Winter i enlarged the circle digged the year before, 8 or 9 yards in diameter, as i found the small roots required it. &

the increase of the Beech (at 5 feet) was 3 inches & 2 tenths. Sixteen Beeches of the same age, viz. all i had measured except some i had digged round before, produced very little above one inch a Tree. Therefore about 3 to one gained. Now tho' the expense of digging cost much more than the worth of the timber gained, yet it affords me much more pleasure, than i could have felt, if i had not digged them, as i do not feel the want of the digging money. You see 'tis like Dean Swift in Gulliver of propagating a breed of Sheep with hair instead of wool. But here is no injury, but to self. By the bye i received a letter last post, informing me of a hollow Oak within a few miles of Warwick 55 feet round at 3 feet. I tell you honestly i do not believe it.—I know there is a Baronet of the name of Cullum in Suffolk, but i have never seen him. I have been to very few of the public meetings of Suffolk, & none in these last 50 years.

Octr 30. My infirmities force me to write by instalments, & *Madam Procrastination* will command the use of my pen. My man has just now shot me a bird, which was flying about my house: i am confident i have never seen its likeness before. But on application to Willughby, i conclude it is the Wall-creeper, or Spider-catcher. I find he had not seen it in England*. It is very beautifully coloured, 'tho' the chief is cinereous; but the shades of red on the wings, & the large spots of white & yellow on the quil feathers, are uncommonly pleasing†. You see Willughby does not mention them.

I have asked several members for the Report, &c., but yet without success: however, i have a few more in store.—I am surprised that Mr Etty should hear the English language at Canton. If the Chinese can read English, it will be their fault as well as misfortune, if they do not read the Hist. of Selborne. I had the pleasure of recommending a Vol. to

---

* [Willughby's words are :—" In Anglia nostra eam invenire aiunt, quamvis nobis nondum fuerit conspecta " (*Ornithologia*, 1676, p. 99). Ray Englishes them :—" *They say it is found in* England; *but we have not as yet had the hap to meet with it* " (p. 143). Who the authors were who made such an assertion I do not know.—A. N.]

† [An exquisite drawing of two wing-feathers of the bird accompanied a subsequent letter from Marsham (see pp. 294 and 297).—T. B.]

Northumberland.—I will not say i am glad you are older, but i may say, i am a gainer, that you had lost the furor which you had in 1756. I believe your people might smell the powder from Bagshot; for i think i have smelt the smoke of London at Windsor; & Gunpowder is more pungent than culinary smoke.

My dear Sir, pray pardon me for saying you ought to love your Spaniel as well as if you still was a sportsman. Dogs deserve to be loved for their Virtue, more than their usefulness!—You say your Firs have made surprising leading shoots. I last Autumn removed some large Hornbeams & Beeches viz. about a yard round, & they grow well; one of the Beeches has shot 38 inches. I remain, with great esteem, dear Sir, your obliged servant, R: MARSHAM.

Nov. 1st yesterday my Turkey laid her 15th egg. so 113 this year.—I have measured an Oak this day (at 5 feet) which i planted an Acorn in 1719, 8 feet & 6 inches round. I shall be glad to know if the Wall-creeper lives near you.

[Franked by " W. Fellowes," 3d November.]

LETTER XV.

WHITE TO MARSHAM.

Selborne: Novem^r 3. 1792.

DEAR SIR,

AN extract from the Natural History of Gibraltar by the late Reverend John White.

"In the first year of my residence at Gibraltar which was 1756, it appeared extraordinary to me to see birds of the *Swallow* kind very frequent in the streets all the winter thro'. Upon enquiry I was told that they were *Bank Martins*: & having at that time been but little conversant in Nat. Hist., they passed with me as such for some years without any farther regard. At length, when I had taken a more attentive survey of the physical productions of this climate, I soon discovered these birds to be none of the common *British* species described by authors; & I farther found that they were never seen in G. thro' the whole course of the *summer*; but constantly & invariably made their first appearance about the 18 & 20th, & once as early as the 12th of $Octob^r$ & remained in great abundance until the beginning of *March*.

"These phænomena awakened & alarmed my curiosity as events entirely new & unheard of among the body of Ornithologists, & induced me to be particularly exact & attentive in my observations on every part of their conduct. Early in the autumn vast multitudes of these martins congregate in all parts of the town of *Castillar*, which is situate on the summit of a precipice most singularly lofty & romantic, about 20 miles north of *Gibraltar*. Hence it may be inferred that they build & breed on the inland mountains of *Andalusia* & *Grenada*. But on the approach of winter, when their summer habitations become bleak & inhospitable, (for all those mountains are then usually covered with snow) they retreat to these shores, & remain there 'till the snow is gone next spring. A few are always to be seen about our hill by the middle of $Octob^r$, shifting round to all sides of the rock at times to avoid the wind. $Novem^r$ 2, 1771, I saw several, with some young ones among them sitting in groupes, on the cliffs, where the old ones came & fed them."

Thus have I, for y^r amusement, according to promise, sent You an extract concerning this new & unnoticed *swallow*, which my Brother, with great propriety, in his work has called *Hirundo hyemalis*; & has given several particulars concerning it, & a description of it, too long for the compass of a letter.

Permit me just to hint to You, that I wrote to you some time ago in answer to your last letter, which gave me much satisfaction.

I forgot to mention in the extract, that these *winter Swallows* usually leave Gib. about the beginning of March, unless deep snow (as is sometimes the case, and was particularly so in 1770 & 1772) fall in Spain about that time; & then they linger there till the latter end of the month.

Surely my dear Sir, we live in a very eventful time, that must cut-out much work for Historians & Biographers! but whether all these strange commotions will turn out to the benefit or disadvantage of old England, God only knows! We have experienced a sad spring, summer, & autumn: & now the fallows are so wet, & the land-springs break forth so frequently, that men cannot sow their wheat in any comfort. Our barley is much damaged; & malt will be bad.

Have you read Mr. Arthur Young's "travels thro' France"? He says p. 543, when speaking of the French clergy—"One did not find among them poachers, or fox-hunters, who having spent the morning in scampering after hounds, dedicate the evening to the bottle, & reel from inebriety to the pulpit." Now, pray, who is Mr. Young; is he a man of fortune, or one that writes for a livelihood? He seems to reside in Suffolk, near Bury St. Edmund; so probably You can tell me somewhat about him.

Pray do *wood-peckers* ever damage & bore your timber-trees? not those, I imagine, of your own planting, but only those that are tending to decay. I had a brood this year in my outlet hatched, I suspect, in the bodies of some old willows. My dissertation on the *Caprimulgus* is almost finished.

I remain, with all due respect, & esteem,

   Your most obedient & obliged servant,
         GIL. WHITE.

LETTER XVI.

WHITE TO MARSHAM.

Dear Sir,

Our two last letters seem as if they had crossed each other on the road; but whether they conversed when they met, does not appear.

If you have got the *Certhia muraria*, or true *Wall-creeper*, you are in possession of a very rare & curious bird. For in all my researches here at home for 50 years past, & in all the vast collections that I have seen in London, I have never met with it. No wonder that the great Mr. Willughby is not very copious on the subject, for he acknowledges fairly that he had not seen it; tho' he supposes it may be found in this island. The best person I can refer you to is Dr *John Antony Scopoli*, a modern, elegant, foreign Naturalist, born in the *Tyrol*, but late deceased in Pavia, where he was professor of Botany. This curious & accurate writer was in possession of one in his own Museum, & gives the following description of his specimen in his "*Annus primus historico-naturalis:*"—"that it's bill is somewhat longer than it's shanks, slender, & somewhat bent; the tongue is bifid; & the feet consisting of three toes forward and one behind." Again he adds, "that the upper part is cinereous, the throat whitish; the abdomen, wings in part, tail, & feet, black: the wings at their base, & the quill feathers at their base on one side reddish." "It was taken in Carniola." "It is the size of the common *Creeper**, or *Certhia familiaris:* it's nostrils oblong; tail cinereous at the point; the first four quill feathers distinguished on the inner side by two white spots." He concludes thus,—"Migrat solitario sub finem autumni; turres & muros ædium altiorum adit; araneas venatur; saltitando scandit; volatu vago & incerto fertur volucris muta."—You are sure, I trust, that your bird is not the *Sitta Europæa*, or *Nut-hatch*.

I have written so soon, that you may examine y^r bird well again, before the specimen decays. Y^r Lady's Turkey-hen is a most prolific dame; & must, I think, lay herself to death. You persist very laudably in y^r curious experiments on trees. Whenever You recommend my book, which begins to be better known, you lay me under fresh obligations. I am writing my account of the Fern-owl, & endeavouring to vindicate it from the foul imputation of being a *Caprimulgus*. My letter

---

* [This is a slip of White's pen. Scopoli's words (*op. cit.* p. 51) are "Statura *sittæ*," that is, the size of the Nuthatch, which is nearly true. —A. N.]

will make a fierce appearance with a quotation from *Aristotle*, & another from *Pliny* : but whether the R. S. will read it : or whether afterwards they will print it, I know not.

With all good wishes for your health and prosperity, I remain

Your obliged & humble servant,

GIL. WHITE.

Selborne : Novr 20th, 1792.

LETTER XVII.

MARSHAM TO WHITE.

Stratton : Dec. 10. 92.

Dear Sir,

My thanks are justly due to you for the favour of your obliging letter of the 20th of Nov^r & for Scopoli's description of the *Wall-creeper*. Although several articles answer exactly, yet i must think him a careless describer. e. g. the Bill is somewhat longer than its shanks ; but he does not say the length of either, leaving the reader to suppose what he likes. I tell you the Bill is above an inch, about one tenth. He does not name the hind-claw being above double the length of the fore-claws. Colour has a large share in the beauty of Birds! He says the four quil-feathers are distinguished on the *inner* side with two white spots. These spots are on the *upper* side, & in the two quils next the body ; the upper spots are white & the lower are yellow ; which he ought not to have overlooked. You will judge better by the enclosed painting*, than my poor description. A young Lady drew them for me, & they appear to me to be very exact copies, & charmingly executed.

* [This painting in water-colours has been kindly lent to me by Prof. Bell. It represents with much accuracy two of the primary quill-feathers, the fifth and seventh, I believe, from the left wing of a female or young male *Certhia*, or, as it is now more commonly called, *Tichodroma muraria*, leaving no doubt as to the correctness of the determination of the specimen by Marsham and White.—A. N.]

I had occasion to write to the Duke of Portland[*]; and i ventured to recommend the Nat. Hisst. of Selborne to his Grace.

I think there is no doubt, but the R. S. will print your account of the Fern-Owl. If they do not, i (for one) shall be ashamed of F. R. S. to my name. It has been matter of wonder to me, that (since my Indications of Spring were printed) many people have asked me, what is the Fern-Owl? 'Tis a strong proof of the shameful ignorance of a set of people that live a great part of the year in the Country!—As you have left off sporting I hope you will not think me too cynical, if i wonder that a rational creature can make the chief pleasure of his life to consist in causing, and seeing harmless creatures in the agonies of death. The poulterer's killing-boy & the Lamb-butcher, follow their trade, & perhaps with pity; the Nobleman's and gentleman's, is clear pleasure: from causing pain & death. I am sorry to find by the Meeting advertised that you have scoundrels & rascals in Hampshire, as we have in Norfolk. Besides the real danger of these villains they confirm the bad opinion i am forced to have of human nature. I may say every man in the village is obliged to me; yet 13 of them are of these Clubs. But they do me one service, viz. they mortify my vanity, as i thought i could have led them all. One man in particular, to whom & his family i had been very kind, i believe to hundreds of pounds; & saved his father from hanging: & this is the grateful return!

But no more on this vile subject. I have just begun a new Wood of some acres, now i am near 85 years old; which i attend twice a day; & i feel great pleasure in the work. You remember Evelyn's[†] story of the Emperor Maximilian II. asking an old man, why he planted Dates, which would require an hundred years to make them produce fruit? He answered i have children, and i hope they will have children. But having children or none, the work to me is pleasing.

[*] [William Henry Cavendish Bentinck, Duke of Portland, born 1738, and twice First Lord of the Treasury, died 1809.—A. N.]

[†] [Vol. ii. p. 206. Hunter's edition (*ut supra*).—A. N.]

Dec. 21. I am interrupted by the friend that directs this, & can only add that i am always, with great esteem, your obliged & obedient servant, R: MARSHAM.

[This letter was franked by "Suffield."—21st December.]

LETTER XVIII.

WHITE TO MARSHAM.

Selborne. Jan. 2.
1793.

DEAR SIR,

RAIN IN 1792.

	Inch. Hund.
Jan.	6–7
Feb.	1–68
Mar.	6–70
Apr.	4–8
May	3–0
Ju.	2–78
July	5–16
Aug.	4–25
Sep.	5–53
Oct.	5–55
Nov.	1–65
Dec.	2–11
	48–56

My best thanks are due for your kind letter of Decem^r 21, to which I shall pay proper attention presently. But I shall first speak of the margin of this, which contains the rain of last year, which was so remarkably wet, that You may be perhaps glad to see what proportion the fall of water bears to that of other uncomfortable, unkindly years. The rain in 1782, as you see in my book, was 52 inches; in 1789, 42 inches; & in 1791, 44 inches: yet these wet seasons had not the bad influence of last year, which much injured our harvest; damaged our fallows; prevented the poor from getting in their peat & turf, which lies rotting in the Forest; washed & soaked my cleft beechen wood, so that it will not burn; it prevented our fruits from ripening. The truth is, we have had as wet years, but more intervals of warmth and sunshine.

I am now perswaded that your bird is a great curiosity, the very *Certhia muralis*, or *Wall-creeper*, which neither Willughby nor Ray ever saw; nor have I, in 50 years attention to the winged creation, ever met with it either wild, or among the vast collections that I have examined in London. It seems to be a South Europe bird, frequenting towns, & towers, &

castles: but has been found, but very seldem indeed, in England. So that you will have the satisfaction of introducing a new bird of which future Ornithologists will say,—" found at Stratton in Norfolk by that painful, & accurate Naturalist, Robert Marsham, Esq." You observe that Scopoli does not take notice that the hind-claw is about double the length of the fore-claws: but Linnæus corroborates your remark by saying " Ungues validi, præsertim posticus." You seem a little to misunderstand. Scopoli respecting the spots on the *inner-side* of the quill feathers: by the *inner side* he does not mean the *under side* of the wing next the body; but only the *inner* or *broader web* of the quills, on which those remarkable spots are found, as appear by the drawing. I am much delighted with the exact copies sent me in the frank, & so charmingly executed by the fair unknown, whose soft hand has directed her pencil in a most elegant manner, & given the specimen sa truly delicate & feathery appearance. Had she condescended to have drawn the whole bird, I should have been doubly gratified! It is natural to young Ladies to wish to captivate men: but she will smile to find that her present conquest is a very old man.

My best thanks are due for all your good offices respecting my work, & in particular for your late recommendation to the Duke of Portland.

You did not in y^r last, take any notice of my enquiries concerning *wood-peckers*, whether they ever pierce a sound tree, or only those that are tending to decay. I have observed that with us they love to bore the edible chest-nuts; perhaps because the wood is softer than that of oak. They breed in my outlet, I think in old willows. You have not told me anything about Arthur Young. You cannot abhor the dangerous doctrines of levellers & republicans more than I do! I was born & bred a Gentleman, & hope I shall be allowed to die such. The reason you having so many bad neighbours is your nearness to a great factious, manufacturing town. Our common people are more simple-minded & know nothing of Jacobin clubs.

I admire your fortitude & resolution; & wonder that you

have the spirit to engage in new woods & plantations! Our winter, as yet, has been mild, & open, & favourable to your pursuits. Pray present my respects to your Lady, & desire her to accept of my best wishes, & all the compliments of the season, jointly with yourself. I have now squirrels in my outlet: but if the wicked boys should hear of them, they will worry them to death. There is too strong a propensity in human nature towards persecuting & destroying!

I remain, with much esteem, Your's, &c.

GIL. WHITE.

LETTER XIX.

MARSHAM TO WHITE.

Stratton. Feb. 20.
93.

Dear Sir,

After offering you my hearty thanks for the favour of your pleasing & instructive letter of the 2^d of Jan. i must beg your pardon, for omitting the two articles you had mentioned to me. Indeed i thought i had answered them.—I suppose the wood-peckers do not attack the sound part of a tree; but where a bough has been broke off, & the stump died, & remained some years on the tree before it was broken off; then when the bark skins over the rotten part, these birds attack the skin over those false parts, where they find the holes almost ready made for their use. Several of the edible chestnuts that i have planted, have the woodpeckers holes in them; which i think i remember to have been dead stumps. But i am not certain.—As to Arthur Young, i never saw the man; but by the accounts of others, & from what i have read of his works, i conclude him an abominable coxcomb. We have a story of him, that a foreigner a Russian curious in husbandry, went to see him in Suffolk. He not being at home, the stranger enquired of his wife, how many acres of potatos he had that year, to fatten his swine i think 500? She answered none!

They did not use potatos.—He, you know, gives some descriptions of Noblemen's & Gentlemen's houses, & places. Several of which i have seen, where he is very erroneous.—I had minuted down some articles of his observations, & a friend told me, that no dependence could be had on his veracity. Lies in a pettyfoging writer, such as Farmer Young, do not signify much (tho' he is a voluminous man). But when you find men of fame dealing in lies, or false quotations (which are the worst of lies) they are shocking to an honest mind. Evelyn, e.g. who had perhaps a larger share of it than he deserved, abounded with both. But Addison's false quotation from Bp Burnet's travels * offends me most, as it gave occasion to others to abuse the Bp for lying. I conclude Addison was drunk in the evenings when he wrote his Travels; but as they passed several Editions both he & Evelyn, should have had the honesty to have corrected their errors as a duty they owed to the public.—I wish your friend Daines Barrington was not sometimes inaccurate. e. g. in his zeal against the migration of birds, he urges an instance which makes directly against his opinion. viz if Woodcocks crost the Sea, they would beat themselves against the Lighthouses. This, i am well informed, they do, every Autumn in Norfolk. And he is unlucky when he names the yellow-hammer in Hasselquist's ship †; one is left to suppose the only bird; when you may

* [It would seem that Marsham's memory had deceived him, and that he must have been thinking of some other author than Addison, whose character cannot be affected by what is above said of him. I have examined his 'Travels' without being able to find therein any reflexion on Burnet, to whom, indeed, as the Rev. W. Elwin has kindly pointed out to me, a high compliment is paid in the preface. " Among the authors of our own country we are obliged to the Bishop of Salisbury [Burnet] for his masterly and uncommon observations on the religion and governments of Italy." Mr. Elwin, and there can be no better authority, is fully persuaded of the groundlessness of the charge against Addison. Nor can that against Evelyn be maintained. Marsham's advanced age must be his excuse.—A. N.]

† [Hasselquist, born 1722, died at Smyrna in 1752. His journal and other literary remains were published by Linnæus, and afterwards translated into English, ' Voyages and Travels in the Levant, &c.' (London: 1766). The bird Barrington (Phil. Trans. 1772, p. 276) referred to as a

remember Hasselquist mentions many different birds, on different days, but forgets the poor yellow-hammer.—Mr Barrington concludes Monsr Adanson's birds to be martins, *because they roosted on the Sea-shore.*—But Adanson says after, when he lived by the Gambia, *great numbers of European Swallows came every evening into his hut, & past the night upon the rafters.* Now if these birds roosting on the sands proved them martins, does not their roosting on the rafters prove them swallows? From pieces of quotations you may prove blasphemy from the Bible, as you may remember finely proved by Pulteny (afterwards E. of Bath) against Thomson in the H. of Commons *.—I honour & love Mr Barrington; but i wish every man i love would be careful of what he commits to the public notice. Your friend Pennant has been too careless.

I thank you for your account of the rain of last year, as i do not measure it, i could only observe there has fallen a great deal. If the Squirrels did you as much harm as they do me, you would think your self obliged to the boys that destroy them. I paid for above 80 one year. They bite off the young shoots of my Trees.—Indications of Spring in 1793. Snowdrop Jan 15. Thrush sings Feb. 15. Hawth. l. Mar. 2. Ringdoves coo Feb. 22. Rooks build & stock doves coo Mar. 4. Hepatica F. Feb. 16. Yellow butterfly Feb. 24. Larch l. Mar. 9.

I hope you have presented your account of the fern-owl to the R.S. I am hungry for it. I am glad you liked the drawing of the two feathers. I hinted my wish for the whole bird; but she lent a deaf ear: & in that manner, all young Women have treated me (when i ask favours) since i was turned of 40.

I congratulate you upon the cheque given to the cruel

Yellow Hammer was most likely that which Hasselquist himself called *Emberiza africana* (pp. 14 and 206 of the English translation) and identified by Linnæus with his *Loxia chloris* (Syst. Nat. ed. 10, i. p. 174, no. 20), *i.e.* our Greenfinch.—A. N.]

* [This allusion is quite beyond me, nor can Mr. Elwin throw any light upon it.—A. N.]

french*, & remain with great esteem my dear Sir, your most humble & obliged servant,

R. MARSHAM.

N.B. you see the mournful power the Hag has over me. Feeling my hand not very shaking, i begin a letter & write 'till i am weary; lay it by, and wait 'till i feel myself willing to write again. So i have sometimes found more than a month slide away, before i seize my pen again. My strong comfort is that nobody suffers by my infirmity but myself. 'Tis like drinking; which 'tho' not my weakness, i think very pardonable in those under its influence. Mar. 15. this day Toads sing. I cannot remember a Winter having passed more mildly than the last.

In the Gent. Magazine of last Feb. is a letter against the torpidity of Swallows. Symptoms point as if it might be written by you. I had the lie about the toad in the block of stone in the Phil. Trans. fairly detected †. But i have also a proof of torpidity of Swallows in Yorkshire, that i cannot doubt. If you wish for the particulars, i will transcribe them for you. Again Adieu.

LETTER XX.

WHITE TO MARSHAM.

Selborne: June 15.
1793.

DEAR SIR,

FROM my long silence You will conclude that Procrastination has been at work, & perhaps not without reason. But that is not all the cause: for I have been annoyed this spring with a

* [Towards the end of the preceding year Frankfurt had been retaken by the Germans, and the French compelled to recross the Rhine.—A. N.]

† [I am unable to find any reference to this circumstance, nor can Mr. White, the Assistant-Secretary of the Royal Society, who has kindly made search for me, throw any light upon it.—A. N.]

bad nervous cough, & a wandering gout, that have pulled me down very much, & rendered me very languid & indolent.

As you love trees, & to hear about trees, You will not be displeased, when You are told that Your old friend the great *Oak* in the *Holt* forest is, at this very instant, under particular circumstances. For a brother of mine*, a Man of Virtù, who rents Lord Stawell's beautiful seat near the Holt, called *Morelands*, is at this very juncture employing a draughts-man, a French Refugee, to take two or three views of this extraordinary tree on folio paper, with an intent to have them engraved. Of this artist I have seen some performances; & think him capable of doing justice to the subject. These views my Brother proposes to have engraved, & will probably send a set to You, who deserve so well of all lovers of trees, as You have made them so much your study, & have taught men so much how to cultivate & improve them†.—I have told You, I believe, before, that the great *Holt Oak* has long been known in these parts by the name of the *grindstone* Oak, because an implement of that sort was in old days set up near it, while a great fall of timber was felled in it's neighbourhood.

After a mild, wet winter we have experienced a very harsh, backward spring with nothing but N. & N.E. winds. All the *Hirundines* except the sand-martins were very tardy; & do not seem even yet to make any advances towards breeding. As to the sand-martins they were seen playing in & out of their holes in a sand-cliff as early as April 9th. Hence I am confirmed in what I have long suspected, that they are the most early species. I did *not* write the letter in the Gent. Mag. against the torpidity of swallows: nor would it be consistent with what I have sometimes asserted, so to do. As to your recent proof of their torpidity in Yorkshire, I long to see it. But as much writing is sometimes irksome, cannot

---

* [His brother Benjamin, who, on leaving his business in Fleet Street, resided at Marelands, where he died. See memoir.—T. B.]

† [Whether these drawings were ever engraved or not I have no information. The artist could not have been Grimm, who was not a French refugee.—T. B.]

You call in occasionally some young person to be your Amanuensis?

There has been no such summer as this, so cold & so dry, I can roundly assert, since the year 1765. We have had no rain since the last week in April, & the two first days in May. Hence our grass is short, & our spring-corn languishes. Our wheat, which is not easily injured in strong ground by drought, looks well. The hop-planters begin to be solicitous about their plantations. Here I shall presume to correct (with all due deference) an expression of the great Philosopher Dr. Derham. He say in his Physico-theology, " that *all* cold summers are wet:" whereas he should have said *most*.

Have You seen Arthur Young's " *Example* of *France* a *warning* to *England?*" it is a spirited performance. The season with us is unhealthy.

With true esteem

I remain, Y^r obliged servant,

GIL. WHITE.

[At the head of this letter is the following note in the handwriting of Mr. Marsham:—

"This worthy man died this month."—T. S.]

ON THE
SENSE OF HEARING IN FISHES.

[The following letter was evidently intended for publication, but whether in the series addressed to Pennant or in that to Barrington cannot be ascertained. It is headed, as all the others are, "To the same," and with a number affixed written in pencil, but so worn as to be illegible. There is no date, and the words "Hints but not finished" are prefixed. It is a rough copy, with many verbal corrections.—T. B.]

It has long been a question among naturalists whether *Fishes hear or not*. This subject I should make no scruple to take in the negative; and without being biassed, or indeed without knowing what has been said before, shall proceed to give you my thoughts in my own way. And here I would be understood to mean *Fishes strictly so called*; for it is well known that *cetaceous Fishes*, the *Belluæ marinæ*, are furnished with ears, like quadrupeds, though the perforations are very small.

When people advance that *Fishes do hear*, I would answer that after the strictest examination, the best modern Ichthyologists assure us they are destitute of any kind of organs for that purpose. "Pisces destituuntur auribus auriculisque," says Linnæus.

But then if Fishes do not hear, some will say how do tame fishes in stews and canals come to be fed at the sound of a whistle? That fishes used to be fed will come when their owners whistle cannot be disputed; but they may have many intimations that their masters are not aware of; in the first place from their eyes, which are wonderfully quick and curiously adapted to all the various refractions of their element; and then from their feeling, which is very delicate and can from a distance discern the footsteps of those that approach; and moreover the sound of the whistle possibly may make a sensible impression on the water and awaken their attention. That water is very pervious to sound is known by many experiments; for noises made under water are distinctly heard above, and so *vice versâ*; and moreover sounds raised under water may be heard to an almost incredible distance by an ear placed under water. Now these noises cannot pervade any medium without occasioning a sensible vibration in it, and therefore they may become the object of *feeling*. Where one sense is wanting or impaired by any decay, the others are more alert and their attention is more alive. Thus blind people avail themselves of many little intimations that escape the attention of those who can see; they can remember men's voices as we distinguish their persons, and discriminate each friend as he enters the room by his step or his manner of opening or shutting the door. Hearing and feeling in particular are kindred senses, and the latter often performs the function of the former, as I shall endeavour to prove before I close this letter. On the morning of the 1st of Nov^r, 1755, some people that were busied about the pen-stock of a pond saw the fish agitated in a very unusual manner, and expressing uncommon terror and dismay; but were unable to form the least judgment concerning this novel commotion 'til the next mail from Portugal brought advice of the sad fate of the city of Lisbon, which was destroyed in that most awful moment by a tremendous earthquake.

A deaf person with whom I am very well acquainted, as he sits with his back to the door, can feel people enter the room though he cannot hear them; and some summers past, during the royal review at Spithead, could distinguish every salute by the vibrating of the floor and walls of his parlor and the chair in which he sat, though his hearing was too dull to be affected by the report of the cannons, which were at 30 miles distance.

When the 'Edgar' man-of-war was blown up at Spithead in Queen Anne's time, the concussion and crash, which were rather felt than heard at this place, were so horrible that a team at plow ran away with such fury as to tear the share out of the ground, and to drive it through the body of one of the horses. In a dead calm, with the weather-cock pointing to the N.E., we rather felt than heard the guns of the Tower of London, though at fifty miles' distance.

The following story, which was well authenticated at the time, is much to our purpose. While the French were besieging Bergen-op-Zoom in a late war, it happened that a young gentleman of some college in Cambridge was so affected by the loss of a dear friend that he shunned all society, and indulged his melancholy in lonely and sequestered places. One day, as he was lying at length on the grass in some retired spot, he felt, or thought he felt, a concussion like the discharge of ordnance. When he stood up the sensation ceased, but was repeated again as soon as he returned to his former posture. Struck with the oddity of the occurrence, he ran and called some of his acquaintance, who all declared that while they were on their legs they perceived nothing, but that as soon as they were stretched on the turf they plainly felt a shaking like that from the firing of great guns. These young people examined their watches and attended to the time of day, and were surprised to find by the next Dutch mail that it was the very juncture in which the assailants made a most vigorous attack on the town with a shower of bombs and all the thunder of their heaviest artillery.

(A wonderful effect that a cannonade had in N. America this war by scaring away all the lobsters from a large river where before they remarkably abounded.—Mentioned by Captain Duke of Sarson, who was on the spot at the time.—To enquire what river. It was at Hell-gate near the Island of New York. Hell-gate is a road or arm of the sea in the mouth of the Hudson river.

Sound conveyed along a mast in a dock-yard.—To examine

what Dr. Franklin says concerning sounds made under water (See Derham on sounds made under water but heard above) *.

* [The passage here referred to is in a note near the close of the third chapter of Derham's 'Physico-Theology,' and is as follows:—" But 'tis not the air alone that is capable of the impressions of sound, but the water also, as is manifest by striking a bell under water, the sound of which may plainly enough be heard, but is much duller, and not so loud; and it is also a fourth deeper, by the ear of some great judges in musical notes who gave me their judgment in the matter. But Mersenne saith, a sound made under water, is of the same tone or note, if heard under water; as are also sounds made in the air, when heard under water. *Vide* MERSEN.: *Hydraul.* Having mentioned the hearing of sounds under water, there is another curiosity worth mentioning, that also further proves water to be susceptible of the impressions of sound, viz. *Divers* at the bottom of the sea can hear the noises made above only confusedly; but on the contrary those above cannot hear the Divers below." The most elaborate and interesting investigations which had at this time been made on this subject were those of Anderon, recorded in the Phil. Trans. for 1748, with which Gilbert White does not appear to have been acquainted. He came to the conclusion that fishes are devoid of the sense of hearing, which, however, is scarcely proved by his facts. Franklin's experiments, interesting and conclusive as they are, do not appear to bear upon the question of the hearing of fishes. They show the extent to which sound is conveyed through water, but go no further.—T. B.]

SERMON*.

[I have selected the following sermon of Gilbert White's out of three in my possession, as a fair illustration of the general tone of his parochial instruction, and as an example of the ordinary character of the best village sermons of the period. The list, in his own hand, of the numerous occasions on which it was delivered is prefixed to this and to each of his other sermons; and I find attached to a sermon of his uncle Charles White, the Rector of Bradley and Swarraton, under whom he held his first curacy, a similar list, partly in the handwriting of the uncle, and afterwards in that of Gilbert White, who appears thus to have utilized his uncle's compositions, as heir not only to his secular property, but to his pastoral teaching.—T. B.]

Selborn: Aug. 6, 1758.
Selborn: May 13, 1759.
Farringdon: Septem. 7, 1760.
Farringdon: July 13, 1761.
Chute: May 9, 1762.
Fyfield · May 23, 1762.
Farringdon: July 4, 1762.
Farringdon: Nov. 11, 1764.
Faringdon: Jan. 24, 1768.
Faringdon, & Chawton: Dec. 3, 1769.
Faringdon: Jan. 26, 1772.
Faringdon: May 1, 1774.
Faringdon: April 28, 1776.
Fyfield: May 19, 1776.
Faringdon: Jan. 23, 1779.
Faringdon: April 22, 1781.
Faringdon: Nov. 24, 1782.
Selborne: Nov. 7, 1784.
Selborne: Dec. 1786.
Selborne: Aug. 24, 1788.
Selborne: Aug. 15, 1790.
Selborne: August 19, 1792.

Math: 25: 30. Cast the unprofitable servant into utter darkness: there shall be weeping, and gnashing of teeth.

THESE words are the conclusion of the parable of the talents; and designed by our Saviour to stir up all Xtians to faithfulness, and zeal in the exercise of all those powers, and means, whether outward or inward, natural or supernatural (for by every one of these is meant the talents) which God blesses

* [For this sermon I am indebted to the kindness of the Rev. M. G. Watkins, Rector of Barnoldby-le-beck, Lincolnshire.—T. B.]

them with: least by failing in the due use of them, they should fall under the sentence of the unprofitable servant; and be ejected out of God's Kingdom into most inexpressible miseries. By whatsoever endowments and gifts we may (by a due use of them) bring honour to God, and promote his Kingdom; by neglecting so to manage the same we become unprofitable; that is, do not answer the ends for which God hath fitted us; nor bring him those fruits and profits which he justly expects from those opportunities and means with which he hath so furnished us. It is true that none, even the best of men, do or can help or profit God. He reaps no gain or advantage by any of our doings: and therefore how great proficients soever we are in virtue, and holiness, we are still but unprofitable servants: according to that of our Saviour (Luke xvii. 10) "When ye have done all those things that are commanded you, say, we are unprofitable servants." And doubtless our Lord would not teach us to tell an untruth; and to say we are unprofitable, if we were not really so. It is therefore certain, that we can not be profitable to God: but withall it is as certain that he is pleased to accept us as *such*, when we are faithful, and do our true endeavour to serve his interests, and glory. When therefore we neglect these ends, and do not use the talents wherewith he has entrusted us, to such purposes; we are unprofitable in ye sense of the text, and fall under the condemnation of it. Such are the bounties and liberalities of God, that he is continually filling all things living with his blessings; especially man whom he hath made in his own image; and upon whom he poureth down the most plentiful effusions of his riches and grace. So that he among them, that partakes *least* of his favours, hath no less than a *talent*, a very considerable sum, committed to him; and hath therefore no small obligation to answer for. And the encreasing this talent, which is the return God expects for every benefit which he has conferred, is the using it in the best manner we can, to his honour, and the good of men. And by casting the unprofitable servant, him that did not so improve his talent, into utter darkness, is not meant only the depriving him of this *present life*: tho' darkness be frequently set in the H. S.

in opposition to the light of ye living, and signifies no more than natural death. But the word *darkness here* hath a further meaning; and signifies a much worse thing, viz. Hell, or the place appointed by God to be the prison of damned Angels, and men. And in this sense Darkness is made use of in other parts of S. as Jude v. 13: " To whom is reserved ye blackness of darkness for ever:" and 2 Pet. 2, " To whom is reserved the mist of darkness for ever."

Having thus explained the terms of the text, and thereby shewed what will subject people to the dreadful doom of it: I shall in the next place make it my business to shew more particularly what those talents are by the due use of which we may escape that sentence. And the Talents in general are all advantages and means, endowments, gifts, and faculties, whereby we may glorify God, or be beneficial to men. And these are twofold, either external, or internal. The external, or gifts of fortune, as some call y^m are riches, honour, and power. The internal, or endowments of Nature, are likewise double; either those seated in the body, as strength, and beauty: or those in the mind; as reason, and it's several branches, and faculties, viz. memory, understanding, and judgment. By every one of these we are put into a capacity (if we will but take care rightly to apply them) of doing service to God, and men; and so of becoming profitable servants.

I begin with external gifts, or those of fortune, as some call them; viz: riches, honour, and power. These, if rightly understood, are all of them very considerable helps towards doing good, and gaining God's love: because there are no duties with which he is more pleased than with humility, condescension, charity, and mercy. But to think these talents bestowed upon us only to pamper, and puff us up, and nourish us to a prodigious bulk, that we may be as it were alone on ye earth; such overgrown trees as eclipse all the blessings of Heaven from every thing around them; and suffer nothing to prosper or thrive near or under them; is to forget that there is an over-ruling power above, an higher than ye highest on earth, that considers all things done here, and will call them into judgment. It would be strange indeed, if ye Lord of the Vineyard should long bear such unprofitable loads, and not pronounce the just sentence upon them; "Cut them down, why cumber they the Ground." But if men, more than ordinary favoured with these bounties of God, seriously considering why He should commit five or ten talents to y^m when the generality of their Brethren have but one or two; and perceiving that to whom *much* is given, from them the *more* is required,—shall provide to answer the donor's expectations in the case; and employ their wealth, influence, and dignity to such ends as it may reasonably be presumed He gave them for: if they relieve and comfort the needy and distressed, and assist all people, as far as they can, according to their several exigencies; then do they thereby lay up for *themselves* treasures which may profit in the day of wrath; and bespeak Grace to help in the time of *their own* necessities; and shall have their talents, their riches, honour, and authority increased, and be called to nearer advances to the Divine presence.

The next talents, whereby we may be profitable, are the endowments of Nature, which, as I said before, are twofold, those of the body, and those of the mind. Those of the body are strength, and comliness of parts; by a right use of which we may do honour and service to the ever-blessed Giver.

And 1st our bodily strength we may employ, as Samson did his, in the behalf of God's friends, and subduing his enemies: or as Moses (tho' the meekest man on earth) did his, in vindicating those that are wronged, and delivering them from the injuries and oppressions of such, as being stronger than they, would trample them under their feet. The wise man tells us (Prov. 20: 29) "That the Glory of young men is their strength;" what they chiefly delight in. But for the most part, as they use it, it is only the occasion of evil and mischief to them: because they suffer themselves to be exalted thereby to pride, and into contentions and quarrels; only upon presumption that they shall have the advantage in such engagements, as being ye strongest: or else they show their strength in wicked and immoral practices; as excessive drinking, and fulfilling the lusts of the flesh; and glorying to out-do and conquer others in such vile and irrational emulations: never considering that all such glory is the height of their shame, and proves them only the more degenerate and brutish. They ought to be mindful how contrary all such uses of it are to the intents **for which God gave** it them; viz: that they should **exert it in undergoing more** abundant labours, and enduring **more hardships for his** sake: and so much as they **excell others in** strength, be the so much more mighty in resisting temptations, and overcoming the wicked one; and in fulfilling God's commandments, and exalting his praise, as the H: Angels, which excell in strength, we read, are: and in acts of piety, faith, devotion, and zeal; that they may have power with God, and be able to prevail with him for blessings, on **themselves and friends.** If thus we use our strength: **then out of the strong will** come forth sweetness: **for we shall thereby confirm and** increase our inward powers and spiritual graces, and likewise our everlasting reward.

And then 2[17] as for beauty, or the comeliness of our outward parts; we may thereby serve God acceptably, and endear ourselves to the Gracious Donor of them; as Esther did her's, to the benefit of the true Religion and welfare of God's faithful people. But if our hearts be lifted up within us because of it, and we are inclined to grow vain, and to despise others upon that account; if we use it only as an incitement to lewdness, and wicked **purposes, and to** multiply iniquity in ourselves and others, as is the practice with too many: if this be the best use we make of our fair proportions and beautiful frame; it would have been much better for us that we had been born the most ugly and deformed creatures in the world: since no outward deformity would render us hateful to God: but beauty, so abused, will be of all things the most odious, and abhorred in his sight: if we serve only Satan, and our own vile affections by our gracefulness of person, and not God and virtue; we shall certainly be esteemed unprofitable; and be sentenced, how splendid and gay soever we may have been **here, to** utter darkness, and weeping, and wailing, and gnashing of teeth.

But 3dly the next talent whereby we may profit, and ingratiate ourselves with our Alm: Lord, and Master, are the endowments of the mind, viz. *Reason*, with all its branches, and faculties; as Memory, Understanding, and Judgment. And these are more noble Instruments than the former, of serving God, and doing good; as those by which we may attain to the knowledge of the adorable perfections and will of the most High, in all needful instances; and be affected with the wonders and efficacy thereof in ourselves, and communicate them to others: and may thereby learn many useful arts and sciences; and thereby improve and help ourselves and neighbours. And therefore sure[ly,] to bury so beneficial a talent in Sloth, Intemperance, or Luxury; or to stifle it with the cares of this World, is most grievous Ingratitude, and unprofitableness, and must be exceedingly displeasing to the Giver. Such is the bounty, and generosity of God, the best and supreme of Masters, that tho' his family be numberless, and comprehending the whole race of mankind; yet is there no one servant, or dependant of his, (let the place or office, which he is employed in, be ever so mean and low) but hath at least one, or two, or more talents committed to him to trade and profit withall. And the most universal one is that of *Reason*, which God, as a common badge, bestowes on all his domestics in general, and without distinction, even the most inferior retainers to Him. This, notwithstanding its commonness, is so rich a gift, and carries with it such an air of divinity, and similitude of the All-perfect Donor, that there is nothing in nature of price enough to compare with it. It is this which distinguishes angels and men from beasts; and the eternal and surviving part of the Creation from the temporary and perishing: that which, like a celestial flame, sparkles, and shines, and spreads out its lustre every way; and extends itself to all parts of the Universe: and attracts to it not only present, but also past, and future objects, those in Heaven above, and in the earth beneath, and even under it. This is the principle of all Knowledge, both of things in the world, and those above it: that light which God has set up in the breast of every partaker of Humane Nature, whereby (as refiners do by fire) to try and find out, from among ye gross heap of dross and rubbish, good from evil, and truth from falsehood. A talent, which tho' but *one*, is capable of being multiplyed into manifold, and innumerable treasures. When reason is first sowed in infants, it is a very small seed indeed, the least of all seeds, scarcely perceptible; but wonderfully vigorous and apt to encrease; and by degrees, if rightly cultivated, shoots up into a mighty tree, the tree of knowledge, blossoming into arts and sciences, and speculations; and fructifying, first into moral actions, and practices; and then, as it advances to maturity, into divine habits, and graces. For "first is that which is *natural*, and *afterwards* that which is spiritual." And he that is faithful in little will be faithful in more: and, because he hath, shall have more given him, and have abundance, and grow from natural (if he be not wanting to make a due improvement with them) to supernatural and spiritual attainments.

This was the highest and brightest talent of natural light and conscience (before ye coming of Xt) which God committed to ye world; except to the Jews, who alone of all nations were acquainted with divine revelation, and some degrees of spiritual light: and by a due use of this, viz. of their rational faculties, and natural conscience *might* have been happy, and known the eternal power and goodness of God, and demeaned themselves acceptably towards him. But while they neglected strictly to follow the direction of this Heavenly Guide, and sought out to themselves many inventions in their religious services, which they could not justify by reason; and thought themselves wise therein, they became fools; and by dishonouring God with their will-worship, that is, with human inventions, instead of that which their own light and judgment, if not perverted, would have led them to, - - - became unprofitable servants: and, for darkening their own hearts, and acting against their own innate knowledge, worthy to be delivered up to a reprobate mind, and cast into præternatural, and utter darkness. Rom. i. 20, 21, 22, & 28.

The excellence, or highest improvement of this talent, reason, is to attain thereby to true wisdom; an ability to direct ourselves and others in the choice and pursuit of our proper end, everlasting happiness. For surely, **of** *all* **advantages, this will be found the greatest to ourselves**; and God will esteem it so too; because thereby our own, and probably other's souls will be gained **to** Him; which is the only **gain** that he accounts of. The **wisdom** of directing our own ways aright, **viz. being wise for ourselves is** doubtless the prime point of all wisdom: according to that of Solomon: (Prov. 14: 8) "The wisdom of the prudent is to direct his way." And whoso is wise will make the knowing and securing of his own eternal happiness his *main* business: and being sensible, (as he presently **must, that at all considers this matter)** that without a truly religious life, and a pure and holy conversation no man *can* be acceptable *to God*, or admitted into his joys; - - will labour above all things after sanctification, to please God both in body and soul: **that if he cannot** do any *further service* **to** his maker, he may be *sure however* to glorify him in working out his *own* salvation. But withal knowing that such a *private* spirit is very short of that of Xtianity (which would have *all* **men to** be saved) will find himself obliged *moreover* to become EXEMPLARY in goodness, that he may by the loveliness **of his ways** win *others* **to the** *like*, **and** yᵉ **service of God, and righteousness.**

GILBERT WHITE'S ACCOUNT-BOOK.

[The following transcript from one of Gilbert White's account-books affords so many interesting traits of his character at the period to which it belongs, that I have been induced, at the wish of many friends to whom I showed the original, to print it *literatim*. It has always struck me as exhibiting in its simplicity that combination of genial kindliness and generous hospitality with habitual prudence, punctilious formality, and methodical habits which was so characteristic of the whole of his after life. As an indication of some phases of ordinary college life of the time it is not without some amusing interest.—T. B.]

Expences preparatory to & during my year of Proctorship in the University of Oxon, 1752.

		Li: s: d:
March 20. 21.	On the road from Selborn to Oxon: & hire of Boy, & Horse	01 01 11
	Coffee-house	00 00 07
	Two Quire of paper, & this Book	00 03 00
25.	Subscription to the Concert	00 10 06
	Provost's, & Mrs. Croke's Man	00 02 00
	Pair of Norway-Doe Gloves	00 01 08
	Pound of Candles	00 00 06
	Cook's shop	00 00 05
28.	Tin-Boiler; & Chocolate pot, & mill	00 04 06
31.	Going to the Concert, choral night	00 01 00
	A feather-top'd grizzle wig f^m London	02 05 00
	Half pound of Hyson-tea f^m Har: Woods	00 08 00
	Half pound of Congo from Do.	00 04 00
31.	3 pounds of Chocolate from Do.	00 10 06
	Pr of Norway-Doe Gloves	00 01 08
	Cook's-shop	00 00 06
April 2.	Mr Smith, Senr Proct^r Man	00 01 00
	Large washing Bason	00 01 00
4.	Six large polished tea spoons	01 06 00
	Carried forward	07 03 09

		Li: s: d:
1752.	Brought forward	07 03 09
April 4.	Engraving my Crest on Do.	00 03 00
4.	Car: of two Hampers of Mountain from Southampton	00 15 00
	Porterage to Coll:	00 01 00
	Cinder-sifter, & hearth-brush	00 02 04
	Junr Proctor, Mr Dickens's Man	00 01 00
4.	6 doz: of Mountain-wine, half pints, half quarts, from Mr Atherley of Southampton: very old, & good..	04 16 00
	Bottles, Corks, & Hampers for Do.	01 12 06
6.	President of Trinity's Man	00 01 00
7.	Senr Proct^{rs} Man	00 01 00
8.	An 100 p^d weight of biscuit to treat the Masters of Art in Oriel Hall	05 00 00
	entered on my office then.	
	Paid the Porter for two weeks waiting	00 02 00
9.	Ringers, & Musick	00 10 00
	Alms-men of St. Barthol^{ws}	00 02 06
	4 p^{ds} of Candles	00 02 00
	Washing-pan, & wainscot-brush	00 00 08
	Tobacco, & pipes	00 01 01
	A Plate of Olives	00 01 06
	A bowl of rum Punch from Horsmans	00 02 06
	Two Sevil-Oranges	00 00 03
	A Sallad from Mason's Garden	00 01 00
	Taylor's man	00 01 00
10.	P^d my Predecess^r Mr Dickens	03 12 00
	To be repaid by my success^r	
11.	Took a Commons in port-mead	00 07 06
	Sallad from Mason's	00 00 06
	Odd matters	00 00 08
13.	Extraordinary Choral night	00 01 00
	For reading the 3rd & 4th Vol: of Amelia	00 00 06
14.	Mrs Croke's man	00 01 00
16.	Large Pier-Glass, second-hand, from London, bought by Jenny Croke	03 10 00
	Packing, & Carriage	00 06 00
	Porterage	00 00 06
	3 Eggs from Cook's shop	00 00 03
18.	Sallad from Mason's	00 00 06
	Gave Mr Parker's man of Trin: Coll:	00 01 00
18.	3 pair of black ribbed-stockings	00 18 00
19.	Spent at Engham	00 01 00
	Mouse-trap, & two Oranges	00 00 09
	Carried forward	30 02 03

			Li: s: d:
1752.		Brought forward	30 02 03
Apr. 20.	Present to the Vice-Chan: a loaf of Double Refin: Sugar 7 lbs. at 13d. With six bottles of Wine.		00 07 07
20.	Brother Chapman's Man		00 01 00
	Quire of whited-brown paper		00 00 04
	Plate of Olives		00 01 00
	Radishes		00 00 02
	Bottle of Ink		00 00 03
	2 Sevil Oranges		00 00 02
	A riding Cane		00 00 06
25.	Going to Bensington to meet Sister Becky*, & Mr Snooke		00 03 00½
26.	Mrs Croke's man		00 01 00
	President of Trinity's man		00 01 00
27.	Choral night		00 01 00
	Raisins & almonds		00 00 06
	Plate of Olives		00 02 06
	Mr Dike's man of Ch: Ch:		00 01 00
	Shewing Sister Becky Radclif's Library		00 01 00
29.	A Sallad from Mason		00 00 09
	Loaf of Single refined Sugar 9 lbs. at 9d		00 07 01
	Gave Brother Barker's Coachman for his care of Mouse, while he wintered in Rutland		00 02 06
	Mrs. Croke's Man		00 01 00
	Shewing Sister Becky great Tom		00 00 06
30.	Going to Woodstock with Sister Becky in her way to Rutland		00 05 00
	Shewing my Sister the Picture Gallery		00 01 00
	2 doz. of Corks		00 00 04
May 1.	Mr Dickens's Man		00 01 00
	Coffee-House		00 00 06
2.	Odd matters		00 00 04
3.	Provost's man		00 01 00
	Spent in journey to London to settle Mr Holt's Executorship-matters with Mr Butcher, & to Sunbury, & Selborn, from May 4 to May 26		04 19 09
	Cast Sheffield Razor of Will: Yalden		00 01 06
	2 Tea Canisters		00 00 08
9.	P^d Share of the expence for Mr Butcher's release when we settled accounts		00 10 06
		Carried forward	37 17 08½

* [His sister Rebecca, who married Henry Woods, Esq., of Shopwyke House, near Chichester.—T. B.]

GILBERT WHITE'S ACCOUNT-BOOK. 319

		Li: s: d:
1752.	Brought forward	37 17 08½
May 9.	Gratuity, my Share to D^{os} Clerks	00 13 01½
21.	P^r of Shoes of Geo. Tanner	00 05 06
27.	**Coffee-house**, & Mrs Croke's Man	00 01 06
28.	**Gardener** at the Physick-Garden	00 01 00
	Coffee house	00 00 04
	Gave Black Jack	00 01 00
	4 Lettuce from Mason's	00 00 06
June 1.	Large Iron-Chafingdish	00 02 06
	Going to the Concert	00 01 00
	6 Bottles of Olives bought by Benjⁿ in London at 2s. 6d. p^r bot. & pack: 6d.	00 15 06
	Seeds by Do.	00 00 09
2.	Ray's History of ye Rebell: in 1745	00 03 06
	Pot of Coffee, & Br: & Butter	00 01 02
	Coffee-House	00 00 06
	Shewing Nanny Yalden, Benjⁿ & Will: Yalden * the Museum, & Magd. Coll:	00 01 06
4.	Shewing N: Yalden Monday's Organ	00 02 00
	Charcoal	00 02 02
	Odd matters paid for by Joe	00 03 01
5, 6.	Expences in going to Stow Gardens, S^r Cl: Cotterels, & Blenheim with Nan: Yalden, Benjⁿ &c.	00 15 06
	Pair of Woodstock Gloves	00 02 00
9.	Vice-Chanc^{rs} **man**	00 01 00
	Basket of **Strawberries**	00 00 04
	Coffee-House, & **Strawberries**	00 00 10
	2 Lettuce, & **oatmeal**	00 00 04½
14.	The President of Trinity's man	00 01 00
	A Lobster	00 01 02
	Lettuce, & Cream	00 00 05
15.	The Concert, choral night	00 01 00
	A Tart	00 00 03
16.	Mr Chapman, Broth^r Proct^{rs} man	00 01 00
17.	Nash of Worcester's man	00 01 06
	Cherries, & Strawberries	00 00 10
19.	Strawberries, & Lettuce	00 00 08
	Gardener at the Physic-Garden	00 00 06
19.	Carriage of Olives, & **porter**	00 01 02
	Carried forward	42 03 10½

* [Children of the Vicar of Newton Valence and his own brother Benjamin.—T. B.]

		Li:	s:	d:
1752.	Brought forward	42	03	10½
June 19.	Shewing M^r & Mrs Whiston All: Souls Library*	00	01	00
	Coffee-House	00	00	08
19.	Punch for Bappy Isaac†	00	02	00
	Coffee, Candles, & milk	00	01	02½
	Coffee	00	00	05
29.	Gave ye Drawer at ye Blue Boar at ye Barbers Feast	00	01	00
30.	Gave an old man	00	00	06
	Hogshead of Cyder from the Southams of Devon; brought in April 27	04	00	00
	Car: in London to the Carrier	00	02	00
	Car: from London to Oxon by the waggon	00	15	00
	Porterage into the Cellar	00	02	00
30.	A Crab, Lettuce, & Milk	00	01	01¼
July 1.	Coffee-House, & raspberries	00	01	03½
2.	Vice-Chan: Man at Commemoration-Dinner	00	01	00
	Tom Warton's Commem: Ode	00	00	06
3.	Gave at Physick-Garden	00	01	00
	Fruit	00	00	06
	Bell & wire	00	01	00
	Coffee-House: tooth-powder	00	01	06
5.	Gave at St. Ebbe's Church at the Sacrament which I received to qualify me for my office	00	01	00
	Stamped parchment instrument	00	01	04
	Gave the Clerk, & other Witness	00	02	00
	Fee at the sitting when I took the oaths	00	04	00
6.	Provost's man: & weekly concert	00	02	00
	Coffee-House	00	00	09
8.	Dr Wanley, the Compound^r of Worcester's Servant	00	01	00
9.	Gave Dr Goddard's man when I sold my mare	00	01	00
9.	Gave the Judges' servants	00	02	00
	Gave Barret's man	00	02	00
10.	Gave Bat Piegley's man	00	01	00
	Punch for Mr Mulso, & Tom ‡	00	01	06
13.	Gave Black Jack, who broke his leg	00	01	00
	Odd matters bought by Joe	00	01	05
14.	Gave Vice-Chan: man	00	01	00
15.	Black leathern-breeches with linings	00	12	00
	Carried forward	49	12	07

---

* [Mr. Whiston was a descendant of the celebrated William Whiston, who was uncle to Mr. Barker. See memoir.—T. B.]

† [His cousin.—T. B.]

‡ [The father and brother of Mrs. Chapone. See memoir.—T. B.]

			Li:	s:	d:
1752.		Brought forward	49	12	07
July 16.		P^d for 6 fan-back'd chairs, with leathern bottoms ..	03	12	00
		For two great-armed Ditto	01	16	00
		Butter print for my Un: White................	00	02	00
	17.	P^d Common-room bill for Port, & Madeira to July ye 4th	03	14	07
	18.	P^d Barret's Bill for keeping ye Mare, & Black Horse; & some Hire: to June 23rd	04	10	00
	17.	Punch for Bappy Isaac	00	02	00
		Quire of paper	00	01	00
		Odd matters bought by Joe	00	00	05½
	20.	Farrier's Bill for shoing to that time	00	09	04
	20.	Barret's Bill for keeping Horse to that time	01	02	06
	20.	200 of Broccoli plants, & basket	00	02	04
		Elder Rob, & conserve of Ilips	00	00	08
	20. 21.	Expenses from Oxon, to Selborn	00	09	06
		Barret's portmanteau-Horse	00	10	00
	22.	Joe's Expenses back to Oxon................	00	03	02
Selborn.					
	23.	Dr Bristow's man...................	00	01	00
	23.	Bleeding Mouse	00	00	06
		Sending Jack Wells to Alton, & Bradley	00	00	09
		John Carpenter's Horse to Bradley	00	00	06
	25.	Robin Tull in the Garden	00	03	06
	27.	Two loads of Hay laid up in my Father's rick	02	06	00
		A Quarter of Oats from Dr Bristow	00	16	00
	28. 29.	Going to meet Dr Bentham, & Mr Barners at Alton; and going with y^m to Farnham................	00	14	05
	30.	Mr Hinton's man of Chawton	00	01	00
Augt 1.		Mr Battin's man	00	01	00
		Jack Wells, an errand........................	00	00	02
	3.	Pair of Shoes from George Tanner	00	05	06
	4.	Mouse, two shoes before. remove behind	00	01	03
	4.	Gave my Un: White's servants........	00	02	00
Oxon.					
	5. 6.	Spent in Journey thither without a Serv^{nt} to meet the Mulsos	00	07	01
	7.	Fruit...	00	00	08
	8.	Horse at Woodstock: ye Mulsos treated..........	00	00	06
		Punch for the Mulsos........................	00	05	00
		Shewing Wadham Chappel to D^o...............	00	00	06
		Weekly Concert	00	01	00
	11. 12.	Expenses to Stow Gardens with ye Mulsos	00	14	01
		Carried forward	72	10	06½

		Li:	s:	d:
1752.	Brought forward	72	10	06½
Aug^t	Fruit	00	00	06
11. 12.	Oxon Butter Print, a present for Mrs Batten	00	02	00
13.	A square Cap, at my going into Office	00	07	00
	Hat for myself, at D°	00	15	00
	Two Hats for my men at D°	01	00	00
	Hat box	00	00	06
	Fruit	00	00	03
15.	Pair of Shoes of Remmet's man	00	07	00
15.	Parson's bill, for Glasses, and stoneware	01	19	06
16.	Mrs Croke's man	00	01	00
	Gardener at ye Physic Garden for two melons	00	01	00
	Spinage-seed, garlick, & half a Gallon of Mazagon Beans from Mason ye Garden^r	00	01	04
	Keeping Horse at Barret's, & shoing	00	09	10
17.	Mrs Witherington for painting my room, & a Hearth Cloth	01	16	00
	Gave Bet Bull	00	01	00
17.	Barret's Boy	00	00	06
	Odd matters bought by Joe	00	01	05½
	Quire of wrapping-paper	00	00	04
	Gave the porter	00	00	06
17. 18.	Spent in Journey to Selborn	00	12	02
	Portmanteau Horse to D°	00	10	00
	Joes expences back	00	03	06
Selborn.				
20.	John Neal mending Cloaths	00	00	11
	Six pounds of shot	00	01	00
22.	Jack Wells to Bradley	00	00	06
	Tanner's Horse to D°	00	01	00
	Goody Tolvery for washing	00	00	08
	Robin Tull for 300 Savoy plants	00	01	06
27.	John Lasham bringing S^r: Becky's Letter	00	01	06
28.	Mr Batten's Butler	00	01	00
31.	Meeting Jenny Croke, & Sister Becky at Basingstoke	00	18	06
Septem^r 14 N.S.	P^d then my Sister Becky what my Brother Barker expended for Mouse's winter's run, farriering, & shoeing in Rutland	02	14	02½
	Half pound of Gunpowder	00	00	08
	Mending breeches	00	00	04
19.	Mouse remov'd all round at Bradley	00	00	06
	William for cleaning my Gun	00	00	06
22.	Mr Batten's Butler	00	01	00
	Carried forward	85	04	08½

		Li:	s:	d:
1752.	Brought forward	85	04	08¼
Sept* 22.	Gave Tom Ruffel for shewing me some quails	00	00	06
	Bill Cosens to hold up her head	00	00	06
26.	Servants at Bradley	00	02	00
	Corn at Alton, & chambering saddle	00	01	00
	Mending Girth	00	00	06
29.	Gave towards my Br: John's Ziczac up the Arbour Hill	00	01	00
Octob* 1.	Sent R: Tolvery with my Father's mare from Selborn to Bradley	00	01	00
	Two 100 of tacking nails	00	00	08
6.	Mrs Yalden's maid	00	01	00
7.	A petticoat for Tull's naked wench	00	02	06
13.	Mr Batten's Servants	00	02	00
14.	Beckhurst, 4 days & half in ye Garden	00	04	06
13.	Set of Shoes for Mouse, one bar	00	02	06
15.	Gave the old man at Mr Henley's Gate	00	00	06
	Second Subscript^a to the Ziczac	00	01	00
	Sending Boy to Alton	00	00	03
18.	Gave Dr Bristow's Servant	00	01	00
	Lost at Commerce	00	01	00
19.	Mending Cloaths	00	01	00
20.	Gave among the poor of Selborn	00	13	00
	Ned Aldred for shaving	00	00	06
	Jenny Baker for mending shirts	00	01	03
	Dame Turner for washing &c.	00	01	00
Oxon.				
25. 26.	Spent in Journey from Selborn to Oxon in a post-chaise with Jenny Croke	01	03	11
25.	Gave Jenny Croke a round China-turene, being prevented paying for ye post-chaise	01	16	04
	The post-boy	00	02	06
29.	Hire of Horse to Glimton	00	02	00
	President of Trinity's man, & Ostler	00	01	06
30.	As Junr Proctor, to the Savilian Profess^{rs}	04	10	00
30.	The Concert, choral night	00	01	00
	Coffee House	00	01	03
31.	Pair of Norway-Doe Gloves	00	01	08
31.	Mr Nash's Servant, & Coffee house	00	01	04
Novemr 4	Coffee-House	00	00	08
5.	Sacrament at St. Maries 1s. Mrs Croke's man 1s.	00	02	00
	Bottle of ink	00	00	03
6.	Lost at Cards in the Common-room	00	01	00
	Carried forward	95	10	03¼

Y 2

			Li:	s:	d:
1752.		Brought forward	95	10	03½
Novr 8.	Coffee-House		00	00	06
8.	Vice-Chan: man		00	01	00
	Pair of yarn Gloves		00	01	00
10.	Gave Black Jack, who broke his leg		00	01	00
11.	4 bottles of French-Olives from London		00	15	00
	Quart of fine oyl, & stone bottle		00	02	10
	Quart of vinegar, bottle, & basket		00	01	02
	2 Westmoreland Hams, w^t 35 lbs. at 7^d		01	00	05
	6 p^d of Sturgeon, pan, & basket		00	03	00
13.	Choral-night, & Coffee-house		00	02	00
14.	A door-mat		00	00	04
	Two pounds of common Candles		00	00	11
	Odd matters		00	00	04½
15.	Horse-hire to Woodstock		00	02	00
	Spent there		00	02	07
16.	Shewing Mrs Lort Radclif's Library		00	01	00
	A small lanthorn		00	01	04
17.	Car: & porterage of the above things f^m London		00	03	04
	Taylor ye Carpenter's bill for Jobs		00	14	00
	Dumb bell in my mens room		00	05	00
17.	2 cut-top'd Cruets		00	03	00
17.	Mason's Bill for Hearth-stone, &c.		01	15	06
17.	Bought from Woodstock turn-pike, a small beautiful liver-coloured Spaniel-Bitch * of the Blenheim-breed, one year old		00	07	06
19.	Gave at the Sacrament		00	01	00
21.	Horse-hire for an airing		00	02	00
22.	Gave the printer, who brought my present of six Oxon-Almanacks		00	01	00
23.	Mr Biesley's man		00	01	00
24.	Sadler's Bill for Horse-cloth, &c.		01	00	00
25.	Half pound of Souchong from H: Woods		00	04	00
	Car: & port: of Turene, & tea		00	01	01
	Box for the Turene, & Canister		00	00	10
26.	Mrs Croke's Servant		00	01	00
27.	Pair of ribbed yarn stockings		00	02	06
27.	Concert, Choral night		00	01	00
28.	Provost's man		00	01	00
30.	Coffee-house		00	00	08
Decr 1.	Plaisterer's bill for white-washing, &c.		00	04	06
		Carried forward	104	01	08

* [Fairey Queen.]

			Li:	s:	d:
1752.		Brought forward..................	104	01	08
Decr 2.	Taylor's Bill for Proctor's Gown, Cassock, mens suits,				
		mens Cloaks, &c:.........................	03	08	00
2.	Dr Durnfort's, Gr: Comp^r of Wadham Coll: man		00	01	00
3.	President of Trinity's man...................		00	01	00
	Candles		00	02	01
4.	Paid Boswell in part for altering Br: Harry's study				
		into a Servants room	01	01	00
5.	Iron-monger's Bill, for cleaning Grate, &c:		00	11	06
	A trivet, & fork from D°........................		00	05	00
5.	Lost at Cards		00	01	00
6.	Com: room wine-bill from July 7th to Decr 6		01	18	05
6.	Battles* in Lady-Day Quart^r		01	15	11
	„ in Midsum^r Quart^r.....................		12	14	08
	„ in Mich: Quart^r		07	15	02
	Odd matters		00	00	03
7.	Coffee House		00	00	08
8.	Coffee-House		00	00	04
10.	Mrs Croke's man		00	01	00
11.	Mr Nash's man...............................		00	01	00
14.	Oxon Almanack & 3 explanations.................		00	01	01½
	D° & 1 D°		00	01	00½
14.	Provost's man		00	01	00
	Lost at Cards		00	01	00
15.	President of Trinity's man......................		00	01	00
16.	Mending Barret's saddle which I borrowed........		00	01	04
18.	1 Quart of white Dutch kidney-beans		00	01	00
18.	Bet Bull's bill for cream, bread, & butter, making				
		towels, &c: to Decem^r 13th..................	00	10	11
	Mrs Croke's Bill for 20 yards of blue check'd-linen				
		for window-curtains at 20^d..................	01	13	04
18.	P^d Mr Ward for putting-up draw-Curtains		01	11	09
	„ to D° for a Cushion...........................		00	03	03
	Mrs Croke's bill, for two cloth-frocks, one D° waist-				
		coat, p^r of sheets, 3 table cloths, &c:............	10	19	06
	Her Bill for Proctor's Velvet-sleeves, silk grogram				
		cassock, silk sash, &c:.....................	10	13	10
	Her bill for two mens broad-cloth suits, & cloaks, &				
		p^r of stockings each.........................	13	08	05
18.	5 doz: of Corks to bottle out the bottom of my hogs-				
		head of Cyder	00	00	10
18.	Men, pair of Shoes each		00	10	00
		Carried forward	173	19	00

* [The name for College bills. Usually spelt battels.—T. B.]

		Li:	s:	d:
1752.	Brought forward	173	19	00
Decr 19.	Flask of Ink for my Father	00	01	03
18. 19.	Boy, & Horses at Barret's	00	03	10
	Barber Xmas Box	00	01	00
	Barret's man	00	01	00
	Coffee House	00	00	08
17. 18.	Boy's expences from Selborn to Oxon	00	01	07
	Bull's maid	00	01	00

Bradley and Selborn.

		Li:	s:	d:
19. 20.	Expences on the road f^m Oxon to Bradley	00	10	00
	Boy's Hire	00	03	06
24.	Gave John Appleton at Bradley	00	01	00
25.	„ Goodman Townsend at Swarraton	00	01	00
27.	Third subscription to the Zigzag	00	03	00
	Trimming little Jack, given me by my Uncle White	00	00	06
29.	Mr Johnson'n maid, & lost at Cards	00	01	02
	Velvet for Cape to a Frock	00	01	06
	Mending a frock	00	00	06
	Advertising, & crying Fairey	00	03	06
	Reward to Bernard Bailey at Swallowfield, whether she was strolled	00	07	00
	News-man for bringing her to Selborn	00	01	00
1753.				
Jan:	Letters about her, & sending ye Oxon news-man out of his way	00	01	08
1.	Mending powder-horn, & girth	00	00	03
2.	Mouse remove, & second-hand shoe	00	00	07½
2.	Ten yards of Irish from Lee, at 3^s p^r y^d	01	10	00
	Two thirds of Lawn at 6^s p^r yard	00	04	00
	Thread, tape, & buttons	00	00	07
	Jenny Baker making three shirts	00	03	00
	Making three stocks	00	00	06
2.	Lost at Cards	00	01	06
4.	4 pounds of shot, & quart^r p^d of powder	00	01	00
	Will: Carpenter two Days, & half in Garden	00	02	06
	Lost at Cards	00	00	06
	Lost at Cards	00	00	06
10.	Gave my Un: White's maid	00	01	00
	Washing at Bradley, & Selborn	00	01	01
	Boy to Oakhanger	00	00	02
10.	Tanner for soling, &c: a pair of thick shoes	00	01	03
12.	Lost at Goose	00	00	06
13.	2 Quarts of early-pease, & an ounce & half of Carrot-seed f^m Farnham	00	01	04½
	Carried forward	178	15	00

		Li:	s:	d:
1753.	Brought forward	178	15	00
Jan: 13.	Half gallon of broad-beans	00	00	03
13.	A small saddle bought of Tanner	00	06	00
15.	Will: Carpenter in the Garden	00	01	00
	Peck of Barley-meal for Fairey	00	00	06½
17.	Gave Mr Newlin's maid	00	01	00
	Lost at Cards	00	01	00
18.	Sent Boy to Oakhanger	00	00	02
19.	Leek, radish, and parsley-seed f^o Farnham	00	00	08
19.	Removing little Jack's shoes	00	00	06
24.	Will: Carpenter in the Garden	00	01	00
24.	Tanner soling thick shoes	00	01	02
„	Chrystal to a watch	00	01	00
„	mending Fairey Queen's Collar	00	00	04
26.	Sent boy to Hawkley about Grass for Jack	00	00	03
	Lost at Cards	00	00	05
27.	Gave Tanner for putting Mouse to winter	00	01	00
28.	Gave my Un: White's Servants	00	02	00
28.	Gave Mr Batten's D^o: lay at his house	00	03	00
29.	Hire of Tanner's mare to Reading	00	02	06
	Hire of Jack Wells to D^o	00	01	06
	Pint of ale, & turnpike	00	00	03½
30.	Boy's expences back	00	01	04
30.	Expences at Reading	00	10	07
30.	Post-chaise to Bensington. & Boy 1^s	00	12	03
	Spent at D^o	00	00	09
	Return post-chaise from D^o to Oxon	00	04	00
	Boy	00	00	06
Oxon.	Cook's shop	00	00	06
31.	Bed at Blue Boar, & Chamber-maid	00	01	06
Feb: 3.	Plate of cold veal from Cook's shop	00	00	04
4.	Gave Mrs Croke's man	00	01	00
5.	Gave little Xtian	00	01	00
6.	„ Mr Nash's Man of Worcester Coll:	00	01	00
	Odd matters	00	00	04
7.	Gave Barret for the use of his Saddle	00	01	00
9.	Mr Chapman's man	00	01	00
10.	Gave old Bull for Xmass-box	00	02	06
	Washing-bason	00	01	00
14.	Paid Mrs Barnes's Bill for wood and coal to Feb: 5.	03	11	06
13.	Bowl of Punch for the Master, Wardens, &c: of the Barber's Company	00	02	06
	Pipes, & tobacco for D^o	00	00	07½
	Carried forward	185	15	00½

		Li:	s:	d:
1753.	Brought forward	185	15	09½
Feb: 13.	Pound of Candles; & oatmeal	00	00	07
15.	Spent at the King's Head; being obliged to be much in yᵉ High-street on account of an Election-treat	00	04	06
17.	Coffee-House	00	00	05
19.	Paid for the paper of Mʳ Kennicott's dissertation on 1st Chron: ii. Chap.	00	01	02
	Binding Dᵒ	00	00	06
	2 sticks of sealing-wax	00	00	06
19.	Concert, common night	00	01	00
	Coffee-house	00	00	04½
22.	Gave Craddock's maid, who brought me Mʳ Nowell's present of 2 brace of woodcocks	00	01	00
	Gave a sick man	00	00	06
26.	Concert, Choral-night; & Coffee-house	00	02	00
March 1.	Lowth's Lectures stitched in paper, a present to Mʳ Scrope of Castle-comb	00	12	06
	Car: of Dᵒ	00	00	03
	Oysters	00	00	02
3.	Coffee-House	00	00	04½
4.	Provost's man	00	01	00
5.	Oysters	00	00	03
6.	Gave a poor Frank from Constantinople	00	00	06
7.	Coffee-House, an evening	00	01	06
8.	Pʳ of strong shoes from Remmet's man	00	07	00
8.	Gave Judge's Servants	00	02	00
9.	,, the Girl at Mʳ Mulso's Lodgings	00	01	00
10.	Coffee-house	00	00	06
11.	Gave the Printer who brought the lent-scheme	00	01	00
11.	Mʳˢ Croke's man	00	01	00
12.	A Sallad from Mason's	00	00	06
12.	Subscription to the Concert for 1753	00	10	06
12.	Common-night	00	01	00
	For Candles, & brown-paper	00	01	02
	Odd matters	00	00	06½
13.	Gave Mʳ Bosworth's Servant	00	01	00
16.	Mʳ Nash's Servant	00	01	00
17.	Coffee-house	00	00	05
17.	Pair of large silver-buckles	00	17	00
19.	Paid for the paper of Lowth's Poet[1] lectures	00	02	02
	For Dᵒ of Holloway's Letter & spirit	00	01	01
19.	Binding both	00	01	06
	Quire of paper	00	01	00
	Carried forward	189	16	06

			Li:	s:	d:
1753.		Brought forward....................	189	16	06
Mar: 19.	The Concert		00	01	00
	21.	A Commons on Port-mead......................	00	07	06
		Coffee-house........................	00	00	04
	24.	Oysters for Mr Nash	00	00	10
	26.	Common Concert; & a negus	00	01	04
		Putting piece of flannel in riding breech⁸..........	00	00	06
	28.	Gave Mr Burrough's man of Trin:.............	00	01	00
	30.	Paid Mr Benjⁿ Burrough, Junr of the Act, for 64			
		Regent A:M: at 1ˢ 3ᵈ pr man....................	04	00	00
	30.	Gave Mr Gearing's man of Trinity................	00	01	00
		Tooth-powder........................	00	00	04
Apr: 1.	Gave Mrs Croke's man...................		00	01	00
		Quarter of a pound of Bohea.....................	00	02	00
		Carpenter's Job	00	00	03
	4.	Pr of thick shoes	00	07	00
		Sausages; & gave away	00	01	00
	5.	Shewing Brothr Thoˢ Physick-Garden.............	00	01	00
	6.	Shewing Dᵒ the Theatre......................	00	01	00
		Sallad, & fruit	00	00	08
	9.	Horse hire to Chalgrave, & Mrˢ D: Servant........	00	03	00
	10.	Candles, & odd matters bᵗ by Joe.................	00	03	03½
		2 Quarts of marrow-fat pease.....................	00	01	00
		Ink, & quills..............................	00	00	07
	11.	Mr Nash's man, & Coffee-House	00	01	04
		Gave Cook the Gardener.....................	00	00	06
	12.	Horse-hire to Woodstock wᵗʰ Br: Tho:	00	02	00
		Spent there	00	05	08
	13.	Spent at yᵉ 3 Goats in a party	00	02	06
12. 13.	Will: Deweys expences with Mouse, & John Carpenter's Horse to Oxon....................		00	06	00
		Odd matters bought by Joe	00	00	07
	14.	Mouse 2 new shoes before, 1 bar	00	01	02
		Expences for Boy, & horses at Barret's	00	02	00
		Gave Barret's man	00	01	00
		Coffee-house...........................	00	00	02
	14.	Pr of tan-leather boot-straps	00	01	06
		Paid more at Barret's.......................	00	01	10
14. 15.	Expences from Oxon to Selborn		00	09	00
		Boy's hire, and little Horse	00	06	06
Selborn.					
		Removing Mouse before his Journey	00	00	06
		Br: Tho: seeds fᵐ London	00	04	00
		Carried forward	197	19	01½

		Li:	s:	d:
1753.	Brought forward....................	197	19	01½
Apr: 20.	Men in the Garden	00	07	06
	Gave my Father's man	00	02	00
	Jenny Baker mending shirts	00	01	00
	Sending Boy to Hawkley, & Newton	00	00	05
	Paper, & oil for Hot-bed.................	00	00	03
	Mending Cloaths.......................	00	00	03
	Mouse 20 weeks run in Mr Butler's Grounds at 6^d p^r week................................	00	10	00
	Little Jack 10 weeks, at Merchants at Hawkley at D°...............................	00	05	00
	Gave Merchant's boy	00	00	06
20.	2 Silver, & 1 Scotch fir, planted in the upper end of the Ewel-Close	00	01	06
23. 24.	Spent in Journey from Bradley to Oxon	00	09	06
	Gave Timothy Pound at Speenham	00	01	00
Oxon.				
25.	The Provost's, & Mrs Croke's Servant	00	02	00
26.	Gave at Charity Sermon........................	00	00	06
27.	Gave Barber.................................	00	00	03
28.	Gave Xtian Motley for making Bro: Tho: Bed in Harry's room	00	02	06
29.	Gave Mr Carne's servant	00	01	00
30.	„ at the Sacrament at St. Mary's	00	01	00
30.	Paid Boswel for altering Harry's study into a servant's room; which with £1 1^s 0^d paid before is in full..................................	00	12	00
	Half pound of Sugar	00	00	06
30.	Concert, choral night	00	01	00
May 1.	Gave at the Physick-Garden	00	00	06
	Provost's man	00	01	00
2.	Mr Twynehoe's man. Went out of my office......	00	01	00
4.	Gave Mr Jennings's servant	00	01	00
	Battles* in St Tho: Quart^r 1752	04	18	11
	„ in Lady-Day Quart^r 1753	04	13	02
	P^d Mr Diesley of Trin: my Sr Pro: for his assistance being defrauded of the Logic-Lectureship	21	00	00
4.	Bowl of Punch for the Proctors	00	02	06
	Quart^r of p^d of Bohea.............................	00	01	09
4.	Half Hogshead of Southam-Cyder as a present to my Father	01	17	06
	Half Hogsh: of D° to my Uncle White	01	17	06
	Carried forward	235	15	09½

* [See note, p. 325.]

		Li:	s:	d:
1753.	Brought forward	235	15	00½
May 4.	Cartage in London to the Waggon	00	02	02
	Biscuits at the Vice-Chan: at settling accounts	00	01	02
	To Mr Beaver, & Freeman for chanting	01	01	00
	Bet: Bull bed-making for the year	01	00	00
	Mr Benjn Burrough 3 Regents-fees	00	03	00
	Keeping & breeding-up two of Mab's puppies......	00	11	04
	Xtian Motley 3 quart{rs} washing	03	03	00
	Taylor's Bill......................	00	12	00
	Keeping Horse one week	00	06	00
	Shaving in Proct{rs} year	01	02	06
	Wood, & coals.................................	02	00	04
	Exceedings in St Tho: Quart{r}....................	01	06	11
	„ in L: Day	01	00	02
		£248	04	08½

Money received from my Fellowship, &c.: 1754.

		Li:	s:	d:
Octr 18.	Of Mr Frewen Dividend due Nov: 1753	04	02	0
22.	Of Mr Nowel, 1 Year's room rent to Midsum{r} 1754..	08	08	0
	1 Year's rent of 2nd room to Mich: 1754	05	00	0
	By fines from Mander, Sr Treas{r}	26	05	8
	By Dividend from D{o}..........................	23	02	0
	By Bal: from Mander in 1752: 1753..............	05	08	6
	....Savings in 1754	02	14	4
	Dirge	00	01	0
Nov: 24.	Surplice-fees at Durley	00	08	4
Decemr 28.	For supplying Durley-Church an year from Septemr 9. 1753. to D{o} 1754..........................	24	00	0
1755. Mar: 9.	For supplying D{o} half an year to yt time..........	12	00	0
		£111	09	10

Money received. 1753. 1754.

		Li:	s:	d:
June 3.	From Mr Fyler for presenting him to ye Degree of A:B:	01	01	00
	From Mr Musgrave on his putting-on a Law-Gown.	01	01	00
	From Mr Edgehill on D{o}	01	06	00
	Library-fee from Mr Musgrave...................	00	05	00
	Carried forward	03	13	00

		Li:	s:	d:
1753.	Brought forward	03	13	00
June 3.	From Mr Nowel for A:M: Degree	01	01	00
	Presenting Wickham, and Vaughan	02	02	00
	Wickham's Library fee	00	05	00
	Vaughan's Do	00	05	00
	Fyler's Do	00	05	00
Octr 18.	By 7 fines from Senr Treasr	38	4	00
	Dividend from Do	21	0	00
	Dean's Stipend	02	0	00
	Livery	02	10	00
	Mr De Chair's fee for presentation to Degree of M:A: in Mich: term 1753	01	01	00
1754.				
Feb: 25.	Wedding at Durley	00	05	00
May 4.	Mr Taylor's present: fee for A:M: Degree			
Nov. 6.	Wedding at Durley	00	05	00
12.	Sold Mr Nowel 2 doz: of Mountain wine	02	02	00
		£74	18	00

Money received arising from my Fellowship, Deanship, &c., in 1752 & 1753.

		Li:	s:	d:
Mar: 20.	Brought with me from Selborn	19	17	6
July 9.	Sold Flora, my little bay Mare	15	15	0
11.	Received of Mr Bosworth Senr Treasurer	14	15	2
18.	Bal: from Mr Davies late Treasurer	05	10	11
Novr 25.	Sold Basil Cane a second-hand Saddle	00	10	06
Dec: 6.	By Fines, & St Luke's dividend of J: Bosworth	39	07	11
18.	Salary as Collectr Reditm	02	00	00
March.	From Mr Bower for presenting to determine	00	10	06
1753.	From Mr Wyat for Do	00	10	06
	From Mr Still for present: to degree, & determ:	01	11	06
	From Do as Librarian	00	06	06
24.	A dirge from Sr Treasr	00	00	10
26.	Mr Cane Law-gown, & Library fee	01	06	00
May 5.	Presenting Mr Smith, & Library fee	01	06	00
22.	From my Father; lent him in 1750	12	03	06
		£115	12	04

Money received arising from my Proctorship, 1752.

Easter-term.

		Li:	s:	d:
May 27. From a petty Compounder............................		00	02	00
28. From Proceed^rs in Divinity in Easter-term........		02	16	00
28. At examining the Musæum		00	10	06
June 4. From a petty Compounder............................		00	02	00
25. From a petty Compounder............................		00	02	00
July 1. From a petty Compounder............................		00	02	00
6. From three petty Comp^rs		00	06	00

Act term: Mr. Eyton.

1 Med: Bac: Grand: Comp:	01 18 08
M:D: 2 D^rs act fees	01 06 08
64 Regents fees	40 00 00

Act term: Mr. Beaver.

D:D;LL: non resid: 2	01 04 00
D:D: act fees......2	01 06 08
B:LL: pet: Comp:..1	00 12 00
B:B;LL: ord:......5	02 10 00

Act term: Mr. Walker.

1 B:D: G: C:.................................	01 18 08
1 B:D: P: C:.................................	00 12 00
3 B:D: Ordin: each ten shill:	01 10 00
1 D:D: G: C:.................................	01 18 08
2 D:D: Pet: C: each 12^s	01 04 00
1 D:D: Gr: Comp: act fees	01 06 08
7 D:D: act fees: each 13^s 4^d	04 13 04

Michaelmass-term.

Novr 4. From a petty Compounder........................	00 02 00
8. For visiting at the Bodlean Library.............	02 10 00
Dec: 1. From a petty Compounder........................	00 02 00
18. From a petty Comp^r	00 02 00

Michaelmass-term: Mr. Walker.

2 B:D: G: C: each Li:1 18s. 8d...................	03 17 04
2 D:D: G: C: each Li:1 18s. 8d...................	03 17 04
1 B:D: Ordin:	00 10 00
1 D:D: Ordin:	00 12 00

Carried forward	77 14 06

Mich. Term: Mr. Beaver.

	Li:	s:	d:
Brought forward	77	14	06
1 B:L:L: Ord:	00	10	00
1 B:L:L: Non Comp:	00	12	00
2 D:L:L:	01	04	00

Mich. Term: Mr. Eyton.

1 Dr Phys: Grand Comp:	01	18	08
Act-fees for D^o	01	06	08

Lent-term.

Mar: 13.	From Determiners	00	02	00
16.	From D^o & 1 petty Comp^r	00	04	00
20.	From D^o	00	02	00
20.	From 80 Determ: Batch^m at 4^s p^r man	16	00	00
21.	From Determ^{rs}	00	02	00
23.	From D^o	00	02	00
20.	2 Gracious-days, & pet: Comp:	00	06	00
Apr: 3.	Gracious Day	00	02	00
5.	Gracious Day	00	02	00
6.	Gracious Day	00	02	00

Mr. Beaver.

1 B:LL:	00	12	00

Mr. Walker.

3 B:D: Pet: Comp: each 12	01	16	00
1 D:D:	00	12	00

Mr. Eyton.

1 D:M:	00	12	00
15 Determ: A:B:	03	00	00

May 14. Of the Vice-Chan: at settling our accounts at his Lodgings	14	00	08
11 Determ: A:B: omitted before	02	04	00
3 Regents fees........D^o	01	17	06
Out of a pract: Phys: licence	00	01	00
	125	05	00
1 Regent's fee still due p^d April: 1755	00	12	06
	£125	17	06

The Reverend Mr. White to James Gibson Dr.

	Li:	s:	d:
To 1 years Board due the 8th of September 1754	20	0	0
serving his Church 3 Sundays at 9s 3d p Sunday, which is in proportion to £24 a year	1	7	9
2 horse hires, to 2 Burials, when my horse was lame		2	0
	21	9	9
Recd in part	14	0	0
paid. Remains due £	7	9	9

Expences from May 2, 1753.
The day I went out of my Proctorship.

		Li:	s:	d:
May 5.	Gave Mr Jennings's Servant	00	01	00
6.	Spent at Woodstock	00	01	03
	Coffee-house	00	00	08
7.	A Lobster for Cowper, & Skeeler &c:	00	00	11
9.	Mr Proctr Robinson's man	00	01	00
11.	Soling pair of Shoes	00	01	06
13.	Gave Farmr Howel's man, & a poor woman at Wolvercot: & Coffee-House	00	01	10½
13.	3 Coss-lettuce for ye President of Trin: &c.	00	00	06
14.	Concert, Choral-night	00	01	00
	Coffee-house	00	00	06½
15.	Vice-Chanrs Man	00	01	00
18.	Mr Nash's man	00	01	00
	Coffee-house twice: & Eynsham-ferry	00	01	07
20.	Coffee-house	00	00	06
21.	Coffee-house	00	00	08
22.	Mrs Darling's Boy; & Cook's shop	00	00	09
23.	Ferry, & Turnpike to Eynsham	00	00	03
26.	Provost's man	00	01	00
	Shearing Copper	00	00	06
27.	President of Trin: man	00	01	00
28.	Barret's man, & Porter	00	01	00
27.	Candles, & odd matters by Joe	00	04	02½
	Spent in Journey to London, Sunbury, & Selborn from May 28 to June 28	05	00	08
	Carried forward	06	04	04

		Li:	s:	d:
1753.	Brought forward	06	04	04½
May 27.	Cut-grizzle-wig in London	02	00	00
	Offices of Burial &c:	00	01	00
June 29.	Gave Will: Kelsey for coming up to carry down my Dogs	00	14	00
	Allowed to feed the Dogs	00	00	06
	100 of Broccoli plants to send into ye country	00	01	00
	Pr of dog-couples	00	01	00
29.	Gave Mason for walking in his Garden this spring, & last	00	05	00
	Coffee-House, & tart &c	00	01	07
July 2.	Concert, Choral night	00	01	00
	Coffee-house	00	00	09
	Bet Bull for Cream &c:	00	04	03
	Do Quarter's Bed-making to Midsumr 1753	00	05	00
	Gave Do	00	02	06
	Coffee-House	00	00	08
	Gave Knight the Shoemaker for describing Mr. Holt's arms	00	01	00
	Odd matters laid out by Joe	00	03	00½
	6 weeks waiting by Do	00	06	00
5.	Xtian Motley 1 quartrs washing in full to Midsumr 1753	01	01	00
	Taylor's Bill till Do	00	08	03
7.	Going to Wallingford to see Mrs Gifford	00	01	11
	Coffee-house	00	00	10
	Keeping Horse at Barrets to Midsumr	01	18	00
	Coffee House	00	00	04
9.	Odd matters bought by Joe	00	01	00
	Barret's man	00	01	00
	Seeing Dr Bacon's Gardens	00	01	00
	Carr: of a trunk to Winton	00	02	06
9.	Castle's portmanteau—Horse to Malford	00	14	00
	Car: of Box from Winton	00	01	00
	Expences in Journey to Malford; & a 5 weeks season at the Hot well at Bristol from July 9: to Aug: 30th *	16	12	00
Aug: 31.	Powder-horn spring	00	01	00
	Cleaning Gun	00	00	06
	Carried forward	31	17	01

---

* [I find no intimation of any attack of illness which could have necessitated this visit to these once celebrated waters. It is, however, not improbable that his health might have been injured by the attack of small-pox in 1747.—T. B.]

		Li:	s:	d:
1753.	Brought forward	31	17	01
Aug: 31.	Gun-powder	00	00	06
	Expences at Petersfield	00	03	10
Sept: 10.	A set of Shoes for Mouse	00	02	00
	Tea at Waltham	00	00	06½
	Sugar	00	00	08½
	Mr Batten's Servant	00	01	00
	Mending Cloaths	00	00	07
	Powder & shot	00	01	08
	Washing at Bradley, & Selborn	00	03	00
	4 pecks of Barley-meal for Dogs	00	02	06
	Savoys, & spinage-seed	00	01	01
17.	Horse & Boy to Bradley	00	01	00
	Beckhurst for watering firs	00	01	00
	Keeping Horse at Waltham	00	06	07
	Gallon of small beans from Oxon	00	02	00
	3 p^d of Shot	00	00	03
20.	P^r of Ram-skin breeches from Newbolt	00	08	00
	Washing at Selborn	00	01	02½
	Set of Shoes from Scrub	00	01	04
22.	Boy to Waltham, & his expences	00	00	08
	Odd matters	00	00	11
	Washing	00	00	11
	Hyson-tea, & sugar	00	01	07
	Powder, & shot	00	01	00½
	Gave Goody Fig	00	01	00
Octr 3.	Days shooting, & Boy	00	01	06
	Car: of Game to Mr Mulso	00	01	00
	Mending of Linnen	00	00	10½
6.	Gave Thomas	00	01	00
6.	Gave Mr Gibson's Masons	00	01	00
	Congo tea	00	00	06½
	Keeping Horse to the 6th	00	04	08
Sep: 18.	Six Gallons of Wine from Fareham at 5^s 6^d p^r Gall.	01	13	00
	Car: to Waltham	00	01	06
Octr 8.	Peck of Nonparels, & D^o of Gold^n rennets			
	Odd matters	00	00	05
	Gave Baines's Ostler	00	01	00
	Dog-chain	00	00	10
10.11.12.	Journey to Southtōn with Sist^r Becky, Harry, & Will: Yalden	00	17	01
13.	Set of Shoes for Mouse	00	02	00
13.	Quart^r of a pound of Congo	00	02	03
	Pound of Gun-powder	00	01	02
	Carried forward	37	11	10

VOL. II.   Z

		Li:	s:	d:
1753.	Brought forward	37	11	10
Octr 13.	Washing at Waltham	00	01	01½
16. 19.	Post-chaises to & from Basingstoke to Oxon when I went to resign my Deanship	03	06	00
	Drivers, ostlers, & turnpikes	00	08	01
	Expences on the road	00	02	03
	Horse left at Basingstoke, & bill there............	00	08	07
17.	Barber, washing, & Bedmak^r at Oxon	00	03	00
	Joe, & potter	00	02	00
18.	Mrs Croke's bill for Mast^{rs} Gown, satten wastecoat, Great-coat &c.	07	03	00
	Gave a sick man	00	01	00
	Mrs Costard's bill for shaving.....................	00	12	06
	Wood, & coal in spring	00	04	02
	Taylor's Bill .... reckoned elsewhere	00	00	00
	Common room wine	00	00	00
	Battles* in Midsum^r Quart^r 1753.................	05	19	04
	...... in Mich.......... D^o	00	18	11
	Midsum^r Exceedings	01	06	00
18.	Mr Frewen reading in Chappel	00	04	00
	Letter	00	00	04
18.	Wood, & coal to air my room			
21.	Gave the Clark of Durley	00	01	00
	Miller's Gardener's Diction^{ry} new edit: half bound in exchange from Br: Benj:.....................	01	14	06
	Butler's Sermon's & analogy	00	11	00
	Raij Methodus...............................	00	03	06
25.	From Lee at Alton 4 Yards ½ fine diaper	00	09	00
	40 Y^{ds} fine Irish for Shirts at 3^s	06	00	00
	1 Y^d superfine d^o...........................	00	04	00
	2½ Y^{ds} Long Lawn at 4^s for stocks	00	10	00
	1 Y^d of D^o for Bosoms	00	05	00
	Keeping Horse at Waltham, &c.	00	00	03
	A monthly Grass for Scrub in Hartley ground	00	03	06
26.	Set of Shoes for D^o	00	01	06
	Black leathern Breeches from Newbolt	00	12	00
	Beckhust in the Garden	00	03	00
	Mending Cloaths, & watch-string.................	00	01	08½
	Barley-meal	00	00	08½
	Gave G: Dotterel, & Tull	00	03	06
27.	Boy to Waltham..............................	00	00	06
29.	Washing at Bradley	00	01	03
	Carried forward	70	07	00½

* [See note p. 325.]

		Li:	s:	d:
1753.	Brought forward	70	07	00½
Oct' 29.	M' Batten's man	00	01	00
31.	Sending Ruffel to Selborn for the spaniels	00	01	00
	Pollard Bran for Dogs	00	00	03¼
Nov: 3.	Servants at Bradley	00	02	00
5.	M' Hampton's servant	00	01	00
	Gave away	00	00	06
	Powder & shot & paper	00	01	03½
	Half p^d of Sugar	00	00	04½
7.	M' Allanson's man at Upham	00	01	00
9.	M' Hale's man, & spent at Hambledon	00	01	06
	Odd matters	00	00	07
12.	Baines's ostler, M' Yalden's Man	00	02	00
	Gave Goodman Hammond	00	01	00
13.	Soling Boots	00	01	03
	Mending Shirts, & stocks	00	01	06
14.	Piece of fine colour'd Cambrick of Mrs Croke for 6 Handk: at 4^s each	01	04	00
	Mending my Frock	00	00	09½
	P^d of Gun-powder from Johnson	00	01	04
	Sending Girl to Oakhanger	00	00	03
	Making 12 Shirts, & 12 Stocks	00	17	06
	...... 6 Handk: & 6 Caps	00	01	06
17.	Spring to powder Horn, & gun-scrue	00	00	08
	New webbing my Saddle-girths	00	01	06
	Currier for suppling thick boots	00	01	00
19.	Pint, & Quart Decanter a present to Bradley	00	02	06
24.	Keeping Horse to that time	00	15	04
	Boy spent at Waltham	00	00	07½
	Meat, & meal for Dogs	00	01	06
19.	Set of Shoes for Mouse; & nailing &c	00	02	02
	Yarn Gloves	00	00	08
24.	Odd matters	00	00	02
	Washing at Waltham	00	03	11
26.	Lost at Cards 1^s & ink	00	01	03
Dec: 2.	Gave a man, & woman at Waltham	00	02	00
5.	Soling a pair of Shoes	00	01	04
	Odd matters	00	00	03½
5.	2 Ounces of Congo	00	01	0
5. 6.	M' Kent's, & M' Clewer's servants	00	02	0
8.	P^d Barber to that time	00	03	0
9.	Horse to Durley: Mouse's heel bruised	00	01	0
10.	P^r of yarn stockings, & yarn to lengthen them	00	01	8
	Half Quire of paper	00	00	5
	Carried forward	75	12	8½

			Li:	s:	d:
1753.		Brought forward	75	12	8½
Dec: 10.	Thread, tape, & shirt buttons for Shirts &c:		00	03	1
	Beckhurst, & Tull's girl		00	00	9
	Boy to Bradley		00	01	0
	Sermon Case from Oxon		00	01	0
	Quart of French beans from D⁰		00	00	9
	Peck barley-meal; & mending breeches		00	01	2½
14.	Gave Sarah Xmass		00	05	0
15.	Gave Thomas		00	01	0
16.	Gave a sick woman at Durley		00	01	0
18.	Peck of pollard at Bradley; & odd matters		0	00	5
22.	Pᵈ of Breakfast-sugar		00	00	8
26.	Bohea, & Green-tea		00	02	2
29.	Set of Shoes for Mouse		00	02	0
	Spent at Alresford		00	01	0
1754.	Washing at Bradley		00	00	9
Jan: 5.	Gave Servants at Bradley		00	05	0
	Odd matters		00	00	4
8.	Gave Mʳˢ Hammond's maid; & lost at Cards		00	02	1½
11.	Pʳ of yarn rib'd stockings		00	02	0
16.	Letter from Bro: John		00	00	4
17.	Quartʳ of a pound of Bohea		00	01	4
18.	Mʳ Hampton's Servant: & letter fᵐ B: Isaac		00	01	7
21.	Quire of paper		00	00	9
22.	Mʳ Yalden's servant		00	01	0
	Beckhurst		00	01	6
	Tanner's Jobs; & shot		00	01	3
	Mending Cloaths		00	01	5
	Deal-plank of Edm: Yalden		00	03	6
	John Carpenter making two frames for Cucumber-lights		00	03	0
	22:½ square feet of Glass for Glazing D⁰		00	13	1
	Mending an old one		00	01	2
26.	Keeping Horse to that time		02	02	0
28.	Washing to that time		00	03	4½
	Bushel of Barley-meal for Dogs		00	02	6
	Quarter of an Horse for D⁰		00	00	6
Feb: 4.	2 Pᵈˢ of Shot		00	00	5
6.	Barber to that time		00	02	0
6.	Gave a poor woman		00	01	0
	Letters sent by the post		00	00	4
12.	6 pounds of Sturgeon from London		00	08	0
	Car: to Wickham, & Waltham		00	01	4
	Garden-seeds		00	01	5½
	Carried forward		81	16	9½

			Li:	s.	d.
1754.		Brought forward	81	16	9½
Feb: 14.		Sugar, & tea	00	03	4½
		Dog-pan, & string	00	00	3½
	14.	Letter from Br Tho:	00	00	4
	15.	Entertaining ye Waltham Gentry	00	17	4½
18. 23.		Spent at Alresford to & from Bradley	00	00	10
	21.	Mr Stockwel's Servant	00	01	0
		Quire of whited-brown paper	00	00	3½
		Gave a poor old-man	00	01	0
	25.	Set of shoes; & frost nails	00	02	2
		Gave Baines's Ostler	00	02	0
		Mending Cloaths; & errants	00	00	6
Mar. 1.		Going with Ladies to puppet-shew	00	01	6
		Letter from Brother Barker	00	00	7
	4.	Pd keeping horse to that time	01	12	0
		Half Bushel of Barley meal	00	01	3
	5.	Mending Cloaths, & odd matters	00	00	6
	7.	Half Bush: of B: meal at Selborn for dogs	00	01	3
		8 pots for hot-beds 8d: & 4 cramps for frames	00	01	8
	8.	Work done in the Garden	00	09	6
	9.	Gave Sarah Xmass	00	02	6
	11.	Gave old John at Bradley; & washing	00	01	6
		Powder, & shot 1s & seeds 5d	00	01	5
	14.	Mr Lisset's servant	00	01	0
	15.	Cleaning watch	00	01	6
	19.	Mrs Yalden's maid	00	01	0
	25.	Car: of Box of Cloaths from Oxon to Winton, & Waltham	00	02	7
		Hat from Evans Oxon	00	15	0
		Gave old Edgehill	00	01	0
		Wristbanding shirts	00	00	9
		Tull in the Garden	00	02	0
		Pease-haulm for screen to Cucumbers	00	01	4
		Paper & oil for melon lights	00	01	0
		Gave Will: Wells for cockshooting	00	01	0
		Strengthening Cucum: frames	00	01	3
		Washing at Selborn	00	01	11
		Webbing Girths at Alton	00	1	0
		Half bush: of Barley meal	00	01	2
April 7.		Poor Woman at Durley	00	02	6
	8.	Keeping Horse to that time	00	09	0
		Cucumr mats of Johnson	00	00	4
	11.	Boy & expences to Northwarnboro'	00	00	10½
		2 firs, 2 larches, 6 laurels from Do	00	03	6
		Carried forward	88	09	4

			Li:	s:	d:
1754.		Brought forward	88	09	4
Apr: 11.	Lost at Cards towards cleaning zigzag...........		00	01	6
	Beckhust for work in Garden...................		00	04	0
	New frame for a Cucum^r Light		00	02	0
	Odd matters.................................		00	01	2
	Seeds..		00	00	6
21.	Sunday; spent at Alresford; Allenson's man messenger to Durley		00	02	0
22.	Barber to that time...........................		00	01	3
24.	11 foot & half of Glass for Cucum^r light.........		00	06	8
	Spent at Botley		00	00	4
26.	Sack of oats at Selborn		00	07	6
	Half quire of paper		00	00	5
27.	Boy to Waltham		00	00	6
29.	Fitting-out, & sending little Horse to Mulso		00	04	10
	8 Weeks grass for D^o at Butlers		00	04	6
May 6.	Set of shoes for Mouse		00	02	0
6.	Ribband for watch; & spent at Soberton		00	00	9
	Gave old Lee		00	00	6
10.	Work in the Garden		00	04	3
	Half Bush: of Barley-meal.......................		00	01	3
	Small watering-pot		00	02	0
	7 large flower-pots for Cockscombs		00	02	2
11.	Little Horse returning from Sunbury		00	02	9
15.	Gave Mr Dacres's Gardener		00	01	0
	Barber		00	00	6
17.	Tooth powder		00	01	0
18.	Entertaining Ladies at the pond		00	00	8
19.	Cauliflowers from Soberton		00	01	1½
18.	Ounce of tea.................................		00	01	2
	Odd matters		00	00	6
	G: Tanner helping about ye Cockscombs		00	01	0
	Washing		00	01	6
24.	Mr Newlin's Maid		00	01	0
25.	Work in Garden		00	05	1
27.	Keeping Horse, & dogs to that time..............		00	19	11½
	Wine at Baines's..............................		00	01	6
	Apothecary's bill for Rhubarb, tooth-powd^r		00	04	6
27.	Spent at Alresford		00	00	6
28.	Mr Batten's servant		00	01	0
30.	Spent at Visitation at Alton		00	04	6
31.	Servants at Bradley...........................		00	02	0
	Cabbadge plants		00	01	3
	Carried forward		93	11	11

GILBERT WHITE'S ACCOUNT-BOOK.

		Li:	s:	d:
1754.	Brought forward	93	11	11
May 31.	Two pots	00	00	4
June 3.	Hund: of **Savoys** at Waltham	00	00	6
3.	Keeping Horse to that time	00	02	0
3.	Boy to Waltham, & Horse	00	02	5½
	Letter	00	00	6½
5.	Trimming Mouse	00	01	0
	Gave Will: Marshal	00	01	0
	Painting bench, & Gate in Father's field	00	04	4
6.	Working in Garden	00	02	6
	Letter, & Soap	00	00	4½
7.	Barley meal	00	01	2
	Journey to London, & Sunbury from June 7th to ye 28	04	04	5
	Large Mahogany table from London a present to Un: White	03	03	0
	Packing D^o	00	01	6
	A Bonnet & tippet from D^o for Polly Gibson	00	07	6
	Sending a puppy to Bradley, &c.	00	01	6
July 1.	Set of Shoes, remove, & oiling H^s shoulder	00	03	0
	Sending to Hill pound	00	01	0
	Black leathern breeches begin: of June	00	12	0
	Half Bushel of Barley-meal	00	01	1½
5.	P^r of Boots of Tanner	00	16	0
6.	Work in Garden	00	01	0
	Washing at Selborn	00	01	11
8.	Mr Hampton's Servant	00	01	0
9.	Spent at the Milberries	00	00	10½
10.	2 ounces of Congo	00	01	0
11.	Mr Missen's Servant	00	01	0
13.	P^d M^{rs} De la rose washing to that time	00	06	2½
	Odd matters	00	00	6
13.	Spent at forest-green	00	01	0
14.	Mr Allanson's Man	00	01	0
15.	Sending to Hill-pound	00	00	6
15. 20.	Spent at Alresford	00	00	8
	Washing at Bradley	00	00	6
18. 19.	Spent at Basingstoke race	00	01	5
	Work in the field	00	01	0
	Soling p^r of shoes	00	01	2
	Car: of Broccoli to Alton	00	01	0
26.	Gave Goodman Grant at Swarraton	00	01	0
27.	Servants at Bradley	00	05	0
	Carried forward	105	06	11

		Li:	s:	d:
1754.	Brought forward	105	06	11
July 27.	Gave away	00	00	6
	Spent at Alresford	00	00	4
	Odd matters	00	00	6
Jul: 30 to				
Aug: 3.	Servants at Chilgrove & Chichester	00	06	0
	Gave at seeing needle-making at D°	00	01	0
6.	Removing Mouse's shoes	00	00	6
	Odd matters	00	00	9
	Gave away	00	01	0
12.	Mr Cutler's Servants	00	02	0
	2 ounces of Spinach-seed	00	00	3
13.	Gave Thomas for cutting first Melon	00	02	6
	Barley meal	00	01	1½
	Mending Cloaths	00	01	0
17.	Tea, sugar, & letter	00	01	10
19.	Gave old Lee	00	01	0
19.	Set of Shoes for Mouse	00	02	0
19.	Keeping Horse to that time	01	09	0
	Gave Ostler	00	01	0
21.	Boy & Horse to Bradley to carry a melon	00	01	6
	Odd matters	00	01	1½
29.	Gave old John at Bradley	00	01	0
30.	Gave Mr Batten's man at returning Gun	00	01	0
	Car: of Cloaths from Oxon	00	01	6
Septr 2.	Tea, & letter	00	01	2
	6 p^{ds} of shot	00	01	3
6.	Mr Hampton's man	00	01	0
	Gave away	00	01	0
	Altering Cloaths	00	01	2
7.	Going to Southampton	00	03	9
9.	Powder, & shot; & odd matters	00	03	0
13.	Gave Sarah Xmass	00	02	6
21.	Gave to sufferers by fire	00	01	0
26.	Tun of Hay laid up in my Father's rick	01	12	6
	15 Loads of melon-earth from Dorton	00	08	0
27.	Odd matters to Octob^r 14	01	01	11
Oct: 14.	Post-chaises from Bradley to Oxōn on Mr Whiting's Death	02	06	3
	Mr Nourse for attending on my Knee	00	10	6
	Mr Malbon Apoth: bill in 1753	00	12	0
	Taylor's Bill	01	09	0
	Wine Bill in 1753	04	00	0
	Carried forward	121	01	4

			Li:	s:	d:
1754.		Brought forward..................	121	01	4
Oct: 14.	Poundage to Mander, & Beaver...................		01	05	5
	Exceedings in Midsum^r 1754.....................		00	14	0
	Reading in Chappel supply'd.....................		02	02	0
25.	Mrs Croke's bill to that time.....................		05	14	0
	Barber, washing, waiting		00	16	0
	Common room wine		00	11	11½
	Coals, & wood, 6^s 6^d: & gave Bet: Bull 5^s		00	11	6
	P^r of Indian Doe breeches from Haines		00	16	0
	Odd necessary Expences at Oxon from Octob^r 14: to Novem^r 15		02	06	7
Nov: 15.	Expences in post-chaises from Oxon to Bradley the Day after Harry's Election to B^p Robinson's Exhibition...................................		02	05	10
	P^r of Boot-straps.............................		00	01	6
	Odd matters		00	01	9½
18.	Set of Shoes for Mouse, by Boxall		00	02	0
18.	Keeping Horse before Journey		01	08	0
	Wine at Baines's.............................		00	01	9
	Barley-meal.................................		00	01	2
22.	Altering & partly throwing open ye little Garden & plot behind		00	07	0
23.	Gave Thomas for looking after horse		00	02	0
	Odd matters.................................		00	05	6
24.	Clark at Durley for collecting surplice fees		00	02	4
	Allanson's, & Hampton's men		00	02	0
	Odd matters.................................		00	02	1
	Tea, & sugar................................		00	02	8
29.	Washing to that time.........................		00	08	2½
29.	P^d Gibson for a Year's board from Septem^r 8th 1753: D^o 1754.......................................		20	00	0
	D^o for supplying my Church 3 Sund:		01	07	9
	His Horse hire to Burials		00	02	0
30.	P^d Mr Futcher for 55 dinners from Septem^r 8th 1753: to Septem^r 8. 1754		02	15	0
Dec. 1.	A warm wastecoat for old Lee		00	02	0
3.	Two large pullets.............................		00	01	6
3.	Mr Guernier's Gardener for melon-seeds..........		00	02	6
	Odd matters.................................		00	02	9½
9.	Shoes, & removes, & cleaning Gun		00	02	0
12.	Expences to Waverley, & Farnham..............		00	04	0
	Gave Sarah Xmass		00	02	6
16.	Farmer Turner for bringing fairey		00	02	6
	Carried forward		166	17	2

		Li:	s:	d:
1754.	Brought forward	166	17	2
Decr 16.	Odd matters	00	02	8
	Piece of Brawn, & pot of Sausages from Oxōn	00	17	10½
	Gave Tom Ruffell, & Mr Batten's man	00	03	00
26.	Entertaining the Gentry of Waltham exclusive of Port wine	00	13	3½
1755.	Several odd matters	00	11	11
Jan: 13.	Keeping Horse to that time	02	01	0
	Barley-meal, & gave Ostler	00	03	10
	Altering necessary House, & throwing open the little Garden at Selborn	00	06	0
	Servants, & lost at Cards	00	03	9
24.	Set of Shoes, & remove	00	02	3
	Several odd matters	00	12	11
	4 planks for new frames, & car:	00	16	0
	Garden seeds	00	03	11
Feb: 2.	Gave Dr Durnford's Servant at Harting	00	03	0
	Mending lights, & altering frames	00	05	1
11.	Making my new melon-frame	00	10	0
	10 Iron tenons for D^o	00	01	8
18.	23 feet & half of tiled Glass hot-house fashion for D^o at 8^d p^r foot	00	15	6
21.	3 large mats for melon frames	00	03	0
	Lost at Cards	00	03	9
March 1.	Gave Mr Missing's servants	00	12	0
	Odd matters	00	05	6
5: 8:	Expences with Edm: Yalden down to Dene in Wilts	00	11	1
	Shoing 2^s 6^d & washing 5^s 10^d	00	08	4
9.	P^d Futcher for 25 Sunday's dinners	01	05	0
11.	Keeping Horse at Waltham	01	02	0
	Half year's board to Gibson	10	00	0
	P^d him for serving my Church	01	07	9
	Wine of D^o	01	02	3
	Joints of meat for Harry & Cane in Feb:	00	05	9
	Gave his Maid	00	10	6
11.	Boy & Horse at leaving Waltham	00	05	1
	Hire of screen	00	02	0
	Odd matters	00	07	3
15.	Two p^r of Shoes of Tanner 11^s: & mending	00	12	2
21.	Shrubs from Waverley	00	11	11
	Odd matters	00	06	2
22.	5 more Hot-bed-mats	00	05	0
	Total	£195	17	4

GILBERT WHITE'S GARDEN KALENDAR.

[The anxiety with which **Gilbert White** watched every phase of his horticultural operations, and **the methodical manner in which he details** the daily work of his garden, is so minutely described in his "Garden Kalendar," and is so characteristic of his habits, that I have thought it would not be uninteresting to the reader to have a portion of these notes in their primitive form. It is therefore printed verbatim from his MS. One of the most amusing features of this record is the interest with which he watches the growth of his Cantaloupe melons, then a novelty to him, his alternate hopes and fears as they advanced, and the disgust with which he contemplates their ultimate failure. A letter from Philip Miller[*], the author of the celebrated 'Gardener's Dictionary,' is not only interesting in itself, but as showing the source whence he obtained those precious seeds, and I have therefore thought it worth while to prefix Miller's **letter to the Kalendar.**—T. B.]

SIR,

I AM much obliged to you for your favourable opinion of my performance[†]: if what **I have** published has **been of** public utility I shall think myself happy.

The Cantaleupe Melon seeds here inclosed, are from Armenia, which is the country from whence the seeds were first brought to Cantaleupe. I have had the seeds from thence several years, and have found them much better than any of those which were sent me from Cantaleupe.

---

[*] [Philip Miller was born in 1691, and succeeded his **father as gar**dener to the Chelsea Gardens in 1722. He was an excellent botanist, and became a correspondent of Linnæus. He was a Fellow of the Royal Society, **and** a member of some of the scientific societies on the Continent. He died in 1771.—T. B.]

[†] [It appears by an entry in his account-book of 1749 that in that year he purchased his copy of Miller's 'Gardener's Dictionary' for eighteen shillings.—T. B.]

I have made trials several times of Tanners bark for raising of Melons, and sometimes have had good success with it, but I have found in hot dry seasons the plants of Cantaleupe have hung their leaves, and sometimes their roots have perished before all the fruit were ripe: so that I prefer good dung for the heat and a proper depth of Loam for the roots to strike into, but this, in my situation, is very difficult to procure; for we have very little Loam within a reasonable distance.

I do not know if you have seen the last edition of the Gardeners Dictionary, which has been published in weekly numbers and is now almost finished; in which there are all the improvements that have come to my knowledge in the culture of the Cantaleupe Melon; there is also a plan of a small stove for Pines, which is not very expensive to erect, and where Tan and Fuel are cheap, may be maintained for a small annual sum.

If in any thing I can contribute to your laudable pleasure you may freely command, Sir,

Your most obedient humble servant,
PHILIP MILLER.

Chelsea, Feb. 14, 1759.

P.S. Your letter did not come to Chelsea till yesterday.

GARDEN KALENDAR.

May 1st, 1759.

May 1st. Pulled away the hedge round the fir-quincunx, and hoed the ground clean.

2. The Hanger out in full leaf; but much banged about by the continual strong east wind that has blown for many days. The buds and blossoms of all trees much injured by the wind. The ground parch'd and bound very hard. The cold air

keeps the nightingales very silent. No vegetation seems to stir at present.—Disbudded some of the vines. The buds are about an inch long.

May 3rd. Made second annual bed with six barrows of grass and weeds only; no dung.

Planted out the five hand-glasses with the great white Dutch Cucumbers 4 plants in a hill. The plants are pretty much drawn. This evening the vehement east wind seems to be abated; and the air is soft and cloudy. Ground bound like a stone.

4. Sowed a pint, four rows, of small dwarf white kidney-beans in the lower field-garden.

Earthed the Cantaleupes* the third time: found all the plants in a very flourishing way, and the fibres extended to the very outsides of the hills. Cut away the plants to one in some of the hills; and left two in some, stopping down the worst plant very short towards the bottom of the runners, for experiment's sake, to see what the small wood about the stems will do. Some of the plants offer for male bloom.

Saw the first Redstart and Cherrysucker †. Sowed about two doz. of the large white Dutch cucumber seeds for yᵉ latter hand-glasses: the first sowing got full tall and big.

Delicate soft rain all the afternoon and all night, which soaked the ground well to the roots of all vegetables.

5. Fine growing weather.

Several of the Cantaleupes have male blossoms fully expanded.

7. Disbudded all the vines according to Hitt. Almost every shoot shows bloom. Housed 21 barrows of the last prepared Cantaleupe loam: by means of the late rains it is in the most delicate order and crumbles into dust.

9. Berriman sowed Baker's Hill with Barley, and after it 8 pounds of clover, and two bushels of white seed or Rye Grass. The ground cold and cloddy, and pretty full of daisey roots and grass, and not in very fine order. Added since 8 pᵈˢ more of clover.

* [See the Letter from Philip Miller.—T. B.]
† [Spotted fly-catcher.]

May 10. Several Cantaleupe plants shew fruit and grow away at a great rate. Pricked out the annuals into the second hot-bed. Fine showery growing weather.

12. Gave the Cantaleupe hills a full barrow of loam each: the fourth time of earthing. Cut away the plants to one on a hill.

14. One Cantaleupe fruit in full bloom. Made three hills for large white cucumbers in Turner's garden.

15. Sowed the second pint of french-beans, large white Dutch; soaked them in water over night.

18. Sowed a crop of white, green and black Coss-lettuce. All my Savoy seed and Boor Cole fails this year: not one plant appears.

20. Strong sunshine for many days, and a sharp east wind. Cold white dews in the mornings. Our clay ground as hard as a stone. This burning sun, as usual, makes the Cantaleupes look not quite right. Most of the fruit as soon as it appears turns yellow. The single fruit that is out of bloom not likely to stand.

The dwarf french beans are come up pretty well.

The lettuce that stood the winter are finely leaved. This unkind weather stops the setting of the Cucumbers.

21. Earthed the Cantaleupes the last time within their boxes. Finding the Cantaleupes much exhausted and dryed by the fierce heat of the Sun, and the dry air, I watered them all over, leaves and all, with one small pot of water. The leaves all hang down, and have a dry paper-like feel, and look woolly; and the fruit all turns yellow: I remember they had all just the same appearance at this time last year; the sunshine and east wind being as vehement.

Planted 100 of late cabbages.

26. The burning sunny weather continues. The gardens suffer much by the drought.

29. Frequent showers. The watering the Cantaleupes twice over the leaves seemed to refresh them very much; but has occasioned one of Mr. Hunter's plants to grow a little mouldy at a joint on one of the leaders near the stem. So that water, though never so much wanted, is dangerous near the stem.

The Armenian plants in general have small leaves and vines: and one in particular so fine and wire-drawn that one would imagine it would never be able to carry any fruit to perfection. The rest are healthy, and are disposed very regularly in their frames, and are full of fruit. No fruit set yet.

Took off the glasses from the early cucumbers and annuals to give them ye benefit of the showers.

May 28: 29. Housed four loads of peat in most excellent dry order. The uncommon dryness occasions some waste by making the bats crumble.

Gathered two scarlet strawberries. The early beans have large pods. The early pease are well blown.

30. The rain on the 29th very heavy for some hours; so as to make the cart way run. Raked all the rough-dug ground that was, 'till moistened, like an heap of stones. Pricked a pot of Celeri.

31. Sowed a pint more of large French beans. The first sowing strangely devoured by snails. Tull gathered a bowl dish three quarters full in one evening: and still the plants were almost covered with them the next. Cold winds and frosty nights since the rain.

Hoed the strawberries that were planted last autumn, and filled up the vast cracks in their beds. At least half the autumn planted pine-strawberries are dead. The scarlet will have some fruit; and so will the few plants of Collison's. The Nova-Scotia will not bear this year.—Stringed the bearing pine-strawberries, which are full of bloom. The Autumn sown and Capuchin and brown-Lettuce, now in high perfection. I have a very poor crop of Coss lettuce this spring.

June 1. Distant thunder and fine showers all the evening and part of the night.

May 31: June 1st: 2nd. John tacked all the vines for the first time this year according to Hitt. Those vines that were dressed in that method last year, are now full of fruit; those that have been trained only this year have little or none.— Frequent good showers. The ground is now finely soaked. Continued picking vast quantities of slugs from the french beans, which are in a poor way.

June 3. Continued heavy showers all night and all day. The ground is now well soaked.

5. Lined out the Cantaleupe bed with twelve dung-carts of hot dung. The bed is now 12 feet broad and 40 feet long. Continued showers all day; so that no loam could be laid on ye bed but what was already housed in the earth-houses. The fig tree has plenty of fruit which grows apace.

Such a violent rain and wind all the evening and most part of the night that they broke down and displaced the pease and beans and most of the flowers; and tore the hedges and trees and beat down several of the shrubs.

6. Continual rain all day. The lining of the Cantaleupe bed, which is not yet earthed, in danger of losing its Heat by being so thoro'ly soaked.

8. Earthed the lining of the Cantaleupe bed, and raised the frames to the top of the earth. The Waverley plants had filled the frames with their roots; the fibres of ye Armenian sort had not extended themselves so much.

Sowed a pint more of dwarf kidney-beans in the room of those that were devoured by snails. Fine summer weather. Turned down the three forward basons of cucumbers from out their hand-glasses.

9. Gathered first beans, a large mess.

10. Fine soft weather for some days; now a soaking rain.

11. Finished off the borders in the new garden, by cleansing raising and laying a good coat of fine peat dust, finely sifted in order to make them light and dry. Sowed the first plot of Endive, and a plot of Lettuce, green and white Coss.

12. In the evening began a vast storm which continued all the night, and tore and destroyed the things in the Garden worse than the former: it broke down vast boughs in the Hedges, and had like to have overturned the Limes in the Butcher's yard. If the Annuals had been planted out, they must have been quite whipped to pieces. The hedges look bare and unsightly by being lashed and banged by the wind; and the ground is strawed with leaves.

13. The middle Waverley Cantaleupe has some decayed

rotten runners; Quæ: if occasioned by those two waterings all over their leaves in that scorching weather in May.

The leaves of the Armenian Cantaleupes have a much blacker aspect than those of the Waverley.

June 14. Planted the empty basons in the field, and two borders in the new Garden with annuals, French and Afr: Marrygolds, Sunflowers, Nasturtiums, pendulous Amaranths, and China Asters. Hot growing weather; vast showers about.

15. Planted 150 Savoys from Alton.

16: 18. Lined out the Cantaleupe bed with loam very deep quite down to ye Ground on each side: the fibres may now, if they please, extend themselves 16 feet. The plants look in a most thriving way, and are loaded with fruit; but they hold off from setting strangely: no one set yet. Cut off a great branch of one of the Waverley Cantaleupes that was quite rotten.

19. Planted out crop of leeks and some late Coss Lettuce. Furious hot summer weather.

20. To be planted pint of french beans, and an early row of Celeri to be trenched. All the former crops of french beans like to come to nothing.

23. Called in upon Mr. Miller at Chelsea, and found that he had 18 lights of Armenian Melons in excellent order. There were about two brace and half of fruit to a light, full-grown, and very rough and black. He pushes his lights, it seems, quite down in dry weather: and says the defect of male bloom is owing to the seeds being of some age.

30. On my return from Sunbury I found my Cantaleupes in very bad plight indeed: two of the Waverley plants were quite rotten, and corrupted at the stem, and one of the Armenians, the day after I came home, withered away, tho' perfectly sound; and dyed as if eaten off at the root; tho' upon search no grub could be found in the mould. And what is stranger, no one fruit was set upon any plant, tho' hundreds have dropp'd away. There certainly is a want of male bloom in the Armenians to a degree: but then the Waverley plants over abounded and yet cast all their fruit.

I found a vast crop of pease thro' the dripping season; and

(had) green pease soup every day. The first hand-glass cucumbers are in full bearing: I intend to save 4 more (the large white Dutch) for seed. The small forward beans have an unusual crop. The fourth and fifth crop of french beans like to come to good.

July 2. Planted out a vast bed of Holy-oaks.

6. Not one Cantaleupe set yet. Planted out about 50 Polyanths raised this Spring from seed given me by Mr. Hale.

7. Finished my Hayrick in most excellent order. The weather has been so perfectly hot and bright, for these five days past, that my Hay was all cut and made in that time. The crop was so great that Kelsey's people made 8 carryings of it; and the burden in the great mead was supposed to be considerably greater than was ever known. To my own stock I added two tons from Farmer Lassam, which in all made a considerable rick.

Finished cutting the hedges round Baker's Hill.

21. On my return from Dene on this day I found I had but one Cantaleupe set and that a fig-shaped one not likely to come to good. The plants are in uncommon vigour; and grow unaccountably, and are full of fruit still; but strangely deficient in male bloom. The void spaces in the frames are quite filled out with the remaining plants. Mr. Cane's Cantaleupes were all burned up, with a noble crop on them, about ten days before the fruit would have been ripe. He had a fine crop: but the intense heats scorch'd off all the fibres thro' his light dusty earth. Tull planted out Endives and lettuce in abundance during my absence; he pronged up the bulbous roots against Parsons's, planting annuals in their room. John trimmed and nailed the vines in a very handsome manner according to Hitt. Those vines that have been managed in that manner for two years, have a noble crop of fruit very forward. My crops of beans and pease are very extraordinary this year. The annuals against the broad walk in the new Garden are uncommonly large.

23. Gathered 36 cucumbers. Earthed up the chinks round the hand glasses with melon loam.

Unusual hot summer weather for three weeks past. Wheat harvest has begun in some places.

July 26. Pulled up another of the Armenian Cantaleupes which was rotten at stem. So now I have lost four plants out of nine. The fruit begins to set now at a vast rate on the remaining plants, as fast as ever they fell off before.

The hot vehement season continues: the ground is wonderfully burnt.

31. Now a great rain after several weeks drought.

Aug. 1. On examination I found above 20 brace of Cantaleupes set: about 10 brace on one of the Armenian plants; about 3 brace on another Armenian; 2 brace (one a full-grown fruit) on another: and one Armenian is quite barren. The Waverley plant is infected with the rot that destroyed the rest, which I endeavour to stop by wiping and dust. It is observable that those plants that bear so prodigiously are those which (their fellows being rotten) have the space of two or three lights to run in. Had the fruit set in this manner a month or six weeks ago (when it all dropp'd off) there had been a noble early crop.

10. The first set Cantaleupe, tho: unpromising at first, now a fine beautiful large fruit, just like Miller's. The rest of later date come on apace. Prodigious hot sunny weather. Sowed half pound of Spinage, mixed with Capuchin and Dutch Lettuce, and white turnep-Radishes. Trenched four rows more of Celeri: and planted out about 150 more Savoys. Tyed about 20 of the Endives.

Sowed a little more Endive seed.

14. Lost the third and last Waverley Cantaleupe with a crop of 4 brace of fruit on it. I have now lost five plants out of nine. The four Armenians now remaining have 10 brace of fruit likely to come to good. Pulled off two brace and half of fruit, some of a considerable size. Dry, hot weather still.

16. Sowed a crop of Coss Lettuce and Endive to stand the winter. Trimm'd the side shoots of the vines for the last time. The clusters are unusually large and forward. Perfect Summer weather but cooler.

27. Cut a vast quantity of white Dutch cucumbers. One

that was young and eatable weighed 2 pounds 5 ounces, and measured 12 inch: and half in length. The Canker continues to spread among the Cantaleupes, and is likely to destroy plants full of beautiful fruit within a fortnight of being in perfection.

Aug. 28. Planted on the bank several large white Lilly roots, Crown Imperials, and double white rockets. Cut the first Endive.

Septem^r 4. Planted some tree primroses on the bank. It has been very wet, blowing weather, for several days past.

8. Tyed up about two doz. of the best bunches of Grapes in Crape-bags.

11. Cut ye first Cantaleupe: it was finely emboss'd, and weigh'd 3 p^{ds} 11 ounc: but when it came to be cut up it had hardly any flesh, and was rank and filthy.

Tyed up more Endive.—Uncommon sunny sultry day.

15. Tyed on 18 more Crape-bags on the best bunches of Grapes. Fine dry weather with pretty cold dews.

29. All the Cantaleupes cut. Not one in perfection; tho' many were finely embossed and looked wonderfully promising. The canker I suppose had prevented their drawing any nourishment, and getting any thickness of flesh. Fine dry weather for a long time past, and the roads perfectly good. The small bunches of Grapes are very good: the large ones not yet ripe against the wall.

Octob. 1. Tyed up last crop of Endive.

The largest Cantaleupe was finely embossed, and tho' almost all rind, weigh'd 4 pounds 2 ounces.

3. Now a vast rain after many weeks fine Autumn weather.

5. Gathered the two first bunches of bag'd Grapes: they were a little mouldy; but the sound part of the bunches were perfectly ripe, and sweet.

8. Now perfect summer weather again, after one wet day. The Grapes in the bags unusually fine; and both bunches and single Grapes are as large again as usual. It is to be observed that this new culture swells the berries so much; they are apt in this cluster-sort to press too hard on each other, and prevent ripening, and occasion mouldiness: there-

fore if the Grapes were thinn'd-out the beginning of the summer with the points of a pair of scissars, it would certainly prove an advantage.

Oct. 10. Planted two rows of Crocuss along the borders under the dining-room windows; both borders, especially that that hath the vines in it, were made very light and mellow with an abundance of sand and blacksmith's cinders. Weeded and cut down the leaves of the strawberries and mended out those beds that failed with the pine sort. Now very dry, and warm: but there are great tokens of rain.

11. Now great rains and wind.

Tunn'd three quarters of an Hogsh: of raisin wine. The quantity of raisins in the mash vat were 1 hund: and half of Smyrnas, and 3 quarters of an hundred of Malagas. The quantity of water put up was 18 3 gallon buckets; which made sufficient quantity without any squeesing. The colouring was 14 quarts of Elder syrop. The weather was so hot that it stood but eleven days to ferment in the vat. The Elder juice was boiled up with 14 pounds of sugar.

16. Finished off the bank in the new Garden and planted the front row of the additional part with pinks both red and pheasant-eyed: laid it with turf some days agon. On measuring the great oak in the meadow which was measured in ye spring, I found it to be encreased in girth about one inch.

18. The mornings begin to be frosty, yet the Grapes continue in high perfection.

19. Finished a broad brick walk thro' ye new wicket at the end of the dining room; and carryed a narrow one up by the side of ye pitching to the orchard walk: rectifyed the broken pitching and turned the gutter at the brewhouse door, so as to get a 12 inch border four feet long for a white muscadine vine.

22. Planted a row of Coss Lettuce *touching the wall* along the vine-border under the dining-room window to stand the winter. Planted a row of Holyoaks against the boards of the woodhouse.

24. Planted the irregular slip without the new wicket in the Garden with first two rows of Crocuss; a row of pinks; several sorts of roses; Persian Jasmine and yellow D°. several

sorts of Asters, French-Willows; a curious sort of bloody wall-flowers; double Campanulas, white and blue; double Daisies; and a row against the hedge of good rooted Laurustines. Planted the back row of the part of the bank newly length'ned-out with blue and white Double Campanulas; and the border under the dining-room window with the bloody Double wall-flowers. Planted a bason in the field with french willows. Planted many dozens more of Coss Lettuce against the buttery wall, and down the wall against the yard.

Oct. 25. Planted a large layer of the musk-rose from Mr. Budd against the boards of the old barn.

Wet season after very dry weather.

26. Trimm'd and tack'd the bottoms of the vines according to Hitt: the lower parts of those under the Dining-room window are deficient in wood, 'till more can be got from ye stems. Began curving two shoots in order to reduce two of the vines to regular shapes from the bottom by degrees.

Novem' 5. Planted my Hyacinths, Narcissus's, Ranunculus's, Tulips, Crown Imperials, and Anemonies in the border against Parsons's. It had been trenched very deep with a good quantity of rotten tan, and was in perfect dry order when the roots were put in.

Planted a small thriving larch at the east corner of Baker's Hill; two well-grown Provence-roses in the field shrubbery and two monthly roses in the Orchard walk; all from North Warnboro'. Fine, dry, sunny weather. Planted two rows of hardy lettuce under the filbert hedge against Parsons's.

6. Trimmed and tack'd the fig tree, leaving a leading bough in the middle to fill the wall by degrees quite up to the eaves. This tree is full of young wood and fills the wall well; and may be carry'd by a second stage according to Hitt, up to the tiles. Planted a number of Gooseberries and Currans from Mr. Johnson, good plants, in the Orchard-walk and among the rasps. The grapes lasted in good perfection 'till the beginning of Novem': those that were hung up in the study are very sweet but shrivelled up like raisins, notwithstanding a grape was stuck on the stem of each Cluster.

12. Plunged the seven pots of Pyram: Camp: in the border

against Parsons's under y*e* Filbert hedge. Planted a nursery border of small bulbous roots. Dug up a decaying Cluster pine, and parsley-elder in the shrubbery, and put in a two-thorned Acacia and Judas tree in their room. A most delicate summer-like day.

Nov. 14. Transplanted the striped Epilobium into a fresh bason. Planted about 20 fraxinellas, seedlings from Mr. Budd, in a nursery. Planted several Laurels in the gaps of Hedges round Baker's Hill.

The potatoes raised from about 14 large ones cut in pieces turned out a fine crop of about 3 Bushels: several single ones weigh'd about a pound. Put by about 30 of the finest as a supply for a crop next year.

Planted some cuttings of parsley-elder, with some cuttings of fine white Currant.

15. Planted in the new Garden two standard Duke's Cherries; an espalier Orleans plumb; an espalier green-gage plumb; a duke cherry against the north-west wall of the brewhouse; and a standard muscle plumb in the orchard. These trees came from Forster of North Warnboro' and seemed to be good in their kind; were planted the day they were taken out of the nursery, in basons, which being prepared before, were in excellent crumbling order.

16. Planted 3 pints, 7 rows of small early beans in the lower field garden.

DESCRIPTION OF DUFOUR'S FIRE-ESCAPE.

[That the interest of Gilbert White was not confined to the investigation of the objects of nature and the ordinary pursuits of a man of scientific and literary taste, but that he was fully alive to any improvement in the useful arts of life, is shown by the following account of Dufour's Fire-escape, which I have found among his papers. It is in his own handwriting, but without date or any indication of its having been intended for any especial object beyond that of a personal memorandum. The description of the apparatus is in the same clear and simple language which constituted much of the special charm of his writings. Previous to Dufour's invention, the "Fire-escape" seems to have been limited to "*a pole, a rope, and a basket.*" It appears from the records of the Patent Office that Dufour's patent is dated 1788, and the experiment described in the following paper was probably the first public test of its efficiency. —T. B.]

A PATENT machine, known by the name of the Fire escape was brought along fleet street. It consisted of a ladder, perhaps 38 feet in length, which turned on a pivot, so as to be elevated or depressed at will, and was supported on framed work, drawn on wheels. A groove on each side of this ladder-like construction admitted a box or hutch to be drawn up or let down by a pulley at the top and a windlass at the bottom. When the ladder is set up against a window the person in danger is to escape into the hutch, and so to be let down. That the ladder may not catch fire from any flames breaking out below, it is defended with a sheathing of tin.

Several people, it seems, had illiberally refused the patentee the privilege of trying his machine against their houses; but my brother*, on application, immediately consented, when the ladder was applied to a sash on the second story and a

* [Benjamin White, of Fleet Street.—T. B.]

man was immediately hoisted up, and let down with great expedition and safety, and then a couple of boys together.

Some spectators were of opinion that the hutch or box was too scanty and shallow, and that for security it ought to be raised with a treillis of strong wire, or Iron work, lest people in terror and confusion should miss of their aim and fall over to the ground. This machine was easily drawn by four men only. The inventor's name is Mr. Du Four. The ladder, the owner told us, would reach to the third story, when more elevated.

LISTS OF THE MORE NOTEWORTHY

ANIMALS AND PLANTS

OBSERVED IN SELBORNE AND THE NEIGHBOURHOOD.

MAMMALIA.

CHEIROPTERA.

Noctule bat.	Scotophilus noctula.	In the Park and Lithe.
Pipistrelle.	—— pipistrellus.	Cottage and barn roofs.
Reddish-grey bat.	Vespertilio Nattereri.	Cottage roofs.
Daubenton's bat.	—— Daubentonii.	In my cellar.
Long-eared bat.	Plecotus auritus.	Very rare.

INSECTIVORA.

Hedgehog.	Erinaceus europœus.	
Mole.	Talpa europæa.	
Common shrew.	Sorex vulgaris.	
Water shrew.	Crossopus fodiens.	Stream by the Grange.
Oared shrew.	—— ——, var. remifer.	In my garden.

CARNIVORA.

Badger.	Meles taxus.	Great wood near Alton and Theddon.
Common otter.	Lutra vulgaris.	Stream at Priory, and at Froyle.
Ermine or Stoat.	Mustela erminea.	Often partially white.
Common weasel.	—— vulgaris.	
Polecat.	—— putorius.	Monkswood; very rare.
Common marten.	Martes foina.	Stated to have been found at Woolmer by Geo. Cannons.
Common fox.	Vulpes vulgaris.	

BIRDS FOUND AT SELBORNE.

RODENTIA.

Common squirrel.	Sciurus vulgaris.	
Dormouse.	Myoxus avellanarius.	Scrubs, &c.
Harvest mouse.	Mus minutus.	In wheat ricks.
Field mouse.	—— sylvaticus.	Enters houses in winter.
Common mouse.	—— musculus.	
Brown rat.	—— decumanus.	
Water vole.	Arvicola amphibius.	Stream at Dorton.
Common field vole.	—— agrestis.	
Bank vole.	—— glareolus.	Bank at Temple.
Hare.	Lepus timidus.	
Rabbit.	—— cuniculus.	

BIRDS.

[In the following list of the birds which have been seen in Selborne and the neighbourhood, I have included a large number which were observed in or near Alton by the late Dr. John Curtis, many of which are in the Alton Museum. The letters W., B., C. indicate those attested by Gilbert White, by myself, and by Dr. Curtis. The comparative rarity of their occurrence is indicated by the letters r, rr, rrr. The nomenclature is principally that of Yarrell's 'British Birds.'—T. B.]

Peregrine falcon.	Falco peregrinus.	B., C.	rrr	Empshott. Alton.
Hobby.	—— subbuteo.	B., C.	rrr	Same.
Kestrel.	—— tinnunculus.			
Sparrow-hawk.	Accipiter nisus.			
Kite.	Milvus ictinus.			Formerly.
Osprey.		C.	rrr	Lasham.
Common buzzard.	Buteo vulgaris.	C.	rr	Medstead.
Honey buzzard.	Pernix apivorus.	W.	rrr	Selborne.
Hen harrier.	Circus cyaneus.	W.,B.,C.	rr	Faringdon. Alton.
Montagu's harrier.	—— cinereus.	B., C.	rrr	Faringdon.
Long-eared owl.	Asio otus.	B., C.	rr	Tisted.
Short-eared owl.	—— accipitrinus.	B., C.	rr	Selborne and Alton.
Barn-owl.	Aluco flammea.			
Brown owl.	Strix aluco.			
Great grey shrike.	Lanius excubitor.	C.	rrr	Alton.
Red-backed shrike.	—— collurio.	W.,B.,C.		Selborne and Alton.
Woodchat.	—— auriculatus.	W.	rrr	Near Selborne (Gould).
Spotted flycatcher.	Muscicapa grisola.			
Missel thrush.	Turdus viscivorus.			
Fieldfare.	—— pilaris.			
Song-thrush.	—— musicus.			
Redwing.	—— iliacus.	W.		
Blackbird.	—— merula.			
Ring-ousel.	—— torquatus.	W.,B.,C.	rr	Selborne and Alton.
Hedge accentor.	Accentor modularis.			
Redbreast.	Erithacus rubecula.			
Redstart.	Ruticilla phœnicura.	W.,B.,C.	r	Selborne and Alton.
Black redstart.	—— tithys.	C.	rrr	Alton. 1 sp.
Stonechat.	Saxicola rubicola.	W.,B.,C.		Selborne and Alton.

English name	Latin name			Location
Whinchat.	Saxicola rubetra.	W.,B.,C.		Selborne and Alton.
Wheatear.	—— œnanthe.	W.,B.,C.	r	Same.
Grasshopper warbler.	Acrocephalus nævius.	W., C.	rrr	Selborne and Worldham.
Sedge warbler.	—— schœnobœnus.	W., C.		Selborne and Alton.
Reed warbler.	—— streperus.	W., C.		Same.
Nightingale.	Daulias luscinia.			
Blackcap.	Sylvia atricapilla.	W.,B.,C.		Selborne and Alton.
Whitethroat.	—— rufa.	B.	r	Selborne.
Lesser whitethroat.	—— curruca.	B.	rr	Same.
Dartford warbler.	Melizophilus undatus.	B.	rr	Woolmer.
Golden-crested regulus.	Regulus cristatus.	W.,B.,C.	r	Selborne and Alton.
Fire-crested regulus.	—— ignicapillus.	C.	rrr	Alton.
Willow wren.	Phylloscopus trochilus.	W., B.,C.		Selborne and Alton.
Chiff chaff.	—— collybita.	W.,B.,C.		Same.
Wood wren.	—— sibilatrix.	W., B.	r	Selborne.
Great tit.	Parus major.			
Blue tit.	—— cœruleus.			
Coal tit.	—— ater.	B., C.	r	Selborne and Alton.
Marsh tit.	—— palustris.	W.	rr	Selborne.
Long-tailed tit.	Acredula caudata.	W.,B.,C.		Selborne and Alton.
Bohemian waxwing.	Ampelis garrulus.	C.	rrr	Holybourne (once).
Pied wagtail.	Motacilla lugubris.			
Grey wagtail.	—— sulphurea.	B., C.		Selborne and Alton.
Yellow wagtail.	—— flava.	B., C.	r	Hawkley Mill.
Tree pipit.	Anthus trivialis.			
Meadow pipit.	—— pratensis.			
Skylark.	Alauda arvensis.			
Woodlark.	—— arborea.	W.,B.,C.	r	Selborne and Alton.
Snowbunting.	Emberiza nivalis.	C.	rrr	Faringdon.
Yellow bunting.	—— citrinella.			
Common bunting.	—— miliaris.			
Cirl bunting.	—— cirlus.	B., C.	rr	Selborne.
Chaffinch.	Fringilla cœlebs.			
Bramble finch	—— montifringilla.	B., C.	r	Selborne and Newton.
Greenfinch.	Coccothraustes chloris.			
Hawfinch.	—— vulgaris.	W.,B.,C.	rr	Selborne and Newton.
Goldfinch.	Carduelis elegans.			
House sparrow.	Pyrgita domestica.			
Siskin.	Carduelis spinus.	C.	rrr	Alton.
Common linnet.	Linota cannabina.			
Mealy redpole.	—— canescens.	C.	rr	Alton.
Lesser redpole.	—— linaria.	C.	rr	Same.
Bullfinch.	Pyrrhula vulgaris.			
Common crossbill.	Loxia curvirostra.	W., C.	rr	Newton and Alton*.
Starling.	Sturnus vulgaris.			
Raven.	Corvus corax.	W.,B.,C.	r	Selborne Common.
Carrion crow.	—— corone.			
Hooded crow.	—— cornix.	C.	rr	Shalden and Binswood.
Rook.	—— frugilegus.			
Jackdaw.	—— monedula.			
Magpie.	Pica caudata.			
Jay.	Garrulus glandarius.			
Green woodpecker.	Picus viridis.			
Great spotted Do.	—— major.	C.	rr	3 or 4 at Alton.
Lesser Do. Do.	—— minor.	C.	rrr	1 at Binsted.
Wryneck.	Yunx torquilla.	C.	r	Alton.

* Has bred at Alton.

BIRDS FOUND AT SELBORNE.

Creeper.	Certhia familiaris.	B., C.	r	Selborne and Alton.
Wren.	Troglodytes parvulus.			
Hoopoe.	Upupa epops.	W.,B.,C.	rrr	Selborne, Newton *.
Nuthatch.	Sitta europæa.	W.,B.,C.		Selborne and Alton.
Cuckoo.	Cuculus canorus.			
Kingfisher.	Alcedo ispida.	W.,B.,C.		Selborne.
Chimney-swallow.	Hirundo rustica.			
Martin.	———— urbica.			
Sand-martin.	———— riparia.			
Swift.	Cypselus apus.			
Nightjar.	Caprimulgus europæus.	W.,B.,C.	r	
Turtledove.	Columba turtur.	B.	r	Selborne.
Stockdove.	———— œnas.	W., B.		Same.
Ringdove.	———— palumbus.			
Pheasant.	Phasianus colchicus.			
Black grouse.	Tetrao tetrix.	W.,B.,C.	rr	Woolmer and Shortheath.
Common partridge.	Perdix cinerea.			
Red-legged partridge.	———— rubra.	C.	rr	Holybourne.
Quail.	Coturnix vulgaris.		rr	Chawton.
Golden plover.	Charadrius pluvialis.	B., C.	rr	Hartley.
Dotterel.	———— morinellus.	C.	rr	Kingsley.
Stone curlew.	Œdicnemus crepitans.	W.,B.,C.	rr	Selborne.
Peewit.	Vanellus cristatus.			Woolmer, &c.
Sanderling.	Calidris arenaria.			?
Heron.	Ardea cinerea.	B., C.	rr	Selborne and Alton.
Bittern.	Botaurus stellaris.	B., C.	rr	Selborne and Woolmer.
Common Curlew.	Numenius arquatus.	B.	rr	Selborne.
Common redshank.	Totanus calidris.	C.	rr	Alton.
Spotted redshank.	———— fuscus.	B.	rrr	Selborne.
Common sandpiper.	———— hypoleucos.	W., C.	rr	Selborne and Alton.
Bar-tailed godwit.	Limosa rufa.	C.	rrr	Faringdon.
Woodcock.	Scolopax rusticola.			
Snipe.	———— gallinago.			
Jack snipe.	———— gallinula.	C.	rr	**Alton.**
Little stint.	Tringa minuta.	C.	r	**Same.**
Land rail.	Crex pratensis.	W.,B.,C.	r	**Selborne.**
Spotted crake.	———— porzana.	C.	rrr	Kingsley. 1 sp.
Water rail.	Rallus aquaticus.	B., C.		Priory and Alton.
Moorhen.	Gallinula chloropus.	W.,B.,C.	r	Combe pond, Selborne.
Coot.	Fulica atra.		r	Alton.
Grey phalarope.	Phalaropus lobatus.	C.		Selborne.
Avocet.			rrr	2 killed at Frencham.
White-fronted goose.	Anser albifrons.	C.	rr	Holybourne.
Egyptian goose.	———— ægyptiacus.	C.	rr	Alton.
Hooper Swan.	Cygnus ferus.	C.	rrr	Headley.
Common Sheldrake.	Tadorna Bellonii.	C.	r	Alton.
Shoveller.	Anas clypeata.	C.	rrr	Greywell.
Teal.	———— crecca.	W.,B.,C.	r	Woolmer and Alton.
Wild duck.	———— boschas.	W.,B.,C.	r	Woolmer, &c.
Wigeon.	Mareca penelope.	B., C.	r	Woolmer and Alton.
Pochard.	Fuligula ferina.	C.	rr	Alton. 2 sp.
Scaup duck.	———— marila.	C.	rrr	Same. 1 sp.
Tufted duck.	———— cristata.	C.	rr	Headley. 3 sp.
Red-breasted merganser.	Mergus serrator.	C.	rrr	King's pond, Alton.
Goosander.	———— merganser.	C.	rr	Froyle. 2 sp.
Little grebe.	Podiceps minor.	C.	rr	Alton.

* See note at p. 31, Vol. I.

Great northern diver.	Colymbus glacialis.	W., B., C.	rr	Woolmer and Medstead.
Little auk.	Mergulus melanoleucos.	B.	rrr	Selborne by Lecourt.
Razorbill.	Alca torda.	O.	rrr	Alton.
Green cormorant.	Phalacrocorax cristatus.	O.	rr	Alton.
Black tern.	Sterna nigra.	C.	rrr	Hartley. 1 sp.
Common tern.	—— hirundo.	O.	r	Alton.
Lesser tern.	—— minuta.	O.	rrr	Same. 1 sp.
Black-headed gull.	Larus ridibundus.	C.	rrr	Worldham. 1 sp.
Great black-backed gull.	—— maximus.	O.	rrr	Alton. 1 sp.
Kittiwake.	—— tridactylus.	C.	r	Same.
Fork-tailed petrel.	Thallassidroma Leachii.	O.	rrr	Same. 1.

[The greater number of the aquatic birds in this list mentioned by Dr. John Curtis as having occurred at Alton were occasional visitors which were observed from time to time on the River Wey as it passes by the town.—T. B.]

REPTILIA AND AMPHIBIA FOUND AT SELBORNE.

Reptilia*.

Viviparous lizard.	Zootoca vivipara.	Woolmer, common.
Slowworm.	Anguis fragilis.	In coppices, common.
Ringed snake.	Natrix torquata.	Common near water.
Common viper.	Pelias berus.	On dry heaths.

Amphibia.

Common frog.	Rana temporaria.	
Common toad.	Bufo vulgaris.	
Natter-jack toad†.	—— calamita.	At Woolmer and in my grounds.
Warty newt.	Triton cristatus.	Pond in Hartley wood.
Common smooth newt.	Lissotriton vulgaris.	Common in ponds.
Palmated smooth newt.	—— palmipes.	In the pond on Selborne Common.

FISHES.

For the Fishes see Vol. I. pp. 32, 56, 57.

---

* [The green lizard mentioned by Gilbert White as having been found in the neighbourhood of Farnham (Vol. I. p. 64) has not, as far as I know, been found near Selborne; but it is not improbable that the species may, in the course of years, have made its way across the Holt to Woolmer.—T. B.]

† See Vol. I. p. 55.

MOLLUSCA.

Conchifera (Bivalves).

Cyclus cornea	Pond at Short Heath.
Anodonta cygnea	Same.

Gasteropoda (Univalves).

Neritina fluviatilis	The stream at Dorton.
Bithinia tentaculata	Same.
Valvata piscinalis	Same.
Planorbis spirorbis	Pond at Short Heath.
—— marginatus	Same.
Physa fontinalis	Stream at Dorton and Priory.
Limnæa peregra	Pond at Short Heath.
—— auricularia	Same.
—— stagnalis	Oakhanger (Dr. J. Curtis).
Ancylus fluviatilis	On leaves of iris, Dorton meadow.
Arion empiricorum	Garden.
—— hortensis	On the lawn.
Limax flavus	Cellar.
—— agrestis	Garden.
—— maximus	Same.
—— arborum	Beeches in the Hanger.
Testacella haliotoidea	In my kitchen-garden.
Succinea putris	Meadow by Combe Wood.
—— elegans	Same.
Vitrina pellucida	Under moss on the Hanger.
Zonites cellarius	Under stones.
—— alliarius	High Wood on shrubs and trees.
—— crystallinus	Among moss at the foot of the Hanger.
—— fulvus	Same, rare.
Helix aspersa	Everywhere.
—— nemoralis	Scrubs, **Hanger**, &c.
—— hortensis	Same.
—— ——, var. hybrida	(Dr. John Curtis.)
—— arbustorum	Scrubs and Hanger.
—— Cantiana*	S.E. end of Common.
—— rufescens	Hanger, &c., very numerous.
—— hispida	Under stones in Rocky lane.
—— virgata†	Selborne Common, Nore hill, &c.
—— caperata	S.E. end of the Common and Dorton.
—— ericetorum	The Park, Nore hill, &c.
—— pulchella	Among moss, decayed leaves, **&c.**
—— rotundata	Hanger, &c.
—— lapicida	Scrubs and Hanger.

---

* [At the S.E. end of Selborne Common *Helix Cantiana* and *H. caperata* are both tolerably abundant, but each species occupies its own ground without encroaching on the portion appropriated by the other. There is no apparent cause, either as regards soil or food, to account for this selection.—T. B.]

† [On the "Hog's-back," between Guildford and Farnham, *Helix virgata* is found of a very large size. I have taken many specimens there ¾ of an inch in diameter.—T. B.]

Bulimus montanus	On beeches in the Hanger.
—— obscurus	Same; very numerous.
Pupa edentula	On a wall among moss.
—— muscorum	Among moss.
Balia perversa	On beech trees in the Hanger.
Clausilia nigricans	On beeches in the Hanger, &c.
—— laminata	Same.
—— ——, white var.	Same (a single specimen).
Azeca tridens	Among damp moss, in Hanger, &c.
Zua lubrica	Same.
Achatina acicula	Among the roots of moss and grass.
Carychium minimum	Among dead and decaying oak-leaves.
Cyclostoma elegans	Foot of the Hanger, plentiful.

[I am indebted to Earl Waldegrave for the following list of some rare Lepidoptera taken by himself at or near Blackmoor, in the parish of Selborne.—T. B.]

BUTTERFLIES.

Clouded yellow.	Colias Edusa.	Many taken between August and October, 1875. All males but two.
Pale yellow.	—— Hyale.	Blackmoor.
Marbled white.	Melanagria Galathea.	Not uncommon at Blackmoor (plentiful on Selborne hill, T. B.).
White Admiral.	Limenitis Sibylla.	Common in Blackmoor wood.
Duke of Burgundy.	Nemeobius Lucina.	Wheatham Hill and Coldhayes.
Greasy fritillary.	Melitæa Artemis.	Same.
Small blue.	Lycæna Alsus.	Same.
Silver studded blue.	—— Ægon.	Woolmer forest.
The grayling.	Hipparchia Semele.	Woolmer and Blackmoor.

SPHINXES AND MOTHS.

Death's-head sphinx.	Acherontia Atropos.	(The Wakes, Selborne, T. B.)
Convolvulus sphinx.	Sphinx Convolvuli.	Blackmoor (Selborne, T. B.).
Six-spot Burnett.	Zygæna Filipendulæ.	Same, early in August 1875.
Cream-spotted tiger.	Chelonia villica.	One, on June 29, 1875.
Ruby tiger.	Arctia fuliginosa.	One in August 1875.
Grass emerald.	Hemithea cythisaria.	August 1875.
The streak.	Chæsias spartiata.	October 6, 1875.
Broad-bordered yellow underwing.	Triphæna fimbria.	September 1875, 2 specimens.
Grey rustic.	Noctua neglecta.	Several. September 1875.
Double kidney.	Tethea retusa.	August 16, 1875.
Black rustic.	Epunda nigra.	Six specimens. Sept. and Oct. 1875.
Grey shoulder-knot.	Xylina rhizolitha.	October 1875.
Beautiful yellow underwing.	Anarta Myrtilli.	Tolerably abundant, Woolmer. August 1875.
Dark crimson underwing.	Catocala sponsa.	One specimen, August 9, 1875.

[*Vanessa Antiopa* was seen by the Rev. Horsley Palmer at Coldhayes, near Petersfield, and a female of this species was taken by Captain Chawner, of Newton Manor House, in June 1877.—T. B.]

PLANTS.*

Adoxa moschatellina	Nore Hill. "Lanes and coppices." G. W.
Allium oleraceum	Park at the Wakes.
—— ursinum	"Bradshott Wood." Ld. S.
Anagallis tenella	"Short Heath and Woolmer." W. W.
Antirrhinum orontium	Short Heath and Temple.
Aquilegia vulgaris	"Below S. side of Nore Hill." Mrs. de J.
Astragalus glycyphyllus	W. W.
Bartsia viscosa	Between Short and Long Lithe.
Betula alba	Boggy ground, Woolmer.
Bromus secalinus	"Poundfield and Temple." G. W.
Bryonia dioica	Hanger and hedges.
Callitriche autumnalis	Ditch between Temple and Woolmer, rather rare.
Campanula glomerata	Selborne Hill. "Lanes." G. W.
—— patula	Woolmer. "Bradshott." W. W.
—— trachelium	Scrubs. "Temple, &c." Ld. S.
Carduus nutans	Selborne Hill, plentiful.
Carlina vulgaris	"Selborne Down." G. W.
Caucalis arvensis	"Own fields." G. W.
Centunculus minimus	Short Heath.
Chenopodium bonus Henricus	Blackmoor and the Wakes.
Chlora perfoliata	Kingsfield. "The same." G. W.
Chrysanthemum segetum	Short Heath.
Cnicus acaulis	Selborne Common, plentiful.
Comarum palustre	"Woolmer." W. W.
Conium maculatum	"Binsted Wyck." W. W.
Convallaria multiflora	"Lane leading to Bradshott Mill." Ld. S. "Binsted Wyck." W. W.
Conyza squarrosa	Week-Hill hanger. "Sutton." W. W.
Crocus vernus	"Holywater near the brook." Ld. S.
Cuscuta europæa	"Bean's bog." G. W.
Cynoglossum officinale	Oakhanger.
Daphne laureola	Scrubs, Park and High Wood, &c.
—— mezereon	Scrubs, rare.
Dianthus armeria	"Near Bentley." W. W.
Dipsacus pilosus	Dorton and Short Lithe. "Binsted Wyck." W. W. "Lythe." G. W.
Drosera longifolia	Woolmer and Short Heath.
—— rotundifolia	Same places. "Bean's bog." G. W.
Eleocharis acicularis	Holywater and Woolmer.
Epilobium angustifolium	Hedges at Dorton, &c. "Forest." G. W.
—— palustre	Short Heath and Oakhanger.
—— roseum	Dorton and Oakhanger.

---

* I have already stated in the Preface that the majority of the plants in this list have been found by my relative Dr. Bell Salter, by the late Dr. Bromfield, the botanist of Hampshire, and by myself. I also possess a catalogue in the handwriting of Gilbert White, including a few which are not contained in the XLIst letter to Barrington. I am greatly indebted to Lord Selborne and to William Wickham, Esq., of Binsted Wyck, for considerable additions, and to Mrs. de Jersey, of Empshott Vicarage, for notices of several rare and interesting species. These additions are respectively distinguished by the initials G. W., Ld. S., W. W., and Mrs. de J.

Erigeron acre	"Road near Norton." W. W.
—— canadense	"Once at Binsted Wyck." W. W.
Euonymus europæus	Hedge near the Grange.
Eupatorium cannabinum	"Bradshott Wood." Ld. S. "Binsted Wyck." W. W.
Fedia dentata	Nore Hill.
Filago minima	Short Heath and Oakhanger.
Fumaria capreolata.............	Oakhanger.
Galanthus nivalis................	"Holywater; long copse, Wickhill." Ld. S. "Between E. and W. Worldham." W. W.
Galeobdolon luteum	Park, plentiful.
Galeopsis ladanum	"About Selborne." Dr. Bromfield.
Gentiana amarella	Zigzag. "Same place." G. W.
Geranium pratense	Priory, near the end of the Lithe.
Helleborus fœtidus	High Wood.
—— viridis	"Norton Lane." G. W.
Helosciadium inundatum	Woolmer and Short Heath.
Hieracium sylvaticum...........	Woolmer and rocky lanes.
—— umbellatum	Rocky lanes by the Grange.
Hydrocotyle vulgaris	"Forest." G. W.
Hypericum androsæmum	"Temple Wood." Ld. S. "E. Worldham." W. W. "Hollow lanes." G. W.
—— elodes	"Oakhanger and Woolmer pond." Ld. S.
—— humifusum	"Between Selborne and Liss." W. W.
Hypochœris glabra	Short Heath and Oakhanger.
Jasione montana	Lithe, Woolmer, and Short Heath.
Juncus squarrosus	Woolmer and Short Heath.
Lathræa squamaria	In a garden in the village. "Church Litton coppice." G. W.
Lathyrus nissolia.................	"Once. Binsted Wyck." W. W.
—— sylvestris	Dorton, &c. "Lythe." G. W.
Leonurus cardiaca	"Forest side." G. W.
Linaria elatine	"Own closes." G. W.
—— minor	"Binsted Wyck." W. W.
—— spuria	"Binsted, in cornfields." W. W.
—— vulgaris	Hedges below Temple.
Linum angustifolium	"Holybourne." W. W.
Lithospermum arvense	"Binsted Wyck." W. W.
—— officinale	Lithe. "Street." G. W.
Littorella lacustris	Short Heath and Woolmer.
Luzula sylvatica	Winchester Wood.
Lycopus europæus	Temple.
Lysimachia nummularia........	Dorton and rocky lanes.
—— vulgaris	"Bean's bog." G. W.
Malva moschata *	On banks, common.
Melica cærulea	Woolmer.
—— uniflora	Chawton Park.
Melissa officinalis................	Dorton, by the stream.
Mentha sylvestris................	The Lithe.
Menyanthes trifoliata	"Bean's bog." G. W.
Milium effusum	Selborne Common and elsewhere.
Mœnchia erecta	"Woolmer." W. W.
Monotropa hypopitys	The hanger, abundant.
Myosotis palustris	Stream from Dorton to Oakhanger.

* Doubtless White means his species when he mentions in his MS. list "*Malva alcœa*" as occurring in the "long lithe," *Alcea vulgaris* being the name given to it by Dillenius and Ray.

PLANTS FOUND AT SELBORNE.

Myosurus minimus	Hollow lane at Norton.
Narcissus biflorus	"Kingsley." Miss Lushington. "Empshott." Mrs. de J. "Coldhayes." **Ld. S.**
—— pseudo-narcissus	"Blackmoor Wood, &c." Ld. S.
Narthecium ossifragum	"Oakhanger and Hogmer." Ld. S.
Nasturtium terrestre	Short Heath.
Nepeta cataria	"Northfield." G. W.
Œnanthe fistulosa	"Same." G. W.
Origanum vulgare	Scrubs. "Floribus **albis, Kingsfield.**" G. W.
Ornithopus perpusillus	"Woolmer." W. W.
Orobus tuberosus	Own beechen grove.
Paris quadrifolia	Combe Wood. "Temple and Snapwood" Ld. S. "Coppices." G. W.
Parnassia palustris	"Oakhanger." Ld. S.
Peplis portula	Short Heath and Woolmer.
Picris hieracioides	"Own fields." G. W
Pinguicula vulgaris	"Woolmer." Ld. S.
Poa nemoralis	Bank at Week Hill.
Polygonum minus	Short Heath.
Populus tremula	"Woods at Selborne." Dr. Bromfield.
Potamogeton lucens	"Woolmer and Holywater." Ld. S.
—— natans	"Combe pond." G. W.
Poterium sanguisorba	Scrubs.
Prenanthes muralis	Rocky lanes, **common.**
Primula elatior	Park, rare. "**Binsted Wyck.**" W. W.
Pulmonaria angustifolia	"Hollow lanes." G. W.
Pyrethrum parthenium	Oakhanger.
Pyrus aria	Scrubs. "Hanger." G. W.
—— aucuparia	Scrubs.
Radiola millegrana	Woolmer and Short Heath.
Ranunculus aquatilis	Short Heath, &c.
—— hederaceus	Same.
Rhamnus catharticus	Hedge near the Grange.
Rhynchospora alba	Short Heath.
Ribes grossularia	"Stubb's farm, Binsted." W. W.
Rubus affinis (rosaceus)*	Lithe.
—— Babingtonii	Week Hill.
—— carpinifolius	Oakhanger.
—— discolor	Various places.
—— Kœhleri	Wood below Week Hill.
—— Lejeunii	Between Temple and Woolmer.
—— leucostachys	Various places.
—— nitidus	Priory.
—— rudis	On the road to Alton.
—— Schleicheri	Temple.
—— tenuis (macrophyllus)	Various places.
—— cæsius	Various places.
Ruscus aculeatus	"Forest side." G. W. "Alice Holt." W. W. "Harting Combe." Ld. S.
Sambucus ebulus	**Park** and scrubs. "Own fields." G. W.
Saponaria officinalis	Priory. "Street." G. W.
Scirpus sylvaticus	Oakhanger, &c.
Sclerochloa rigida	"Selborne." Dr. Bromfield.

* I give the names and habitats of the genus *Rubus* as they were communicated by Dr. Bell Salter, who, as is well known, made the genus a special study.

Scutellaria galericulata	Short Heath.
—— minor	Peaty bogs, Woolmer.
Sibthorpia europæa	Short Lithe.
Silaus pratensis	Between Priory and Oakhanger.
Sison amomum	Rocky lanes. "Prædio meo." G. W.
Tamus communis	Scrubs and elsewhere.
Teesdalia nudicaulis	"Kingsley." W. W.
Trifolium arvense	Blackmoor.
Tulipa sylvestris	Park.
Ulex nanus	Woolmer.
Ulmus montana	"Woods at Selborne." Dr. Bromfield.
Vaccinium myrtillus	Woolmer. "The forest." G. W.
—— oxycoccos	"Forest bogs." G. W.
Valeriana dioica	Scrubs. "Own fields." G. W.
Verbascum nigrum	Common on banks.
—— Thapsus	Bank on the road to Newton.
Veronica anagallis	Short Heath.
—— montana	Chawton Park.
—— officinalis	"Hollow lane." G. W.
—— scutellata	Short Heath.
Vinca minor	Hanger. "Temple woods." Ld. S.
Viscum album	On Apple, Hawthorn, Maple, and Lime at the Wakes.

ORCHIDS.

Aceras anthropophora	"Nore Hill." Mrs. de J.
Epipactis ensifolia	Under beeches in the Park, rare.
—— grandiflora	Same and the Hanger, plentiful.
—— latifolia	Hanger. "Binsted Wyck." W. W. "High Wood." G. W.
—— media, Bab.	Park and Hanger.
—— purpurata	Hanger.
Gymnadenia conopsea	Kingsfield. "Empshott." Mrs. de J.
Habenaria bifolia	Park, plentiful.
—— chlorantha	Same, rare. "Binsted Wyck." W. W.
Listera ovata	Park and Hanger.
Neottia spiralis	Selborne Common. "Pastures below Temple." Ld. S. "Dorton." G. W.
—— nidus-avis	Hanger and High Wood. "Long Lithe and Dorton." G. W.
Ophrys apifera	Park, High Wood, and Nore Hill.
—— muscifera	Same localities.
Orchis maculata	Priory meadow, &c., common.
—— mascula	Park, &c.
—— morio	Same.
—— pyramidalis	Kingsfield, rare.

FERNS.

Asplenium adiantum-nigrum	Lane leading to Empshott.
—— ruta-muraria	Church wall (formerly).
—— trichomanes	Temple Lane.
Athyrium filix-fœmina	Lane leading to Temple.
Blechnum boreale	Coppice on Temple Hill.

Botrychium lunare	S. end of common, very rare.
Ceterach officinarum	Church wall (formerly).
Lastrea dilatata	Temple Lane.
—— filix-mas	Rocky lanes.
—— oreopteris	Dorton Wood towards Priory.
Lycopodium inundatum	Short Heath and Woolmer.
Ophioglossum vulgare	Park. "In meadows." G. W.
Osmunda regalis	"Ditch at Oakhanger, on Woolmer Forest." Ld. S.
Polypodium vulgare	Rocky lanes.
Polystichum aculeatum	Same.
—— angulare	Honey Lane.
—— lobatum	Rocky lanes.
—— lonchitis	"Kingsfield coppice." Ld. S.
Pteris aquilina	Selborne hill, &c.
Scolopendrium vulgare	Rocky lanes.

THE GEOLOGY OF SELBORNE.

By WILLIAM CURTIS, Esq.

The village of Selborne stands just upon the junction of the Chalk Marl with the Upper Greensand. The bed of Chloritic Marl, probably not ten feet thick, though rarely distinctly visible, exactly marks the line of junction. It may be seen at each extremity of the village where the road leaves it for Newton Valence at one end, and Empshott at the other. It passes through the village, giving a darker appearance to the soil in some of the gardens, and is called by Gilbert White the "Black Malm," in contradistinction to "White Malm," the term applied to the soil generally over the Upper Greensand.

The springs mentioned by Gilbert White as arising at the extremities of the village issue from the Chloritic Marl, or sand, as it might more appropriately be called. That to the south-east, called Well Head, works a small flour-mill, with an overshot-wheel eighteen feet in diameter. The mill stands in a little deep gully, excavated by the action of water in the Malm rock; and, opening into the Priory valley at Dorton, the rivulet meets the little stream from the north-west end of the village.

The high Chalk ridge coming off from Newton Valence terminates abruptly on the south-west side of the village, and there forms the beautiful beech-covered "hanger" known as Selborne Hill. From this one may look down upon the quiet village, its church and great yew tree, the parsonage-house and plestor, and in the foreground, just at the foot of the hill, the unpretending residence and pretty garden and grounds formerly of Gilbert White, now of his worthy admirer Mr. Bell. May this sweet spot never be spoiled by improvements!

The narrow strip of land between the foot of the hill and the village street consists of the Chalk Marl. The north-eastern side of the village stands upon the Malm rock, the provincial name of the Upper Greensand. This formation is cut into deeply by the Priory valley, so that the Gault is exposed in the bottom of it some distance up towards the church. The Gault everywhere underlies the Upper Greensand, and separates it from the Lower. Gilbert White states that the wells in Selborne average a depth of sixty-three feet. This appears to represent the thickness of the Upper Greensand, which having been pierced, the water retained by the Gault-clay basin is reached. Descending towards the Priory, the Malm rock rises on the left hand into the Lythe, Week Hill, and Hartley "hanger," and the valley opens out on the Gault flat towards Oakhanger. On the right it stretches away for about a mile, gradually rising until it ends in an abrupt "hanger," clothed with oak timber, upon the extremity of which stands Temple farm.

At an average distance of about half a mile the Gault is succeeded by the Lower Greensand of Blackmoor, Woolmer Forest, Oakhanger, and Short Heath in the parish of Selborne, and of the adjoining parishes of Greatham and Kingsley. Over the comparatively level district which it here presents there are numerous ponds, such as Woolmer Pond (about sixty acres in extent), and Oakhanger Pond in the parish of Selborne, besides many others at a greater distance. Bin's or Bean's Pond, described by Gilbert White in Letter VIII. to Pennant, is, I believe, now quite dry. These sheets of water appear to express a general water-level in the sandy strata.

In regard to the land-slips caused by the undermining of the Upper Greensand and softening of the Gault by the agency of the springs, Gilbert White has described the best example of the kind, which occurred at Hawkley in the year 1774. Nothing like it appears to have happened in the parish of Selborne; but there are spots close to the emergence of the Gault from beneath the Malm rock where the clay appears to have been thrust forward by the superincumbent pressure. A considerable slip of one of the Binsted hangers took place about forty years ago.

It may be here observed that the hollow lane between Hartley and Selborne, in some parts nearly twenty feet deep, with almost perpendicular sides, is cut by the joint action of water and the wear of traffic through some of the upper beds of the Malm rock. These beds consist of alternations of hard blue argillaceous ragstone, one or two feet thick, and of softer ones of sandstone, called Firestone, four or five feet thick. The lower beds of the Upper Greensand are of a marly character.

A few general observations on the fossils from the beds in question may here be added. The Chalk in the vicinity of Selborne is so little exposed that I have obtained few fossils from it. Gilbert White speaks of large " *Cornua Ammonis* " being found when cutting an inclined path up the Hanger. These must have been in the Lower Chalk, and in a bed corresponding with one near Alton, in which I have found large Ammonites of several species, the largest, in the museum of that town, measuring 27 inches in diameter. With these occur smaller Ammonites and small *Nautili*. The large *Nautili* mentioned by Gilbert White as occurring at the northwest end of the Hanger belong to the Chalk marl.

These *Nautili* of the marl (*N. elegans*) are the largest species found above the chloritic bed. The most abundant fossil in the Chalk marl is the *A. varians*, and the most characteristic, as it is small and scarce in the other beds. In the side of the lane turning up the hill from Fisher's Buildings I procured two species of Turrilite, *costatus* and *tuberculatus*, and one of *Micraster*. I have several specimens of the " *Mytilus Cristagalli* " (*Ostrea carinata*), figured in the 'Natural History of Selborne,' which I did not find *in situ*; but I believe they belong to the Chalk marl.

The chloritic marl is a sandy slightly coherent bed, clearly distinguished by its black and green particles. After heavy rains these may be seen spread over the bottom of the little stream flowing from Well Head. This bed may still be seen in the " lane above Well Head in the way to Emshot," where Gilbert White describes it as a " darkish sort of marl." He speaks of the soil it produces—the " black malm " as a "warm, forward, crumbling mould," and of the "white malm" as "becoming a manure to itself." The qualities here alluded to and the general fertility of these particular soils depend on the existence, in addition to lime, of a large percentage of soluble silica and minute quantities of the alkalies and phosphates in the rocks which produce them.

In this bed are found ramose Sponges, Ventriculites, Choanites, and many traces of other species of the lower organisms, a *Micraster*, *Pecten orbicularis* and *quinquecostata*, several Lamellibranchiates, *Pleurotomaria*, and Cephalopoda; the last rare (the Alton Museum contains but one specimen, an imperfect *Am. varians*).

In the Upper Greensand a few traces of plants and bored wood are met with. It contains several species of Sea-urchins, and I have a single specimen of the Starfish from the Selborne Firestone. Brachiopoda are rare, the Mollusca numerous. The Alton Museum possesses about twenty species of Lamellibranchiata, five of Gasteropoda, and ten or twelve of Cephalopoda. The *Pecten orbicularis* is the only species of which the individuals are abundant. The Cephalopoda form the most conspicuous feature amongst the organic remains of the Upper Greensand of Selborne. Baculites and Hamites are rare, Ammonites numerous (the species *rhotomagensis*, *varians*, *rostratus*, *catillus*, and probably three or four others). *Nautilus pseudo-elegans* and a larger one (probably a distinct species, sometimes fourteen inches in diameter) are not uncommon.

The *Am. rostratus* presents three forms of the rostrum, which may indicate specific differences. The shells of the Cephalopoda are mostly found pressed more or less out of their natural form.

The *Belemnitella* are rare; they present a delicate nacreous covering. Some imperfect remains of Crustaceans, a few fish-scales and teeth of fishes and saurians have been obtained from the Malm rock.

The Gault is so little exposed that I have obtained very few fossils from it, and none from the Lower Greensand, within the bounds of Selborne parish.

W. C.

APPENDIX.

ON THE
ROMAN-BRITISH ANTIQUITIES
OF
SELBORNE.

By LORD SELBORNE.

THE conclusion drawn by White, from the discovery of Roman coins during the first half of the last century in the bed of Woolmer Pond, that Selborne was not unknown to the Romans ("Antiquities," Letter I.), has been abundantly confirmed by other and more recent discoveries.

About the year 1774 (as appears by a letter, dated in August 1777, from Mr. Sewell, then residing at Headley, to Mr. White, for the communication of which I am indebted to the kindness of Professor Bell) a large pot of coins or medals was also found in Woolmer Pond, from which Mr. Sewell obtained a complete series of all the Roman Emperors, from Claudius the First to Commodus (both inclusive), and the two Faustinas, and Crispina, the wife of Commodus, extending over nearly 150 years, from A.D. 43 to A.D. 194. There were none, he says, later than Commodus. And I learn from Mr. Prettejohn (now residing at Yanston, in Devonshire), who lived for more than thirty years near Woolmer Pond, and was "foreman" of the Forest for a period including the reign of George the Fourth, that in his time Roman coins were occasionally found in the gravel and sand of Woolmer Pond, on the Blackmoor side, and sometimes also in the old roads and paths in the open Forest, and within the present grounds of

Blackmoor House. He himself and other members of his family have found more than twenty among the siftings of gravel dug to repair the turnpike-road by the side of the pond, four of which (being all that he has retained) he has had the goodness to show me. They are much defaced, and the legends are wholly obliterated; but one can be recognized as of the younger Faustina, and one as of Crispina, the Empress of Commodus.

In 1865, having purchased the Temple and Blackmoor estates, I chose for my residence the spot then occupied by Blackmoor Farm House. The name "Blackmoor" properly belongs to the western and northern parts of the sandy ridges (raised considerably above the lower level of Woolmer Forest, and themselves overlooked from the west by the escarpments of the Upper Greensand and the still loftier chalk summits behind them) by which the basin of Woolmer Forest, where it is crossed by the main road between Petersfield and Farnham, is enclosed. To the north-east and east the ridges of Blackmoor connect themselves with those of Hogmoor, White Hill, and Wall Down, between which and the south-eastern and southern ridges, dividing this forest-basin from the valley traversed by the road between Greatham and Liphook (on which stand fir-plantations belonging to the crown), rises the conspicuous landmark of Holy-Water (or Holly-Water) Clump. The intermediate low ground, covered with rough heather, and interspersed here and there with pools of water at certain seasons, is in breadth about a mile and a half from north to south by about two miles in length from east to west. In a depression at the narrowest point between the government plantations to the south-east and the most southerly part of the Blackmoor ridges lies Woolmer Pond, a shallow lake, nearly always fordable by man or horse in every part, and varying with the seasons from a large and broad sheet of water to a bed of sand, almost entirely dry in times of prolonged drought.

All these ridges, and the basins below them, are upon the formation called by geologists the Lower Greensand, which is naturally barren or covered only with furze and heath, though now planted in many places, chiefly with Scotch fir. But the westerly ridge of Blackmoor extends back as far as the Gault clay, on which there is abundance of oak and other wood. At the exact point of junction between these two formations, at the east end of Blackmoor Wood, and within the limits of the present gardens of Blackmoor House, is a small square island, surrounded by a moat of water; and behind, and higher than Blackmoor House, to the north (also included within the present gardens) is a piece of land formerly called the " Chapel Field." Here, while the foundations were being dug in 1867 for a kitchen-garden wall, the first discovery of Roman or Roman-British remains was made. A large sepulchral earthenware vase was dug up, much broken in the upper part, in which were contained a small bronze cup, enamelled in various colours, nearly perfect, and the remains of a bronze patera of extreme thinness; also one large bronze coin, much worn, which is pronounced by competent authority to be of Lucius Verus. There were in this vase some small remains of bones.

In other parts of the garden and grounds, and in digging the foundations for the house and offices, there were found many fragments of various articles of Roman pottery, including some of Samian or imitated from Samian ware; some Roman tiles (probably roof-tiles), many of which were in the island already mentioned; a bronze celt or axe-head; a large leaden ring, such as might have been run through a staple fixed into a post or wall; and two iron axe-heads, an iron socket for receiving the head of an axe or other weapon, a large iron cattle-bell, and fragments of iron nails, &c. The dates of these leaden and iron articles (all which were much oxidated) I do not profess to determine.

In 1868 the moat round the small island was cleaned out, and at the bottom of it were found a large earthenware water-vessel and a small earthenware drinking-cup, both in excellent preservation.

A reservoir for the storage of water was constructed under the Temple " Hanger " in 1869-70; and in digging-out this reservoir some further fragments of Roman pottery were found.

In the spring of 1870, in the garden of a cottage on the western side of the road ascending from Eveley corner to Hogmoor, a number of bronze weapons, or parts of weapons (Roman or Roman-British), were found under peat, free from rust or oxidation. They consisted of twenty-seven fragments of sword-blades, some of which, when put together, made complete swords; two fragments of sword-sheaths; one grooved socket for connecting a spear-head, or perhaps a standard, with the shaft; eighteen large and six small spear-heads; two spear-points; three rings; and two fragments of uncertain use. Most of the sword-handles had bronze nails (evidently intended to fasten the iron part of the handle to some covering material) remaining perfect in their holes; and in the cavities of several of the spear-heads the wooden points which had been inserted to fix them in sockets connecting the head with the shaft of the spear were still remaining. Some of the edges of these weapons were hacked and notched in a manner which could hardly have resulted from use; and of the sword-blades, some had been forcibly bent before being broken, proving that those who buried them had first taken pains to render them useless.

In the same cottage garden there have also since been found, in a fragment of a small earthenware pot, nearly 100 copper coins, much defaced, chiefly of the elder Tetricus, but including a few of his son, and of Gallienus and Victorinus.

The next discovery was that of two large earthenware vases, which, when perfect, must have contained considerably more than 30,000 Roman and Roman-British coins, the number of those which still remained in them when found, or which were recovered by myself from the surrounding earth, having been counted at 29,802. They were buried at a spot rather less than halfway between Blackmoor House and Woolmer Pond, where they were found, covered by about two feet of soil, on the 30th of October, 1873, by some workmen employed in trenching ground for a plantation. The upper parts of both vases were much broken, probably by agricultural operations at some distant date. The coins in them were closely caked together, and completely filled what was left of the vases.

They were all coated, more or less, with green oxide of copper. Some fragments of the broken parts of the vases and a small piece of the bottom of a Roman mortar were soon afterwards found near the same spot, but nothing else was there discovered.

The coins, on examination, were found to be chiefly bronze, varying from a size rather larger than a shilling to less than sixpence, those of the same size being often of very unequal thickness and weight. There were also a large number, principally *denarii*, of or plated with the base metal called by numismatologists "billon." Of the whole quantity, about one third only have been cleaned; the whole have now been sorted (an operation which was not complete when this paper was first prepared), and the result is as follows*:—

Gordian the younger (emperor A.D. 238–244)	2
Philip the Arabian (emperor A.D. 244–249)	1
Otacilia (wife of Philip)	1
Gallus (emperor A.D. 252–254)	1
Volusian (son and associate of Gallus)	1
Valerian (emperor A.D. 254–260)	25
Valerian the younger (son of Valerian)	2
Gallienus (son and associate of Valerian, and sole emperor from A.D. 260 to 268)	3475
Salonina (wife of Gallienus)	331
Saloninus (son of Gallienus)	7
Julius Gallienus (son of Gallienus), doubtful	2
Postumus (tyrant in Britain and Gaul, A.D. 258–265)	331
Lælianus (ditto, A.D. 265)	8
Marius (ditto, A.D. 265)	60
Victorinus (ditto, A.D. 265–268)	5450
Tetricus Augustus (ditto, A.D. 268–271)	10195
Tetricus Cæsar (son of Tetricus Augustus)	3833
Claudius Gothicus (emperor A.D. 268–270)	4213
Quintillus (brother of Claudius, emperor A.D. 270)	188
Aurelian (emperor A.D. 270–275)	175
Severina (wife of Aurelian)	14
Tacitus (emperor A.D. 275, 276)	206
Florian (brother of Tacitus, emperor A.D. 276)	18
Carried forward	28,539

---

* A catalogue of these coins will be found in the 'Numismatic Chronicle,' new ser. vol. xvii. pp. 90–156.

Brought forward	28,539
Probus (emperor A.D. 276–282)	431
Carus (emperor A.D. 282, 283)	12
Carinus (Cæsar A.D. 282; emperor A.D. 283–285)	24
Numerian (brother and colleague of Carinus)	14
Magnia Urbica (wife of Carinus)	2
Diocletian (emperor A.D. 285–305)	75
Maximian (colleague of Diocletian, A.D. 286–305)	53
Constantius Chlorus (Cæsar A.D. 292; became emperor A.D. 305)	1
Carausius (emperor in Britain A.D. 286–294)	545
Allectus (ditto, A.D. 294–296)	90
Total	29,788

The remaining fourteen cannot be distinguished.

Among these coins there are many which must have come from the mint in an imperfect state, some of them having either no heads or no reverses, one having the same head on both sides, some twice struck, either with the head of the same prince or with the head of one prince on a coin previously bearing that of another.

With respect to the condition of these coins, it is worth observation that those of Valerian, Gallienus, Salonina, Claudius, Victorinus, the two Tetrici, and Carausius are generally the most worn and defaced—a fact which, as to those of Carausius (almost the latest in the whole series), seems remarkable. All the imperial coins of later date than Aurelian (as also those of Severina and many of Aurelian himself) and the coins of Allectus are comparatively unworn and in fine condition, except when (as has happened in a few cases) they have sustained accidental damage, from excessive oxidation or adhesion while underground, or in the processes of separation and cleaning. In the legends and reverses there is great variety. They include 726 varieties which have, and 367 which have not, been described in Cohen's 'Catalogue of the known Imperial Roman Coins.'

This is understood to be the largest deposit of Roman or Roman-British coins ever yet found at one time in Great Britain; and it is rendered still more remarkable by the fact (already referred to) that in the last century other large quantities (the number has not been recorded) were found within a quarter of a mile of the same spot, in the bed of Woolmer Pond, some in a large pot, probably similar to the vases above mentioned, and others (being those mentioned by White) not enclosed in any vessel, but appearing to have been hastily thrown or poured into the water in a large heap or heaps. These appear to have been, if not wholly, in part at all events, of earlier date; and they were probably (at least in part) of greater size and value than those found at Blackmoor; for Mr. Sewell speaks of medals and White of medallions as well as coins; and White describes those which he saw as having been in very good condition.

This account of the antiquities discovered in the parish of Selborne would be imperfect without adding that, on the ridges surrounding the forest basin, of which a description has been given, there are thirty-five or more circular tumuli, or sepulchral mounds, some larger than others, but none of very large size, of which eleven are at or near Hogmoor, to the north-east (seven together in one place, three near together in another, and one by itself apart); four are on White Hill, to the east (three together, close to the high road, and one at a little distance apart); one is by itself on the south-easterly projection of the northern Blackmoor ridge (the ridge on which the church and vicarage-house now stand); five are in a line together at the southern extremity of the western Blackmoor ridge (close by the high road, overlooking Woolmer Pond); six, close together, are at the top of the opposite hill, on the other side of Woolmer Pond; four, close together, are in the government fir-plantations, about a quarter of a mile eastward from the east end of Woolmer Pond; three are in the highest part of the same plantations, to the north-west of the high road from Greatham to Liphook (one apart from the others, to the south-west, the other two close together); and one, remote from all the rest, is on the summit of Weaver's Down, close to the extreme southern boundary of Selborne parish. Some of them appear to have been much, and all or almost all of them more or less disturbed—with what results I have no information, except what I have obtained from Mr. Prettejohn, who was present at the opening of five of them in 1829.

He states that Mrs. Barlow, a lady then residing at Midhurst, by the permission of the proper authorities, caused that examination to be made. The first four mounds appeared to have been previously explored; and nothing was found in them except pieces of charcoal, ashes, calcined bones, and (in one of them within the Brimstone-Lodge enclosure) some small fragments of an urn, "old, rotten, decayed, crookey," and seeming to have been sun-dried, and not regularly burnt in a potter's kiln. In the fifth (being the smaller of the two upon " Cold-down hill, not far from Hogmoor Pond and Binn's Pond ") an urn was found, placed on the original level of the ground, covered by a flat stone, and containing (as I infer) calcined human bones or ashes. Mr. Prettejohn describes it as " of a bilged shape, something between a pitcher and a flower-pot," about eleven or twelve inches high, and capable of containing two or three quarts. It was " in appearance, weak;" but it was, with care, sent off "by two men to Midhurst" (a distance of twelve miles), " carrying it on a sling on a pole." Mrs. Barlow supposed it to be not only a relic of much interest and value, but of antiquity far greater than Roman-British times; but a friend, learned in these subjects, whom I have consulted, is led by the description given to doubt the soundness of that opinion. No coins were found in any of the tumuli thus examined.

With respect to earlier explorations, all that I can gather, through the recollections of old inhabitants, is, that some of the tumuli on the Forest were opened by a gentleman named Butler, certainly not less than sixty years ago. I have myself lately opened the largest of those not covered by plantations on my own property; nothing, however, was found there, except traces of former disturbance of the ground down to the natural level, and a cavity which might, not improbably, have once contained a sepulchral urn.

It occurs to me also to mention in this place (though their origin, nature, and purpose is obscure) that, immediately to the south-west of the five tumuli on the Blackmoor Ridge, overlooking Woolmer Pond, are a series of ancient parallel trenches (six or seven in number) of some depth, running nearly north and south from the top of the ridge down to the present high road. They can hardly be the result of natural or artificial drainage; and from their number and proximity to each other they are not likely to represent ancient tracks or ways. Whether they could, under any circumstances, have been intended for military defence, I do not know.

From the pottery and other remains found at and near Blackmoor House, it may be concluded with certainty that, on or close to that site, there once stood Roman or Roman-British buildings of some importance; and the name of the adjoining parish, Greatham, may perhaps indicate the situation (at least as early as Saxon times) of a hamlet or village more considerable than others in that neighbourhood. Mr. Sewell, in his letter of 1777, already referred to, speaks of Roman and British entrenchments as visible at that time on Headley Heath and Common; and he also describes, as a known historical event (I know not on what authority), a march by Vespasian, as general under Claudius, about A.D. 47, from the neighbourhood of London towards Porchester, Southampton, and the Isle of Wight, by way of Headley and Woolmer; adding that he (Vespasian) then fixed, at or near Woolmer Pond, "an abiding station or city, which remained near 150 years, when they seem to have been expelled thence by the Britons, or perhaps by an earthquake, or some other cause." I have not myself met with any mention of what Mr. Sewell calls "the Roman station or city of Wulmere in Hants" in any writer, ancient or modern, with whose works I am acquainted; and it is possible (as the end of the period of "near 150 years," which he assigns for its continuance, coincides with the time of Commodus, whose coins were the latest which had been found in Woolmer Pond) that his statements, however historical in form, may have been founded upon conjecture.

From the condition of the fragments of weapons found at Hogmoor, and from the circular tumuli on the ridges surrounding the forest basin, it seems, further, to be a probable conjecture that this part of the parish of Selborne was a battle-field in Roman-British times; and the burial of so large a quantity of money in one spot, and the burying and casting away of another quantity (perhaps more valuable) in the water within a quarter of a mile of the same spot (on both sides of which water tumuli now appear), seems to tell a tale of panic and flight. If we ask how so large a number and variety of coins, thus hidden and cast away, came to be brought together (including, as they do, some so imperfectly minted that they can hardly have been issued for circulation), it occurs to me, as a not improbable supposition, that they may have been hastily collected and carried off from some station in which there was a military chest, and perhaps also a mint, either to provide for the pay of a retreating army, or to prevent them from falling into the hands of an approaching enemy. The Roman Clausentum (now Bittern, near Southampton) was a garrison town, in which there was also a mint, in the times of Carausius and Allectus, some of whose coins, found at Blackmoor, bear the letter C on the exergue, which I understand to be the mint-mark of that place. The latest in date of all the coins found (if one, which may have become casually mixed with those of this hoard, and which is at least seventy years later, is excluded) are ninety of Allectus and a single coin of Constantius Chlorus—of which the legend is "FL. VAL. CONSTANTIUS NOB. C." (Flavius Valerius Constantius Nobilis Cæsar), and on the reverse, "VIRTUS AUGG." (Virtus Augustorum), with the device of Hercules leaning on his club and holding a bow, with the lion's skin over his arm—plainly one of his early coins, before his accession to the empire. The date, therefore, of their deposit cannot have been earlier than the reign of Allectus; and if it had been later than the reconquest of Britain by Constantius, it is not probable that only one coin of that prince would have been found.

On the other hand, there would be nothing in the occurrence among this treasure even of several coins of Constantius, while only Cæsar, inconsistent with the hypothesis that it may have belonged to Allectus himself, and may have been buried and cast away at the time when his retreat from the coast was intercepted by Asclepiodotus, the Prætorian prefect of Constantius, and when the engagement took place in which Allectus lost his life. Constantius was made Cæsar by the Emperor Diocletian A.D. 292, four years before his invasion of Britain, while Carausius was living; and nothing is more probable than that during that interval coins struck with the effigy of Constantius might obtain currency in Britain.

My own conclusion is, that in the basin of Woolmer Forest, and in the neighbouring ridges and hills, we have probably the scene of important events, of which a narrative, strictly contemporaneous, has been preserved to us in the panegyric of the orator Eumenius, pronounced in honour of Constantius Cæsar on his recovery of Britain.

Carausius, a native of the country between the Meuse and the Scheldt, of the same Belgic race by which, as early as the time of Julius Cæsar, Hampshire and the adjoining maritime parts of England were peopled, and a man of high reputation in naval warfare, was intrusted by Diocletian, soon after his succession to the empire, with the defence of the northern coast of Gaul from the incursions, then already frequent, of Saxon and Scandinavian corsairs. This he did successfully; but being accused of permitting the corsairs to commit depredations, with the view of appropriating the spoil when recaptured to his own use, Maximian ordered him to be put to death. Carausius then (A.D. 286) declared himself independent, and established an empire of his own in Britain, retaining also Boulogne and other neighbouring places in Gaul. To Britain he carried over with him the fleet under his command, which had been equipped for the defence of the opposite coast; and he built other ships of war in British ports, manning them with merchant seamen from various parts of Gaul, and with fighting men, attracted to his service from different barbarous nations, whom he instructed in naval as well as military warfare. The Roman legion, or legions, stationed in Britain acknowledged his sovereignty, which seems, from traces still remaining in various parts of the island, north as well as south, to have extended throughout Great Britain. The condition of this island, improved by two centuries and a half of Roman civilization, was at that time highly prosperous. "Non mediocris," says Eumenius, "jactura erat reipublicæ terra, tanto frugum ubere, tanto læta munere pastionum, tot metallorum fluens rivis, tot vectigalibus quæstuosa, tot accincta portubus, tanto immensa circuitu." Carausius became a considerable potentate—in naval power, especially, superior to the Romans, who, since their conquest of all the countries bordering on the Mediterranean, had neglected maritime warfare. Maximian in vain attempted an expedition against him; and in A.D. 289 terms of peace were agreed to, by which that prince and Diocletian recognized him as (in Britain) their partner in the empire.

When, however (A.D. 292), Constantius and Galerius were created "Cæsars" (or presumptive successors to the empire), Constantius, to whom the government of Gaul, Spain, and Britain was assigned, lost no time in attacking Boulogne, and reuniting to the empire that and the other continental possessions which Carausius still held. But no invasion of Britain appears to have been then apprehended.

In A.D. 294 Carausius was assassinated by his friend and minister Allectus, who himself assumed the purple in Britain. Preparations were now made by the Roman emperors for an invasion; and in the third year of Allectus (A.D. 296), Constantius, having collected two fleets of transports, one at Boulogne and the other at the mouth of the Seine, set sail with a considerable force from both ports simultaneously (himself embarking at Boulogne), with contrary winds, and in thick, foggy weather. Part of the expedition lost its way, and eventually sailed up the Thames to London; the main body, with Constantius himself and his Prætorian prefect Asclepiodotus, made for the British coast opposite the Isle of Wight, near which the navy of Allectus was on the look-out for them. Under cover of the fog, that part of the force which was under the command of Asclepiodotus passed unseen by the British fleet, and effected a landing, setting fire immediately afterwards to their ships. Allectus, who was in possession of the neighbouring port (doubtless Portsmouth), and encamped upon the shore, hastily abandoned his position, and retreated inland as soon as the sails of the ships which followed with Constantius came in sight. His retreat was cut off, and his army surprised, after it had advanced some distance into the interior, by the force under Asclepiodotus. The British troops were totally routed, and Allectus and many of his followers were slain, whose bodies, distinguished by their long fair hair and gay barbaric apparel, were found dispersed over hill and plain in various directions, while scarcely one Roman soldier perished. The remnant of the British army made its way to London, intending first to pillage, and then to abandon that city; but, meeting there with those troops of Constantius who had sailed up the Thames, it was put to the sword. And thus Britain was recovered to the Roman empire.

Such (supplying only from other sources some of the introductory facts, with the names of Asclepiodotus and of Carausius, whom the orator calls the "arch-pirate," and Allectus, whom he styles a "satellite" of Carausius and the "standard-bearer" of the rebel party) is the substance of what we learn from Eumenius. The passages most material to the question of the identity of the battle-field with Woolmer Forest are subjoined, in the original Latin.

"Ad tempus ipsum tantæ se dorso maris nebulæ miscuerunt,
"ut inimica classis, apud Vectam insulam in speculis atque
"insidiis collocata, ignorantibus omnino hostibus præteriretur.
". . . Jam vero idem ille vestro auspicio invictus exercitus,
"statim atque Britanniæ litus invaserat, universis navibus
"suis injecit ignes. . . . Ipse autem Signifer nefariæ fac-
"tionis, cur ab eo litore, quod tenebat, abscessit, cur classem
"portumque deseruit, nisi quod te, Cæsar invicte, cujus im-
"minentia vela conspexerat, timuit jam jamque venturum?
". . . Te tamen illo fugiens, incidit in tuorum manus; a te
"victus, a tuis exercitibus oppressus est. Denique adeo tre-
"pidus, et te post terga respiciens, et in modum amentis
"attoniti properavit in mortem, ut nec explicaret aciem, nec
"omnes copias quas trahebat instruxerit, sed cum veteribus
"illis conjurationis auctoribus, et mercenariis cuneis bar-
"barorum, tanti apparatûs oblitus, irruerit. Adeo, Cæsar,

"hoc etiam reipublicæ tribuit vestra felicitas, ut nemo fere
"Romanus occiderit, Imperio vincente Romano. Omnes enim
"illos, ut **audio**, campos atque colles non nisi teterrimorum
"hostium corpora fusa texerunt. Illa barbara, aut imitatione
"barbariæ olim cultu vestis et prolixo crine rutilantia, tunc
"vero pulvere et cruore fœdata, et in diversos situs tracta,
"sicuti dolorem vulnerum fuerant secuta, jacuerunt. Atque
"inter hos ipse Vexillarius latrocinii, cultu illo quem vivus
"violaverat sponte deposito, et vix unius velaminis repertus
"indicio. Adeo verum, ubi dixerat, morte vicinâ, ut inter-
"fectum se nollet agnosci.

"Enimvero, Cæsar invicte, tanto Deorum Immortalium tibi
"est addicta consensu, omnium quidem quos adortus fueris
"hostium, sed præcipue internecio Francorum, ut illi quoque
"milites vestri, qui, per errorem nebulosi (ut paulo ante dixi)
"maris abjuncti, ad oppidum Londiniense pervenerant, quid-
"quid ex mercenariâ **illâ** multitudine barbarorum prœlio
"superfuerunt, cum direptâ **civitate fugam** capessere cogi-
"tarent, passim totâ urbe **confecerint**, et non **solum** pro-
"vincialibus vestris in cæde hostium **dederint salutem**, sed
"etiam in spectaculo voluptatem."

The inferences to be drawn from this narrative appear to me to correspond with those which I derive from the evidence of the buried weapons and coins, and the tumuli upon the ridges surrounding the basin of Woolmer Forest. If, as is manifestly probable, Asclepiodotus landed between Portsmouth and Chichester, and if Portsmouth was the harbour near which Allectus took up the position which he so hastily abandoned, he would naturally fall back upon Clausentum (Southampton) and Venta (Winchester) by the ordinary Roman "iter;" and, after collecting whatever treasure he found in those places, the more southerly road, corresponding with that which now **goes by way** of Alresford* and Alton†

---

* A writer on the antiquities of the neighbourhood of Bicester, Oxon., in Kennett's 'Parochial Antiquities,' supposes (somewhat fancifully) that the first syllable of the name of Alresford and of some other places was derived from Allectus.

† Farnham was a military station; whether identical with "Vindomis"

towards Farnham and London, would probably be that which he would take, as offering the best chance of escape, if he were closely pursued. From Alton, if he heard that Constantius was following him, by turning a few miles to the southward, to the station or settlement which (as has been seen) existed at or near Blackmoor, he would obtain the protection of a country, probably then more difficult of access, in the immediate neighbourhood of the great **Forest** (Sylva Anderida), **which** certainly extended as far north-west as a part of **Rogate**, near the southern boundary of Selborne parish, and possibly further. In order to account for his meeting there with the Roman army under Asclepiodotus, nothing more is required than that we should suppose Constantius, soon after landing, to have ordered his Prætorian prefect to cross the hills, through the country of the Meanvari, in the direction of Alton or Farnham, for the purpose of cutting off the **communication between Allectus and the military stations to the east and north-east** of Winchester. The route which Asclepiodotus would follow in the execution of such orders would naturally take him, by Porchester and West Meon* (both Roman stations), either to the valley of

---

or not is a matter of controversy. Alton was certainly a Roman town. About thirty or forty years ago some interesting remains were found there, in ground now occupied as a timber-yard by Messrs. Dyer, some of which are still in the possession of the Messrs. **Dyer** and others are in the British Museum. They **consisted of several sepulchral vases, set in** dishes or saucers; two **lachrymatories; a small wooden dice-box; a** small lamp; and a signet-ring of onyx set in gold, which was still (when found) on the calcined bone of the wearer's finger. On this seal are engraved four small figures, set upright, parallel to each other, those in the centre representing an amphora and an ear of bearded corn, between an axe with fasces on one side and a quiver with arrows on the other. There were also some small pieces of Samian, or British Samian, ware.

* There is an earthwork on Old Winchester Hill, at West Meon, supposed to have been the *castra æstiva* of a Roman garrison in the country of the Meanvari, a tribe whose appellation is still preserved in the names of East and West Meon and Meonstoke. At the meeting of **the** Archæological Association held at Winchester in 1845, Colonel Greenwood exhibited a Roman terra-cotta lamp found within this en**campment, and some fragments** of Roman pottery found in a barrow near

Petersfield, up which he would move to Woolmer Forest (reversing what Mr. Sewell describes as Vespasian's march), or along the upper level of the chalk hills to Selborne or some point near it, from which he might descend suddenly upon the enemy in Woolmer Forest, unprepared for his approach. The expressions of the orator, "te fugiens," "te post terga respiciens," "incidit in tuorum manus," favour the hypothesis of such a countermarch by Asclepiodotus; and nothing can better agree with the character of the ground on which I suppose the two armies to have met than the words " omnes illos campos atque colles," which "teterrimorum hostium corpora fusa texerunt." The dispersion of the bodies of the fallen " in diversos situs tracta " agrees also with the positions of the tumuli (some in groups and some isolated), which, if my identification of the battle-field is correct, may perhaps now cover, or formerly have covered, some of their remains.

S.

Blackmoor, November 1874.

[The following is the letter from Mr. Sewell to Gilbert White referred to by Lord Selborne in his Lordship's paper. The original letter was communicated to me by Algernon Holt White, Esq.—T. B.]

Rev. Sir,

Out of a large pot of Medals (about 3 years since) which were found in Wulmere Pond, I collected a series from Claudius Drusus to Commodus included; that is medals of all the Rom^n Emp^{rs} from An^o Dom^i 43 to 194 with those of the two Faustinas and Crispina Empress of Commodus; and after Commodus I found no more. Also among the rest I found that of Trajan's famous stone Bridge over the Danube, below Belgrade; which, if it had been found when the three Bridges at London were first plann'd (viz: Westminster, London and Blackfriars Bridges) would then have been of very great

it, together with some remains of Roman weapons found at Bramdean, a few miles further north, in the same high chalky district.

value. Vespasian a general under Claudius Drusus, about A.D. 47, marched down with a Roman army this way from the Parts where London now is, towards Porchester, S. Hampton and the Isle of Wight. It is beautiful on Headley Heath and Common to observe the Entrenchments of the Romans and Britons, over against each other, the first advancing the other retreating. The Romans crossed Headley River at Hanford and advanced to the place where now is Wulmere Pond; and there fixed an abiding station or City, which remained near an 150 years; when they seem to have been expelled thence by the Britons, or perhaps by an Earthquake, or some other cause. Great treasures lie buried even now in that Pond of Roman Antiquities, of Coins and medals, of Instruments of War and Husbandry, and various Utensils for various uses. Of the vast quantity of Medals found there, as you mention, about 40 years since, no kind of historical use was ever made that I ever heard of; when this plain, and obvious Historical Truth might easily from thence have been deduced—the commencement, continuance or duration of the Roman Station or City of Wulmere in Hants. I believe from thence may be traced vestiges of Rom: roads to Porchester, Winton &c. The R^t Honble M. Legg got a great Quantity of these Coins; and with him they lye dormant: as also a great Quantity with — Whitehead of Liphook, and with Mr Hugonen. And this is the misfortune of most Antiquities that they frequently fall into hands that can collect nothing from them; in whose coffers they are more buried than if they were to lye in the depth of a Mine or of Wulmere Pond. The greatest curiosity hereabouts is, as I said, the advancement of the Roman Army to the S.W. over Hindhead and over Headley Heath and Common. What may be observed of this kind by way of Liphook over Hindhead, I have not yet searched and examined.

     I am, Sir, most respectfully,
         Your obed^t Servt,
           WM. SEWELL.

Headley, Aug. 7, 1777.

NOTE

ON SOME

RECENT DISCOVERIES IN SELBORNE CHURCH,

AND

THEIR BEARING ON THE HISTORY OF THE SUDINGTON PRECEPTORY OF THE KNIGHTS TEMPLARS.

Some very interesting discoveries have been made in Selborne Church in the course of its restoration, which has taken place during the progress of the second volume of this work through the press. These, while generally confirming the views which I ventured to express in a note at p. 287 of the first volume*, have thrown new light upon the history of some parts of the building, and particularly as affording important illustrations of the relation which existed between the parish church and the Knights Templars of Southington (Sudington) Preceptory.

The introduction of this celebrated military order into England took place early in the reign of Stephen, about the middle of the twelfth century. On their establishment in London, their first home was in the district of Oldbourne (the site of the present Southampton Buildings), which, in the reign of Henry II., was exchanged for the piece of ground to which the name of the order has become permanently attached, and which constituted the headquarters of the order in England until its dissolution. It is not necessary here to

---

* I must here correct a mistake which I made in the note referred to. I stated that there is no piscina in the chancel or the nave. On removing the wainscot, however, which had for ages covered this part of the wall, a good piscina of the early English style was exposed, which had been entirely concealed.

enter into the general history of the Knights Templars*. As regards their connexion with Selborne, all that was known with any certainty is told by Gilbert White in his usual full and interesting manner†. But still further illustrations of this connexion have been brought to light in the course of the recent explorations.

It is to the east end of the south aisle of the church that the principal interest attaches with reference to this subject. I have, in the note already alluded to, mentioned that in this part exist all the essentials of sacramental furniture. Gilbert White states that the east end of this aisle was called the South Chantry, and adds that, " till within these thirty years " (therefore within his recollection), it was " divided off by an old carved Gothic framework of timber, having been a private chantry." I have also stated that its boundary was still further defined by its being raised above the general level of the church floor by a stone step about 4 or 5 inches high, not only across the aisle from north to south, but also enclosing the area of the chapel by a similar step from west to east. We have then full evidence that the east portion of the south aisle formed a distinct chapel or chantry, separated by being on a higher level, and by a carved wooden screen, and furnished with an altar, a piscina, and a niche. The question then arises, to whose use was this separate place of worship appropriated? The question I believe to be solved by the recent researches.

Gilbert White states‡ that "two narrow stone coffin-lids composed part of the floor " of the north transept. At present, he says, "they have no coffins under them;" and from this circumstance he very naturally concludes that this was not the position which they originally occupied, but that

---

* Of the atrocious persecutions, the tortures, and slaughter to which the Knights Templars were undeservedly subjected on the demolition of their order, mainly from the avarice and through the machinations of Philip the Fair of France and Pope Clement V., I need only refer to the full and interesting account in Mill's 'History of the Crusades,' vol. ii. p. 366 &c. (4th edit.).
† Vol. I. p. 316 &c.
‡ Vol. I. p. 284.

Wrdes' Selborne

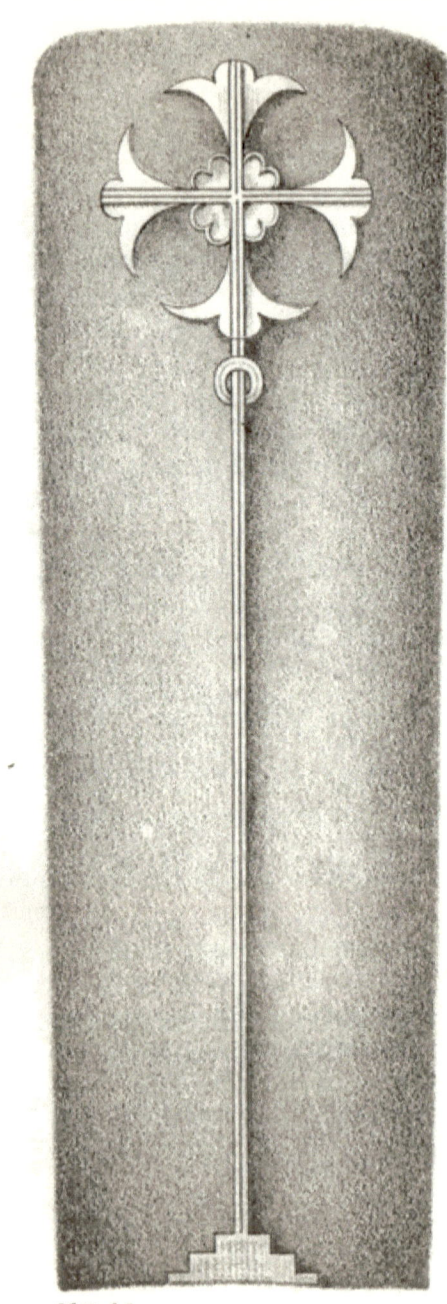

M.H. del.

they were brought hither from some part of a former church. On one of these lids, he tells us, "is to be discerned a *discus*, with a cross on it, at the end of a staff or rod, the well-known symbol of a Knight Templar."

The discovery of no less than five stone coffin-lids in this transept, not one of which had a coffin under it, confirms the opinion that this was not their original situation, but that they were brought to this spot by some graceless restorer to serve as paving-stones. At what period this was done it is impossible to say. There were no stone coffins found in the transept, but a grave lined with stone, containing the decayed remains of a wooden coffin and the bones of a man.

It is to the south chantry that we have to turn for the probable solution of the question. Here were found two stone coffins, each covered with a lid. One of the coffins was about two feet below the floor, exactly at the northern boundary of the chantry; the other partly built into the south wall. Each is formed of a solid block of Sussex stone, and each contained the skeleton of a man; the workmanship was throughout that of a skilled stonemason. There is in each, as is usual in stone coffins of that period, a hollow for the head, and in each case the skull occupied its original position within it. There was also in each of them the usual hole at the bottom of the coffin to drain off the moisture produced by the decay of the body. The coffins are somewhat narrower at the foot than at the head[*], which is also the case with most of the lids of which the coffins have not been found. In both the skeletons were perfect; in the larger of them the tibia had been broken and badly set, the two broken portions overlapping each other. The other coffin is somewhat smaller and more tapering.

I have now to describe those lids which are ornamented with crosses. The most perfect of these covered one of the coffins

[*] The dimensions of this coffin are as follows:—Total outside length 6 feet 10 inches, breadth at the head 1 foot 10 inches, at the foot 1 foot 4 inches, the thickness of the stone parietes averaging about $3\frac{1}{2}$ inches; the horseshoe-shaped cavity for the head is $9\frac{1}{2}$ inches in diameter and 7 inches deep, being 1 inch above the floor of the coffin. The length of the interior is 6 feet 3 inches. The other coffin is a little smaller.

which was found within the precincts of the south chantry. The cross (see Plate facing p. 397) is of the form designated in the language of heraldry the cross *flory*, and is so circular in its outline as to give the impression that it is figured on the *discus* of the Templars' symbol. There is a ring on the staff immediately under the cross, which is also seen on another of the crosses. On this cross is an element which I have never before seen: at the intersections of its four angles are four hearts, with the apices towards the centre. On one of the lids is a simple cross *pátée* (Maltese), without staff or any other adjunct; the sides of the lid are broadly and deeply moulded. Nearly a hundred tiles were found at a short distance below the surface, evidently belonging to the thirteenth century; almost the whole of them are of the usual size, about $5\frac{1}{2}$ inches; six examples of these are figured in the opposite Plate. There is one of a most extraordinary pattern, fully $6\frac{1}{2}$ inches square, which is also figured. These tiles undoubtedly paved the space in front of the altar. All these relics appear to me to point conclusively to the adaptation of this chantry or chapel to the service of the Knights Templars. T. B.

M.H. del.

INDEX.

Account-book, Gilbert White's, ii. 316.
Adanson, M., ii. 245.
Addison's 'Travels,' ii. 299.
Air, humming in the, i. 452.
Albinism in birds, i. 45.
Alfred, king, chapel founded by, i. 318.
Allectus, battle between Constantius and, ii. 389.
Alton, Roman remains found at, ii. 392.
——, stag-hunt at, i. 449.
Ameria, wife of Adam Gurdon, i. 307.
America, Seneca on the discovery of, ii. 43.
Ampelis garrulus, i. 37.
Amphibia, breeding of, i. 5.
—— and reptilia found at Selborne, i. 53 and *note*, ii. 366.
Andalusia, climate of, ii. 7.
Anderson, Rev. James, ii. 175.
Anecdote of a field-mouse, i. 146.
—— of Mr. Pink, ii. 156.
—— of Gilbert White, i. 369.
Animal productions of Southern Europe, ii. 67–94.
Animals, στοργη of, i. 145.
——, influence of food on the colour of, i. 45, 481.
—— and plants, Mr. Banks's collection of, ii. 99.
Anne, Queen, visit to Wolmer forest to see the red deer, i. 18.
Antiquities, i. 275, ii. 378.
Ants, migration of, i. 462.
Aphides, shower of, i. 245, 462.
Architecture of Church, i. 287 *note*, ii. 395.
Aristotle, extract from, on the *Caprimulgus*, ii. 224.

Armament, on the late (poem), i. 506.
Arno, the river, frozen over, ii. 121.
Arnold, Miles, Selborne parsonage leased to, i. 364.
Ash trees, i. 470.
Ashford, Thomas, elected prior, i. 352.
——, pension granted to, i. 360.
Attachment of animals of different kinds to each other, i. 200.
Aurora australis, ii. 140.
—— borealis, i. 479.
Auk, little, i. 99 and *note*.
Ayles or Alice Holt, i. 25.

Badeisley, preceptory at, i. 317, ii. 131.
Bagshot, review at, ii. 284.
Balloon, Mr. Blanchard's, ii. 154.
Banks, Joseph, account of a visit to, ii. 97.
——, letter from Gilbert White to, ii. 241.
Barker, Miss Mary, letter from Gilbert White to, ii. 176.
——, Mrs., letters from Gilbert White to, ii. 107, 109, 117, 135, 154, 165, 178.
——, Samuel, letters from Gilbert White to, ii. 96, 100, 105, 110–116, 118, 124–129, 133, 136, 138–142, 161, 163, 168, 173, 180.
——, ——, letter from John White to, ii. 103.
——, Thomas, letters from Gilbert White to, ii. 95, 101, 119, 123, 166, 171.
Barometers at Selborne and Newton compared, i. 259.
Barragons manufactured at Alton, i. 15.

Barrington, Hon. Daines, letters from Gilbert White to, i. 113–274.
——, controversy with Dr. Ducarel, ii. 269.
Bat, great, if really a distinct species, i. 92.
——, ——, description of, i. 93.
——, ——, method of feeding, i. 77.
Batrachia at Selborne, i. 50.
——, breeding of, i. 50, 53, 55, 58.
Bats, habits of, 34 and *note*.
—— species of, at Selborne, i. 33 and *note*.
——, tame, 34.
Battle of Woolmer forest, ii. 390.
Beachy Head, Cornish choughs found at, i. 96.
Beans sown by birds, i. 473.
Beaufort, Bishop of Winchester, i. 334.
Beeches, remarks on, i. 470, ii. 247, 249, 252, 258, 265, 268, 271, 281.
Bees, cucumbers set by, i. 474.
——, fondness of an idiot boy for, i. 189.
Benefactors to Selborne priory, mass ordered to be celebrated for, i. 361.
Bernes, Peter, appointed prior, i. 341, 348.
——, indenture of certain things put into the custody of, i. 340, 399.
——, reduced to poverty, i. 351.
——, resignation of, i. 343, 349.
Binn's or Bean's pond, i. 22, ii. 375.
Birds, albinism in, i. 45.
——, beans sown by, i. 473.
——, change of colour in, cause of, i. 128.
——, choosing fresh mate after losing the first, i. 82.
——, different voices of, i. 222.
—— dusting themselves, i. 130.
—— found at Selborne, ii. 363.
——, hard-billed, more easily imported than soft-billed, i. 84.
——, migration of, i. 87.
——, non-migrating, food of, i. 104, 106.
——, numerous species at Selborne, i. 103.
——, observations on, i. 423.
—— of passage, list of, i. 48.
—— of prey, boldness and rapacity of, i. 434.
——, soft-billed, which remain, i. 114.
——, summer, i. 113.

Birds that sing as they fly, i. 118.
——, their various kinds of flight, i. 220.
—— which are silent at midsummer, i. 117.
—— which sing in the night, i. 116.
—— which sing till past midsummer, i. 117.
—— which sing only in early spring, i. 117.
——, winter, i. 115.
—— with some note but no true song, i. 118.
Black game, i. 18.
—— spring, severe season known by the name of, i. 479.
Blackcap, i. 29.
——, bird of passage, i. 29, 480.
——, its song, i. 102, 120.
Blackmoor, i. 22.
——, Roman remains found at, ii. 379.
Blackthorn, i. 472.
Bog-moss used for brooms, i. 188.
Bog-oak at Wolmer, i. 17, *note*, 256.
Bohemian chatterer, i. 37.
Bombylius medius, i. 460.
Botanizing excursion through Wales, ii. 234.
Botany, on the study of, i. 215.
Botetourt, Lord, on civility, ii. 210.
Bourn well head, ii. 207.
Brambling, migration of, i. 75.
Bridge over the rivulet at Oakhanger, i. 364.
Brimstone Lodge, Wolmer, i. 21.
Brydone, P., ii. 276.
Bull issued by Pope Innocent VIII., i. 359.
—— issued by Pope Martin, i. 337.
Bullfinch, change of colour in a, i. 45, 98, ii. 101.
Bunting, cirl, i. 40, *note*.
——, common, rare at Selborne, i. 40.
Bustard, habits of the, i. 89, 482.
Butcher-bird, i. 96.
——, red-backed, i. 60.
Butt-wood close, i. 363.
Butterflies found at Selborne, ii. 368.

Calendar, Gilbert White's garden, ii. 347.
——, naturalist's, comparative view of the, kept at Selborne and Catsfield, i. 405.
Cancers, toads used for curing, i. 57.
Cane or Kine, a small variety of weasel, i. 44.

Canons of Selborne fond of hunting, i. 328.
Caprimulgus, extract from Aristotle on the, ii. 224.
Carausius establishes an empire in Britain, ii. 388.
Carnivora found at Selborne, ii. 362.
Carp retire in winter, i. 102.
Carpenter, Richard, preceptor of Sudington, i. 320.
Castration, its effects, i. 198.
Cat, young squirrels suckled by a, i. 449.
Catalogue of animals sent to Linnæus by John White, ii. 85.
Catsfield, naturalist's calendar kept at, i. 405.
Cattle resorting to water, i. 23.
———, fatal effects on, from eating leaves and twigs of the yew-tree, i. 292, ii. 260.
Chaffinch, separation of the sexes in their migration, i. 39, 46.
Chaffinches, flocks of female, i. 98, 132.
Chalk of Selborne, fossils found in the, ii. 376.
Chandler, Dr., ii. 61.
———, letter from, ii. 132.
Chantry, Selborne priory reduced to a, i. 362.
Chapel of Whaddon, i. 364.
Chapone, Mrs., ii. 108.
Charter for the foundation of Selborne priory, i. 375.
——— respecting the choosing of a prior, i. 323, 377.
Chaucer, the clergy ridiculed by, i. 338.
Cheiroptera found at Selborne, ii. 362.
Chestnut, magnificent Spanish, at Tortworth, ii. 253.
———, old London built of, ii. 266, 269.
——— timber, i. 471.
Chif-chaf, remarks on the, ii. 280, 286.
Chloritic marl of Selborne, fossils found in the, ii. 376.
——— marl, springs issuing from the, ii. 374.
Church, recent discoveries in Selborne, ii. 395.
——— bells, i. 288.
——— yard, i. 289.
Churton, Rev. R., correspondence between Gilbert White and, ii. 186-230.
Cicada, chirping note of the, ii. 42.

Cimex linearis, breeding-habits of, i. 455.
Clausentum, the Roman, ii. 387.
Cleanliness in sacred matters, i. 331.
Cobwebs covering the ground, i. 180.
———, shower of, i. 180.
Coccus of the vine, i. 243.
———, its history, i. 244.
Cockchaffers, damage done by, i. 452.
Cockroaches, swarms of, i. 454.
Coffin-lids, stone, found in Selborne church, i. 284, ii. 397.
Coins found in Woolmer pond, i. 24, 277, 278, ii. 378.
Colour of animals, influence of food on the, i. 45, 481.
Conchifera found at Selborne, ii. 367.
Condensation, test of, ii. 115.
Conduit wood, spring of water in, i. 363.
Congregating of birds, causes of, i. 133, 140.
Constantius, battle between Allectus and, ii. 389.
Conveniences enjoyed by the priory, i. 372.
Copulation of frogs, i. 51, ii. 245, 248, 252, 270.
Corn-mill at Selborne priory, i. 365.
Cornish choughs at Beachy Head, i. 96.
Cornua Ammonis, localities where found, i. 8, 480.
Cornwallis, the Hon. E., ii. 47.
Court-leet held at the Grange, i. 371.
Courtney, Peter, Bishop of Winchester, i. 360.
Cowthorpe oak, ii. 247.
Cricket, field, i. 230.
———, house, i. 233.
———, mole, i. 235.
Crickets, supposed rumination of, i. 236 and note.
Crocus, on the blowing of the (poem), i. 504, ii. 195.
Crossbill, i. 32 and note, 480.
——— at Ringmer, i. 131.
Cuckoo, its habits, i. 122, 123, 125, 130, 483, ii. 255, 256.
———, supposed anatomical cause of its not incubating, i. 195.
———, ditto, refuted, i. 197.
——— and fern-owl, resemblance between, i. 112.
Cucumbers set by bees, i. 474.
Cullum, Sir John, ii. 287.
Cundyth wood, i. 363.
Curlew, stone, migration of the, i. 438.

Curtis, William, on the geology of Selborne, ii. 374.
Cypselus melba in England, i. 88, *note*.

Daw, power of flight of a, ii. 130.
Deer, fallow, in the Holt forest, i. 26.
——, red, in Wolmer forest, i. 18, 19.
——, suborbital glands of, i. 43, 44.
—— stealers, i. 19 *et seq.*
Derham on sounds made under water, ii. 307.
Dew condensed by ponds, i. 194.
Discovery of the harvest-mouse, i. 36, ii. 26.
Dissensions between religious orders, i. 317.
Diver, great speckled, observations on, i. 435.
Dodecatheon media, ii. 233.
Dog, Chinese, i. 254.
Dogs, anecdotes of, ii. 283, 286.
——, peculiar habits of, i. 255.
Drought, dripping weather after, i. 478.
Dryden and Pope, ii. 106, 111.
Ducarel, Dr., ii. 266, 269.
Duck with arms of the king of Denmark on its collar, i. 136.
Dufour's fire-escape, description of, ii. 360.

Earthenware vases found at Selborne, ii. 381.
Earthworms, i. 464.
——, beneficial, i. 201, 202, *note.*
Ecclesiastical tiles found in Selborne church, ii. 398.
Echoes, i. 209.
——, Lucretius's description of, i. 212, 213.
—— of firing cannon, i. 258.
Eels, breeding of, i. 100.
Ela Longspee, i. 321.
Election of a prior, mode of, i. 334.
——, dispute about the, i. 345.
Elm, extraordinary large, ii. 273, 274, 278.
Empedes, swarms of, i. 462.
Emperors, coins of Roman, found at Selborne, ii. 382.
Empshott, etymology of, i. 1, *note.*
England, floods in, ii. 105.
English and a Norman ship, quarrel between the crews of an, i. 314.
—— poetry, sentiments on, ii. 106, 111.
Epitaph of Rev. Andrew Etty, i. 286.
—— of Mr. Ray, ii. 223.

Epitaph of Gilbert White, i. 286.
Estates, tenure of the Selborne, i. 372.
Eumenius on the battle of Woolmer forest, ii. 390.
Europe, Southern, animal productions of, ii. 67–94.

Fair held at Selborne, i. 372.
Fairwise, Thomas, appointed prior, i. 345.
Fairy rings, i. 475.
Falcon, peregrine, i. 35, 253, 480.
Fauna Calpensis, Gilbert White's sentiments on the, ii. 45, 49.
Fern-chafer, i. 102.
Fern-owl, habits of the, i. 439, ii. 251.
——, migration of the, ii. 273.
——, torpidity of the, ii. 246.
Ferns found at Selborne, ii. 372.
Field-cricket, i. 230.
Field-fare, i. 79.
—— breeds in Sweden, i. 134.
Field-mouse, anecdote of, i. 146.
Fire-escape, description of Dufour's, ii. 360.
Fish, gold and silver, i. 246.
——, sense of hearing in, ii. 304.
——, sleep of, ii. 139.
——, species of, at Selborne, i. 32 and *note*, 56, 57.
Flea of sand-martin, i. 169 and *note.*
Flies, observations on, i. 461.
Flight of birds, various kinds of, i. 220.
Floods in England, ii. 105.
Flora of Selborne, i. 217, ii. 369.
Flowing of sap, i. 469.
Fly-catcher, i. 29, 48.
——, its habits, i. 103.
Fog, reflection of, i. 477.
Food, influence of, on the colour of animals, i. 45, 481.
—— of the ring-dove, i. 433.
—— of the cuckoo, ii. 113.
Forest-fly, i. 151 and *note.*
Forms respecting the choosing of a prior, i. 323, 377.
Forster on the aurora australis, ii. 140.
Fossil wood of Woolmer forest, i. 256.
Fossils found at Selborne, i. 7, ii. 376.
Foundation of the priory of Selborne, charter for the, i. 375.
Franklin, Dr., on sounds made under water, ii. 307.
Freestone, i. 8.

INDEX.

Frog, green, i. 53 and *note*.
Frogs coming out in rainy **weather**, reason for, i. 52, **481**.
———, copulation **of**, i. 51, ii. **245, 248**, 252, 270.
Frost, partial, **i.** 476.
———, remarkable, in 1776, i. 263.
———, remarkable, in 1784, i. 267
Frozen **sleet, i.** 477, ii. 40.

Galls of Lombardy poplar, i. 470.
Garden kalendar, Gilbert White's, ii. 347.
Gardens for the poor, importance of, i. 207.
Gassendi, effects of music, i. **251, ii.** 145, 193.
Gasteropoda found at Selborne, ii. 367.
Geology of Selborne, ii. 374.
Gibbon, Mr., ii. 120.
Gibraltar, **on** the natural history **of**, ii. 290.
——— quail, ii. 6, *note*.
Gilpin, William, ii. 276.
Glowworms, i. 464.
Goatsucker, habits of the, i. **439**.
———, Pennant's mistake **about its** noise, i. 65, *note*, 67, 93.
Godesfield, preceptory at, i. **317**, ii. 131.
Gold **and** silver fish, i. 246.
Gossamer, i. 180, 182 and *note*, ii. 116, 142.
Gough, **Mr.**, ii. 211.
Gracious-street, **a term not understood**, i. **371**.
Grange, **the** priory, **i. 371**.
Grasses, a knowledge of, useful, ii. 127
Grasshopper-lark, i. 48, 50 *note*.
Graves, supposed, of Knights Templars, i. 284, ii. 396.
Great speckled diver, observations on, i. 435.
Grebes, erroneous ideas respecting, i. 438.
Grimm, **S. E.,** ii. **48**.
Gross-beaks, i. **32 and *note***.
———, food of, i. 446.
Growth and **size of trees**, i. **467, ii.** **247, 249, 252, 257, 258, 264, 270, 273, 275, 277, 278, 281, 288**.
Gurdon, **Sir Adam, i. 306**.
———, made **warden of Wolmer forest**, i. 312.
Gypsies, i. 184.

Habits of the old family tortoise, i. 373.

Habits of thrushes, i. 426.
Hales, Dr., ii. 244, 248, 261, 263.
———, on dew, i. 195.
Hanger, the, i. 2.
Hare, Francis, ii. **253**.
Hare, white or Scottish, i. 75 and *note*.
Hartley Mauditt, orthography of, i. 2, *note*.
Harvest-bug, i. 89, *note*.
Harvest-mouse, i. 29, 35, 36 and ***note***, 42.
———, discovery of the, i. 36, ii. 26.
Harvest scene (poem), i. 503, ii. 197.
Harwood, Sir Busick, ii. 211.
Hawfinch, i. 32 and *note*.
Hawk killed by poultry, i. 225.
Hawkley, landslip at, i. 227, ii. **27**, 103, 375.
Hawks, nesting-places of, i. 100.
Headley Heath, Roman and British entrenchments on, ii. 386, 394.
Hearing in fishes, on the sense of, ii. 304.
Heat, extraordinary, in 1781 and 1783, i. 270.
Heath-fires, why **lighted, i. 21, 480**.
Hedgehogs, their **habits, i. 78**.
Hedge-sparrow, **habits and food of,** i. 105.
Heliotrope, suggestions for a, i. 225.
Hen harrier, boldness of a, i. 434.
Heronry at Cressi Hall, i. 64, 67.
Hesiod on the note of the *Cicada*, ii. 42.
Hibernation of swallows, **i.** 142.
Himantopus, i. 237, 238 *note*.
Hippobosca hirundinis, i. 151.
Hirundines, on various, ii. 6, 22, 30, 33, 35, 127, 246, 249, 257, 272, 291, 302, 443.
Hirundo rupestris of Scopoli identical with *H. hyberna*, i. 86.
Hobart, John, ii. 275.
Hobby on Nore hill, i. 254, *note*.
Hogmoor, fragments of weapons found at, ii. 386.
Hollow lanes, i. 11.
Holt, Ayles, account of, i. 25.
Holt forest, i. 25, 26.
——— forest, large **oak** in, ii. **247, 302**.
Honey-buzzard, **i. 108**.
Honey-dew, origin **of**, i. 478, 485.
———, **cause** and effect of, i. 270.
Hoopoe, i. 31 and *note*.
Hop-fly, i. 245.
Hop-gardens, humming sound heard in, 114, 121.

Hops, culture of, i. 472.
Horne, George, ii. 287.
Horse, instinct shown by a, i. 449.
House-cricket, i. 233, 445.
House-martins, flocks of, ii. 272.
——, nidification of, i. 152.
House-pigeon, origin of, i. 109.
House-swallows partial to water, i. 252.
Humming in the air, i. 452.
Hunter, Mr., on the sight of the nightingale, ii. 256.
Hunting, canons of **Selborne** fond of, i. 328.
Hurtsmonceux castle, ii. 268.
—— park, beeches in, ii. 265.
Huxham's remarks on rain, i. 258.
Hybrid pheasant, description of a, i. 430.
Hyde abbey, i. 318, 355.
Hyla viridis, i. 53 and *note*.

Ichneumon fly, spider attacked by a, i. 459.
Idiot boy, his fondness for bees and immunity from their stings, i. 189.
Immunities and privileges enjoyed by Selborne priory, i. 366.
Impropriation of Selborne **priory,** i. 355.
Indenture of certain things put into the custody of Peter Bernes, sacrist of Selborne priory, i. 340, 399.
Indians, South-Sea, instruments &c. used by, ii. 98.
Insectivora found at Selborne, ii. 362.
Insects, birds of prey occasionally feed on, i. 424, 485.
——, noxious, i. 89, 91 *notes*.
——, on various, ii. 4, 8, 37.
—— and Vermes, observations on, i. 451.
Instinct, modifications of, i. 250.
Invitation to Selborne (poem), i. 499, ii. 36.
Ireland, natural history of, i. 106.
Iron-stone, remarkable forms of, i. 10, *note*.
Italy, on a tour through, ii. 224.
Ivy, insects supported by, i. 451.
Ivy-berries, i. 472.

Jackdaws, nesting-places of, i. 62, ii. 217, 218.
Japan plants thriving in our climate, i. 484.
Jekyll, Sir Joseph, ii. 263.

Kalendar, Gilbert White's garden, ii. 347.
Kent, Nathaniel, ii. 276.
King John's hill, i. 22.
Kite's hill, tumulus known as, i. 371.
Knights Templars, i. 316.
—— ——, supposed graves of, i. 284, ii. 396.

Lakes in Wolmer, names of, i. 21, 23.
—— in Wolmer forest, wild fowl frequenting, i. 33.
Land-rail, observations on a, i. 431.
Lands and manors pertaining to Selborne priory, value of the, i. 401.
Landslip at Hawkley, i. 227, ii. 27, 103, 375.
Langelande, Robert, the clergy ridiculed by, i. 338.
Langrish, Nicholas, **pension granted** to, i. 362.
Lathræa squammaria, ii. 241.
Lavants, i. 166.
Leaves, renovation of, **i. 470.**
Leigh, Dr., ii. 283.
Leprosy, case of, i. 205.
Leveret nursed by a cat, i. 200.
Leverian museum, i. 164 and *note*.
Licentiousness of religious societies, i. 338.
Lightfoot, Rev. John, letters from, to Gilbert White, ii. 231, 233.
Lime-blossoms, i. 471.
Linnæus, correspondence between the Rev. John White and, ii. 67-94.
List of the priors of Selborne Priory, i. 353.
Living of Selborne, i. 294.
Lizard, green, i. 64, 67.
Loach, description of, i. 57.
Lombardy poplar, galls of, i. 470.
London, old, built of chestnut, ii. 266, 269.
—— smoke, i. **477.**
Longevity at Selborne, i. 15 and *note*.
Lucomb's oak, ii. 54.

Madagascar, tridactyl quail from, ii. 6.
Magdalen College, grants to, i. 311, 355.
Malm, black, i. 3.
——, white, i. 4, ii. 376.
—— rock, hollow lane cut through the, ii. 376.
Mammalia found at Selborne, ii. 362.
Manors and lands pertaining to Selborne priory, value of the, i. 401.

Markwick, W., naturalist's calendar kept by, i. 405.
——, observations on various parts of nature, i. 421.
Marsham, Robert, correspondence between Gilbert White and, ii. 243–303.
Martins, house-, search for **hibernation** of, i. 241, 248.
——, second broods of, i. 154.
Mass ordered to be celebrated for benefactors to Selborne priory, i. 361.
Mayflies, myriads of, i. 457.
Medals and coins found in Woolmer pond, ii. 378.
Meteorological diary, i. 476, ii. 143.
Middleton on modern Rome, ii. 181.
Migration discussed, i. 135, 136, 137.
—— disputed by Barrington, i. 135.
—— not wholly on account of food, i. 133.
—— of birds, i. 39, **41, 42, 481,** ii. 245.
—— of frogs, i. 52.
—— of swallows, i. 67, 68.
—— of the Grallæ, **i.** 139.
Military orders of the religious, i. 316.
Miller, Philip, letter from, to Gilbert White, ii. 347.
Miscellaneous letters, ii. 231.
Missel-thrush breeds near houses, **i.** 179 and *note*.
Mist, called London smoke, i. 477.
Mole-cricket, i. 235.
Mollusca found at Selborne, ii. 367.
Monastic societies, licentiousness of, i. 338.
Montagu, Lieut.-Col., letters from, to Gilbert White, ii. 236, 239.
Monument to the Rev. A. Etty, i. 286.
—— to Mr. Ray, ii. 223.
—— **to** Gilbert White, i. 286.
Moose-deer, description of, i. 79, 83.
Morning clouds, i. 478.
Morton, John, elected prior, i. 343.
Moss, Charles, ii. 282.
Mosses, sexuality of, ii. 124.
Motacilla ficedula, ii. 16.
Moths found at Selborne, ii. 368.
Mulso, Miss Hecky, Timothy the Tortoise to, ii. 183.
Munificence of Bishop Wykeham, i. 332.
Music, its effect on the mind, i. 251, ii. 145, 193.
Musical keys of the voices of birds, i. 139.

Mustelinum, supposed species of the genus, i. 44, 481.
Natter-jack, i. 55.
Naturalist's calendar kept at Selborne and Catsfield, comparative view of the, i. 405.
—— summer-evening walk (poem), i. 70.
Nature, on various parts of, i. 421.
Nephew, letters from Gilbert White to his, ii. 143, 170.
New Forest, German boars in the, ii. 480.
New-Zealanders, customs of the, ii. 98.
Newton Valence, origin of name, i. 2, *note*.
Nidification **modified by circumstances,** i. 250.
—— of the osprey, ii. 246.
—— of rooks, i. 425.
—— of swallows, i. 152, 161.
Nightingales, different sounds of, i. 100.
——, limits of their visit, i. 137.
——, sight of, ii. 256.
Norman ship, quarrel between the crews of an English and a, i. 314.
Nose-fly, torture caused to horses by the, i. 459.
Notitia Monastica, extracts from Bishop Tanner's, i. 366.
Nuthatch, i. 50 and *note*.

Oak on the Plestor, i. 5.
Oaks at Blackmoor and Temple, i. 6.
——, remarks on, ii. 247, 249, 252, 258, 264, 268, 270, 273, 274, 277, 282, 289.
Oakhanger, rivulet at, i. 364.
Œdicnemus crepitans, i. 45 and *note*.
Œstrus curvicauda, i. 459.
Omens, on deriving, from accidental events, ii. 152.
Orchids found at Selborne, ii. 372.
Osprey at Frinsham pond, i. 96.
——, nesting of the, at the lake of Killarney, ii. 246.
Ostrea carinata, i. 8, *note*.
Otter found at Selborne, i. **83.**
Owl, barn or white, i. 33.
——, barn, occasionally hoots, i. 148.
——, brown, i. 33.
——, eagle-, i. 76.
Owls hoot in various keys, i. 138.
——, pigeons attacked by, i. 82.
——, species of, in the neighbourhood of Selborne, i. 149, *note*.

Owls, structure of wing-feathers of, i. 149, *note*.
——, their **habits** of feeding, &c., i. **148, 484.**
Oxen, fatal effects on, from eating leaves and twigs of the yew-tree, i. 292, ii. 260.

Paradyss mede, i. 362.
Parliamentary acts respecting Wolmer forest, i. 312.
Parsonage of Selborne leased, i. 364.
Partial frost, i. 476.
Partridge, solicitude **for its young,** i. 429.
Passus Decimus of Piers Plowman, extract from, i. 339.
Peacock, tail of, its true position, i. 92.
Peat cut in Wolmer forest, ii. 279.
Pennant, Thomas, letters from Gilbert White to, i. 1–112.
Peregrine falcon shot near Wolmer forest, i. 253.
Pettichaps, remarks on the, i. 252.
Phalæna quercus, damage done to oaks **by**, i. 456.
Pheasant, description of a hybrid, i. **430, 485.**
Phenomena in 1783, i. 271, 485.
Philip the Hardy, i. 314.
Piers Plowman, the clergy ridiculed by, i. 338.
Pigeon, house-, origin of, i. 109.
Pigeon-hawk, ii. 240.
Pigeons attacked by owls, i. 82.
Pink, Mr., anecdote of, ii. 156.
Plants found at Selborne, i. 217, ii. 369.
——, **various times of flowering,** i. 219.
—— and animals, **Mr. Banks's** collection of, ii. **99.**
Plestor, the, **i. 5, 310.**
Poems, i. 499.
Ponds in Wolmer forest named after extinct animals, i. 23, *note*.
Pope Innocent VIII., bull issued by, i. 359.
Pope Martin, bull issued by, i. 337.
Population of Selborne, i. 13, 14.
Portland, Duke of, ii. 295.
Position of the church, i. 290.
Pottery, Roman, found at Blackmoor, ii. **380.**
Poultry, sagacity shown by, i. 427.
Preceptores and preceptorium, meaning of, i. 320.

Preceptories in Southampton, i. 317.
Prediction, remarkable, concerning religious houses, i. 339.
Prettejohn, Mr., on Roman-British remains found at Selborne, ii. 378, 385.
Prior, dispute about the election of a, i. 345.
——, forms respecting the choosing of a, i. **323, 377.**
Priors, list of the, of Selborne priory i. 353.
Priory of Selborne, **i. 299, 375.**
——, impropriation of the, i. 355.
—— lands leased out, i. 362.
——, privileges and immunities enjoyed by the, i. 366.
——, the, a source of prosperity to Selborne, i. 373.
——, Wayneflete endeavours to reform the, i. 354.
Ptinus pectinicornis, damage **done to** furniture by, i. 453.
Puckeridge, cause **of, i. 439, ii. 213,** 216, 250.

Quadrupeds, observations on, i. 448.
Quail, tridactyl, from Madagascar, ii. 6.

Rabbits, **finest** turf made by, i. 448.
Rain, measurement of, i. 12, 488, ii. 167, 173, 176, 178, 194, 206.
Rainbow, on the (poem), i. 502, ii. 147, 149.
Rapacity of birds of prey, i. 434.
Raven-tree, the, i. 6.
Ray, Mr., epitaph of, ii. **223.**
Redbreast, song of, i. 101.
Redshank, spotted, i. 59, *note*.
Redstart, its **song and habits,** i. 103.
Redwings breed **in Sweden, i. 134.**
Reed-thrush of Latham, ii. **9,** *note*.
Reflection of fog, i. 477.
Register, Beaufort's, i. 334, 336.
——, Wayneflete's, extracts from, i. 341–349.
Registers of Gilbert White's family, ii. 95.
Relics of Selborne priory, i. 370.
Religious, military orders of the, i. 316.
—— houses embarrassed, i. 333.
——, remarkable prediction concerning, i. 339.
—— orders, dissensions between, i. 317.
Renovation of leaves, i. 470.
Reptilia, species of, at Selborne, i. 53, ii. 366.

Reservoir in Conduit wood, i. 363.
Revenues of Selborne priory, i. 337, 342.
Rhodian children, as they go a swallowing (poem), i. 505.
Ring-dove breeding near house, i. 179, *note*.
——, food of the, i. 433.
Ring-ouzel, i. 37.
——, migration of, i. 60, **63, 69, 72,** 75, 84, 95.
—— in Sussex, i. 131, 159.
—— shot in Norfolk, ii. 254.
Ringmer, crossbills at, i. 131.
Rivulet at Oakhanger, i. 364.
Road, on a bad, ill-mended (poem), i. 506.
Rock-dove, origin of house-pigeon, i. 109, 110.
Roman-British antiquities of Selborne, ii. 378.
Rome, difficulties started at, respecting Selborne priory, i. 359.
——, information sent to, respecting the priory, i. 336.
Rookery at Ringmer, i. 160.
Rooks, nidification of, i. 425.
——, their evening voices, i. 257.
—— accompanied by other birds, i. 141, 483.
Ruins of Selborne priory, i. 369.
Rushes used for candles, i. 186, 188, *note*.

Sagacity of a willow-wren, i. 146.
—— shown by poultry, i. 427.
Salicaria, i. 69, 73, 76.
Samford, Robert, grants made by, to Selborne priory, i. 319, ii. 133.
Sand-martin, its history, i. 167, &c.
——, nidification of, i. 442.
Sandpiper, three species of, found at Selborne, i. 59, *note*.
Sandwich, Lord, ii. 262.
Sap, flowing of, i. 469.
Satire, fragment of a, i. 506.
Scarabæus fullo, i. 69.
Scheik Sefi, interview between Tamerlane and, ii. 153.
Scopoli's 'Annus Primus,' mistakes in, i. 85.
Scotland, a visit to, ii. 231.
——, its natural history and geography, i. 107.
. Scrutiny, mode of electing a prior by, i. 346.
Sedge-bird, i. 99, ii. 12.
Seed lying dormant, i. 473.

Selborne a Saxon village, proof of, i. 279, *note*.
——, extent of parish, i. 11.
——, its extent and boundaries, i. 1–4.
——, its streams, i. 3.
——, Lord, on Roman-British antiquities, ii. 378.
——, naturalist's calendar kept at, i. 405.
——, variously spelt and etymology of, i. 279, *note*.
—— church, description of, i. 282.
—— church, recent discoveries in, ii. 395.
—— fair, i. 372.
—— hanger (poem), i. 501.
—— parsonage leased, i. 364.
—— priory, charter for the foundation of, i. 375.
—— priory granted to Magdalen college, i. 355.
—— priory, list of the priors, i. 353.
—— priory, privileges and immunities enjoyed by, i. 366.
—— priory, value of the manors and lands pretaining to, i. 401.
—— priory, sequestration of, i. 342.
—— priory, Wayneflete endeavours to reform, i. 354.
Self-defence, early instinct of, i. 197.
Sermon by Gilbert White, ii. 308.
Serpents, three species of, at Selborne, their different habits and food, i. 55, *note*.
Sewell, W., on Roman remains found in Woolmer pond, ii. 393.
Seymour, Francis, ii. 275.
Sharp, John, elected prior, i. 350.
——, priory lands leased to, i. 362.
Sheep, embarassment shown by, i. 448.
——, different breeds of, i. 158.
Sheffield's, Mr., account of a visit to Mr. Banks, ii. 97.
Shivering wren, ii. 12.
Short-winged birds, migration of, i. 158.
Shrew-ash, i. 191.
Silbury hill, ii. 159.
Silk, electricity from, ii. 201.
Silver and gold fish, i. 246.
Size and growth of trees, i. 467, ii. 247, 249, 252, 257, 258, 264, 268, 270, 273, 275, 277, 278, 281, 288.
Skinner, Mr., letter from, to Gilbert White, ii. 234.
Sleet, rooks frozen by, i. 477, ii. 40.

Smith, W., on the migration of swallows, ii. 245.
Snails and slugs, i. 465.
Snake, its odour when irritated, i. 74.
Snake's slough, i. 465.
Snipes, sound produced by, in descending, i. 98 and *note*.
——, voice of, i. 50.
Sociality of animals, i. 183.
Soil, effect of, on thermometers, i. 271.
Song, influence of the male bird's, i. 482.
Sounds made under water, ii. 307.
South-Sea Indians, instruments &c. used by, ii. 98.
Southington, preceptory at, i. 317, ii. 131.
Southwell, T., on some incidents in the life of T. Marsham, ii. 243.
Sow, remarkably prolific, i. 199.
Spanish chestnut, magnificent, at Tortworth, ii. 253.
Sparrow-hawk, i. 108.
Sparrows, building-places of, i. 101.
Sphinxes found at Selborne, ii. 368.
Sphynx ocellata, habits of, i. 457.
Sponge, experiment with, ii. 115.
Sponsors and their god-children, relationship between, i. 330.
Spoonbills, flock of, ii. 43.
Spring of water in Conduit wood, i. 363.
Sprout-cale, i. 207, 484.
Squirrels, young, suckled by a cat, i. 449.
Stag-hunt at Alton, i. 449.
Star-sluch, ii. 193, 196.
Stawell, Lord, ii. 260.
Stepe, prior of Selborne, i. 340, 341.
Sticklebacks, i. 32, 56.
Stilt-plover, i. 237, 238, *note*.
Stoat, pied specimens of, i. 450.
Stockdove, i. 96, 109.
—— breeds at Selborne, 97 *note*, ii. 254.
Stone coffin-lids found in Selborne church, i. 284, ii. 397.
Stone-curlew, i. 46, 61, 88.
——, nocturnal flight of the, i. 257.
——, migration of the, i. 438.
Stoneleigh park, fine oaks in, ii. 258.
Storm of wind, ii. 141.
Strangers appointed priors, i. 344, 346, 350.
Stratford, bishop of Winchester, i. 324.
Stuart, Sir S., letter from, to Gilbert White, ii. 264.

Sudington preceptory, relation between Selborne church and, ii. 395.
Summer birds, migration interrupted, i. 81.
Superstitions at Selborne, i. 190, 192, *note*.
Sussex downs described, i. 157.
Swallow, chimney, early arrival of, i. 160.
——, ——, habits of the, 162, 163, *et seq.*
——, ——, its nest-places, i. 161 and *note*.
——, its second brood, i. 162.
——, remarkable situation of the nest of a, i. 164.
—— tribe, on the annual increase in the, ii. 246, 249.
—— washing, i. 97.
Swallows congregate before leaving, i. 37, 444.
——, difference in the tails of the different sexes, i. 100.
——, migration of, i. 67, 68.
——, reappearance of, i. 28, 204.
——, their history, i. 150, 158, 169-172.
——, their supposed torpidity, i. 27, 28, 38, 95.
——, time of arrival at different places, i. 178, 483.
Swift, delayed departure of, i. 242.
——, Gibraltar, found occurring in England, i. 88, *note*.
—— drinks on the wing, i. 99.
——, its history, i. 171, &c., 175 *note*, 213.
——, number of eggs laid by, ii. 33, 35.
—— of a different genus from swallows, i. 176, *note*.
——, time of its arrival, i. 98.
——, time of departure, i. 94, 175, ii. 272.
Swine, various names for, ii. 158.
Sycamores, i. 470.
Sylvester, Thomas, Selborne parsonage leased to, i. 364.
Systema Naturæ, proposed new edition of, ii. 66, 77, 89.

Tabanus bovinus, ii. 116, 142.
Tamerlane, interview between Scheik Sefi and, ii. 152.
Tan-house garden, i. 363.
Teals taken at Oakhanger ponds, ii. 12, 15.
—— taken at Wolmer, i. 99.

Tempest near London, ii. 102.
Tenure of the Selborne estates, i. 372.
Test of condensation, ii. 115.
Tiles, ecclesiastical, found in **Selborne** church, ii. 398.
Timber, large fall of, **in the Holt,** i. 26.
——, value of, in **Wolmer forest,** ii. 279.
Titmouse, habits of different species, i. 105, 106.
——, notes of different species, i. 101.
Thaws, observations on, i. 476.
Thrushes, habits of, i. 426.
Thunderstorm, account of, i. **272.**
Toad, a tame one, i. 52.
——, poisonous exudation from **skin,** i. 51, *note.*
Toads used for curing cancers, i. 57.
Torpidity of swallows, i. 204, 443.
Tortoise (Timothy), i. 131, ii. 182.
—— (——) become Gilbert White's property, i. 239.
—— (——), its **habits,** i. 143, 144, 484.
—— (——), letter **from,** to Miss H. Mulso, ii. 183.
——, more particulars **respecting the** old family, i. 373.
—— at Ringmer, i. 159.
Tortoises, various forms of sternum in, i. 241, *note.*
Tortworth, magnificent **Spanish chest**nut at, ii. 253.
Townsend, Joseph, ii. 269.
Townson, Dr., ii. 209, 224.
Trees act as "alembics," i. 192.
——, on the size and growth of, i. 467, ii. 247, 249, 252, 257, 258, 264, 268, 270, 273, 275, 277, 278, 281, 288.
——, order of losing their leaves, i. 467
Tremella nostoc, i. 475.
Truffles, i. 474.
Tumuli **at Selborne,** ii. 384.
Turkey, **fertility of a,** ii. 288, 290.
Turtle-dove **at Selborne,** i. 97, *note.*
Tylehouse **grove,** i. 363.

Ulmus montana, i. 5, *note.*
Upper Greensand **of Selborne,** fossils found in the, ii. 377.

Value **of the** manors and lands pertaining to Selborne priory, i. **401.**
Vase discovered in the priory **ruins,** i. 370.

Vases, earthenware, found at Selborne, ii. 381.
Vegetable food, **value and increase of,** i. 207.
Vegetables, observations on, i. 467.
Vegetation, influence of south-west exposure on, ii. 120, 122.
Vermes and insects, observations on, i. 451.
Versification, the art of, ii. 106, 111.
Vespasian, station of, at **Woolmer** pond, ii. 386, 394.
Vicars, list of, i. 294.
Viper, early instinct of self-defence, i. 197.
Vipers swallowing their young, i. 54 and *note.*
Virgil's allusion to the swallow, i. 165, 166.
Visitation held at Selborne priory by Wykeham, i. 326, 381.
Voices of birds, i. 222.

Wager, Admiral Sir C., ii. 245.
Wagtail, food of the, i. 446.
——, yellow, i. 98, *note.*
——, young cuckoo **fed by a,** ii. 248.
Walden lodge, i. 21.
Wales, a visit to, ii. 233, 234.
Wallcreeper, remarks on the, ii. 289, 293, 294, 296.
Walpole, George, ii. 245.
Warm weather in early spring, its effects, i. 203.
Wasps, damage done by, i. 270.
——, nidification of, i. 458.
Water-rat, i. 30 and *note.*
——, its stores, i. 76.
Water-shrew, i. 76, *note.*
Water-snails, buoyancy of, ii. 125.
Wayneflete, bishop of Winchester, i. 339.
——, death of, i. 360.
——, **intercedes for Peter Berne,** i. 351.
Weapons, fragments of, **found at Hog**moor, ii. 386.
Weather, full account of, i. 260, 487.
Well-head, i. 3.
Wells, **average depth of,** at Selborne, ii. 375.
Whaddon chapel, i. 364.
Whales in the Mediterranean, ii. 58.
Wheat, effect of heat on, i. 474.
Wheatear, i. 41, 153.
——, localities where **taken,** i. 159, 484, ii. 10.
Whinchat, winter food of, i. 106.

White, Gilbert, account book of, ii. 316.
——, correspondence between the Rev. R. Churton and, ii. 186-230.
——, correspondence between Robert Marsham and, ii. 243-303.
——, correspondence with his family, ii. 95-185.
——, garden kalendar of, ii. 347.
——, letter from Rev. J. White to, ii. 64.
——, letters from, to Hon. Daines Barrington, i. 113-274.
——, letters from, to T. Pennant, i. 1-112.
—— miscellaneous letters to, ii. 231-241.
——, naturalist's kalendar kept by, i. 405.
——, sermon by, ii. 308.
White, Miss, letters to, from Gilbert White, ii. 137, 145-148.
White, Rev. Edmund, letter to, from Gilbert White, ii. 150.
White, Rev. John, correspondence between Linnæus and, ii. 67-94.
——, letters from Gilbert White to the, ii. 1-64.
——, letter from, to Samuel Barker, ii. 103.
White, Thomas, letter to, ii. 131.
White-throat, habits of, i. 102.
Wickliffe, doctrines of, i. 338.
Wild bee, i. 457.
—— boars in Holt forest, i. 26.
Willow-wren, notes on a, ii. 237, 239.
——, sagacity of a, i. 146.
——, the smallest uncrested, i. 439.
——, three species of, i. 47, 58.
Winchester, bishop of, summoned to parliament, i. 314.
Wind, storm of, ii. 141.
Windham, William, ii. 277.

Winter, swarms of insects observed in, i. 452.
——, warm weather happening in (poem), i. 504.
Winter-martin, doubt respecting the, ii. 5.
Wolmer forest, i. 16, 22.
—— ——, formerly frequented by deer, black game, &c., i. 24.
—— ——, limits of, i. 22.
—— ——, parliamentary acts respecting, i. 312.
—— ——, Sir Adam Gurdon made warden of, i. 312.
—— ——, visited by Ed. III., i. 281.
—— pond, i. 24.
Woodcock carrying its young with its beak, i. 85 and *note*.
Woodcocks breed in England, i. 133.
—— breed in Tirol, i. 134.
——, their migration, i. 134.
Woodpeckers, damage done by, ii. 292, 297, 298.
Wood-pigeons, flocks of, i. 110.
——, food of, i. 110.
Worldham, etymology of, i. 2, *note*.
Wren, golden-crested, migration of, i. 104.
——, shivering, ii. 12.
Wryneck, food of the, i. 44.
Wych-elm, i. 5 and *note*.
Wykeham, bishop, munificence of, i. 332.
——, visitation held at Selborne priory by, i. 326, 381, ii. 136.
Wynchestre, John, elected prior, i. 334.
Wyndesor, William, elected prior, i. 345.

Yew-tree in churchyard, i. 291.
——, fatal effects on cattle from eating leaves and twigs of the, i. 292, ii. 260.

www.ingramcontent.com/pod-product-compliance
Lightning Source LLC
Chambersburg PA
CBHW030549300426
44111CB00009B/917